A Practical Approach to Teaching Reading

Second Edition

DOROTHY RUBIN
Trenton State College

ALLYN AND BACON
Boston London Toronto Sydney Tokyo Singapore

With love to my understanding and supportive husband, Artie,
my lovely daughters, Carol and Sharon,
my precious grandchildren, Jennifer, Andrew, and Melissa,
my charming son-in-law, Seth,
and my dear brothers and sister.

Series Editor: Virginia C. Lanigan
Production Administrator: Annette Joseph
Production Coordinator: Holly Crawford
Editorial-Production Service: Judith Ashkenaz, Total Concept Associates
Cover Administrator: Linda K. Dickinson
Cover Designer: Suzanne Harbison
Manufacturing Buyer: Megan Cochran

Copyright © 1993, 1982 by Allyn and Bacon
A Division of Simon & Schuster, Inc.
160 Gould Street
Needham Heights, MA 02194

Library of Congress Cataloging-in-Publication Data

Rubin, Dorothy.
    A practical approach to teaching reading / Dorothy Rubin. — 2nd ed.
        p. cm.
    Includes bibliographical references and index.
    ISBN 0-205-14215-X
    1. Reading. I. Title.
LB1050.R8   1993
428.4′07 – dc20   92-21969
                                                                        CIP

Printed in the United States of America

10 9 8 7 6 5 4 3 2 1   97 96 95 94 93 92

Text credits:
        pp. 36–38 reprinted with permission of Doris Ching and the International Reading Association.
        pp. 364–380 from *Teacher Edition of A New Day* of the *World of Reading* series, © 1991 Silver, Burdett & Ginn Inc. Used with permission.
        p. 473 from *Home Connections Letters, Levels 1–3* of the *World of Reading* series, © 1991 Silver, Burdett & Ginn Inc. Used with permission.

CONTENTS

9   Reading and Study Skills I: An Emphasis on Content-Area Reading   284

10   Reading and Study Skills II: An Emphasis on Content-Area Reading   321

Part III   The Reading Program in Action   **357**

11   Reading Approaches   **357**

12   Whole Language   **391**

13   A Diagnostic-Reading and Correction Program   **411**

PREFACE

Literacy for all is the goal of *America 2000,* and without reading, there is no literacy. Most information is still passed through the written word, and anyone who finds reading difficult is seriously handicapped in the civilized struggle for a place in the world. Children who come from homes where they are surrounded by print material usually do better in reading and subsequently in school achievement than children who do not come from such environments. Teachers cannot change their students' home environment or socioeconomic status, but they *can* make a difference.

In *A Practical Approach to Teaching Reading*, Second Edition, I present the knowledge, skills, and strategies that preservice teachers need to become effective teachers of reading. Reading is looked upon as a complex, dynamic thinking process, and word recognition is regarded as the foundation of comprehension because without word recognition there is no reading. The emphasis throughout is on having teachers help students become more strategic readers while at the same time instilling in students a love of reading.

In this book, I provide teachers with many suggestions and strategies to help them become better interactive teachers and good role models, and I present the various approaches and movements vying for their attention. In particular, I discuss the whole language movement and how teachers can integrate various aspects of this movement with different programs to achieve a modified, eclectic program that is practical.

The book is divided into three parts. Part I deals with the foundation of reading. Because a definition of reading determines the kind of reading program that is presented, I start with a global definition of reading and discuss the process of reading and the interrelationship of reading with the other language arts. The other three chapters in Part I deal with individual difference factors, the role of the teacher in reading, and the importance of instilling a love of reading in children. Unless teachers are aware of the individual differences of their students, understand how reading is related to the other language arts, have an insight into their role, and are knowledgeable about good literature, they will not be able to implement the proposed reading program very well.

Part II concerns the subject matter of reading. In this part, I discuss children's emergent literacy or early literacy development, word recognition, comprehension, vocabulary expansion, and reading and study skills. The chapters in Part II usually contain explanations, sample activities, model lesson plans, and diagnostic checklists.

Part III presents approaches to the teaching of reading, including a chapter on whole language, as well as how to organize for reading in a diagnostic-reading and correction program. This part also contains chapters on special children and on parents as partners in their children's learning.

Every chapter begins with a scenario, key questions, and key terms and is filled with other scenarios to illustrate the concepts presented. Each chapter also contains a running glossary that explains key terms. Each chapter ends with a graphic summary of the chapter and a listing of the key concepts presented. The graphic summaries and other techniques used in this book help make reading this textbook a more interactive experience for the reader.

A Practical Approach to Teaching Reading, Second Edition, presents a balanced approach in discussing whole language, literature-based basal readers, and skill development. It helps teachers acquire the information they need on word recognition, comprehension, vocabulary expansion, and study skills, as well as the methods and approaches for teaching them.

D. R.

1

An Introduction to
A Practical Approach to Teaching Reading

SCENARIO: MS. HART—A NEW TEACHER

Ms. Hart was just informed that she will be hired to teach the fourth grade in the school system of her choice. Ms. Hart is ecstatic. She knows that competition for her teaching position had been very keen and that each one of the prospective teachers who had been interviewed had excellent qualifications because the principal had said so. When the principal who had interviewed her phoned to tell her that she was to be hired, he told her that the reason he chose her rather than the others was because of her strong background in reading and her recognition that reading is an integral part of the language arts. He was impressed with her views concerning the teaching of reading. He felt that, of course, it was important to be able to implement one's views, but in order to be able to do this, a person must first have ideas and knowledge—must have the necessary preparation, motivation, and intelligence. The principal felt that she, Ms. Hart, had all the attributes necessary to become an excellent teacher and that she was particularly strong in the area of reading and knowledgeable of its relationship to the other language arts areas. He told Ms. Hart that in this school system, great emphasis is placed on the teaching of reading through the grades and on the reading–writing connection. Because the school authorities feel strongly that every teacher is a teacher of reading, they screen every candidate very closely to make sure that he or she has the special qualifications that they want. He felt that she, Ms. Hart, had the necessary qualifications, so she was hired.

Ms. Hart sat down in a daze. When the phone call came for her, she was just opening the door, and she was a little out of breath. When she heard whom the call was from, she held her breath because she was literally afraid to breathe. She now let out a long sigh of relief. "What luck!" she thought, "to get the position I want." Ms. Hart was going to rush out to tell her friends her marvelous news, but she decided to phone her parents first. They would be so proud of her.

She had wanted to be a teacher all her life, and now she finally would have the opportunity to be one. She was grateful for the opportunity.

Ms. Hart was also grateful for the opportunity to have gone to a school that stressed the importance of reading as an integral part of the language arts. Her instructors had impressed upon her the need to understand the purposes of what one is doing, to have skills at one's fingertips, and to have strategies to directly teach reading. It was actually her ability in these areas that had given her the edge over the other candidates.

Ms. Hart decided to sit down for a moment to go over in her mind's eye the questions that the principal had asked her concerning reading. She vividly remembered the first one: "How do you define reading?" She remembered going into a discussion of how difficult it is to define reading, but she did give a definition of reading, and she explained why she gave the definition that she did. When he questioned her on how she would teach reading as an integral part of the language arts, she was very well prepared to answer this question.

The principal then queried her on other topics he felt were very important, such as study skills and higher order thinking. As she spoke, the principal shook his head vigorously in agreement and smiled. When she finished, he cleared his throat, gave her an encouraging smile, and asked her what she thought about the whole language movement and if she was prepared to teach in a situation that embraced many of its beliefs.

Ms. Hart was prepared for these questions. Her reading professor had been an eclectic pragmatist, who believed that the best elements of whole language can live very comfortably under the same roof with a strong sequentially developed reading skills program, as well as with a basal reader program. Fortunately for Ms. Hart, her professor not only discussed and explained how this could be done but also modeled sample lessons that gave students insights into how to implement such an eclectic program.

Ms. Hart became quite animated when she presented her views about reading because her professor had imbued within her the idea that regardless of the approach teachers use to get students to read, they must help instill a love of books in their students. And they must give their students many, many opportunities to read.

Ms. Hart remembered feeling drained after the interview; she felt as though he had tapped her brain. It wasn't until she had left the principal's office that she realized how knowledgeable she was about reading. It was interesting that the principal had not just asked her questions about theories and research, but he was concerned that she had knowledge of how to help students to attain the various skills and that she was well versed in the subject matter. The principal had told her that it isn't until a teacher is on the job that one can really tell how well he or she can do, but one thing was sure—a teacher who did not have the proper background would not be able to be a competent teacher.

This chapter will introduce you to *A Practical Approach to Teaching Reading*, Second Edition, and discuss how the definition of reading influences the reading program. In addition, this chapter emphasizes the interrelatedness of reading with the other language arts.

KEY QUESTIONS

After you finish reading this chapter, you should be able to answer the following questions:

1. How was reading perceived in ancient times?
2. Who is considered a literate person?
3. What is the relationship of the definition of reading to the reading program?
4. What is meant by "reading as a total integrative act"?
5. What is metacognition?
6. What are some reading literacy objectives?
7. How is reading related to the language arts?
8. What are some reading theories?
9. What should teachers know about reading terminology?
10. How can story maps integrate reading and writing?

KEY TERMS IN CHAPTER

You should pay special attention to the following key terms:

affective domain	metacognition
bottom-up reading models	perception
cognitive domain	perceptual domain
interactive reading models	reading
language arts	reading process
listening vocabulary	story map
literate person	top-down reading models

Literacy for All

Literate person
One who can read and write.

A literate person is one who is "able to read and write."[1] In ancient times reading was considered a mystery that only priests could unravel; it was considered a special gift of the gods. As the centuries passed, others besides priests learned the mysteries of reading, but it was learned by a select few. In Aristotle's time the education of a freeman was a liberal education, which was undertaken for its own sake rather than for any useful purpose. Aristotle did recommend, however, that freemen be taught to read, even though it was useful. In the seventeenth century in Massachusetts, parents were commanded to teach reading to their children to

[1] *Webster's New World Dictionary of American English.* Third College Edition, Victoria Neufeldt, ed. (Cleveland: Webster's New World, 1988), p. 789.

foil the deluder Satan, who tries to keep persons from knowledge of the Scriptures. Reading, therefore, was taught for religious purposes.

Today everyone is expected to learn to read, and literacy is essential for survival. Our world is a complicated and competitive one; to stay on it comfortably, we need understanding. To understand more than our individual experiences can teach us—to deal with modern society and technology, that is, on terms better than those of primitive man—we must be able to get and give information. The harsh fact is that most information is still passed through the written word, and anyone who finds reading difficult is seriously handicapped in the civilized struggle for a place in the world.

Even though some children learn to read before they come to school, school is usually looked upon as the place that children learn to read, and teachers are looked upon as those key persons who help children to unlock the mysteries of the written word. To take a child by the hand and help to lead him or her into the world of books is an exciting, worthwhile, and rewarding endeavor. All teachers want to be able to do that. However, the path leading to the world of books may be fraught with many obstacles. The only way that teachers can overcome these is to be as well prepared as possible.

Defining Reading

A definition of reading is necessary because it will determine the goals of the reading program and influence the kind of reading program it will be. Most people agree on this. The problem is that not everyone agrees on the definition of reading.

Read the following examples. After each, stop and ask yourself whether you feel the person is reading.

1. Tess can read aloud very well. She reads with expression and observes all punctuation marks. She can't answer any questions on what she has read. Is she reading?
2. Sara stumbles on a few words when she reads aloud, but she can answer all the comprehension questions. The information is familiar to her. Is she reading?
3. Craig's assignment is to read Chapter 2 in his textbook. He counts the number of pages he has to read, groans, and then reads his whole assignment. When he's finished, he gives out a long sigh of relief, and prepares to go on to his next assignment. Unfortunately, he can't remember a thing about what he has just read. Is he reading?
4. Tom is reading something with which he completely disagrees. He is so furious that he completely ignores the writer's message. Is he reading?
5. Jordan can't make head or tail of the article he is reading for his history class because it is so poorly organized. As a result, he can't figure out the writer's message. Is he reading?
6. Anna has trouble decoding the words on the printed page. Is she reading?

The answer to these questions obviously depends on our definition of reading. Determining the answer is not as easy as it sounds because, as stated previously, not everyone agrees on a definition of reading. A teacher who views reading as a one-way process, consisting simply of decoding symbols or relating sounds to symbols, will develop a different type of program from that of a teacher who sees reading as a dynamic interactive process that requires the getting of meaning from the printed page.

Reading
A complex, dynamic process that involves the bringing of meaning to and the getting of meaning from the printed page.

Even though a single, agreed-upon definition of reading does not exist, there is a broad definition that has been widely used, one that takes into account both the reader and the printed page: Reading is a complex, dynamic process that involves the bringing of meaning to and the getting of meaning from the printed page.

This definition implies that readers bring their backgrounds, their experiences, as well as their emotions, into play (see Figure 1-1). Students who are upset or physically ill will bring these feelings into the act of reading, and this will influence their interpretive processes. A person well versed in the topic that is being read will gain more from the material than one who is less knowledgeable. A good critical thinker will gain more from a passage that requires critical thinking than will someone who lacks this ability. A student who has strong dislikes will come away with different feelings and understandings from one with strong likings. And certainly, if the print material is disorganized or not well written, this too will affect the ability of the student to "get the message."

If we define reading as *a complex, dynamic process that involves the bringing of meaning to and the getting of meaning from the printed page*, then Sara is

FIGURE 1-1   Andrew brings his background of experiences to what he reads.

the only child who is reading because she is the only one who understands what she is reading. She is the only one who is interacting with the text so that she is able to integrate information from the printed material with her background of information and experiences. Stumbling on a few words does not prevent her from getting the message.

It's obvious that Anna is not reading because she can't pronounce the words on the printed page. For some of the others, however, it's less obvious. Although Tess can pronounce all the words, she is not reading because she either doesn't know the meanings of the words or cannot assimilate them into a meaningful message. Craig is not reading, even though his eyes have scanned the pages of his textbook, because he does not remember anything he has "read." Tom, too, is not reading because his strong feelings have interfered with his getting the writer's message, and Jordan is not reading because the writer has done a very poor job of presenting the material.

From the preceding paragraphs, we can see that reading is a complex process that includes an interaction between the reader and the text to produce meaning and that there are a number of factors that can influence whether an individual will get the message from a printed page. Motivation, skill, background of knowledge, purpose for reading, and the writer's ability to present his or her information in a clear, logical, and readable form are merely a few of these factors.

Reading as a Total Integrative Process

Reading process
Concerned with the affective, perceptual, and cognitive domains.

By using a broad or global definition of reading, we are looking upon reading as a total integrative process that includes three domains: (1) the *affective,* (2) the *perceptual,* and (3) the *cognitive.*

Affective domain
Includes the feelings and emotional learnings that individuals acquire.

The affective domain includes our feelings and emotions. The way we feel influences greatly the way we look upon stimuli on a field. It may distort our perception. For example, if we are very hungry and we see the word *fool,* we may read it as *food.* If we have adverse feelings about certain things, these feelings will probably influence how we interpret what we read. Our feelings will also influence what we decide to read. Obviously, attitudes exert a directive and dynamic influence on our readiness to respond.

Perceptual domain
Part of the reading process that depends on an individual's background of experiences and sensory receptors.

In the perceptual domain, *perception* can be defined as giving meaning to sensations or the ability to organize stimuli on a field. How we organize stimuli depends largely on our background of experiences and on our sensory receptors. If, for example, our eyes are organically defective, those perceptions involving sight would be distorted. In the act of reading, visual perception is a most important factor. Children need to control their eyes so they move from left to right across the page. Eye movements determine a reader's reading rate[2] and influence what the reader perceives.

[2] Dorothy Rubin, *Diagnosis and Correction in Reading Instruction,* 2nd ed. (Boston: Allyn and Bacon, 1991), p. 97.

Although what we observe is never in exact accord with the physical situation,[3] readers must be able to decode accurately the graphemic (written) representation. If, however, readers have learned incorrect associations, this will affect their ability to read. For example, if a child reads the word *gip* for *pig* and is not corrected, this may become part of his or her perceptions. If children perceive the word as a whole, in parts, or as individual letters, this will also determine whether they will be good or poor readers. The more mature readers are able to perceive more complex and extensive graphemic (written) patterns as units. They are also able to give meaning to mutilated words such as

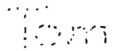

Perception
A cumulative process based on an individual's background of experiences. It is defined as giving meaning to sensations or the ability to organize stimuli on a field.

Perception is a cumulative process that is based on an individual's background of experiences. The perceptual process is influenced by physiological factors as well as affective ones. As already stated, a person who is very hungry may read the word *fool* as *food*. Similarly, a person with a biased view toward a topic may delete, add to, or distort what is being read.

Cognitive domain
Hierarchy of objectives ranging from simplistic thinking skills to the more complex ones.

The cognitive domain includes the areas involving thinking. Under this umbrella we would place all the comprehension skills (see Chapter 7 on reading comprehension). Persons who have difficulty in thinking (the manipulation of symbolic representations) would obviously have difficulty in reading. Although the cognitive domain goes beyond the perceptional domain, it builds and depends on a firm perceptual base. That is, if readers have faulty perceptions, they will also have faulty concepts.

The development of faulty concepts would interfere with the process of reading because reading is a thinking act. Because *A Practical Approach to Teaching Reading* emphasizes reading as a thinking act and because there is often confusion concerning *concepts,* a special section on concepts is presented in Chapter 8.

Metacognition

Metacognition
Thinking critically about thinking; refers to students' knowledge about their thinking processes and ability to control them.

Metacognition literally means thinking critically about thinking. It has been used "to refer to both students' knowledge about their own cognitive processes and their ability to control these processes."[4]

When metacognition is applied to reading, readers are active learners and consumers of information. They use good monitoring strategies whereby they

[3] Julian E. Hochberg, *Perception* (Englewood Cliffs, N.J.: Prentice-Hall, 1964), p. 3.

[4] Claire E. Weinstein and Richard E. Mayer, "The Teaching of Learning Strategies," in *The Handbook of Research on Teaching,* 3rd ed. (New York: Macmillan, 1986), p. 323.

establish learning goals for an instructional activity, determine the degree to which these goals are being met, and, if necessary, change the strategies they are using to attain the goal.[5] In other words, good readers who have metacognitive ability know what to do, as well as how and when to do it.

The "what to do" includes such strategies as "identifying the main idea, rehearsing (repeating) information, forming associations and images, using mnemonics, organizing new material to make it easier to remember, applying test-taking techniques, outlining, and notetaking."[6] Good readers have good reading, learning, and study skill techniques.

The "how and when" includes such strategies as "checking to see if you understand, predicting outcomes, evaluating the effectiveness of an attempt at a task, planning the next move, testing strategies, deciding how to apportion time and effort, and revising or switching to other strategies to overcome any difficulties encountered."[7]

Good readers are good thinkers.

Reading Literacy Objectives

Reading literacy objectives should be those that describe what good readers do. The 1992 National Assessment of Educational Progress (NAEP) for their reading assessment put forth a number of objectives that guide what they assess. These objectives are being given here because they are not dependent on any specific approach or program, and they are in accord with the definition of reading that this text embraces: Reading is a complex, dynamic process that involves the getting of meaning from and the bringing of meaning to the printed page. Good readers do the following:

1. They exhibit positive reading habits and value reading.
2. They can read with enough fluency that they can attend to the meaning of what they are reading rather than focusing all their attention on figuring out words.
3. They form an understanding by using what they already know and interacting actively with the text; they extend, elaborate, and critically judge the meaning of what they read.
4. They plan, manage, and check the progress of their reading and use effective strategies to aid understanding.[8]

---

[5] Ibid.

[6] Anita Woolfolk, *Educational Psychology,* 4th ed. (Englewood Cliffs, N.J.: Prentice-Hall, 1990), p. 252.

[7] Ibid.

[8] *Reading Framework: 1992 National Assessment of Educational Progress Reading Assessment,* 1992 NAEP Reading Consensus Planning Project (Princeton, N.J.: Educational Testing Service, 1990), p. iii.

Reading: An Integral Part of the Language Arts

Language arts
Listening, speaking, reading, and writing.

The language arts are listening, speaking, reading, and writing. Can you imagine any school day devoid of listening, speaking, reading, and writing?

Read the following to see how Mr. Jones integrates the language arts in his sixth-grade class:

Mr. Jones's class is studying the habits of various animals. He has divided his students into a number of groups, and each group is charged with becoming "experts" on different types of animals. To do this, they are to read a variety of materials and take notes on what they read. Then each group is responsible for presenting a talk to the whole class on what they have learned.

During the talk the listeners are responsible for taking notes on the talk, which they use after the talk to summarize the presentation orally.

Commentary

Visitors watching the students' presentations marvel at how smoothly everything goes and how adept the students are in their almost flawless performances. As any teacher knows, however, a lot of work went into getting students to reach this level. Mr. Jones's students are lucky because he recognizes that reading is an integral part of the language arts and tries to incorporate this in his teaching. In addition, he has helped them gain the necessary reading, listening, learning, and study skill strategies that were so evident in their polished performance.

The fundamental interrelatedness of the language arts can be deduced from observations of children's development of oral and written expression, which usually follows the sequence of listening, speaking, reading, and writing. Because of this developmental sequence, a problem encountered in one segment of the language arts will often carry over to another; likewise, proficiency in one area will usually facilitate the acquisition of skill in another area. For example, in order for children to be able to speak correctly, they must be able to hear sounds correctly, and the sounds must convey meaning for them. If children have difficulty with a concept in listening and speaking, this difficulty will usually also carry over to the areas of reading and writing. The "Peanuts" cartoon shown in Figure 1-2 illustrates this very well.

Reprinted by permission of UFS, Inc.

FIGURE 1-2   How can Sally be expected to diagram a sentence if she has no conception of what the term means? (Perhaps Sally is smarter than we think—studies suggest that diagramming sentences does not help students become better writers.)

Listening and Reading

The child's earliest learning of language comes through listening. It is the foundation for the sequential development of language arts. If children do not listen effectively, they almost certainly will have difficulty in all other areas of the language arts.

In order to be able to recognize expressions in print, students must have heard these phrases correctly in the past. Reading comprehension depends on comprehension of the spoken language. Students who are sensitive to the arrangement of words in oral language are more sensitive to the same idea in written language. Listening helps to enlarge a student's vocabulary. It is through listening that pupils learn many expressions they will eventually see in print. Listening takes place all the time. Teachers orally explain word meanings and what the text says. Students listen to other children read orally, talk about books, and explain their contents.

In the elementary grades, students of low and average achievement usually prefer to listen rather than to read independently. These children gain more comprehension and retention from listening because of the important added cues they receive from the speaker, such as stress given to words or phrases, facial expressions, and so on.[9] Children who are very able and who have had success in reading achievement prefer to read rather than listen because these children can set their own rate of reading for maximum comprehension and retention. They don't wish to be constrained by the teacher's fixed oral rate of word production.

The case of students who can understand a passage when it is read to them orally but cannot understand it when they read it themselves, indicates that the words are in the students' listening vocabulary, but that the students have not gained the skills necessary for decoding words from their written forms.

Listening vocabulary
The number of different words one knows the meaning of when they are said aloud.

It may be that some words are in the children's listening vocabulary (for example, they know the meaning of the individual words when they are said aloud), but they still might not be able to assimilate the words into a meaningful concept. The instructor will have to help these children in concept development and in gaining the necessary reading comprehension and listening skills. A person who does not do well in listening comprehension skills will usually not do well in reading comprehension skills. "Good readers tend to be good listeners and, conversely, poor readers tend to be poor listeners."[10] This is especially true at the more advanced levels of reading.[11] Help in one area usually enhances the other because both listening and reading contain some important similar skills,[12]

[9] Robert Ruddell, "Oral Language and the Development of Other Language Skills," *Elementary English* 43 (May 1966): 489–498.

[10] Meredyth Daneman, "Individual Differences in Reading Skills," in *Handbook of Reading Research*, Vol. II, Rebecca Barr, Michael L. Kamil, Peter Mosenthal, and P. David Pearson, eds. (New York: Longman, 1991), p. 526.

[11] Ibid.

[12] Thomas Jolly, "Listen My Children and You Shall Read," *Language Arts* 57 (February 1980): 214–217.

and research going as far back as the 1930s seems to support this view. For example, an investigation done in 1936 found that children who did poorly in comprehension through listening were also poor in reading comprehension.[13] Research in 1955 on the relationship between reading and listening found that practice in listening for detail will produce a significant gain in reading for the same purpose.[14] Studies have also found that training in listening comprehension skills will produce significant gains in reading comprehension[15] and that reading and listening involve similar thinking skills.[16]

Although there are many common factors involved in the decoding of reading and listening — which would account for the relationship between the two language arts areas — listening and reading are, nonetheless, separated by unique qualities, the most obvious being that listening calls for *hearing,* whereas reading calls for *seeing.* As has already been stated, in the area of listening, the speakers are doing much of the interpretation for the listeners by their expressions, inflections, stresses, and pauses. Similarly, the listeners do not have to make the proper grapheme (letter)–phoneme (sound) correspondences because these have already been done for them by the speakers. It is possible for students to achieve excellent listening comprehension while not achieving as well in the area of reading.

Readers must first make the proper grapheme–phoneme correspondences and must then organize these into the proper units to gain meaning from the words. Readers must also be able to determine the shades of meaning implied by the words, to recognize any special figures of speech, and finally to synthesize the unique ideas expressed by the passage.

The relationship between listening and reading ability is summarized succinctly by these four rules:

1. When auding[17] ability is low, reading ability tends more often to be low.
2. When auding ability is high, reading ability is not predictable.
3. When reading ability is low, auding ability is not predictable.
4. When reading ability is high, auding ability is, to a very small extent, predictable — and likely to be high.[18]

[13] William E. Young, "The Relation of Reading Comprehension and Retention to Hearing Comprehension and Retention," *Journal of Experimental Education* 5 (September 1936): 30–39.

[14] Annette P. Kelty, "An Experimental Study to Determine the Effect of Listening for Certain Purposes upon Achievement in Reading for Those Purposes," *Abstracts of Field Studies for the Degree of Doctor of Education* 15 (Greeley: Colorado State College of Education, 1955), pp. 82–95.

[15] Sybil M. Hoffman, "The Effect of a Listening Skills Program on the Reading Comprehension of Fourth Grade Students," Ph.D. dissertation, Walden University, 1978 [ED 157 029].

[16] Thomas G. Sticht, Lawrence J. Beck, Robert N. Hauke, Glenn M. Kleiman, and James H. James, *Auding and Reading: A Developmental Model* (Alexandria, Va.: Human Resources Research Organization, 1974); Walter Kintsch and Ely Kozminsky, "Summarizing Stories after Reading and Listening," *Journal of Educational Psychology* 69 (1977): 491–499.

[17] *Auding* refers to the highest level of listening. It is listening with comprehension. The term *listening* is frequently used to mean auding.

[18] John Caffrey, "The Establishment of Auding-Age Norms," *School and Society* 70 (November 12, 1949): 310.

Listening and Speaking

Studies with deaf and hard-of-hearing children reveal that their speech has been severely retarded. Many children with hearing problems have often been improperly diagnosed as being mentally retarded because of their language difficulty. It would not be far off the mark to say, "We speak what we hear." (See Figure 1-3.)

From descriptive studies of children's acquisition of language, it has been found that they learn language from the speech around them. Children learn the rules that govern usage of words so that they can comprehend and produce properly constructed speech. Because skill in listening is so very closely related to speech development and, subsequently, to effective oral development, knowledge of the various aspects of listening becomes essential for the proper understanding of the development of speech.

Speaking and Reading

Students read with greater ease things that they have talked about. Oral statements in class discussion can be recorded and become reading material for pupils. Through oral language, teachers can learn about the interests of students and build on these in choosing books. Students share favorite stories and passages with others by reading aloud. Many times, pupils will dramatize a story they have found in their reading. Voice sound production activities are based on words in the reading selections. Discussion topics also may emanate from stories.

A good teacher does not have to be a speech expert to be aware of the relationship of speech to other language arts areas. A child who has difficulty in speaking will have difficulty with reading, writing, spelling, phonics, and so on.

If a wide gap exists between the language used by the child every day and the language of the books which he is trying to read, he cannot possibly succeed until that gap is closed. The beginner who says, "Me dot one"; the older child who persists in saying, "I seen," "This one is gooder," "I've gaven it to him," makes slow progress in reading until spoken language improves. [19]

Reprinted by permission of UFS, Inc.

FIGURE 1-3   Having fun and learning should not be mutually exclusive; also, for Sally, "the Mona Lisa" did not make sense, so she heard it as "Ramona Lisa."

[19] Gertrude Hildreth, "Interrelationships among the Language Arts," *The Elementary School Journal* 48 (June 1948): 539.

Although there is no definitive evidence to make the statement that an oral language deficit causes a reading problem, there is ample evidence to conclude that children who have oral language problems also seem to have reading problems. In other words, language problems and reading problems seem to coexist.[20] (See the sections entitled "Language Development and Home Environment" in Chapter 2 and "Language Development, Concept Development, and Reading" in Chapter 8.)

Reading and Writing

The report from *America's Challenge: Accelerating Academic Achievement* shows that "our present education performance is low and not improving."[21] The summary of findings from the National Assessment of Educational Progress states that

> *taking the results of both the age- and grade-level (9-, 13-, and 17-year-olds) reading assessments into account, it appears that most students develop the ability to read for surface understanding as they progress through the school years. That is, they can identify specific information and the "gist" of the material. Yet, when either the material or the reading tasks themselves become more challenging, as suggested in our national goal, far fewer students display competency. In particular, they appear to have considerable difficulty analyzing and synthesizing what they have read.[22]*

The results of the writing assessment are even more worrisome than those for reading:

> *Looking across the three grade levels (grades 4, 8, and 12) and the different types of writing tasks given in the assessments, one finds that many students have difficulty communicating effectively in writing. No more than 47 percent of the students at any grade level wrote adequate or better responses to the informative tasks, and no more than 36 percent of the students wrote adequate or better responses to the persuasive tasks. Although performance was somewhat better on the narrative writing tasks, no more than 56 percent of the students wrote adequate or better responses.[23]*

The summary of writing results should not be surprising, because if students lack higher order thinking ability in reading, they would lack this ability in writing also. In addition, in the early 1980s many decried the fact that writing,

---

[20] Phyllis L. Newcomer and Patricia Magee. "The Performance of Learning (Reading) Disabled Children on a Test of Spoken Language," *The Reading Teacher* 30 (May 1977): 896–900.

[21] Ina V. S. Mullis, Eugene H. Owen, and Gary W. Phillips, *America's Challenge: Accelerating Academic Achievement,* National Assessment of Educational Progress (Princeton, N.J.: Educational Testing Service, 1990), p. 3.

[22] Ibid., p. 16.

[23] Ibid., p. 18.

which is a fundamental skill that is closely related to reading, is often treated as the stepchild of the English curriculum. At that time it was reported that "for every $3,000 spent on children's ability to receive information, $1.00 was spent on their power to send it in writing,"[24] and "for every two hours spent in teaching reading, only five minutes are spent on teaching writing."[25] There were also reports at that time about how far behind writing was in relation to reading in terms of research. But what was most devastating was the report on teacher preparation in writing. It was reported at that time that elementary teachers have little formal training in writing;[26] it should not be surprising, then, that when students advance to the upper grades, many lack writing skills.

It is disappointing that after all the clamor for writing across the curriculum and an emphasis on the writing process, the results over the past decade remain relatively the same; that is, "there has been little overall change."[27]

Because this is a book on reading instruction, some readers may wonder about my concern over the state of writing in the schools. First, it is important to say that concern over the status of writing in the schools is justified because of the interrelatedness of the language arts. Without writing there would be no reading. Writing reinforces word recognition and sentence sense and increases familiarity with words. Through writing students are able to gain a better understanding of the author's task in getting his or her ideas across. Writing makes students keener analyzers of reading; it is a thinking process. As a writer, you are also a reader looking over your shoulder and trying to determine whether what you have written makes sense and whether it accurately expresses what you wanted to convey. If you read widely, you will have a broad range of topics from which to draw for your own writing. Also, through reading you will come to recognize what skills are necessary to be a good writer. Reading helps you acquire knowledge and often furnishes the stimulus for creative writing. Reading helps you to develop vocabulary and a language sense and helps you to become familiar with a variety of sentence structures used in both speaking and writing. Reading good literature exposes you to the beauty of language when it is written so that it seems to capture a sentiment or a thought perfectly.

Both reading and writing need time; that is, students must be given the

[24] Donald H. Graves, "A New Look at Writing Research," *Language Arts* 57 (November–December 1980): 914.

[25] Donald H. Graves, "We Won't Let Them Write," *Language Arts* 55 (May 1978): 638.

[26] Sean A. Walmsley, "What Elementary Teachers Know about Writing," *Language Arts* 57 (October 1980): 733.

[27] Arthur N. Applebee, Judith A. Langer, Ina V. S. Mullis, and Lynn B. Jenkins, *The Writing Report Card, 1984–88,* National Assessment of Educational Progress (Princeton, N.J.: Educational Testing Service, 1990), p. 6; Ina V. S. Mullis, John A. Dossey, Mary A. Foertsch, Lee R. Jones, and Claudia A. Gentile, *Trends in Academic Progress,* National Assessment of Educational Progress (Princeton, N.J.: Educational Testing Service, 1991), p. 150.

opportunity and time to spend in reading and writing. Students also need instruction in both as well as knowledge of results. It seems that one effective way to make the best use of time would be to integrate the teaching of reading and writing.

The integration of reading and writing would be a modification of the language experience approach, and it would be useful in the intermediate and upper grades as well as the primary grades. Special emphasis is being given to this area because I feel that this is a viable approach that can help students to be both better readers and writers. An integrated reading–writing approach stresses the teaching of the two together in such a way that each acts as a stimulus and aid for the other. (See Figure 1-4 and "The Language Experience Approach" in Chapter 11.)

FIGURE 1-4   This child is going over one of his stories with his teacher. He has written an exciting adventure for a character from one of his favorite books. Eventually he will share the story with his classmates.

Scenarios That Integrate the Language Arts

SCENARIO 1

Mrs. Tracy Integrates the Language Arts in Her First Grade

Just before Halloween, Mrs. Tracy has her children listen to the audio cassette "It's Alive," a wonderful Halloween tale by Frances E. Caffrey. After introducing the audio cassette and discussing "trick or treating," she tells her students that the tape is often called "Black Bubble Gum." She asks them to listen carefully to figure out why.

Mrs. Tracy plays the audio cassette. After the tape is finished, she discusses with them why they think the story is often called "Black Bubble Gum." She also asks them if they would have chewed the black bubble gum. She then asks them what they would have done to get rid of the bubble gum.

After discussing the story, Mrs. Tracy asks her students to write what else they think came out of the "trick or treat" bag. She also tells them that after they finish writing their stories, they will read them to the class. (Mrs. Tracy goes over each story with each child, and after they read aloud their stories to the class, she puts the children's stories on the outside bulletin board for everyone to read.)

SCENARIO 2

Mr. Drake Uses a Story Map with His Fourth-Graders to Integrate the Language Arts

Mr. Drake has a very strong integrated language arts program in his class. He gives his students many opportunities to listen, speak, read, and write every day, and today is no exception. Mr. Drake decides to have his students listen to an audio cassette of "It's Alive" because it is close to Halloween, and he knows that most of his children go "trick or treating." After introducing the story and setting purposes for it, he has the students listen to the tape.

Story map
A guide that uses questions to help children gain meaning from a story; it logically represents the major ideas of the story; it can also be a guide in writing a story.

After the children finish listening to the story, Mr. Drake goes over the story using a story map. (A story map is a guide that uses questions to help children gain meaning from a story; it can also be used as a guide in writing a story.) Mr. Drake has used story maps with his children before (see Table 1-1 for a story map they had previously done together), so this is not new to the children. He puts the title of the story in the middle of the chalkboard and then asks the children to list the characters in the story and to state its setting. Mr. Drake lists these under the title; then he has the children state the problem, which he also lists. Next, he has them state how the characters in the story try to solve the problem.

Mr. Drake tells his students that they can use a story map as a guide to writing their own Halloween stories. Under Mr. Drake's guidance, they write some wonderful Halloween stories, which they read aloud to the kindergarten children in their school. The kindergarten children draw pictures to go with the stories. Then Mr. Drake displays his children's stories on the class's outside bulletin board for all to read (see Figure 1-5).

Special Notes

1. The main purpose of the story map is to act as an aid in comprehension. Therefore, the teacher must decide the kinds of questions that will help guide the students through the major points of the story. The story map questions will vary based on the age of the children and the complexity of the story. However, the story map must logically represent the major ideas of the story and be related to the central idea of the story.

2. "It's Alive" is the kind of story that can be used with children in the primary grades, as well as in the intermediate grades.

TABLE 1-1   A Sample Story Map

Title: Ming Lo Moves the Mountain by Arnold Lobel
Characters: Ming Lo, wife, wise man
Setting: The bottom of a large mountain
Problem: The mountain blocked the sun from getting to Ming Lo's house.
   The rocks from the mountain made holes in his roof.
How problem is solved: Ming Lo goes to the wise man
   1. Wise man tells Ming Lo to try to knock down the mountain with a tree.
        Ming Lo and his wife try it.
        It doesn't work.
   2. Wise man tells Ming Lo to make lots of noise with pots and pans to frighten the mountain.
        Ming Lo and his wife try it.
        It doesn't work.
   3. Wise man tells Ming Lo to bake lots of cake and bread to give to the spirit of the mountain.
        Ming Lo and his wife try it.
        It doesn't work.
   4. Wise man tells Ming Lo to take apart his house and bind it up. He tells him to carry it and then to do a dance to move the mountain. The dance is one in which he moves away from the mountain.
        Ming Lo and his wife try it.
        It works.
Why did the last solution work: Ming Lo and his wife moved their house away from the mountain. You can't move a mountain, but you can change where you live.

FIGURE 1-5   A display of children's stories based on the tale "It's Alive."

SCENARIO 3

Miss Sherman Uses a Team Approach to Integrate the Language Arts

Miss Sherman's second-graders start writing stories on the day school begins. This is not unusual, but what she has the students do is unique. Miss Sherman teams each child with a partner. First one student and then the other reads aloud his or her story to his or her partner. The child listening to the story must construct four questions for the story. Then the children challenge each other with their questions. As the year progresses, Miss Sherman helps her students construct questions at various levels of difficulty.

Figure 1-6 shows a story that Marc, one of Miss Sherman's second-graders, wrote, followed by the picture he drew to go with his story.

Reading Theory and Terminology

It is difficult to discuss the theory of reading for a number of reasons, not least of which has to do with the term *theory* itself. It has been asserted "that a definition of theory may exist for every published discussion of the topic,"[28] and a perusal of

---

[28] Walter Hill, "Concerning Reading Theory: A Reaction to Carver's 'Toward a Theory of Reading Comprehension and Rauding,' " *Reading Research Quarterly* 13 (1977–1978): 67.

the reading research literature would probably corroborate this view. Dictionaries do not shed too much light on the confusion surrounding the term *theory*. For example, in *Webster's New Collegiate Dictionary* the word *theory* is defined in a number of different ways. Here are some of them: A theory is "the analysis of a set of facts in their relations to one another"; "a belief, policy, or procedure proposed or followed as the basis of action"; "a plausible or scientifically acceptable general principle or body of principles offered to explain phenomena"; "an unproved assumption"; and so forth.

The field of reading is replete with numerous theories, and different catch phrases are sometimes assigned to the same general theories, further confusing the field. An area that has caused much heat and debate among reading theorists

FIGURE 1-6   Marc's story.

FIGURE 1-6   *(cont.)* Marc's picture.

is that of beginning reading. Controversy has centered on whether the reading process is a holistic one (emphasis on meaning), that is, a top-down model of reading, or a subskill process (code emphasis), that is, a bottom-up model, and more recently on whether it is an interactive model, which is somewhat but not entirely a combination of both top-down and bottom-up in that both processes take place simultaneously depending on the difficulty of the material for the individual reader.

Although various types of each reading model have been proposed, and within each group there have been extremists as well as middle-of-the-road advocates, each model has certain unique elements.

Top-down reading models
These models depend on the reader's background of experiences and language ability in constructing meaning from the text.

Top-down reading models depend greatly on the reader's background of experiences and language ability in constructing meaning from the text. In the top-down models readers continuously make predictions about the text based on their prior knowledge, the specific material being read, and the context of the material. For the top-down theorist, "the skilled readers go directly from print to meaning without first recoding print to speech."[29]

Bottom-up reading models
Models that consider the reading process as one of grapheme–phoneme correspondences; code emphasis or subskill models.

The bottom-up reading models, on the other hand, consider the reading process as one of grapheme (letter)–phoneme (sound) correspondences—that is, a decoding process. After the written code has been broken, the reader associates meaning to the written symbols if the words are in the reader's listening experience. For the bottom-up models, the printed material is supposed to supply more information than the reader, which is the converse of the top-down models. Some theorists claim that the bottom-up models describe what readers do when first learning to read and that a top-down model is applicable to more skilled readers.[30]

Interactive reading models
The top-down processing of information is dependent on the bottom-up processing, and vice versa.

The interactive models of reading, which are currently the most widely held, seem to be somewhat but not completely a cross between the top-down and bottom-up models. In these models, the top-down processing of information is dependent on the bottom-up processing, and vice versa. In other words, if the material is difficult to decode, this difficulty will obviously influence comprehension; similarly, if the material is difficult to understand, the impediment will slow down the decoding process. However, there is not "complete agreement among the interactive theorists as to which kind of processing initiates the reading process, or if the processes occur almost simultaneously."[31] There is agreement, however, that "reading involves the skillful combination of linguistic and semantic knowledge with visual information in order to reconstruct the meaning intended by the author."[32]

Practices in classrooms are based on the theories that teachers embrace. Theories often tend to be exclusive; they emphasize their own approach and generally neglect others. The classroom teacher, however, should not accept an either–or dichotomy, but rather should seek a synthesis of all the elements that have proved to be workable; that is, the classroom teacher usually takes elements from each theory based on the individual needs of students. It is not a contradiction of any one of the theories to use elements of each. Good teachers realize that the reading process is a very complex one and that there is no simple answer.

---

[29] Albert J. Harris and Edward R. Sipay, *How to Increase Reading Ability,* 9th ed. (New York: Longman, 1990), p. 13.

[30] Ibid., p. 12.

[31] Ibid., p. 14.

[32] Ibid.

Reading Terminology: A Special Note

When Confucius (c. 551–479 B.C.) was asked what he would do if he had the responsibility for administering a country, he said that he would improve language. If language is not correct, he stated, then what is said is not what is meant; if what is said is not what is meant, then what ought to be done remains undone; if this remains undone, morals and arts would deteriorate; if morals and arts deteriorate, justice will go astray; if justice goes astray, the people will stand about in helpless confusion.

The reading field, like any other professional field, has a special vocabulary. This is understandable because we need labels in order to be able to communicate with one another. The problem is that in the reading field there is disagreement on the use of terms; that is, the same term may be used in a number of different ways. This can be confusing. For example, although the terms *recognition* and *identification* are denoted as synonyms in most dictionaries, persons in the reading field have stipulated a number of different meanings for each, and some are at variance with others.

Another example is the term *whole language.* This omnipresent term has been embraced by teachers, textbook writers, basal reader writers, test makers, and so on. The difficulty is that "whole language" has become a catch phrase that means different things to different people.

Whole language is a set of beliefs that stresses the wholeness of things; it is not an approach, a program, or a set of books. (See Chapter 12 for an in-depth discussion of whole language.)

In *A Practical Approach to Teaching Reading,* Second Edition, I have tried to give principles in practical, comprehensible language as often as possible, for a book overburdened with esoteric terminology tends to obscure rather than clarify concepts. Some explanations cannot be given without names, but whenever I use a technical term or one that is used in various ways by different reading people, I define the term and then use it. I hope readers will find that I have succeeded in cutting down on the number of terms to be learned and that they will benefit from a concentration on practical principles in place of one on terminology.

Graphic Summary of Chapter

Here is a graphic summary of Chapter 1. If you have read the chapter, this graphic illustration should help you remember its main points. Under or beside each heading, you might want to jot down some of the information you recall, as well as some of the key concepts in this chapter. This can act as a good review. You can then check your key concepts against those that follow the graphic summary.

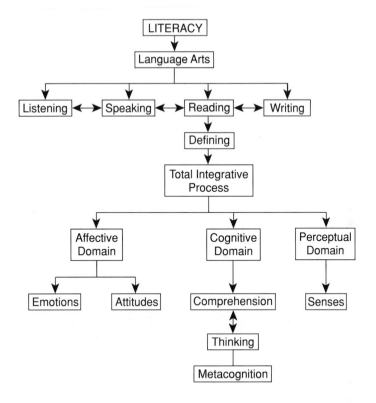

Key Concepts

- Today everyone is expected to learn to read.
- School is usually looked upon as the place where children learn to read.
- Reading is a complex, dynamic process that involves the bringing of meaning to and the getting of meaning from the printed page.
- A number of factors influence whether a reader will get the message from the printed page.
- Reading is a total integrative process that includes the affective, perceptual, and cognitive domains.
- Metacognition helps readers be more active learners and consumers of information.
- Good readers are good thinkers.
- Reading literacy objectives describe what readers do.
- All the language arts are interrelated.
- Reading should be taught as an integral part of the language arts.

- The field of reading is filled with numerous reading theories.
- The top-down reading models depend on the reader's background of experiences and language ability in constructing meaning from text.
- The bottom-up reading models consider the reading process as one of grapheme–phoneme correspondences.
- In the interactive reading models, the top-down processing of information is dependent on the bottom-up processing, and vice versa.

Suggestions for Thought Questions and Activities

1. Observe reading lessons for a one-week period in the same class. From your observations, try to determine the teacher's definition of reading.
2. Try to determine whether the teacher in question 1 views reading as an integral part of the language arts. Keep a record of the kinds of language arts activities the teacher employs if he or she does integrate reading with the other language arts.
3. If the teacher in question 1 does not integrate reading with the other language arts, state the kinds of language arts activities that the teacher could have employed.
4. You have been asked to give a talk to the parents in your school about your definition of reading. What will you say?
5. Explain how the language arts are interrelated.
6. Discuss what is meant by the statement that "reading is a total integrative process."

Selected Bibliography

Dyson, Anne Haas, ed. *Collaboration through Writing and Reading: Exploring Possibilities.* Champaign, Ill.: National Council of Teachers of English, 1989.

Heller, Mary F. *Reading–Writing Connections: From Theory to Practice.* New York: Longman, 1991.

Mullis, Ina V. S., Eugene H. Owen, and Gary W. Phillips. *America's Challenge: Accelerating Academic Achievement,* National Assessment of Educational Progress. Princeton, N.J.: Educational Testing Service, 1990.

Rubin, Dorothy. *Teaching Elementary Language Arts,* 4th ed. Englewood Cliffs, N.J.: Prentice-Hall, 1990.

2

Understanding the Individual Differences of Children

SCENARIO: THE ANIMAL SCHOOL—A CLASSIC FABLE

The classic fable of "The Animal School" illustrates the importance of recognizing that individual differences exist among students.

The Animal School

G. H. Reavis

Once upon a time the animals decided they must do something heroic to meet the problems of a "New World." So they organized a school. They adopted an activity curriculum consisting of running, swimming, and flying. To make it easier to administer the curriculum it was decided that all of the animals should take all of the subjects.

The duck was excellent in swimming. In fact, he was far better than his instructor, but he could not do more than make passing grades in flying and was very poor in running. Since he was so slow in running, he had to remain after school and drop swimming in order to practice running. This was kept up until his web feet were badly worn and he was only average in swimming. But average was acceptable in the school—so nobody worried about that except the duck.

The rabbit started at the top of the class in running, but had a nervous breakdown because of so much make-up work in swimming. The squirrel was excellent in climbing until he developed frustration in the flying class where his teacher insisted that he start from the ground up instead of from the treetop down. He also developed "Charlie horses" from overexertion and then got a "C" in climbing and a "D" in running.

The eagle was indeed a problem child and was disciplined severely. In the

25

climbing class, he beat all others to the top of the tree, but insisted on using his own way to get there. At the end of the year an abnormal eel that could swim exceedingly well, run, climb, and fly a little, had the highest average and was made valedictorian.

The prairie dogs stayed out of school and fought the tax levy because the administration refused to add digging and burrowing to the curriculum. They apprenticed their child to a badger and joined with the groundhogs and gophers to start a very successful private school.

Does this little Fable have a moral?

The moral of the fable is that schools must take the individual differences of students into account and capitalize on their strengths rather than trying to make all students similar.

When young children first come to school, we can wonder what their chances are for success. Will they learn to read, or will they become roll-call statistics in the nonreaders' ledger?

The answers to these questions depend on the children's past experiences, as well as the difference factors discussed in this chapter.

A good reading program cannot exist unless teachers take the individual differences of their students into account. Perceptive teachers sensitive to the uniqueness of each of their students will be better able to plan a program based on their students' needs. Because the principle of providing for the individual differences of students is the backbone of the reading program, this chapter is being presented in Part 1. Throughout this book the necessity of providing for the individual differences of students is emphasized.

Why humans behave as they do is a fascinating question. For example, why is it that two children with similar intelligence quotient (IQ) scores have different achievement behaviors? Even though we cannot discuss the cause of children's behavior in any substantive way in this text (many excellent books are devoted specifically to this topic; see the "Selected Bibliography" at the end of this chapter), it is important for the reading teacher to have some understanding of the various factors that make up individual difference. Some important individual differences that influence language development and, consequently, reading and school achievement are shown in Figure 2-1. (No weighting of the relative importance of the factors is given.)

This chapter will discuss and explain how the factors shown in Figure 2-1 may affect individual school performance and, in particular, reading.

KEY QUESTIONS

After you finish reading this chapter, you should be able to answer the following questions:

1. What individual difference factors affect language development, reading, and school achievement?

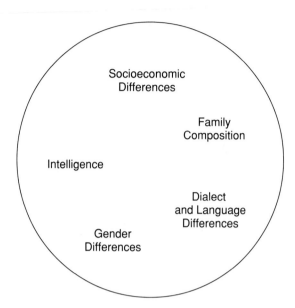

FIGURE 2-1   Individual differences.

2. How is intelligence usually defined?
3. What is the role of intelligence in children's reading achievement?
4. What is the nature–nurture controversy concerning intelligence?
5. What, if any, gender differences exist in reading?
6. How does home environment affect reading?
7. How do socioeconomic factors influence reading achievement?
8. What should teachers know about the cultural diversity of their students?
9. What should teachers know about the dialect and language differences of their students?
10. Who are the at-risk children?
11. What is the role of teachers in providing for the individual differences of their students?

KEY TERMS IN CHAPTER

You should pay special attention to the following key terms:

at-risk students   intelligence
black English   nonstandard English
dialect   second-language learners
home environment   standard English

Individual Differences: Two Case Studies

Read the following scenarios. Which child do you predict has a better chance of succeeding in school? Why?

SCENARIO 1

Lucinda R.

Lucinda, who is three years old, is an only child. She lives with her parents in a large apartment in the city. Her parents love and adore her. Her mother left work after Lucinda was born in order to stay home with her because she wanted to enjoy Lucinda's childhood; she didn't want to miss her baby's first words or her first steps. She has never regretted doing this.

Lucinda's days with her mother are filled with the joy of exploring things together. The wind, the stars, the sun, the sky, the clouds are all wondrous to Lucinda. She constantly questions her Mommy and Daddy about the world around her. Her desire to know is almost unquenchable. Lucinda and her parents talk and talk and talk. (Lucinda's parents had read that young children are egocentric—that is, that they are only concerned with themselves and cannot carry on a conversation involving an exchange of ideas. But this is not so for Lucinda, who can definitely engage in a meaningful dialogue.)

When Lucinda sees her parents reading the newspaper or a book, Lucinda likes to "read" her books, too. She especially loves to have her parents read to her, and her parents love to hear Lucinda retell the story in her own words. Often, Lucinda will "read" a book aloud to her parents and imitate their way of portraying the various characters in the story. Her parents beam with delight when Lucinda stops at a critical point in the story and asks them what they think will happen next or when she stops just before a refrain and waits for them to repeat it exactly. It amazes them that she can remember the story so well. It's as if she really were reading the story aloud (see Figure 2-2).

Lucinda's parents take her out to eat in many different restaurants, so she has been exposed to various types of foods. She knows what a menu is and loves to "read" the menu and order her favorite foods.

She and her parents go to the park, to the zoo, to the science museum, to the museum of natural history, and also to a number of art museums. Lucinda says she wants to be an artist, and at some of the art museums there is a place for children to display their talents.

Lucinda's parents have taken Lucinda to visit different parts of the country. At three, she has flown on a number of airplanes, she has been on a large boat, and she has also been to Disney World. Lucinda is a fortunate child!

FIGURE 2-2   This child is not even three, and she is already "reading." What predictions can you make about her chances for success when she comes to school?

SCENARIO 2 ━━━━━━━━━━━━━━━━━━━━━━━━━━━━

Ronda A.

Ronda A. is also three years old and lives in the same city as Lucinda; as a matter of fact, she lives just five streets away. However, the similarities end there. Their lives and worlds are so different that they might as well be living on two different planets.

Lucinda's apartment house overlooks the park; it stands proud and tall on a tree-lined street. Ronda's house looks like an abandoned building in the midst of a war zone. The building is charred, and the streets are littered with debris and trash. There is no friendly doorman in Ronda's building, and no security guards. Her building is a haven for drug addicts and other undesirables.

Ronda is the next to the youngest of nine children, seven of whom live with their mother in three cramped rooms. Her mother is on welfare, and only three of the children have the same father. There is no father living at home—only a steady stream of "uncles."

Ronda's life is not a happy one. She often doesn't have food to eat, and the food she has is not very nutritious. Nobody listens to her, so she has given up trying to talk to her older brothers and sisters. She spends most of her days listening to her siblings' chatter, taking care of her younger sister, and watching television. When she talks to the baby, she uses expressions she has picked up from her siblings and their friends. Many of the words are X-rated. At three, Ronda has learned about alcohol and drugs. She has learned how to stay out of the way of the police and how to care for her mother when she has a hangover. Ronda is starting life with many drawbacks and is at risk of failing in school before she starts.

At-risk students Those students who because of their backgrounds or other factors are in danger of failing in school.

Commentary

Both Lucinda and Ronda are products of their home environments. When they come to school, they will need teachers who respect individual differences and who will provide a program based on their developmental levels and needs. Lucinda needs a program that will capitalize on her rich background, whereas Ronda needs to gain many of the concepts that will help her succeed in school. Teachers must recognize also that even though Ronda does not have "school-success knowledge," she is not stupid. She is "street-wise" and has an "expressive" vocabulary of her own.

The individual differences between Lucinda and Ronda are quite pronounced at age three, and by the time they come to school the differences will be even greater. "What is particularly striking is that schooling does not reduce the differences among individuals in their reading ability. On the contrary, individual differences are pervasive and persistent and, if anything, become more pronounced with more years of schooling. For example, the differences among the reading achievement of twelfth graders are much larger than the differences among first graders."[1]

The function of the schools is not, as in the "Animal School" fable, to destroy individual differences but, rather, to respect individual differences and try to nip potential problems in the bud, before they become virulent.

What teachers do when children come to school will determine how well their students will do. Teachers are crucial in turning children on or off to learning. Because of this, Chapter 3 of this book is a special chapter on the teacher.

Now let's look at those individual difference factors that play such a significant role in children's literacy development.

[1] Meredyth Daneman, "Individual Differences in Reading Skills," in *Handbook of Reading Research,* Vol. II, Rebecca Barr, Michael L. Kamil, Peter Mosenthal, and P. David Pearson, eds. (New York: Longman, 1991), p. 512.

Home Environment

Home environment
Socioeconomic
class, parents'
education, and the
neighborhood in
which children live
are some factors
that shape children's
home environment.

Socioeconomic class, parents' education, and the neighborhood in which children live are some of the factors that shape children's home environments. Studies have shown that the higher the socioeconomic status, the better the verbal ability of the child.[2] Children who have good adult language models and are spoken to and encouraged to speak will have an advantage in the development of language and intelligence. Similarly, children who come from homes where there are many opportunities to read; where there are diverse reading materials such as magazines, encyclopedias, books, and newspapers; and where the people with whom the children are living read frequently will be better readers than children without these advantages (see Figure 2-3).[3]

Parents who behave in a warm, democratic manner and who provide their children with stimulating educationally oriented activities, challenge their children to think, encourage independence, and reinforce their children are preparing them very well for school.

Children who come from homes where parents have only an elementary school education, where many people live in a few rooms, and where unemployment among the adults in the home is common will usually be at a disadvantage in language learning.

Teachers should also be aware of the adult composition of the child's home environment. Whether a child is reared by both parents, a single parent, a servant, grandparents, or foster parents will affect the child's attitudes and behavior. A child who is reared by a female single parent may behave differently from one reared by a male single parent, for instance. The death of one parent or of another family member will usually cause emotional stress in the child. A divorce can be a traumatic experience for children. Teachers who are aware of the home environment and are sensitive to sudden changes in this important area are in a better position to understand and help such students.

How many children are born into a family and the order in which these children are born affect the achievement levels of individuals, at least to some degree. Research is still being done on these factors, but it has been hypothesized that firstborn children do better both in school and in life than other children in the family. Children without siblings have been shown to be more articulate for the most part than children who are products of a multiple birth (like twins or triplets) or singletons (one child born at a time) who have other brothers and sisters.[4]

---

[2] Walter D. Loban, *Language Development: Kindergarten through Grade Twelve,* Research Report No. 18 (Urbana, Ill.: National Council of Teachers of English, 1976).

[3] Ina V. S. Mullis and Lynn B. Jenkins, *The Reading Report Card, 1971–1988,* National Assessment of Educational Progress (Princeton, N.J.: Educational Testing Service, 1990), pp. 38–39.

[4] Mildred A. Dawson and Miriam Zollinger, *Guiding Language Learning* (New York: Harcourt Brace Jovanovich, 1957), pp. 36–37; Didi Moore, "The Only-Child Phenomenon," *The New York Times Magazine,* Section 6, January 18, 1981, pp. 26–27, 45–48.

FIGURE 2-3   Andrew's mother reads with him every day.

Language Development and Home Environment

Children who are advanced in language development tend to achieve better in school than those who are not. Studies show that high-achieving readers come from homes with enriched verbal environments, whereas low-achieving readers come from homes in which little conversation takes place with the parents.[5]

The home environment obviously plays a significant role in a child's language development. And it is in the area of language development that at-risk children tend to show the greatest literacy lacks. The following report from an English writer emphasizes the importance of having someone to talk to, especially in the crucial years from two to five. It substantiates how closely interrelated are the areas of language, intelligence, early home environment, reading success, and consequently school success.

[5] Loban, *Language Development.*

Twenty-four children of one-and-a-half to two years old, living in an orphanage, were divided into two groups, matched for "measured intelligence"—as far as it could be measured at that age: What is clear is that both groups showed *low* ability. Each of the twelve in one group was sent to be looked after by an adolescent girl living in a mental home; the other group was left at the orphanage. After two years the group that had been living with the girls showed extraordinary increases in measured intelligence (well over twenty points), while those in the orphanage showed a *decrease* of similar proportions. What is more astounding still is that after *twenty-one years,* the experimenter was able to trace the children and discovered that the average of the final school achievement of the group looked after in infancy by the girls was twelfth grade (work normal for seventeen- to eighteen-year-olds), whereas the average for the other group was fourth grade (work normal for nine- to ten-year-olds).[6]

Cultural Diversity

SCENARIO

Mr. Perry Prepares to Meet His Fourth-Grade Class

Mr. Perry awakens with a feeling of both anxiety and excitement. Today is the first day of teaching his very own class. He knows what an important day it is, and he is determined to be the best teacher possible and to make a good impression on his students. In his mind's eye, he has gone over a million times what he will say when he first greets his students and how he will do this. He feels well primed. He also is determined to learn all his students' names as quickly as possible.

Mr. Perry showers, dresses, and has some juice; he is too excited to eat. He picks up his attaché case and dashes to his car. He wants to get to his classroom very early to make sure everything is exactly as he left it the day before.

Actually, Mr. Perry has spent a long time preparing for this special first day. When he was hired, he was told that he would have a number of students for whom English was a second language. He was also told that some of these students knew hardly any English and was asked how he felt about working with such students. Mr. Perry told his principal that he felt it would be a challenge and that he would prepare for this over the summer.

Over the summer, Mr. Perry learned as much as he could about the children he would have in his class, especially those who did not speak English. He prepared a bulletin board for the first day that says, "Hello, I am glad you are here" in twenty different languages, and he left places for the students to put their photos and names. His goal is to make everyone feel welcome and to create an excellent affective environment. He feels strongly that in a nonthreatening envi-

Second-language learners
Children whose parents usually were born in another country and who speak a language other than English; also may refer to a child born in the United States, where English is not the dominant language spoken in the child's home.

6 James Britton, *Language and Learning* (Middlesex, England: Penguin, 1970), pp. 94–95.

ronment children will learn better and feel freer to share and help one another. After all, preparing an individual to live in society has always been a major goal of education. And, today, when one speaks of society, it is the society of the world.

Mr. Perry arrives early. He looks approvingly at his welcoming bulletin board, the round table, and the many shelves filled with various trade books and other print materials he has chosen. He does not have all his learning centers finished because he wants to wait to get input from his students. He looks at the clock. The students will be arriving soon. He sits down at his desk, opens his attaché case, takes out his newspaper, and starts to glance at it. He is really too excited to read. (Through the school year, he will make sure the students see him reading various print materials because he knows how important role modeling is.)

When the school bell rings, he almost jumps out of his skin. He leaps up and goes to the door to greet each arriving student. He smiles and says "Hello" to each. There is no mistaking the warmth of the message; the smile is a universal greeting.

Commentary

The chances are great that Mr. Perry is off to a very good year. He is a teacher who takes nothing for granted, and he is sensitive to the individual differences of his students and will try to provide for these differences. This is an important first step.

The United States is a multicultural nation, and this cultural mix is reflected in our classrooms and among our students (see Figure 2-4). Our students come from different socioeconomic backgrounds, races, and ethnic groups. As has already been stated, these factors greatly shape their lives.

When children enter school, they bring with them the language of their environment, of their family, home, and neighborhood. This first language learning they have acquired is the most deeply rooted, regardless of what other language learning they achieve later in their lives.

Even though most teachers are not linguists or polyglots, effective teachers need to be cognizant of the language differences among their students in order to provide the best possible education for them. The sections that follow should help acquaint teachers with some of the possible differences and language interferences they may encounter in their classrooms.

Dialect and Language Differences

Dialect and language differences are closely related to home environment because the home environment will determine whether the child will speak standard English, a dialect of English, Spanish, Italian, Russian, Chinese, German, French, or some other language. As stated earlier, teachers today have a diverse

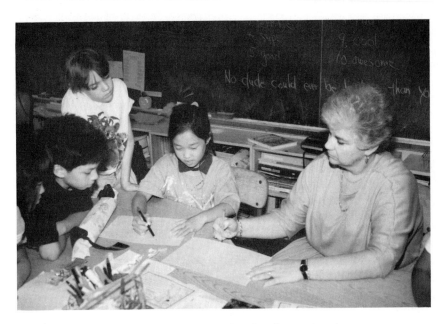

FIGURE 2-4   Most classrooms have a multicultural mix of students.

mix of students in their classroom; the more teachers know about their students' cultural backgrounds, the better able they will be to provide meaningful instruction based on the needs and interests of their students.

Standard English
English in respect to spelling, grammar, vocabulary, and pronunciation that is substantially uniform, though not devoid of regional differences. It is well established by usage in the formal and informal speech and writing of the educated and is widely recognized as acceptable wherever English is spoken and understood.

Dialect
A variation of language sufficiently different to be considered separate, but not different enough to be classified as a separate language.

According to *Webster's Third New International Dictionary,* the term *standard English* is defined as "the English that with respect to spelling, grammar, pronunciation, and vocabulary is substantially uniform, though not devoid of regional differences, that is well established by usage in the formal and informal speech and writing of the educated, and that is widely recognized as acceptable wherever English is spoken and understood."

The term *dialect,* however, is more difficult to define. To some persons, a dialect of English is any variation of standard English; to others, it is merely a means of expressing oneself; and to still others, it is a variety of language related to social class, educational level, geography, gender, and ethnicity. From these definitions, we can see that standard English could then be considered a dialect and that the definition of dialect is obviously intertwined with that of language. If we were to define dialect in a broad sense, we would be concerned with the language of a geographic area; if we were to define it in a specific sense, we would be looking at the language of a neighborhood, a family, or even an individual (*idiolect*). Generally, however, when we refer to dialect, we are talking about a structured subsystem of a language, with definite phonological and syntactic structures, that is spoken by a group of people united not only by their speech but also by factors such as geographic location and/or social status.[7]

[7] Jean Malmstrom and Constance Weaver, *Transgrammar: English Structure, Style, and Dialects* (Glenview, Ill.: Scott, Foresman, 1973), p. 338.

For some people the term *dialect* seems to have negative connotations. This is unfortunate because we all speak a dialect. "Dialects inevitably arise within all languages because all languages inevitably change."[8] If the geographical separation between groups of people is very great, and the separation lasts long enough, "the dialects may diverge from each other so much that they become two distinct languages."[9] (Persons who speak different languages do not understand one another, whereas persons who speak different dialects do.)

In the United States, standard English is considered the "prestige" dialect. Where regional dialects differ very little from each other, perhaps almost exclusively in pronunciation, we would be more likely to speak of an "accent" than a "dialect."[10] In this book, whenever the term *nonstandard English* is used, it refers to a variation of standard English owing to socioeconomic and cultural differences in the United States.

Nonstandard English
A variation of standard English owing to socioeconomic and cultural differences in the United States.

Children speaking in a dialect of English have no difficulty communicating with one another. However, any dialect that differs from standard English structure and usage will usually cause communication problems for children in school and in society at large. Many expressions used by children who speak a variation of English may be foreign to teachers, and many expressions used by teachers may have different connotations for the students. The similarities between the dialects of English and standard English can also cause misunderstandings between students and teachers because both groups may feel they "understand" what the others are saying when, in actuality, they may not. These "misunderstandings" may be especially true for black English vernacular, which is in the class of nonstandard English. Black English and standard English appear similar, but they are not. Labov's research in the 1980s suggests that the differences between black English and standard English are becoming greater rather than narrower. He states that he would not rule out "the possibility that it is contributing to failure of black children to learn to read. How much a little child has to do to translate!"[11]

Black English
A variation of standard English; in the class of nonstandard English.

Here is a sample summary of some possible phonological and grammatical interferences between standard English and black English that may affect reading.

---

1. *r*-lessness. Black English has a rather high degree of *r*-lessness. The *r* becomes a schwa or simply disappears before vowels as well as before consonants or pauses: *r* is never pronounced in *four, Paris* becomes *Pass, carrot* becomes *cat.*

[8] Peter Desberg, Dale E. Elliott, and George Marsh, "American Black English and Spelling," in *Cognitive Processes in Spelling,* Uta Frith, ed. (New York: Academic Press, 1980), p. 70.
[9] Ibid., p. 71.
[10] John P. Hughes, *The Science of Language* (New York: Random House, 1962), p. 26.
[11] William Labov, Professor of Linguistics, Personal communication, University of Pennsylvania, January 11, 1990.

2. *l*-lessness. Dropping of the liquid *l* is similar to the dropping of *r* except that the former is often replaced by a back unrounded glide (*u*) instead of the center glide for *r*. Or the *l* disappears completely, especially after the back-rounded vowels. Examples: *help = hep, tool = too, all = awe, fault = fought.*

3. Simplification of consonant clusters at the end of words. There is a general tendency to reduce end consonant clusters to single consonants, particularly those ending in /t/, /d/, /s/, or /z/. In approximate order of frequency, the /t,d/ clusters affected are *-st, -ft, -nt, -nd, -ld, -zd, -md,* thus generating homonyms such as *past = pass, meant = men, rift = riff, mend = men, wind = wine, hold = hole.* The /s,z/ cluster simplification results in these homonyms: *six = sick, box = bock, Max = Mack, mix = Mick.* Labov found that the simplification of the /s,z/ clusters is much more characteristic of black speakers than of white speakers.

4. Weakening of final consonants. This is another example of a general tendency to produce less information after stressed vowels, so that the endings of words (be they consonants, unstressed final vowels, or weak syllables) are devoiced or dropped entirely. Children who possess this characteristic seem to have the most serious reading problems. Most affected by this are the following: *boot = boo, road = row, feed = feet, seat = seed = see, poor = poke = pope, bit = bid = big.*

5. Possessive deletion. The absence of /-s/ inflection results in: *John's cousin = John cousin, whoever's book = whoever book.* Deletion of /-r/ makes two possessive pronouns identical to personal pronouns: *their book = they book, your = you = you-all.*

6. Verb suffix. Labov believes that the third person singular was not present in black English but was imported from standard English in view of the low percentage of use (only 5 to 15 percent in some cases) and the sharp class stratification between middle and working classes. Some illustrations of the use of the verb suffix in black English are: *Somebody get hurts. He can goes out. He always bes on the beach mosta de time. All our men ares each on side. We goes to church on Sunday. Judy go to school today.*

7. *Be₂* form. There are two forms of *do* and two forms of *have* in English as in "Does he do it?" and "Has he had any?" In the first question, they could be called *Do₁* and *Do₂*. The second form in each class is a normal main verb. *Be* has a main verb *Be₂* which is like other main verbs. The meaning of *Be₂* is so versatile that in some instances standard English has no equivalents:

a. Habitual rather than a temporal or short occurrence. *From now on, I don't be playing. He be sad. I be crying. She always be happy. Guys that bes with us.*

b. Repeated occurrence. Wolfram found between 11 and 16 percent frequency of adverbs with *Be₂*, such as *hardly, usually, sometimes, always, mostly,* and *all the time.*

c. Single nonrepeated activity in the future. This practice is used in all cases where *will* is possible or where an underlying *will* could be elicited in tag questions or in negatives: *Sometime he don't be busy. He be in in a few minutes. I know he will. Sometime he be busy. I know he do.*

   d. Deletion of "would." *She just be talking, and I wouldn't listen. If he didn't have to go away, he be home.*

      8. Copulation. Copula deletion is considered basically a phonological process, but it also has strong grammatical constraints, which are not random. Deletion may occur with verb following, no vowel preceding, but pronoun preceding. Semantically, deletion occurs most often on short active utterances: *Riff eatin. He going. Ricky too old. Jim goin. She real tired. Carol chairman.*

      9. Person–number agreement.

   a. In black English, there is person–number agreement for *I am, you are,* and *he is.*

   b. There is no third person singular marker, as in most languages around the world. The preferred forms are: *He don't. He do. He have. Does, has,* and *says* are used infrequently.

   c. *Was* is the preferred form for past tense of *be.*

      10. Past tense. Phonological conditioning weakens the regular past tense, as in the reduction of /t,d/ inflection: *passed = pass, missed = miss, fined = fine, picked = pick, loaned = loan, raised = raise.*

      11. Negative forms and negation. In black English, *ain't* is used as past negative; for example, *I told im I ain't pull it; He didn't do nothing much, and I ain't neither.* Adults used *didn't* more often than *ain't.* Preteens use *ain't* less often than teenagers. *Ain't* is a stigmatized form but has special social meaning to teenagers.

      In negation, black English seems to carry negative concord principles further than nonstandard Anglo English. Examples: *Nobody had no bloody nose or nosebleed. I am no strong drinker. She didn't play with none of us. Down there nobody don't know about no club.*

Source: Doris C. Ching, *Reading and the Bilingual Child* (Newark, Del.: International Reading Association, 1976), pp. 15–17.

Some Language Difference Interferences

Teachers need to recognize that students who speak a language other than English will usually try to superimpose what they know intuitively about their language on the new language they are learning. Therefore, teachers would be in a better position to help their students if they knew some of the major interferences between standard English and the nonnative speaker's language. This is not easy because most teachers are not polyglots; however, they can seek help from bilingual or English as a second language (ESL) teachers to learn about some of the differences.

Here is a sample of the kinds of problems that Spanish-speaking children have when attempting to learn standard English.

---

1. Certain vowel sounds will be difficult for the Spanish-speaking child: /I/ *bit;* /æ/ *bat;* /ə/ *but;* and /u/ *full.*

2. English relies on voiced (vocal cords vibrate) and voiceless (vocal cords do not vibrate) sounds to establish meaning contrasts, but Spanish does not: *bit–pit; buzz–bus.*

3. The Spanish speaker does not use these sounds in his language: /v/ *vote;* /ð/ *then;* /z/ *zoo;* /ž/ *measure;* /ǰ/ *jump.* Often the speaker will replace these sounds with sounds he perceives as closely resembling them or with sounds that frequently occur in similar positions in Spanish.

4. Words that end in /r/ plus the consonants /d, t, l, p/ and /s/ are pronounced without the final consonant: *card–car, cart–car.*

5. In Spanish the blend of /s/ and the consonant sounds /t, p, k, f, m, n, l/ does not occur, nor does any Spanish word begin with the /s/ + consonant sound. A vowel sound precedes the /s/, and the consonant that follows begins the second syllable of the word. Thus the child has the problem not only of starting the word with the /s/, but also of pronouncing two consonants (star may thus become *estar* and be pronounced *es-tar*). The final consonant clusters /sp/ *wasp,* /sk/ *disk,* and /st/ *last* also present problems in consonant pronunciation.

6. Grammatical differences between the two systems may include the following: subject–predicate agreement (*the cars runs*); verb tense (*I need help yesterday*); use of negative forms (*he no go home*); omission of noun determiner in certain contexts (*he is farmer*); omission of pronoun forms (*Is farmer?*); order of adjectives (*the cap red is pretty*); and comparison (*is more big*).

This summary serves only as an introduction to the teacher to help him or her in being alert to the variations between the Spanish and English languages.

Source: Robert B. Ruddell, *Reading–Language Instruction: Innovative Practices* (Englewood Cliffs, N.J.: Prentice-Hall, 1974), p. 275.

A summary of some of the phonological and grammatical variations between standard English and Chinese are also presented here because of the large population of children in the United States who come from homes where Chinese is the dominant language. The following should help teachers gain a better understanding of some of the difficulties encountered by a number of Chinese-speaking children.

There are many dialects of Chinese, with Mandarin, which is spoken by approximately 70 percent of the Chinese people, as the national dialect. Cantonese, another major dialect, is spoken by most of the Chinese families who come to the United States from Hong Kong, Kowloon, or Macao. Thus, the Cantonese dialect is the one that is discussed here.

---

1. English has many more vowels than Chinese; for example, /ay/ *buy;* /aw/ *bough;* /ɔ/ *bought.* There is specific difficulty with production of certain vowels such as the front vowels /iy/ *beat,* /ey/ *bait.* This results in homophones for a significant number of English words: *beat–bit; Luke–look, bait–bet.*

2. A number of English consonant sounds are not in Chinese: /θ/ *than* /ð/ *that;* /š/ *she;* /n/ *need;* and /r/ *rice.*

3. Many English words end in consonants, but in Chinese many of the consonants are not used in final positions; for example, /f/ is used only initially in Chinese, and the student has difficulty producing it in a final position. Often an extra syllable will be made of the final /f/; *day off* becomes *day offu.*

4. Consonant clusters are nonexistent in Cantonese. Those that occur at the ends of words present difficulty in forming plurals and past tenses using /s, t, d, z/: *cap–caps, laugh–laughed, wish–wished, dog–dogs.*

5. Most grammatical relationships are indicated by word order and auxiliary words: *Yesterday he gave me two books* becomes *Yesterday he give I two book.*

6. Numerical designations or auxiliary words are used to indicate plural forms in Chinese: *two books* is *two book.*

7. A time word or phrase indicates the tense of a verb. An action verb followed by the auxiliary word *jaw* indicates past or completed tense: *He go jaw* means *He went.*

8. Several English word classes—articles, prepositions, and some conjunctions—are reduced or absent in Chinese.

9. The question form in Chinese does not invert the noun and verb forms. Instead, the order is similar to the statement form, but the "empty" words *ma* or *la* are added to the end. For example, *Are you an American?* is *You are American ma?* in Chinese.

10. A subject and a predicate are not required in Chinese when the context is sufficient for understanding. For example, *It rains* may be represented as *Drop rain* in Chinese, while *The mountain is big* may be stated as *Mountain big* in Chinese.

11. Tone or pitch in Chinese distinguishes meanings, but in English pitch combines with intonation to convey sentence meaning.

Source: Robert B. Ruddell, *Reading–Language Instruction: Innovative Practices* (Englewood Cliffs, N.J.: Prentice-Hall, 1974), p. 278.

Special Note

Idiomatic expressions present a great deal of difficulty for all nonnative speakers because idioms are very culturally loaded: the same is true for figurative language; many nonnative speakers will take figurative expressions literally. (A person with limited English who sees a sign that says "Chickens sold—dressed and undressed" would have great difficulty understanding this.)

Teachers' Attitudes toward Nonstandard English

Children who speak nonstandard English may have more problems than children who come from homes in which a foreign language is spoken because more status is generally attributed to a foreign language. It was reported in a large-scale Educational Testing Service study of Title I reading programs that teachers do hold negative attitudes toward nonstandard language.[12] Other studies with similar findings have also reported that the negative attitudes have influenced teacher practices. For example, "teachers tend to rate black English speaking students as lower class, less intelligent, and less able to do well academically than standard English speaking students."[13] In the Ann Arbor school-system case, Judge Charles W. Joiner, a United States district court judge, wrote that "a language barrier develops when teachers, in helping the child switch from the home [black English] language to standard English, refuse to admit the existence of a language that is the acceptable way of talking in his local community."[14]

The rejection of the child's language "may more deeply upset him than rejection of the color of his skin. The latter is only an insult, the former strikes at his ability to communicate and express his needs, feelings—his self."[15] The language of children who do not speak standard English has been an effective means of communication for them until they come to school. If such children are made to feel inferior because of their language by a teacher who constantly attacks their speech as incorrect, they may not attempt to learn standard English.

Intelligence

Intelligence
Ability to reason abstractly; problem-solving ability based on a hierarchical organization of two things—symbolic representations and strategies for processing information.

It is difficult to pick up a newspaper, journal, or magazine without finding some reference to achievement or intelligence. Usually when intelligence—specifically an intelligence test—is brought up, the atmosphere becomes highly charged. Hardly anyone seems to regard IQ objectively.

Intelligence refers to the ability to reason abstractly or to solve problems. It has also been defined as problem-solving ability based on a hierarchical organization of two things—symbolic representations and strategies for processing information. Because intelligence is a construct—that is, it is something that cannot be directly observed or directly measured—testing and research have necessitated

---

[12] Mary K. Monteith, "Black English, Teacher Attitudes, and Reading," *Language Arts* 57 (November–December 1980): 910.

[13] Ibid.

[14] Reginald Stuart, *The New York Times,* July 13, 1979, p. 8.

[15] E. Brooks Smith, Kenneth S. Goodman, and Robert Meredith, *Language and Thinking in the Elementary School* (New York: Holt, Rinehart and Winston, 1976), pp. 46–47.

an operational definition. Such a definition coined in the early part of the century is still much quoted: "Intelligence is what the intelligence test measures."[16] There is a variety of tests designed to measure intelligence, yet no test exists that actually measures intelligence. In other words, intelligence tests cannot adequately determine an individual's absolute limits or the potential of the intelligence. Yet many people, both lay and professional, actually behave as if the intelligence test will tell all.

This state of affairs may be due to the nature–nurture controversy. Advocates of the nature side believe that heredity is the sole determiner of intelligence and that no amount of education or the quality of the environment can alter intelligence. Those who believe in the nurture side claim that intelligence is determined in great part by the environment. For them, intelligence can be affected if the child is exposed to different environments and education. Most professionals take an in-between position, saying that intelligence may be determined by an interaction between heredity and environment. "Heredity deals the cards and environment plays them."[17] Yet the heredity theory dies hard.

The majority position that believes that intelligence is determined by some combination of heredity and environment brings up the question of *which* factor is more important. Conflicting studies reported in this area attribute different percentages to each factor. The controversy continues to rage, as does the confusion surrounding what intelligence tests are measuring.

Most intelligence tests are highly verbal, and studies have shown that persons who do well on vocabulary tests also seem to do well on intelligence tests.[18] If a child has language problems—or if a dialect of English or a language other than English is spoken at home—the child could easily have difficulty in performing well on an intelligence test and in school. IQ tests are valid mainly for a middle-class standard English curriculum, and they predict the ability of an individual to do well in such environments. The positive correlation or agreement between individuals' IQs and their ability to do work in school is neither very high nor low. There are factors other than IQ that determine an individual's success in school. One very important factor for school success is *motivation*—the desire, drive, and sustained interest to do the work.

The IQ test is an imperfect tool that helps teachers and parents to understand the abilities of children better. If students are doing very well in school and if, according to their IQ scores, they are only supposed to be doing average work, one would be misusing the IQ test by thinking, "Stop; you're not supposed to be doing that well."

The IQ test also helps show teachers the wide range of levels of ability in their classes. If teachers are aware of the wide span of mental age of their stu-

---

[16] E. G. Boring, "Intelligence as the Tests Test It," *New Republic* 35 (1925): 35–37.

[17] Lee J. Cronbach, *Educational Psychology* (New York: Harcourt, Brace, 1954), p. 204.

[18] Leona Tyler, *The Psychology of Human Differences* (New York: Appleton-Century-Crofts, 1965), p. 82.

dents, they can design a program based especially on individual needs (see Chapter 15).

However, teachers are cautioned not to see the IQ test as a perfect predictor of a child's ability to do work in school, for there are other factors, some of which are discussed in this chapter, that influence school achievement.

Intelligence and Reading

Because reading is a thinking process, it seems reasonable to assume that highly able persons, who have the ability to think at high levels of abstraction and the ability to learn, should be good readers (see Figure 2-5). To a degree this assumption is so, and many gifted children do learn to read before they come to school (see Chapters 5 and 15). However, studies have shown that not all highly able children become good readers, which confirms the statement made in the previous section that there are factors besides intelligence that contribute to success in reading and, consequently, to school achievement.

Studies have shown also that the correlation between intelligence and reading achievement seems to increase as children go through the grades.[19] Such correlations in the first grade are substantial but not high.[20] This is not surprising, since mental age, which is the child's present developmental level, is more a determinant of reading success when students are involved with reading for information than when they are learning to read. (Of course, while they are learning to read, children are also reading to learn, but the informational load increases as students advance through the grades.) In addition, it is difficult to get a valid IQ score for children seven years old and below.

In the previous section it was stated that intelligence tests are highly verbal and that persons who do well on vocabulary tests also seem to do well on intelligence tests. Studies have also shown that there is a high positive correlation between reading achievement test scores and intelligence test scores.[21] These findings seem to suggest that reading achievement tests and intelligence tests may be measuring some similar factors. Because vocabulary tests correlate highly with intelligence tests and because reading achievement tests depend highly on vocabulary ability, it seems reasonable to assume that a similar and major factor that both kinds of tests have in common is verbal ability. Obviously, reading as a thinking process hinges upon the continuous development of higher levels of verbal ability.

---

[19] Alice Cohen and Gerald G. Glass, "Lateral Dominance and Reading Ability," *The Reading Teacher* 21 (January 1968): 343–348; Dolores Durkin, *Children Who Read Early* (New York: Teachers College Press, 1966), pp. 20–21.

[20] Albert J. Harris and Edward R. Sipay, *How to Increase Reading Ability*, 9th ed. (New York: Longman, 1990), p. 39.

[21] Keith Raynor and Alexander Pollatsek, *The Psychology of Reading* (Englewood Cliffs, N.J.: Prentice-Hall, 1989), p. 395.

Reprinted by permission of UFS, Inc.

FIGURE 2-5   Linus has good reasoning ability; he is a highly able child who should become a good reader. Lucy needs to learn how to control her temper.

Gender Differences

Teachers should know that although studies do not reveal any significant differences between males and females in general intelligence,[22] studies continue to show differences in specific aptitudes.[23] In the earlier studies, it was reported that males in general are superior in mathematical ability and in science, but in rote memory females are usually superior. It also has been consistently shown that girls usually surpass boys in verbal ability. From infancy to adulthood, females usually express themselves in words more readily and skillfully than males do; however, females do not have larger vocabularies than males.[24]

More recent studies seem, for the most part, to confirm earlier findings. An extensive review of the research on gender differences has reported that even though the data on sex differences studies are inconclusive and contradictory, a few generalizations can be made. The reviewers report that "the largest differences appear in tests of mathematical or quantitative ability, where men tend to do better than women, particularly in secondary school and beyond. In recent years, there is some evidence that the gender gap may be narrowing."[25] What is surprising is that the gender gap is narrowing between men and women in the area of verbal skills. "Women have tended to do better than men in many tests of verbal skills (particularly writing), but a number of studies indicate that this superiority has diminished since the early 1970s."[26]

In the 1970s and 1980s females made great inroads into male bastions. Because of this, the results of the latest findings on gender differences may seem confusing, but they should not be. What has happened is that males have gained in verbal skills, so that females seem to be losing their edge in this area, and males have continued to maintain their edge in mathematical skills.

Sex Differences and Reading

A review of the national assessments of reading between 1971 and 1990 reveals that even though, as stated earlier, the traditional female advantage in verbal skills seems to be eroding, "females at all three ages (9, 13, and 17) outperformed their male counterparts in each of the six NAEP reading assessments. . . ."[27]

---

[22] Scottish Council for Research in Education, *The Intelligence of a Representative Group of Scottish Children* (London: University of London Press, 1939); Scottish Council for Research in Education, *The Trend of Scottish Intelligence* (London: University of London Press, 1949).

[23] Gita Z. Wilder and Kristen Powell, *Sex Differences in Test Performance: A Survey of the Literature*, College Board Report No. 89-3 (Princeton, N.J.: Educational Testing Service, 1989).

[24] Tyler, pp. 243–246.

[25] "The Gender Gap in Education: How Early and How Large?" *ETS Policy Notes*, Vol. 2, No. 1 (Princeton, N.J.: Educational Testing Service, October 1990).

[26] Ibid.

[27] Ina V. S. Mullis, John A. Dossey, Mary A. Foertsch, Lee R. Jones, and Claudia A. Gentile, *Trends in Academic Progress 1971–1990*, National Assessment of Educational Progress (Princeton, N.J.: Educational Testing Service, 1991), p. 113.

It should not be surprising then that innumerable studies have found that boys usually outnumber girls in remedial reading classes,[28] and reading disabilities are "from three to ten times more common for boys, depending on how the disability is defined and what population is studied."[29] Researchers have also found "greater variability in reading scores among boys from grades 2 through 7 . . . and boys outnumbered girls among the lowest scores by about 2 to 1 in the lower grades, with the ratio decreasing thereafter."[30]

A number of researchers have suggested that the female superiority in reading in the United States may be due to cultural factors. To determine whether this is so, a number of cross-cultural studies have been done. A much quoted cross-cultural study is Ralph Preston's study comparing the reading achievement of German and American boys and girls. In his study he found that the German boys excelled over the German girls in all reading areas tested except that of speed, and his results for the American children were similar to what researches had previously found; that is, "the incidence of 'retardation' and of 'severe retardation' was greater among the American boys than among the American girls— significantly so in almost all instances."[31] His study supported culture as a major factor influencing sex differences in reading.

A review of many of the cross-cultural studies found conflicting results; that is, many other cross-cultural studies confirm the superiority of girls in reading in countries other than the United States, whereas some studies support the Preston findings in which a cultural bias was found.[32]

Some researchers have claimed that the differences in reading achievement in the early grades are the result of the greater educational readiness of girls for formal reading when they come to school.[33] Both cultural and biological or maturational factors have been put forth as reasons for girls' superior readiness for formal reading. A perusal of the literature seems to lend support to both theories, suggesting that the gender differences in reading may be due to a combination of biological and environmental factors.

[28] Norma Naiden, "Ratio of Boys to Girls among Disabled Readers," *The Reading Teacher* 29 (February 1976): 439–442.

[29] Eleanor E. Maccoby and Carol H. Jacklin, *The Psychology of Sex Differences* (Stanford, Calif.: Stanford University Press, 1974), p. 119.

[30] Ibid.

[31] Ralph C. Preston, "Reading Achievement of German and American Children," *School and Society* 90 (October 1962): 352.

[32] Howard A. Klein, "Cross-Cultural Studies: What Do They Tell about Sex Differences in Reading?" *The Reading Teacher* 30 (May 1977): 880–885; Dale D. Johnson, "Sex Differences in Reading across Cultures," *Reading Research Quarterly* 9: 1 (1973–1974): 67–85; Alice Dzen Gross, "Sex-Role Standards and Reading Achievement: A Study of an Israeli Kibbutz System," *The Reading Teacher* 32 (November 1978): 149–156.

[33] Irving H. Balow, "Sex Differences in First Grade Reading," *Elementary English* 40 (March 1963): 306; Guy L. Bond and Robert Dykstra, "The Cooperative Research Program in First-Grade Reading Instruction," *Reading Research Quarterly* 2(4) (Summer 1967): 122.

A recent book on sex differences by a British writer has caused quite a stir because the author contends that males' and females' brains are structurally different before birth. Because of this structural difference, this writer claims, men's and women's brains process information in different ways, which accounts for their different perceptions, priorities, and behaviors. The structural difference is given as a reason that men have better spatial abilities and women have better language skills.[34]

It is also interesting to note that even though in the past few decades there has been a great emphasis on trying to treat males and females the same, there is

> *ample evidence that boys and girls are treated differently from birth and perhaps even before, in an age of increasing knowledge about the gender of the unborn child. Parents react more positively toward their toddlers when the children are engaged in gender-appropriate behavior. Moreover, parents' behavior is not always congruent with their stated attitudes.*[35]

It may be that parents are more protective of their female children than of their male children and, as a result, spend more time with them. This would result in more verbal interaction between the female child and her parents, which could account for the usual female superiority in verbal skills, despite the recently reported gap erosion. Also, studies done on sex-role standards have shown that American boys look upon reading as "feminine" and not in accord with a masculine role. It has been suggested that this may influence greatly how males will achieve in reading. For example, in a study of an Israeli kibbutz system, where the boys perceive reading as a desirable masculine skill, boys achieve at equally high levels, and boys and girls exhibit an equal amount of reading ability.[36] Preston, in his study, suggests that the apparent superiority of German boys to German girls may be due to the masculinization of the German schools. In German culture, reading and learning are thought to be more in the domain of the male than of the female, and teachers in Germany are predominantly male even in the elementary school.[37]

The *teacher* also has been put forth as a possible cause for boys' depressed reading achievement. Some researchers claim that American teachers expect their girls to read better than their boys and that this expectation influences sex differences in reading achievement.[38] Other investigators suggest that sex differences in reading achievement are the result of classroom teachers' treatment of

---

[34] See Anne Moir, *Brain Sex: The Real Difference between Men and Women* (Secaucus, N.J.: Lyle Stuart, Carol Publishing, 1991).

[35] Wilder and Powell, p. 16.

[36] Gross, pp. 149–156.

[37] Preston, p. 353; Ralph C. Preston, "Letters," *The Reading Teacher* 31 (December 1977): pp. 318–319.

[38] Johnson, p. 85.

boys and girls; that is, "classroom teachers treat boys and girls differently and . . . this difference in treatment is associated with differences in early reading achievement."[39] The sex differences studies in this area are also confusing because different studies seem to find different results. For example, a review of the research comparing male and female elementary school teachers did not find any significant differences between male and female teachers' perception or treatment of boys and girls.[40]

Investigators, however, in analyzing all the available studies dealing with girls in school settings, recently reported that teachers are biased in their behavior toward boy and girl students and that this bias is in favor of the male student. They claim "that girls are not receiving the same quality, or even quantity, of education as their brothers."[41] The researchers report that teachers call on boys more often and give boys more encouragement. They state "that the educational system is not meeting girls' needs. Girls and boys enter school roughly equal in measured ability. . . . Twelve years later, girls have fallen behind their classmates in key areas such as higher-level mathematics and measures of self esteem."[42]

Although it has not been shown that either sex has a preference for the modality of vision or hearing to gain information, Eleanor Maccoby and Carol Jacklin, two noted authorities who have done extensive research on the psychology of sex differences, put forth an "intriguing possibility"—that "modality preferences during the early school years might feed into the development of different subject-matter skills at a later time."[43] Maccoby and Jacklin put forth their "intriguing possibility" based on a study by a researcher who identified individual differences among first- and second-grade children in how they take in information. The study discussed by Maccoby and Jacklin found that the "visual" children do better in reading and the "auditory" children do better in arithmetic. The researcher of the study, however, does not report whether there are sex differences in the perceptual orientations he has identified.[44]

Graphic Summary of Chapter

Here is a graphic summary of Chapter 2. If you have read the chapter, this graphic illustration should help you remember its main points. Under or beside

[39] John D. McNeil, "Programmed Instruction versus Usual Classroom Procedures in Teaching Boys to Read," *American Educational Research Journal* 1(2) (March 1964): 113.

[40] Henriette M. Lahaderne, "Feminized Schools—Unpromising Myth to Explain Boys' Reading Problems," *The Reading Teacher* 29 (May 1976): 776–786.

[41] Susan Bailey et al., *How Schools Shortchange Girls* (Wellesley, Mass.: Wellesley College Center for Research on Women, 1992), p. v.

[42] Ibid., p. 2.

[43] Maccoby and Jacklin, p. 35.

[44] Ibid.

each heading, you might want to jot down some of the information you recall, as well as some of the key concepts in this chapter. This can act as a good review. You can then check your key concepts against those that follow the graphic summary.

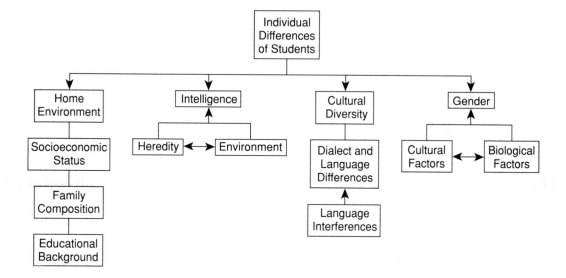

Key Concepts

- Teachers must take the individual differences of their students into account when teaching.
- Children's success in school depends on their past experiences as well as on such factors as home environment, gender, cultural diversity, and intelligence.
- The areas of language, intelligence, early home environment, reading success, and school success are closely interrelated.
- Teachers have a profound effect on children's learning in school.
- Socioeconomic class, parents' education, and the neighborhood in which children live are some of the factors that shape children's home environment.
- At-risk children tend to show the greatest literacy lacks in the area of language development.
- Classrooms in the United States have a multicultural mix of students.
- Teachers should be cognizant of the language differences among their students.
- Intelligence refers to the ability to reason abstractly or to solve problems.
- Most professionals believe that an individual's intelligence is due to a combination of heredity and environment.

- There are factors besides intelligence that determine an individual's reading success.
- Studies do not reveal any significant differences between males and females in general intelligence.
- There appear to be some differences in specific aptitudes between males and females.
- Boys usually outnumber girls in remedial reading classes.
- Cultural and biological factors have been put forth as reasons that there are more males with reading problems than females.

Suggestions for Thought Questions and Activities

1. Given two hypothetical children, X and Y, construct a comparison chart showing how one child's chances for success in school are better than the other child's chances because of certain factors. State five factors, and describe each.
2. Explain how intelligence, language development, and learning to read are all related.
3. You have been asked to give a talk before the Parent Teachers Organization concerning gender differences in reading. Present your talk.

Selected Bibliography

Banks, James A. *Teaching Strategies for Ethnic Studies,* 5th ed. Boston: Allyn and Bacon, 1991.

Langer, Judith A., Arthur N. Applebee, Ina V. S. Mullis, and Mary A. Foertsch. *Learning to Read in Our Nation's Schools: Instruction and Achievement in 1988 at Grades 4, 8, and 12.* National Assessment of Educational Progress. Princeton, N.J.: Educational Testing Service, 1990.

Slavin, Robert E. *Educational Psychology: Theory into Practice,* 3rd ed. Boston: Allyn and Bacon, 1991.

Tiedt, Pamela L., and Iris M. Tiedt. *Multicultural Teaching: A Handbook of Activities, Information and Resources,* 3rd ed. Boston: Allyn and Bacon, 1990.

Wilder, Gita Z., and Kristin Powell. *Sex Differences in Test Performance: A Survey of the Literature.* College Board Report No. 89-3. Princeton, N.J.: Educational Testing Service, 1989.

3

The Classroom Teacher
Making the Reading Connection

> There is no frigate like a book
>   To take us lands away,
> Nor any coursers like a page
>   Of prancing poetry.
> This traverse may the poorest take
>   Without oppress of toil;
> How frugal is the chariot
>   That bears a human soul!
>   —*Emily Dickinson*

SCENARIO: TEACHING IS A SACRED TRUST

Ms. Kerr has been teaching first grade for five years now. She has taught other grades, but she finds teaching first grade the most gratifying. It's probably because most of her children come into this grade not reading, but, by the end of the year, most have unlocked the mystery of the magic symbols and entered the enchanted world of books. How exciting at the end of the year to have children look at samples of their early writing and say, "Oh, I was a baby then. Now I'm grown up because I can read and write."

Fortunately for Ms. Kerr's students and their parents, Ms. Kerr loves children and books, and this love is reflected in her teaching and her classroom, which is filled with books and print material. Ms. Kerr realizes that as a teacher she has a sacred trust: What she does and how she does it can affect her pupils for the rest of their lives. Teaching is an awesome responsibility that she does not take lightly.

This chapter will discuss the kinds of things Ms. Kerr and other good teachers do to make books an integral part of their students' lives and to imbue them with the love of reading. It will illustrate how the teacher is vital to a good reading program.

KEY QUESTIONS

After you finish reading this chapter, you should be able to answer the following questions:

1. What are some characteristics of good teachers?
2. What traits do good reading teachers usually have?
3. What is the relationship of attitudes to learning?
4. How can teachers help students make the book connection?
5. What is self-fulfilling prophecy?
6. What is direct instruction?
7. What is interactive teaching?
8. What is a modeling strategy?

KEY TERMS IN CHAPTER

You should pay special attention to the following key terms:

attitude   reading aloud to children
direct instruction   reading strategy
interactive instruction   repeated reading
modeling instruction   self-fulfilling prophecy

The Teacher

> *It is the supreme art of the teacher to awaken joy in creative expression and knowl-edge.*
>
> *—Albert Einstein*

Teachers are very important people. Unless there are good teachers in the class-room, there will be a travesty of education. Unfortunately, when it comes to the image of teachers, it seems as though time has stood still. For example, if we were to go back through the ages, we would find such familiar comments as this:

> *The teachers today just go on repeating in rigamarole fashion, annoy the students with constant questions and repeat the same things over and over again. They do not try to find out what the students' natural inclinations are, so that the students are forced to pretend to like their studies; nor do they try to bring out the best in their talents. As a result, the students hide their favorite readings and hate their teachers, are exasperated at the difficulty of their studies, and do not know what good it does them. Although they go through the regular course of instruction, they are quick to leave when they are through. This is the failure of education today.*
>
> *—Confucius (c. 551–479 B.C.)*

When he [Abelard's teacher] lit the fire, he filled the house with smoke not with light.

—Abelard (1079–1142 A.D.)

There are a number of factors that profoundly influence children's learning in school. These factors range from the physical plant to materials to methods. The most important variable, however, appears to be the teacher.

Investigators have shown that it is difficult to compare different methods or materials in researches and that students seem to learn to read from a variety of methods and materials.[1] There is, however, one variable that these researchers and others point to as the key in improving reading instruction—the teacher. For example, the authors of *Becoming a Nation of Readers* state that "studies indicate that about 15 percent of the variation among children in reading achievement at the end of the school year is attributable to factors that relate to the skill and effectiveness of the teacher."[2] In contrast, "the largest study ever done comparing approaches to beginning reading found that about 3 percent of the variation in reading achievement at the end of first grade was attributable to the overall approach of the program."[3]

If we want an improvement in reading instruction, we need good teachers who are well versed in reading instruction. The teacher is the key—not materials nor methods. The following scenario illustrates this point.

SCENARIO

Mrs. Powden's and Ms. Davis's Fourth-Grade Classrooms

Mrs. Powden is using a literature-based program in her class that utilizes trade books only, whereas Ms. Davis is using a basal reader series. If you learned this without seeing their classrooms or the teachers in action, you might think they were at opposite ends of the continuum. Actually, these teachers are more alike than different.

When you walk into both these teachers' rooms, you are struck immediately by one thing—books are omnipresent. Their fourth-grade classrooms are filled with all kinds of books at varying readability and interest levels (see Chapter 4 for a discussion of readability and interest levels). Both teachers have special reading corners that are filled with attractive and inviting book jackets and with pictures that students have drawn to illustrate books they have read. In the writing corner there are more books, including children's own "published books."

Both teachers read aloud to their students and provide direct instruction to

---

[1] Guy L. Bond and Robert Dykstra, "The Cooperative Research Program in First-Grade Reading Instruction," *Reading Research Quarterly* 2(4) (Summer 1967): 1–142; Albert J. Harris and Coleman Morrison, "The CRAFT Project: A Final Report," *The Reading Teacher* 22 (January 1969): 335–340.

[2] Richard C. Anderson, Elfrieda H. Hiebert, Judith A. Scott, and Ian A. G. Wilkinson, *Becoming a Nation of Readers* (Washington, D.C.: National Institute of Education, 1985), p. 85.

[3] Ibid.

their students that include the Directed Reading–Thinking Activity (DRTA), interactive reading sessions, and modeling strategies to help their students gain insights into needed concepts. (See the section on direct instruction later in this chapter.) They integrate the language arts with reading and give their students many, many opportunities to read and write. Often during free time or lunch, you can catch both teachers reading a newspaper, book, or journal. Also, when the children go to the library to read or have free reading time in the classroom, these teachers read, too.

In both classrooms, students are animated, actively engaged, and so engrossed in what they are doing that it is difficult to wrest them away. Is it any wonder that parents try hard to get their children into these two teachers' classes?

Some Characteristics of Good Reading Teachers

If we were to ask a number of people to state the qualities they feel a good teacher should have, we might hear the following:

Good teachers need the eyes of an artist to know the varying personalities in their midst. They need a philosopher's insight to know how to deal with each individual. They are blessed with a "democratic spirit" and treat each person as someone worthy of dignity and respect. They have the patience of Job (see Figure 3-1). They help those who need help to become more independent learners. They are astute diagnosticians. Their analytical ability is well developed. Their ebullience and enthusiasm know no bounds. Their experiences are manifold, their knowledge of the highest; and their judgment is superb.

Our Problem—There are only mortals on earth.
Solution—We must work within our limitations—
Be optimistic and strive for the ideal.

Agreement does not exist on what factors affect teaching and learning performance, but most people would agree that the following are some salient characteristics for good reading teachers: verbal ability, a good educational

Reprinted by permission of UFS, Inc.

FIGURE 3-1   Linus recognizes that teachers are human.

background including knowledge of the content of reading, the ability to do higher order thinking, the ability to read with skill oneself, the love of books, good planning and organizing ability, instructional strategies, and positive teacher expectations and attitudes. In addition, a good teacher is enthusiastic, warm, and friendly; knows the interests, needs, and individual differences of students in the class; uses the experiences and interests of the students to plan cooperatively for them; employs a wide variety of materials and resources; and knows adequate techniques for student evaluation.

Studies suggest that teachers who have a good educational background and verbal ability are usually better teachers than those who do not have such abilities.[4] This information makes sense and should not surprise anyone. What is surprising is that there are some teachers who lack necessary reading skills.[5] If teachers have reading deficiencies, this is sure to have an impact on their students. How can teachers involve students in higher level thinking if they themselves are unable to do such thinking? They can't. How can teachers help students gain needed study skills if they themselves lack these? They can't. How can teachers help instill a love of literature in students if the teachers, themselves, do not place a high value on reading? They can't.

Attitudes and Learning

Teachers are interested in making a positive and beneficial difference in the lives of their students; they wish to produce desirable changes in students' learning behavior. How this is done is crucial because in subsequent years students may not remember certain dates or information, but the concomitant learnings such as attitudes will greatly influence whether students will avoid or pursue further learning in an area. This makes sense because attitudes exert a directive and dynamic influence on our behavior.

Attitude
Exerts a directive and dynamic influence on an individual's behavior.

Teachers cannot control their students' home environment or a host of other factors that determine whether students will become good readers and choose to read, but they can control what they do in the classroom. And what teachers do in the classroom can make the difference! Therefore, teachers must be ever vigilant that what they do in teaching reading does not stifle their students' love of reading. They must show through example that they value reading.

4 Charles E. Bidwell and John D. Kasarda, "School District Organization and Student Achievement," *American Sociological Review* 40 (February 1975): 55–70; Eric Hanushek, "The Production of Education, Teacher Quality and Efficiency," Paper presented at the Bureau of Educational Personnel Development Conference "How Do Teachers Make a Difference?" Washington, D.C., February 1970. ERIC No. 037 396.

5 Lance M. Gentile and Merna McMillan, "Some of Our Students' Teachers Can't Read Either," *Journal of Reading* 21 (November 1977): 146; Eunice N. Askov et al., "Study Skill Mastery among Elementary School Teachers," *The Reading Teacher* 30 (February 1977): 485–488.

Teacher Expectations

Self-fulfilling prophecy
Teacher assumptions about children become true, at least in part, because of the attitude of the teachers, which in turn becomes part of the children's self-concept.

The more teachers know about their students, the better able they are to plan for them. However, teachers must be cautioned about the self-fulfilling prophecy—where teachers' assumptions about children come true, at least in part, because of the attitude of the teachers. Studies have shown that teacher expectations about students' abilities to learn will influence students' learning.[6] For example, if a child comes from a home environment not conducive to learning, the teacher may assume this child cannot learn beyond a certain level and may treat the child accordingly. If this happens, then the teacher's assumptions could become part of the child's own self-concept, further reinforcing the teacher's original expectations.

Teachers who are aware of the effect that their expectations have on the learning behavior of students can use this knowledge to help their students. For example, teachers should assume that *all* their students are capable of learning to read (see Figure 3-2); they should avoid labeling their students; and they should use positive reinforcement whenever feasible to help students to become motivated.

FIGURE 3-2   This teacher expects her students to be able to read.

6 Robert Rosenthal and Lenore Jacobson, *Pygmalion in the Classroom* (New York: Holt, Rinehart and Winston, 1968); Douglas A. Pidgeon, *Expectation and Pupil Performance* (London: National Foundation for Educational Research in England and Wales, 1970).

Time Spent in Reading

The National Assessment of Educational Progress has consistently found a positive relationship between achievement and intensive reading experiences. "Students at all ages who read books, newspapers, and magazines most often also displayed the highest reading achievement."[7] Unfortunately, approximately one-tenth of the students who were interviewed in the study said they do not read for pleasure.[8]

Most people agree that reading helps reading (see Figure 3-3) and that teachers cannot control what takes place in students' homes or change students' home environments (see Chapter 2). However, teachers do control what takes place in their classrooms. Therefore, it is disconcerting when studies reveal that teachers do not spend a great amount of time on comprehension instruction and do not look upon a content area such as social studies as a time to help with reading instruction.[9] This is ironic because a problem in a content area, even one like mathematics, may well be a problem in reading.

FIGURE 3-3   Reading helps reading!

[7] Ina V. S. Mullis and Lynn B. Jenkins, *The Reading Report Card, 1971–1988,* National Assessment of Educational Progress (Princeton, N.J.: Educational Testing Service, 1990), p. 43.

[8] Ibid., p. 42.

[9] Dolores Durkin, "What Classroom Observations Reveal about Reading Comprehension," *Reading Research Quarterly* 14(4) (1978–1979): 533.

Another difficulty that studies reveal is that teachers may not give the same quality of reading instruction to poor readers as to good readers. Poor readers are often shortchanged because the amount of reading they accomplish is much less than good readers do, even though they spend an equal amount of time in reading instruction. It appears that teachers have poorer readers spend more time in oral reading and in correcting oral reading errors than on reading in context and in silent reading.[10]

The amount of time one spends exposed to print is related to reading success; this has been stated a number of times. But must the time engaged with print be teacher-guided, or can it be independent reading—that is, reading one does on one's own without teacher assistance or guidance? Both are probably important.

Direct Reading Instruction Strategies

Direct instruction
Instruction guided by a teacher, who uses various strategies to help students understand what they are reading; also referred to as **explicit teaching.**

Reading strategy
An action or a series of actions that helps construct meaning.

Direct instruction is instruction guided by a teacher, who uses various strategies to help students understand what they are reading. There are a number of techniques teachers can use to teach reading directly. The techniques teachers use transcend the kinds of materials they use. In other words, one teacher may embrace whole language and use only trade books in his or her class, whereas another might use a basal reader to teach reading. Both teachers can still employ similar strategies to help students gain needed concepts. (See "Instructional Technique: Guided Reading" in Chapter 11.)

This text advocates a mix of materials, beliefs, and strategies, and the teacher is the one who must decide what is best for his or her students.

Special Note
Explicit teaching is another term used for *direct instruction.*

Interactive Instruction

Interactive instruction
The teacher intervenes at optimal times to enhance the learning process.

In interactive instruction the teacher intervenes at optimal times to enhance learning. The teacher determines when to intervene and what materials and strategies to use to achieve desired learning for the readers with whom she or he is working. "The teacher can modify the text, increase or decrease the demands on reader resources, add to reader resources, set goals that are difficult or easy in relationship to reader resources. Indeed, depending on what the teacher does, the students in one class may be successful in reading while in another class they might fail."[11]

---

[10] Richard L. Allington, "Poor Readers Don't Get to Read Much in Reading Groups," *Language Arts* 57 (November–December 1980): 872–876.

[11] Mariam Jean Dreher and Harry Singer, "The Teacher's Role in Students' Success," *The Reading Teacher* 42 (April 1989): 614–615.

Interactive instruction requires knowledgeable teachers who are good decision makers and who do not use any materials or teachers' manuals as ends in themselves. In addition, interactive teaching can be used in conjunction with other instructional strategies.

SCENARIO

Mr. Smith Uses Interactive Instruction

Mr. Smith teaches social studies and reading to sixth-graders in an inner city. When Mr. Smith finds that the textbook or materials he is using do not fit the needs of his students, he modifies the material so that it is more appropriate for his students. Let's see what Mr. Smith does:

The students with whom Mr. Smith is working are having difficulty reading their social studies textbook because the vocabulary and concepts are too difficult for them. Therefore, Mr. Smith scrutinizes each assignment beforehand to select any technical or nontechnical words he feels students might find difficult, and he breaks up the reading assignments based on the difficulty of concepts presented. (Many good teachers are already using interactive instruction but may not know it. For example, the study guides teachers prepare to help students read content material represent a form of interactive instruction.)

Mr. Smith prepares his students for reading their textbook by going over with them the terms he has culled from their book. He puts each term on the chalkboard in context and goes over each one. He makes sure they can pronounce the word and know how it is used. (He is especially careful to discuss with them words that have multiple meanings because the meaning of these words can only be discerned from context.) He then presents some of the key concepts they will meet in their reading assignment. He also reviews with them a study skills technique he had introduced to them the day before. Mr. Smith gives students some questions to set purposes for their reading and tells them to remember that good readers think about what they are reading and that they should try to relate the new information to what they already know.

After the students have read their assignment, Mr. Smith carefully guides them so that they achieve the desired goals. He asks questions throughout the discussion and encourages students to do the same. Often Mr. Smith uses a modeling strategy to help his students gain insights into what they are reading.

Mr. Smith finds that interactive instruction combined with modeling instruction is very effective in helping his students acquire and retain content concepts.

Modeling instruction
Thinking out loud; verbalizing one's thoughts to help students gain understanding.

Modeling Instruction

Modeling instruction requires teachers to think out loud; that is, teachers verbalize their thoughts to help students gain understanding. This is an exceptionally effective strategy because it helps students gain an insight into the kind of thinking involved in reading comprehension and helps them recognize that reading comprehension is analogous to problem solving (see Chapter 7). Here is a scenario illustrating this technique:

SCENARIO

Mrs. Johnson Uses a Modeling Strategy

Mrs. Johnson and five children in a first grade have been reading a story, "The Hare and the Tortoise." Mrs. Johnson has discussed with the children what a hare and a tortoise are, and she has shown them pictures of both and talked about which animal they would expect to move faster and why. She has gone over all the new words with the children, and before they began to read the story she had them make predictions about who would win the race.

Today she told them that they would do something a little different. They would be detectives. She then asked them if they knew what a detective is. After discussing what a detective does, she told them that they would look for clues in the story to show why Hare lost the race.

She asked the children to reread the story to themselves. After the children finished reading, Mrs. Johnson said she would show them how she goes about finding clues. She told them that she would say aloud everything she was thinking while she tried to answer the question. Here is what she said:

> While I was reading the first two pages, I saw something that told me the rabbit is very sure of himself. I think to myself that this will probably get him into trouble. Hare said, "Rabbits run as fast as the wind." I feel this will get him into trouble because this shows Hare is very sure of himself. It shows that he doesn't take Tortoise seriously. He feels it's silly to think that Tortoise could win. Because of this he feels he can take it easy. Now, everyone look at the next page. Are there any clues there that show us that Hare will lose the race?

Mrs. Johnson calls on different children and elicits from them the reasons for their choices. When they have finished giving all the clues, Mrs. Johnson asks the children if they ever heard the saying "Slow and steady wins the race." She asks them to think about the saying and says that next time they will discuss it.

Repeated reading
Similar to paired reading; child reads along (assisted reading with model or tape) until he or she gains confidence to read alone.

Repeated Reading

Repeated reading is a technique that is gaining favor among a number of teachers to help students who have poor oral reading to achieve fluency in reading. A suggested procedure for repeated readings follows:[12]

Passage length: Short; about 50 to 100 words

[12] Adapted from Sarah L. Dowhower, "Repeated Reading: Research into Practice," *The Reading Teacher* 42 (March 1989): 504–506.

Types of passages: Any reading materials that will be of interest to the child

Readability level of passage: Start at independent level; proceed to more difficult passages as child gains confidence in oral reading; controlled vocabulary is not imperative.

Assisted reading: Use the read-along approach (assisted reading with a model or tape) to help with phrasing and speed; use when speed is below 45 words per minute (wpm), even though child makes few errors.

Unassisted reading: Use when child reaches 60 wpm.

Reading Aloud to Children

Reading aloud to children
An essential activity for building the knowledge and skills eventually required for reading.

"The single most important activity for building the knowledge and skills eventually required for reading appears to be reading aloud to children."[13] A rich oral program is essential for all children because it helps them gain "facility in listening, attention span, narrative sense, recall of stretches of verbalization, and the recognition of new words as they appear in other contexts."[14] Reading a story aloud helps children increase their vocabulary, even if the story is not accompanied with teacher explanation of word meanings.[15]

Reading a story aloud is a beneficial activity for students at all grade levels. Who doesn't enjoy listening to a story well read! For young children it is especially productive and can be an excellent interactive experience if done properly. Here are some steps the teacher can follow in reading a story aloud to young children (preschool and kindergarten):[16]

Preparing for the Story

1. Choose a short storybook that is at the attention, interest, and concept-development levels of the children and that has large pictures that can be seen. Big books with a predictable refrain are especially good to use with a group of children. (See the section on big books in Chapter 4.)
2. Have the young children sit comfortably and in a position that allows them to see the pictures easily.
3. Make sure there are no distractions to attract their attention.
4. State the title and show the book to the children. Ask them if they can figure out what the story will be about from the title.

---

[13] Marilyn Jager Adams, *Beginning to Read: Thinking and Learning about Print—A Summary,* Steven A. Stahl, Jean Osborn, and Fran Lehr, eds. (Urbana, Ill.: Center for the Study of Reading, 1990), p. 46.

[14] Dorothy H. Cohen, "The Effect of Language on Vocabulary and Reading Achievement," *Elementary English* 45 (February 1968): 217.

[15] Warwick B. Elley, "Vocabulary Acquisition from Listening," *Reading Research Quarterly* 24 (Spring 1989): 175–187.

[16] Dorothy Rubin, *Diagnosis and Correction in Reading Instruction,* 2nd ed. (Boston: Allyn and Bacon, 1991), pp. 110–111.

5. Set purposes for the story by telling the children to listen carefully for certain things. (This will obviously be based on what is being read.)

Reading the Story

Read the story aloud to the children (see Figure 3-4). Stop at key points and have them predict what will happen or have them state the refrain if the story contains one. You can state more questions for them to think about while they are listening to the story. If they interject comments during the story, you should acknowledge these—say "good thinking," if it shows they are thinking—and continue reading.

After the Story

When the story is finished, you could have the children answer some of the unanswered questions and do some of the following based on their attention and interest levels:

a. Tell what the story is about.
b. Retell the story in sequence.
c. Discuss whether the story is based on fantasy or reality.
d. Act out the story.
e. Make up another ending for the story.

The Teacher: A Final Note

Throughout this chapter the teacher is presented as the key person in the classroom, a person who is a decision maker and who must be directly involved in his or her students' learning. This view of the teacher as a vital person in the classroom, however, should not be construed as meaning that the teacher should be tyrannical or intimidating.

Good teachers must know when and how much help to give. They must know how to ask questions that will encourage student participation, as well as how to provide a nonthreatening environment that will foster risk taking and question answering.

If teachers want students to be independent thinkers and intelligent question answerers, students must be given the freedom to express their views, even if these views differ from the teachers' opinions.

A good teacher asks questions that stir students to think about what they are reading. The teacher as an "intellectual agitator"[17] pushes students to the limits of their ability. Such a teacher prods students to search for evidence to support their position and continually asks such questions as: "What do you think?" "Why do you think so?"[18] "Can you find evidence in what you read to prove it?"

Good teachers are also good role models (see Figure 3-5)!

---

[17] Russell G. Stauffer, *Teaching Reading as a Thinking Process* (New York: Harper & Row, 1969), p. 26.
[18] Ibid.

FIGURE 3-4 Reading aloud to children is directly related to reading success.

FIGURE 3-5 This teacher is a good role model.

Graphic Summary of Chapter

Here is a graphic summary of Chapter 3. If you have read the chapter, this graphic illustration should help you remember its main points. Under or beside each heading, you might want to jot down some of the information you recall, as well as some of the key concepts in this chapter. This can act as a good review. You can then check your key concepts against those that follow the graphic summary.

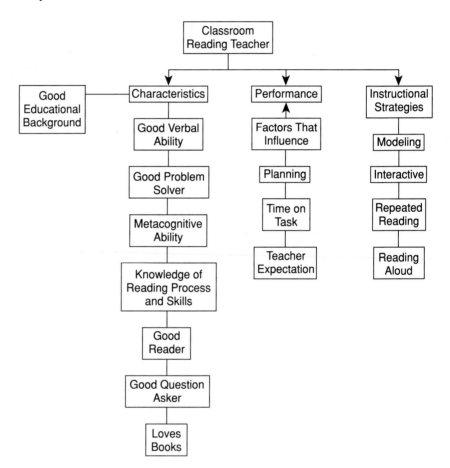

Key Concepts

- Good teachers are vital to a good reading program.
- Teachers should integrate the language arts with reading.
- Classroom reading teachers should possess certain salient characteristics.
- Attitudes exert a directive and dynamic influence on individuals' behavior.

- Teachers should teach reading directly.
- Teacher expectations can influence students' behavior.
- The amount of time one spends exposed to print is related to reading success.
- Direct instruction is instruction guided by a teacher.
- In interactive instruction, the teacher intervenes at optimal times to enhance learning.
- Modeling instruction requires teachers to verbalize their thoughts to help students gain insight into what is being taught.
- Repeated reading helps students who have poor oral reading to achieve fluency in reading.
- Reading aloud to children is an exceedingly important activity for helping children gain the knowledge and skills they need for reading.

Suggestions for Thought Questions and Activities

1. You have been put on a committee to develop criteria to evaluate a reading teacher's performance. What are your views concerning this? What criteria would you recommend? Would you recommend student input?
2. Observe two different teachers of reading for one day. Evaluate these teachers using the criteria presented in this chapter.
3. Generate a number of objectives for teachers in reading that you feel all teachers of reading should accomplish
4. Explain the concept of self-fulfilling prophecy and how you would use it to encourage students to achieve better.

Selected Bibliography

Adams, Marilyn Jager. *Beginning to Read: Thinking and Learning about Print—A Summary,* Steven A. Stahl, Jean Osborn, and Fran Lehr, eds. Urbana, Ill.: Center for the Study of Reading, 1990.

Anderson, Richard C., Elfrieda H. Hiebert, Judith A. Scott, and Ian A. G. Wilkinson. *Becoming a Nation of Readers.* Washington, D.C.: National Institute of Education, 1985.

Ashton-Warner, Sylvia. *Teacher.* New York: Simon and Schuster, 1963.

Harris, Albert J. "The Effective Teacher of Reading, Revisited." *The Reading Teacher* 33 (November 1979): 135–140.

Jackson, Phillip W. *Life in Classrooms.* New York: Teachers College Press, 1990.

Woolfolk, Anita E. "Teachers, Teaching, and Educational Psychology." In *Educational Psychology,* 4th ed. Englewood Cliffs, N.J.: Prentice-Hall, 1990.

4

Teaching for the Love of Books
Children's Literature

SCENARIO: MRS. SMITH HELPS INSTILL A LOVE OF BOOKS IN CHILDREN

Mrs. Smith teaches first grade in an elementary school in a small town in Arkansas. Almost everyone in this town knows Mrs. Smith because of her great love of children and books. The feeling in this town is that if you start with Mrs. Smith as your first-grade teacher, you will always find joy in the world of books.

What is so special about this teacher? What does she do that has such a lasting effect on her students? Let's visit her classroom for a short while to see if we can gain some insights into her success.

Mrs. Smith has arranged her room around a sea of books. In the center of her room there are wrought iron rack shelves that contain books of all sizes and shapes. These racks are on a large circular rug that contains throw pillows. Bookshelves in other parts of the room also contain books at various readability and interest levels. The bulletin boards display children's illustrated stories, and on the walls there are colorful pictures of well-known story characters. The children's desks are in a semicircle around the large rug.

We notice Mrs. Smith working with a group of children at the front of the room. As we look around, we see a number of children reading library books. Some are sitting at their desks while others are on the rug in the center of the room. A few children are standing by the rack browsing in books. Some children are busy writing a story.

What catches your eye immediately is that these young children appear to be so engrossed in what they are doing that they do not even notice your presence.

Mrs. Smith encourages children to go to the bookshelves to choose books to browse through or to read. Her students can do this almost anytime except, of course, while working in a group with her or at other times during direct instruction.

When Mrs. Smith is working with a reading group, she gives the other children in the class two options—they can either read a library book or write their own stories. Mrs. Smith likes to give her children many opportunities to read and write because she believes strongly that the more children are exposed to print, the better readers and writers they will be.

Mrs. Smith has just finished working with a reading group. She thanks the children for doing such good work and tells them to go back to their seats. Then she walks around the room and stops to chat for a moment with each child about what he or she is reading or writing. Finally, she goes to the front of the room and tells the whole class how pleased she is with them. "Now," she asks, "who can tell us what we are going to do next?"

A child named Seth raises his hand and says, "We are going to talk about the books we are reading."

"Good," says Mrs. Smith.

Mrs. Smith has instituted a special "Book Talk" program. Twice a week, the children discuss the books they are reading. They are supposed to share something exciting about their book but not tell the whole story. Their goal is to get the other children to want to read their book.

The children look forward to this activity. It gives them a chance to express their thoughts about what they are reading and to try to be as creative as possible in figuring out how to get other children excited about their book.

It appears that Mrs. Smith's success may be that she actually implements her beliefs about giving children as many opportunities as possible to read and write. You can't fake love; children can see right through deception. The love Mrs. Smith has for children and books fills the room; it's something that cannot be packaged and sold.

This chapter is a crucial one because it helps teachers gain the tools they need to provide a reading for appreciation program for their students, which is essential if reading is to become an enjoyable, lifelong habit.

KEY QUESTIONS

After you finish reading this chapter, you should be able to answer the following questions:

1. What is reading appreciation?
2. What must educators do to show that they value a reading for appreciation program?
3. How would you provide an atmosphere conducive to recreational reading in your classroom?
4. What are some techniques that will interest children in books?
5. How would you help children to select books?
6. What is Sustained Silent Reading (SSR)?

7. What are some criteria for selecting books?
8. What are predictable books?
9. What are "big books"?
10. What is a literature-based program?
11. How can teachers use "big books" with their children?
12. How can literature foster better understanding in a multicultural society?
13. How can children's writing stimulate reading?
14. What is the role of humor in children's books?
15. How can bibliotherapy be used to interest children in books?
16. How are libraries and communities helping to foster recreational reading?
17. How can television be used as a springboard for reading?

KEY TERMS IN CHAPTER

You should pay special attention to the following key terms:

appreciative reading	literature-based programs
bibliotherapy	Newbery Award books
big books	readability
Caldecott Award books	readability formulas
communication	role modeling
creative problem solving	role playing
Drop Everything and Read (DEAR)	starter shelves
good literature	Sustained Silent Reading (SSR)

Good Literature and Reading

Literature-based programs
Reading programs using whole pieces of good literature rather than short excerpts or contrived text.

Good literature
The foundation of any good reading program.

The emphasis in many classrooms today appears to be on literature-based programs, whether teachers use basal readers or not. Rather than reading short excerpts or contrived text, children are being exposed to whole pieces of good literature earlier. This is as it should be because good literature is the foundation of a good reading program.

The question is, what makes something "good literature"? Have you ever read something that excites and stirs you, that makes you feel and experience, that so overpowers you that you cannot stop reading? If so, you have probably been in the presence of good literature.

Good literature captures your soul, your spirit, and your heart. It quenches your thirst for knowledge; it acquaints you with lands and peoples beyond your horizon; it stirs your imagination and helps satisfy your emotional needs. Good literature helps you gain insight into how to cope better with emotional and adjustment problems; it helps you gain emotional strength. Good literature encountered early helps you on the road to lifelong reading.

What Is Reading for Appreciation?

Go to three different dictionaries and you'll probably find a different mix of definitions for the term *appreciation*. *Webster's New Collegiate Dictionary* defines *appreciation* as **"1. a:** sensitive awareness; especially the recognition of aesthetic values; **b:** judgment, evaluation: especially a favorable critical estimate; **c:** an expression of admiration, approval, or gratitude; **2:** increase in value."[1]

The *Random House College Dictionary* defines *appreciation* as **"1.** gratitude . . . **2.** act of estimating the quality of things according to their true worth. **3.** clear perception or recognition, especially of aesthetic quality. . . ."[2]

Webster's New World Dictionary of American English defines *appreciation* as **"1.** the act or fact of appreciating; specif., **a)** proper estimation or enjoyment **b)** grateful recognition, as of a favor **c)** sensitive awareness or enjoyment, as of art **2.** a judgment or evaluation. . . ."[3]

When we talk about reading for appreciation, we are usually talking about sensitive awareness, especially the recognition of aesthetic values. The recognition of aesthetic values includes both enjoyment and the making of a value judgment. Probably because of the evaluation component, some people place appreciation at the highest level in a taxonomy of reading. (See "Reading Comprehension Taxonomies" in Chapter 7.) These individuals believe that a person cannot attain appreciation unless he or she has a complete understanding at the highest level of what is being read.

In this book, appreciative reading is regarded as a separate domain with a hierarchy of its own. It is, therefore, possible for an individual to gain an appreciation for a piece of literature, even though he or she does not have a complete understanding of it. For example, a poem can be enjoyed because of its delightful sounds, rhythm, or language, even though it is not understood. Of course, the greater the understanding, the higher the appreciation, but appreciation is still possible without complete understanding at various lower levels.

Appreciative reading Reading for pleasure and enjoyment that fits some mood, feeling, or interest.

Appreciative reading in this book is defined as reading for pleasure and enjoyment that fits some mood, feeling, or interest. Reading for enjoyment allows readers to experience many adventures vicariously and to engage in "something interesting and exciting."[4] It gives individuals things to discuss with other people, and, very importantly, "reading for enjoyment is associated with reading achievement."[5]

---

1 *Webster's New Collegiate Dictionary* (Springfield, Mass.: G. C. Merriam, 1977), p. 56.

2 *Random House College Dictionary,* Revised Edition (New York: Random House, 1988), p. 66.

3 *Webster's New World Dictionary of American English* (Cleveland: Webster's New World Dictionaries, 1988), p. 67.

4 John T. Guthrie and Vincent Greaney, "Literacy Acts," in *Handbook of Reading Research,* Vol. II, Rebecca Barr, Michael L. Kamil, Peter Mosenthal, and P. David Pearson, eds. (New York: Longman, 1991), p. 88.

5 Ibid.

Roadblocks to Appreciative Reading

Reading helps reading! Everyone agrees on that. The problem is that many students are not reading. It is easy to understand why children with reading problems do not choose to read in their leisure time, but we have a large population of children without any discernible reading problems who also are not reading. Why?

Consider the following familiar remarks:

"Let's go see that new movie."

"Let's listen to my new tape."

"I have a piano lesson."

"I have Little League practice."

"My Brownie troop is meeting."

"I want to watch my favorite television show."

Now read some remarks that children often hear from adults:

"Be well rounded."

"Don't sit around all day long. Go outside and play."

"Socialize."

"Practice the piano."

"It's time for your gymnastics class."

"It's time for your dance class."

It may be that at an early age children are subjected to too many pressures as well as numerous enjoyable activities that vie for their time and attention. In order to become readers, children must have the time and desire to read; they must acquire an appreciation for reading, and they must have a need to read.

The Importance of Providing Time for a Reading for Appreciation Program

Every good reading program must have a component in it dedicated to appreciative reading. Learning to read and reading to learn are important parts of any reading program, but appreciative reading is what determines whether persons will read and continue to read throughout their lives. If children develop an appreciation of books at an early age, it will be more difficult for other activities and media to compete. One important factor is to make the decision to have a reading for appreciation program. Many educators give lip service to the appreciation component of the reading program but do not implement it. The only way that educators can show that they value a reading for appreciation program is by setting aside time for the program. If time is set aside, there is a chance for success. As stated earlier, young people have to contend with many enjoyable activities that compete for their time and attention; reading for pleasure is often given a low priority in the competitive battle. By setting time aside during the school day for reading for enjoyment, educators would be giving students a chance to whet their appetites for books. What is especially encouraging is that the Drop Everything and Read Program (DEAR)[6] or Sustained Silent Reading (SSR) seems to have caught on. Many school systems have initiated DEAR or SSR in their schools, and the response has been excellent. DEAR or SSR is a very simple program to institute, but it needs the backing and commitment of *all* school personnel for it to work, and some adjustments need to be made for it to work effectively in the upper elementary grades.

DEAR or SSR requires that teachers follow certain rules:[7]

Drop Everything and Read (DEAR) Similar to SSR; practice in independent silent reading.

Sustained Silent Reading (SSR) Practice in independent silent reading.

1. Each student must read.
2. The teacher must read at the same time that the students read (see Figure 4-1).
3. Students read for a specified time period.
4. Students are not responsible for any reports on what they have read, and no records are kept of what students have read.
5. Students choose any reading material that they like.

SSR is obviously easier to initiate in the lower elementary grades than in the upper grades where students are more involved in content courses and are usually not in self-contained classrooms. However, it can be practiced in the upper elementary grades if teachers are committed to the importance of having students engage in independent silent reading and if proper provisions are made so that it fits smoothly into the content program. The idea of having a bell ring and everyone from the superintendent to the custodian drop everything and read (DEAR) is intriguing and may work in some school systems; however, common sense dictates that this can cause some difficulties. For example, if a student is intricately involved in a project, the message or bell to drop everything and read can prove to be very frustrating. A student might well develop a negative rather than a positive attitude toward such a reading mandate. Also, what if the bell rang when the children were in a special laboratory or in the gym? Such facilities certainly are not conducive to reading.

DEAR or SSR is an excellent idea, but the program will only work if, as stated earlier, *all* teachers are committed to making it work. All teachers should be involved in planning when the period for SSR should take place in their

[6] Sustained Silent Reading (SSR) rather than DEAR is the more familiar phrase used for practice in independent silent reading. The original phrase was Uninterrupted Sustained Silent Reading (USSR).
[7] Adapted from Robert A. McCracken, "Initiating Sustained Silent Reading," *Journal of Reading* (May 1971): 521–524, 582.

FIGURE 4-1   When her students read during Sustained Silent Reading, this teacher also reads.

classes, and they should provide many types of reading matter for their students. Of course, even if a school system or individual school is not committed to having an SSR program, any individual teacher can initiate and implement one in his or her own class.

Also, teachers can adapt SSR to fit their classes in a number of different ways as long as it does not violate the major purposes of SSR—to get students to read voluntarily and to enjoy what they read. One suggestion is to incorporate discussion as part of SSR.[8] Teachers can set aside some time after reading and have students state in one or two sentences what they liked about what they read. Another variation is to have students meet in groups of four or five and discuss what they are reading, and still another is to have students pair off with a partner and discuss the books between them (see Figure 4-2).

Setting the Environment for the Enjoyment of Reading in the Classroom

Role modeling
An observer imitates the behavior of a model.

Teachers who are enthusiastic about books will infect their students with that enthusiasm. A teacher who is seen to be deeply immersed in a book during the lunch hour is a good role model and will also have a marked influence on stu-

[8] See Richard B. Speaker, Jr., "Another Twist on Sustained Silent Reading: SSR + D," *Journal of Reading* 34 (October 1990): 143–144.

FIGURE 4-2   These children are enjoying a book together.

dents. But the teacher's responsibility does not end there. The teacher must set the stage, provide the materials, and plan with students for recreational reading.

First, the classroom must be an inviting place to read. It should be airy, light, and physically comfortable. The emphasis on books should be clearly visible. For example, bulletin boards should have recommended booklists at all interest and readability levels. Award-winning books, book jackets from a number of popular children's books, students' recommendations and evaluations of various books, and artwork depicting a scene or characters in books should be on display (see Figure 4-3).

Teachers can also heighten students' desire for the books by putting tantalizing captions in front of the books on display to arouse children's curiosity and encourage them to go beyond the covers of the book. In the upper primary grades and above, teachers can challenge students who have read some of the books to make their own captions for these books that would motivate other children to want to read the same books.

Starter shelves
The starting of book collections by teachers to which children can contribute.

Starter shelves, a descriptive term usually used in relation to starting book collections for content areas in secondary school, can also be used by elementary school teachers. The books that are chosen are merely intended to start the students reading voluntarily. The teacher starts the collection, but the children can

FIGURE 4-3   This showcase displays masks children made of their favorite story characters.

contribute to it, and the books are changed periodically on the basis of students' interests, needs, and reading ability levels.

Lots and lots of books should be provided for the children at all interest and readability levels (see the section on selecting books). Newspapers, magazines, and other printed matter of interest to children should be available. Filmstrips, records, and films of favorite stories should also be kept handy for the children's use.

Next, a special place to read is necessary! A section or corner of the room should be readily accessible to all the students, where a few comfortable chairs, some large comfortable pillows, and a scatter rug are placed. This is the reading corner.

Now, time must be provided so that children can read (see the previous section). This book period is separate from the weekly visit to the library and is not dependent on whether children have free time only because they have finished all their "other work." Every day the teacher and children should plan for a book time, when the class just enjoys literature. After the teacher has helped students to choose their books and settle down, as already stated, the teacher, too, should read.

Instilling a Love for Reading in the Early Grades with Big Books

Big books
Enlarged versions of regular children's books; known for their repetitive patterns, which lend to their predictability; they are usually children's favorites.

In preschool and kindergarten programs, the classroom should be full of print, and on display there should be many, many different kinds of books that children can touch and relate to, including "big books," oversized versions of text.[9] Big books can be used in the same way as normal-sized books, but they are much more useful when working with a large group of children. Also, children seem to love to see their favorite stories in an enlarged version (see Figure 4-4).

The big books lend themselves better to interactive sessions with a large group of young children because the pictures and print are so much easier for all the children to see. The children can relate better to the story, and they appear to be more free to ask questions and make predictions about the story.

A key feature of big books is their repetitive patterns, which give them their predictability. Big books are usually children's bedtime favorites, those with which they can associate good feelings. They are books that children like to hear over and over again.

In reading the story, it's a good idea for the teacher to pause during the reading before coming to the repetitive passage or refrain to give the children an

FIGURE 4-4 These children love their big books.

[9] Marilyn Jager Adams, *Beginning to Read: Thinking and Learning about Print—A Summary,* Steven A. Stahl, Jean Osborn, and Fran Lehr, eds. (Urbana, Ill.: Center for the Study of Reading, 1990), p. 69.

opportunity to state it. It is suggested that the teacher point to the words while the story is being read, so the children will gain an understanding of the relationship between the words that are being said and the print on the page, as well as that text proceeds from left to right and from top to bottom.[10] After a few repeated readings, the children will not only state the refrain, but many will be able to recognize it in print.

During the school day, you can often find a number of children reading big books at their desks alone or with another child.

Special Note

The Little Red Hen is an excellent example of a book with a repetitive refrain that appears throughout the book. (See Chapter 12 for an adaptation of *The Little Red Hen*.)

Criteria for Selecting Books

A number of factors should be considered in selecting books for children. Criteria concerned with knowledge of children and what they enjoy in a book include:

1. *Theme:* What the story is all about. It often reveals the author's purpose, and "provides a dimension to the story that goes beyond the action of the plot."[11]

2. *Plot:* This grows out of a good theme. The plot holds the story together; it is the plan of action that should meld the happenings in such a believable and unique way that the reader's interest will remain throughout. Children like heroes and heroines who have obstacles to overcome, conflicts to settle, and difficult goals to win. (It is possible for the characters of a story to determine what direction a story will take and as a result influence the plot, but this is generally within the confines of the theme.)

3. *Characterization:* In good books, characters are multidimensional, real, lifelike, and consistent. As children mature in their reading tastes, they go from enjoying tales of action with stereotyped characters to liking characters who are individual, unique, and memorable.

4. *Style:* This is a difficult quality to define, but its absence is noticeable in books that are repetitious, boring, labored, and so on. The author's style should reflect his or her work and be suitable for the story he or she is writing. Children's authors should recognize that usually children do not like a great amount of description in their stories, but many children can and do appreciate word imagery that is based on their developmental levels.

5. *Point of view:* The author's point of view will influence the plot, the characters, the setting, the style of writing, and so on. The author's mental lean-

---

[10] Ibid., pp. 69–70.

[11] Charlotte Huck, Susan Hepler, and Janet Hickman, *Children's Literature in the Elementary School,* 4th ed. (New York: Holt, Rinehart and Winston, 1988), p. 19.

ing will manifest itself throughout the story. At times, if this is done in a very heavy-handed way, it can interfere with the telling of the story and "turn off" some readers.

6. *Setting:* Concerns time and place of the story. It should enhance the plot, characters, and the theme of the story.

7. *Format:* Deals with the presentation of material, illustrations, quality of paper used, and binding. The illustrations should be attractive and pleasing to the eye as well as consistent with the story. The quality of the paper should not detract from the reading, and the print of the book should be appropriate for the reader.[12]

A book that hinders a child from finding his or her identity, one that portrays the child in a stereotyped role, is a book that would be considered poor reading for all children.

When selecting books for a class library, teachers should try to put themselves in the position of their children and ask: How would I feel if I read this book? Would this book make me come back for another one? Will this book interest me? Are these books on many readability levels? Does the book portray the minority child as an individual? Are the minority adults portrayed in a nonchildlike manner? Are the characters supplied with traits and personalities that are positive? Are the minority individuals in various social positions?

If the answers are "yes," the teacher should choose the book. But even one "no" answer should make the teacher reexamine the book very carefully.

If we were to think of all the different racial, religious, and ethnic groups that live in the United States—Indian, Mexican, Spanish, French, black, and so on—many children would be considered to be culturally different. In the *good* literature books, minorities are not portrayed in a stereotyped fashion. They are presented sympathetically and with sensitivity.

Regardless of the group to which children belong, the books they read must help them to feel good about themselves. They must help children view themselves in a positive light, achieve a better self-concept, and give them a feeling of worth.

Children's Literature: A Bridge to Multicultural Understanding

Teachers have an excellent opportunity to help foster better relations among different peoples of the world by the kinds of books they choose for their classroom libraries.

The importance of learning about other groups of people through literature is aptly expressed in the following:

> *I never felt the world-wide importance of the children's heritage in literature more than on a day when I stood with Mrs. Ben Zvi, wife of the [then] President of Israel,*

---

[12] Ibid., pp. 17–26.

in the midst of the book boxes she had filled for the centers in Jerusalem where refugee boys and girls were gathered for storytelling and reading of the world's great classics for children. "We want our boys and girls to be at home with the other children of the world," she said, "and I know of no better way than through mutual enjoyment of the world's great stories."[13]

Good books can open doors through which can pass better understanding, mutual respect, trust, and the hope of people living together in harmony and peace.

Children's Interests

SCENARIO ——————————————————————————————

Andrew and His Love of Books

Andrew is a reader. He learned to love books at an early age, and even though he is a very active young man, he still takes time each day to read. Andrew is now in the intermediate grades, but his mother or father still reads to him a chapter from one of his favorite books every night before he goes to bed. Nothing gets in the way of this pleasant pastime, not even vacationing at Disney World.

Andrew knows exactly what he likes in books: He likes stories that are fun; he like adventure, and he likes series books with the same characters. Let's look at the kinds of books he has been reading or has had read to him since he was a preschooler.

As a preschooler, in kindergarten, and in first grade, Andrew, like millions of other children, adored the Dr. Seuss books. Another one of his favorite series, which his mother read aloud to him as a preschooler, was the Richard Scarry large picture story books. He loved *Busy, Busy World,* which has pictures to follow the story line (every paragraph on the page has a matching picture). He enjoyed looking at the map of the world at the beginning of the book and following the stories of animals with humanlike characteristics going to different parts of the world. The Mercer Mayer *Little Critter* books were another series that he greatly enjoyed; he had his parents read these to him over and over again until he was able to read the books himself.

The Mayer books deal with a critter family that consists of a mother, father, little boy, who is the protagonist, a younger sister, and grandparents. The titles of the little books are indicative of what the little books portray: *I Just Forgot, Just Go to Bed, Baby Sister Says No, Just a Mess, Just for You,* and a great number of others.

In second and third grade, Andrew met Gertrude Chandler Warner's *Boxcar Children* books, which are all mysteries, and devoured every book in the

---

13 Dora V. Smith, "Children's Literature Today," *Elementary English* 47 (October 1970): 778.

series. In third grade he also read Lynne Reid Banks's *The Indian in the Cupboard, Return of the Indian,* and *The Secret of the Indian,* which have a more difficult concept and vocabulary load than some of the other books he had previously read. In addition, he read the Deborah and James Howe books about talking animals. His favorite is *Bunnicula,* which concerns a bunny who was found at a Dracula movie and consequently was named Bunnicula. Harold, the dog, who is writing the story, and Chester, the cat, together with the bunny, live in a professor's house that has lots of books. Chester learns a lot of information from reading, but he also sometimes gets it confused, which provides humor to the stories. Andrew remembers one incident that especially made him laugh. In the book, Chester is convinced the bunny is Dracula in disguise, and he has just read that you kill a vampire by putting a stake through its heart. Therefore, at dinner, he grabs a steak from the table and puts it on the bunny.

If you ask Andrew why he likes the books he reads, he tells you that he likes stories about animals; he likes adventure stories, mysteries, and funny stories. He also likes to read series books because he like to read lots of books about the same characters in different situations.

Commentary

It appears that Andrew is not alone. Many other children — and adults, too — like to reencounter characters whom they have come to know and like. Many children like the security that series books give them. It is comforting for them to know that there are other books available about their favorite characters.

Andrew came to school with a love of books that his parents helped nourish. He is fortunate in that he has also had teachers who share his love of books. Andrew still loves to read. Let us hope he always has teachers who recognize that one of their major responsibilities is to keep children's love of books alive, as well as to help spark others to want to read for pleasure.

We have already discussed the importance of providing time for reading, reading aloud, and providing an environment conducive to reading. Another essential factor in stimulating children to read for pleasure is for teachers to find out about their students' interests and concerns and then use this information to provide a wide selection of books so that children can choose their own books for recreational reading.

Learning about Children's Interests

There are a number of ways teachers can determine their students' interests. The easiest way is to just ask them in an informal chat or to have them fill out a form on which they state their interests or the books they would like to have in their class library. A less direct way would be to have the children complete incomplete sentences like the following:

Primary Grades

In the early primary grades teachers could read aloud the incomplete sentences and put children's responses on large paper.

> If I could have only one book, I would like _____ .

> I would choose _____ in the book to be my friend.

Intermediate Grades

> I would like to meet another character like _____ in another book.

> If I were asked to take only one book on a flight to another planet, I would take _____ .

Rather than looking at studies that are concerned with what children say they would like to read, teachers should try to find out what children are reading. A study that was done on what children actually borrow from the library, showed that in the early 1970s jokes and riddles were in first place for nonfiction popularity.[14] A reflection of the times was shown in the children's choices of sports books, where judo and jujitsu were the favorites.[15]

Even though there are classics that children of all ages seem to enjoy, such as *Charlotte's Web,* the *Madeline* and *Babar* books, and so on, in each decade there seems to be a particular genre of books that gains popularity. In the 1980s it appeared to be books about romance, divorce, puzzle books (such as the ones in which children create their own endings), self-help books, books with starkly realistic themes, and science fiction books. In the 1990s, it seems that children continue to be interested in books with realistic themes, self-help books, romance books, and science fiction books. However, there also seems to be a greater interest in books that encourage cross-cultural understanding.

Generally, children have many interests. Teachers should be alert to these and not underestimate what children can do or what they will respond to. One eminent literary critic states that "children can respond to tragedy and irony as well as to comedy and romance, and that children want difficulty; if they are practicing jumping over hurdles, they want the highest hurdle they can possibly get over, not a low one that they know they can manage."[16]

Humor and Children's Interests

When Andrew was reading *Bunnicula* in school one day, he laughed out loud so hard that a number of children asked him what was so funny. He told them

---

[14] Donald J. Bisset, "Literature in the Classroom," *Elementary English* 50 (February 1973): 235.

[15] Ibid.

[16] Northrop Frye, "Foreword," in *The Child as Critic* by Glenna Davis Sloan (New York: Teachers College Press, 1984), p. xii.

they had to read what Chester the cat had just done. When some did, they laughed also.

Laughter is infectious, and it often helps us in troubled times. Unfortunately, teachers have not sufficiently exploited the area of children's sense of humor. Children delight in funny words and the way they may be misused, as in the case of Chester the cat. Teachers should choose books that tickle children's funny bone and read these aloud in class, so that children come to realize that the classroom is a place for shared fun and laughter.

One difficulty may be that there are not too many children's books available in which the characters are both "strong and jolly."[17] A well-known authority on children's literature states that "it appears that writers of children's books tend to focus on one or the other trait rather than on both."[18] She presents some examples of books whose main characters embody both traits. For the primary grades, she suggests such books as *Owliver* by Robert Kraus and *Sir Cedric* by Roy Gerrard. For the intermediate grades she recommends *Anastasia* by Lois Lowry, the *Bingo Brown* books by Betsy Byars, and *Do Bananas Chew Gum?* by Jamie Gilson. (In the *Bingo Brown* books and *Do Bananas Chew Gum?* the main characters balance humor with coping with developmental problems; see the section on bibliotherapy later in this chapter.)

Children Like Poetry

Beginning in the early primary grades, teachers should include poetry as part of their literature program. Young children are natural poets; they experiment with words and their sounds to create delightful "poems." They especially love rhymes. Tell them one and they will laugh and tell you one. It may consist of nonsense words, but no matter, as long as it sounds good. Unfortunately, as children go through the grades, many seem to lose this delight in poetry, in the magic of words.

Teachers should try to keep alive children's early love of poetry by reading various types of poems aloud with feeling and understanding. The poems should be read for the sheer joy and delight they bring. As the poet William Yeats once said, "I have just heard a poem spoken with so delicate a sense of its rhythm, with so perfect a respect for its meaning, that if I were a wise man and could persuade a few people to learn the art, I would never open a book of verse."

Teachers should take students' interests into account when choosing poems for their students. Children usually like something they can relate to, humor, a play on words, action, and a lack of moralizing. They also like poems that just "sound good."

One investigator identified a set of poems that primary grade children enjoy listening to and that help to instill positive attitudes toward poetry. Some of these poems are "Spaghetti" (Silverstein); "Miss Hochett" (Anonymous); "The

---

[17] Eileen M. Burke, "Characters—the Strong Ones—the Jolly Ones," Paper presented at the International Reading Association, Las Vegas, Nevada, May 9, 1991.

[18] Ibid.

Creature in the Classroom" (Prelutsky); "Don't Ever Cross a Crocodile" (Starbird); "The Crocodile's Toothache" (Silverstein); and "Rhinoceros Stew" (Luton).[19]

Teachers can also use children's love of humor and rhymes to encourage them to write their own poems and share them with the class. One teacher read the following humorous rhyming poem that she had written to share with her students after they had read *The Cat in the Hat* by Dr. Seuss. After she wrote one with them, she encouraged them to write their own "silly" rhyming poems to share with their peers.

The Teacher's Silly Poem

Have you seen the cat,
Who fell in the hat
And became a rat?
No! No! I mean the rat,
Who fell in the hat
And became a cat.

Oh dear! Could it be a hare?
No! No! It's a deer.
No, I think it's a mare.
Oh dear! oh dear! oh dear!
I really don't care
If it's a hare, or a deer, or a mare.

Something fell in the hat,
which started all of that.
"It's magic," Jennifer said,
While shaking her head.
But now that this has been read,
It's time for Jennifer to go to bed.

See the section on "Phonograms" in Chapter 6 for a "silly" rhyming poem that a teacher and her children wrote cooperatively after reading *The Cat in the Hat* and working with the phonogram *at*.

Children Like Nonfiction, Too

Teachers should capitalize on children's curiosity about the world around them to introduce them to nonfiction. Interestingly, one way to do this is via fiction. When students are studying a particular subject area, the teacher should make available a number of books related to the topic under study. Fiction should "tease" the child's imagination so that he or she will want to find out more about

19 Michael P. Ford, "Selecting Appropriate Poems: The Heart of Poetry Instruction for Young Children," *Wisconsin English Journal* 31 (April 1989): 66.

what the author has written. Nonfiction should be at the students' reading ability levels and able to answer a number of the students' questions.

A unit on the life cycle of a frog can be an excellent stimulus for encouraging reading and for introducing children to informational books. The unit activities help children gain the background they will need for reading informational books; the children learn the technical vocabulary they will meet in print, as well as a conceptual framework about the frog's life cycle. And, probably most important, they want to read more about the frog.[20]

Children Like to Read Other Children's Books, Also

The integration of literature and writing is a natural one that teachers should take advantage of in their classes. Children usually love to read other children's stories. What better place than in the literature program to have this take place! Children who are exposed to a good literature program will have more ideas to write about. They can be encouraged to publish their own books, which can be shared with the class (see Figure 4-5). In addition, a copy of the book can be

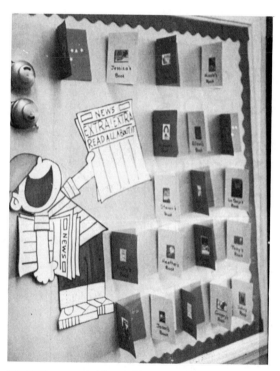

FIGURE 4-5   Children's books on display.

[20] Amy A. McClure, "Integrating Children's Fiction and Informational Literature in a Primary Reading Curriculum," *Reading Teacher* 35 (April 1982): 784–789.

placed in the school library for others to read. When children see that their work is appreciated, they will be encouraged to read and write more. (See Appendix A for "Bookbinding for Books Written by Children.")

Readability and Interest Levels

There are usually one or two books that are very popular and make the rounds of almost all the children in the class. Although such a book may be at the interest level of most of the children, it may not be at every child's reading ability level. There are always a few children who feel left out because they can't read these books. They may take out the books and either walk around with them or make believe that they are reading them. By having the book in their possession they may feel they can gain the esteem they need.

The teacher should not embarrass such students, but should carefully choose substitutes at their reading ability levels, to gain their interest. The teacher should speak individually to such a child and say, "I know how much you like books about heroes. Well, I was looking through this book the other day and I immediately thought of you. I just felt that you would enjoy this book." The teacher should then try to have the student read the first page. Once the child starts by reading the first page, the battle is almost won. The student will usually continue because the book is at both his or her reading ability and interest levels (see Figure 4-6).

The teacher should have an ample supply of books at various readability and interest levels. For help in obtaining a proper selection, teachers can consult the *Elementary School Library Collection.* This reference work gives estimates of children's interest levels and reading difficulties for all the books listed. Having such books available is the essential first part. The other part is helping students choose books based on both their interest and reading ability levels. Unfortunately, as has been shown, a book may be at a child's interest level, but the child may be unable to read it independently.

Readability formulas are used to determine the reading difficulty of written materials. Whereas most readability formulas are based on both sentence length

Readability formulas
Applied directly to the written material to determine the reading difficulty of written material.

Reprinted by permission of UFS, Inc.

FIGURE 4-6   Peppermint Patty is learning the joy of reading.

and syllabication, some may also use word lists. Limitations exist, however. Readability formulas do not take other variables—such as children's experiential background, maturation, purpose of reading, and so on—into account. They also do not measure the abstractness of ideas or the literary style or quality of the written material. Readability formulas are also unreliable, since different formulas on similar material may not produce the same scores. When a readability formula produces a score of grade 4, it does not mean that all fourth-graders will be able to read the book because "one cannot assume that the formula will correctly predict how a particular reader will interact with a particular book."[21] Although readability formulas are imperfect tools, they do have value, for they give some idea of the difficulty of a book for specific groups of readers.

For example, *The Lion* by René DuBois would be of interest to preschool, kindergarten, and first-grade children. According to the Spache Readability formula for grades 1 to 3, however, the book would be near the 3.5 grade level. This means it would have to be read to younger children. At the other end of the scale, there may be students in the upper grades with difficulty in reading, who may be at a reading level as low as preprimer. These students desperately need books at their interest levels. Fortunately, for a while now, more books have been published with the high interest but low readability levels required by such students.

Regardless of which readability formula teachers use, they should be familiar with the methods for estimating readability. Teachers do not have to work out the exact estimates for each book, but by observing the sentence length and syllables, or sentence length and kinds of words—that is, the difficulty of the words used in a paragraph—they can estimate whether a book is at the proper level for their students to read independently. (See Appendix B for an example of a readability formula.)

Although it is difficult to ascertain completely what makes a book easy or hard, the following are "readability pluses" that parents, teachers, and librarians might look for in a book.

Readability
Many variables determine how well an individual will comprehend written material.

Readability is excitement. A punchy beginning. Forceful and colorful language. Variety in style, including both long and short sentences. A subject that appeals to the reader. Interesting pictures and other illustrations.

Readability is familiarity. Plain talk and an informal style, especially for readers with difficulty in standard English. The words and expressions of ordinary speech. The familiar sentence patterns of spoken language. Material that deals with something the reader knows about and has experience with. Unfamiliar ideas explained in terms of familiar ideas.

Readability is clarity. A low percentage of abstract words. Difficult ideas explained and not clumped together. Paragraphs not too long or complicated. Ideas developed in logical order. Introductions and summaries where suitable.

Readability is visibility. Type large enough to read comfortably. Lines not so long that the eye has trouble finding the beginning of the next line. Paper and ink

---

[21] Bob Lange, "Readability Formulas: Second Looks, Second Thoughts," *Reading Teacher* 35 (April 1982): 859.

that lets type stand out sharply—black ink on whitish nonglare paper is best. Plenty of light, without glare. Distance between eyes and print close enough for comfortable reading, but not too close.

Readability is a good book. It's the symmetry and warmth a poem transmits to you. It's a quality that computers find indigestible because it defies precise statistical analysis.[22]

Whetting Children's Appetites for Books

Studies have shown that reading literature aloud to children helps prepare them for reading (see "Reading Aloud to Children" in Chapter 3). During the week there are many opportunities for the teacher to read to students. Books that are chosen to read in full to the children should be those that will interest all children. For example, one fifth-grade class loved Sherlock Holmes stories; however, the vocabulary was too difficult for a number of the students, even though the stories were at their interest level. Therefore, the teacher either used synonyms for difficult words or defined them. There are a number of books in which the authors seem to be able to use imagery to clarify the meanings of unfamiliar words. The techniques that the authors use do not take away from the quality of the story as a story but enhance it.[23]

The teachers must read with expression. They should imagine themselves to be actors or actresses and literally "give it their all." If they are reading effectively, the teachers should have gained the complete attention of the students.

Children love to be told stories. For that matter, so do adults. Storytelling is an art and must be practiced to be effective. It is different from reading, and many teachers find this difficult and very time-consuming; however, it is worth the effort. Some schools have special librarians who are adept at storytelling.

Another technique that teachers can use to interest children in books is to have several students report orally on books they have read that they feel others would also enjoy. In presenting such reports, students must explain why they enjoyed the books, tell about some of the exciting parts, but not give away the endings.

A technique children enjoy using to interest others in books is creative drama. A group of students who have read the same book can present skits highlighting exciting parts in the book (see Figure 4-7).

Peer role modeling is another technique that teachers can use to interest students in books. (See the section on "Television and Reading for Appreciation.") If children see other children reading, they, too, may choose to read. Teachers can display pictures around the room of children reading. One teacher

---

[22] Allen M. Blair, "Everything You Always Wanted to Know about Readability but Were Afraid to Ask," *Elementary English* 48 (May 1971): 443.

[23] For a listing of books and examples, see Dorothy H. Cohen, "Word Meaning and the Literary Experience in Early Childhood," *Elementary English* 46 (November 1969): 914–925.

FIGURE 4-7   These children are highlighting skits from *The Three Bears.*

made a practice of taking photographs of her students while they were reading. Then, these snapshots were placed on a special bulletin board for all to view.

Principals Try to Foster Appreciative Reading

Some principals are very aggressively trying to compete with the many activities that vie for children's time and attention by "going out on a limb to encourage reading."[24] They have found that such programs as the "I-dare-you approach wherein the principal offers the students a wacky reward for meeting reading goals—gets students reading in record numbers."[25] Principals have jumped into pools of Jell-O, sat on a roof for a day, and even worn a monkey suit and sat in a cage in the library all day. Some have actually gone skydiving.

The "wacky dare" program may work for the short term, but will students continue to read on their own and recognize that reading is its own reward? Long-term results need lots and lots of nurturing, and educators know that the key is to instill a love of reading in children at very early ages before they come to school. (See Chapter 16, which deals with parents as partners in learning.) This is the ideal; unfortunately, it does not happen for many of our children. Therefore, one of the responsibilities of teachers of young children, besides promoting awareness

[24] *Reading Today* (Newark, Del.: International Reading Association, April–May 1990), p. 13; see also the October–November 1991 issue, p. 14.

[25] Ibid.

of print in their students, is to help instill in them a love of books. This responsibility does not end, however, with teachers of young children; it must continue all through the grades.

Libraries Try to Foster Appreciative Reading, Too!

Libraries and communities are becoming more aggressive in trying to entice students to read more. For example, some public libraries offer special prizes based on the number of books a child reads. The more books a child reads, the bigger and better the prizes. Prizes range from ice cream sodas to book bags. Very young children can join in the fun and get into the library habit early by having their parents read books to them. Figure 4-8 shows a picture of a preschooler holding her copy of "Lions & Tigers and Books," which is part of the Columbus, Ohio, library promotional program. Her copy has a record of all the books her parents have read to her—and, of course, those that she has "read" to them. She is

FIGURE 4-8   This preschooler loves the "Lions & Tigers and Books" program. She is very proud to be a part of the program.

feeling very good because she has earned the 50 points necessary for the grand prize, a free backpack.

Many public and school libraries have special story hours, book chats, and puppet shows based on favorite storybooks. Often, teachers and librarians work together to choose material that is best suited to the needs and interests of their students (see Figure 4-9).

Special Note

Some people frown on programs such as "Lions & Tigers and Books" because they feel reading should be its own reward. Some critics are also unhappy about the use of prizes like french fries and ice cream sodas. Parents will have to decide for themselves whether they want their children to participate. The key is to get children reading, and these programs seem to be doing just that.

Libraries and Computers

Most libraries across the country are computerized, and a number of the larger libraries are also making terminals available for their patrons to use instead of the card catalogue (see Figure 4-10).

Some libraries also have a program called Dial Access, whereby computer users could access the library's computer database from home or work to determine whether what they want is available.

Bibliotherapy

Bibliotherapy
The use of books to help individuals to cope better with their emotional and adjustment problems.

Bibliotherapy is another technique that can be used to interest students in books. If students see that books can help them, this may encourage them to read more. Also, bibliotherapy encourages students to try to seek answers in a positive, intellectual, and logical manner.

Have you ever felt that you were different from others, that some things bothered only you, that you were peculiar because you liked certain things? Have you ever resented being the smallest or the tallest in class? Have you ever felt guilty because you had bad thoughts about some member of your family? Have

Reprinted by permission of UFS, Inc.

FIGURE 4-9   Lucy is very proud to have her own library card.

FIGURE 4-10   Preschoolers as young as Melissa are learning how to use the computer at the library.

you ever been embarrassed because you were frightened about things nobody else seemed to be frightened about? Have you ever felt that your parents got their divorce because of you? Have you ever worried about death or dying? Have you . . . ?

We could go on and on with the emotions that fill us and the problems that we all may have faced or still may face. Have you ever read a book in which the main character had a problem exactly like yours? Didn't it make you feel good to know that you were not the only one with such a problem? Weren't you relieved?

If you have ever read a book in which the main character had a problem exactly like yours and if the book helped you to deal better with your problem, you were involved in bibliotherapy.

Defining Bibliotherapy

Reading guidance given by teachers and librarians to help students with their personal problems is regarded as bibliotherapy. *Bibliotherapy* is the use of books to help individuals to cope better with their problems. The use of books to help people is not a new phenomenon. As far back as 300 B.C., Greek libraries bore inscriptions such as "The Nourishment of the Soul" and "Medicine for the Mind." In the late 1930s, Alice Bryan, a noted librarian, advocated the use of books as a technique of guidance to help readers "to face their life problems more effectively and to gain greater freedom and happiness in their personal adjustment."[26] However, it probably was not until 1950, when Russell and Shrodes published their articles on the "Contributions of Research in Bibliotherapy to the Language Arts Program," that teachers attempted to bring bibliotherapy into the classroom. Russell and Shrodes discussed their belief that books could be used not simply to practice reading skills, but also to influence total development. They defined bibliotherapy as "a process of dynamic interaction between the personality of the reader and literature—interaction which may be utilized for personality assessment, adjustment, and growth." They also say that this definition

> is not a strange, esoteric activity but one that lies within the province of every teacher of literature in working with every child in a group. It does not assume that the teacher must be a skilled therapist, nor the child a seriously maladjusted individual needing clinical treatment. Rather, it conveys the idea that all teachers must be aware of the effects of reading upon children and must realize that, through literature, most children can be helped to solve the developmental problems of adjustment which they face.[27]

In a definition of bibliotherapy, the term *cope* is important to note. When individuals use coping mechanisms, they are solving their problems by dealing with reality. They are behaving in a positive manner. The coping mechanism used in bibliotherapy is *empathy.*[28] Empathy refers to an individual's being able to project himself or herself into the personality of another and know how that person feels. Unless persons have experienced what someone else feels, either first-hand or vicariously through books, they cannot empathize with the other individual.

Identifying with a character in a story is the important first step in bibliotherapy. *Empathy* is the next step. In this step the reader projects himself or herself imaginatively into the character's "skin." How the storybook character deals with problems and handles his or her emotions can help the reader gain *insights* (the third step) into how to adjust or deal with his or her own real-life problems.

Matching Books to Individuals

Bibliotherapy will not take place by just reading a book, and not all books are suited for bibliotherapy purposes. For bibliotherapy to be effective, there must be a proper match between the individual and a book. Although there are times

---

[26] Alice I. Bryan, "The Psychology of the Reader," *Library Journal* 64 (January 1939): 110.

[27] David Russell and Caroline Shrodes, "Contributions of Research in Bibliotherapy to the Language Arts Program, I," *The School Review* 58 (September 1950): 335.

[28] *Catharsis* is the term usually used by psychoanalysts or psychiatrists to explain the second step in the process of bibliotherapy. The term *empathy* is used here in place of *catharsis* because it is less burdened by clinical connotations.

when some books by pure serendipity do help an individual to cope better with his or her problems, it is best not to leave the selection of the book to chance or accident. Some books are better suited to specific individuals than others. For example, to give a child who is "frightened out of his wits" a book like *Call It Courage* or *Julia of the Wolves* would be ludicrous. A child who is "frightened of his own skin" will not identify with a courageous protagonist. A book depicting a brave character will upset and disturb the frightened child more. This individual needs a book in which the protagonist is frightened by everyone and everything, but learns to deal with his or her problem.

The Uses of Bibliotherapy

Bibliotherapy helps individuals to cope with their problems in a number of ways. It helps people realize that they are not the only ones to have a particular problem. It allows readers to see that there is more than one solution to a problem and that they have some choices. It helps them to see basic motivations of others in situations similar to their own and to see the values involved in human, rather than material, terms. It provides facts needed in solving a problem and encourages the reader to plan and carry out a constructive course of action.[29]

Bibliotherapy can also be used in both preventive and ameliorative ways. That is, some individuals, through reading specific books, may learn how to handle certain situations before they have taken place. Other persons may be helped through books to overcome some common developmental problem they are experiencing at the time. For whatever purpose bibliotherapy is used, it will be of value only if teachers are knowledgeable about *how* to use bibliotherapy in their classrooms.

In order to use bibliotherapy effectively in the classroom, teachers should know about students' needs, interests, readiness levels, and developmental stages.

A word of caution is, however, necessary. Teachers must recognize that they are not psychologists, and they must be careful not to "step on the moral or religious toes of parents" when they introduce bibliotherapy in the classroom. Also, children should never be *forced* to discuss their feelings; children should know, however, that their teachers are available for discussion if they wish to express their feelings.

Bibliotherapy Themes

The kinds of problems that lend themselves to bibliotherapy are varied. For example, being the smallest child in the class, encountering the first day of school, or adjusting to school can be devastating. Being an only child may cause diffi-

---

[29] Alice Bryan, "Personality Adjustment through Reading," *Library Journal* 64 (August 1939): 573–576.

culty for some children. A new baby may bring adjustment problems for others, and going to the hospital may be a frightening event for yet others. Moving to a new neighborhood or simply disliking one's name can cause problems for a number of children. The death of a loved one, the fear of death, or the divorce of parents cause great anxieties on the part of children, and just growing up can be confusing. These are just a few of the problems suitable for bibliotherapy.

The Teacher and Bibliotherapy

By reading books that deal with themes such as those stated in the previous section, children can be helped to cope better with their emotions and problems. Teachers sensitive to their children's needs can help them by providing the books that deal with their problems. However, since teachers are not clinicians, children who are having serious adjustment problems should be referred for help to the guidance counselor or school psychologist. Also, teachers must be careful not to give children who are anxious about a situation a book that would increase their anxiety. A teacher also should not single out a child in front of the class to give him or her a book that points out that child's defects. Such treatment would probably embarrass and upset the child more.

The school librarian and the special reading teacher may be excellent resource persons to help the teacher choose books for bibliotherapy purposes. For best results, teachers should work very closely with them. As was stated earlier, teachers should be familiar with the *Elementary School Library Collection,* which is available in most libraries. It has an annotated bibliography of children's books on all themes with both readability and interest levels indicated, as well as resource books for teachers. Another excellent book with which the teacher should be familiar is Sharon Dreyer's *Bookfinder.*

After teachers use *Bookfinder,* the *Elementary School Library Collection,* or the aid of librarians to identify possible books, they should peruse the books themselves to determine whether they meet certain important criteria. Books for bibliotherapy should deal with problems that are significant and relevant to the students. The characters should be lifelike and presented in a believable and interesting manner. The characters' relationships with others in the book should be equally believable, and they should have motives for their actions. The author should present a logical and believable plot using vivid descriptive language, humor, adequate dialogue, and emotional tone. The situations presented by the author should be such that minor problems can be separated from main problems. The episodes in the book should lend themselves to being extracted and discussed so that students can formulate alternative solutions. Also, the author should present enough data so that students can discern generalizations that relate to life situations. The book should also be written in such a manner that the readers' imaginations are so stirred that they can "enter the skin of another."

A good teacher, one who is perceptive of the students' needs and who recognizes the importance of individual differences, will be in a better position to determine when a problem lends itself to being presented to the whole class, or when it should be handled on an individual basis. As was stated earlier, when a teacher wishes to give individual children books for bibliotherapy purposes, the children should not be singled out lest they feel ostracized or humiliated. One chance to help the children choose books could occur during a school library period or a class library period. The teacher and/or school librarian could make a few suggestions to a child. The student could then decide on one by reading the first page of a few of the suggested books.

Another way to interest individual students in books for bibliotherapy would be to choose an episode from a book to read aloud to the class. The chosen episode should present the main character in a problem situation. Also, the protagonist should be one with whom the teacher feels a number of students can identify. After the episode is read, a discussion should take place on how the character resolves his or her problems. The author's solution should not be given. The book may then be offered to those individuals who would like to read it. The teacher using this technique should have a few copies of the book available because many of the students will want to read it.

Many times a teacher may find that a number of children in the class share a similar problem. Therefore, the teacher might want to introduce the problem in some way to the class and use a bibliotherapy technique to help the students to cope with their problem. One technique to use is bibliotherapy and role playing; another is creative problem solving.

Bibliotherapy and Role Playing

Role playing
A form of creative drama in which dialogue for a specific role is spontaneously developed.

Here is how one teacher combines role playing with bibliotherapy in her class. Over about a week's time, she reads aloud a book that deals with a problem that is common to a number of children in her class. After the book is completed, the children discuss the characters, especially the main character and his or her problem. The students are then encouraged to share their experiences. Next, they are told that they will do some role playing. Each child who would like to plays the role of one of the characters in the story. A scene is set, but no dialogue is given. The children must spontaneously provide that on their own. After each role-playing scene, the teacher discusses with her class what took place and asks for the role players to give their feelings about the parts. If time permits, the children can reverse their roles. It is imperative that only those children who wish to role-play should do so. No child should ever be forced to role-play.

Bibliotherapy and Creative Problem Solving

Creative problem solving
Students using clues are encouraged to generate their own solutions to a problem.

Another technique the teacher could have used is bibliotherapy and creative problem solving. In this method, almost the whole book is read aloud to the class. Before the ending, the students, using clues from the book, try to determine how the main character's problem is resolved. They are encouraged, also, to generate their own solutions. After the ending is read, the students are asked to compare their solutions with the author's. Then they can discuss which they liked better and why.

Books as an Aid in Bibliotherapy

There are a number of excellent books that deal with some of the problems that children may encounter in today's world. Nan Hayden Agle's *Maple Street* is an enlightening story about a young black girl's desire to improve her street and to come to terms with a prejudiced white girl. Mary Calhoun's book *It's Getting Beautiful Now* concerns a boy's emotional problems and drugs. Francine Chase's *A Visit to the Hospital* helps both parents and children in preparing for a stay in the hospital. Gladys Yessayan Cretan's *All Except Sammy* portrays a boy's attempts to win the respect of his musical family.

Perceptive teachers, alert to the needs of their students, should be able to aid them in choosing books to help them cope more effectively with individual problems. As in all matters, the teacher should look for balance in the child's reading habits. A certain degree of escapism is fine, but the child must live in the real world and cannot be in a continuous state of fanciful thinking.

In the latter part of the 1980s children's books began to deal with more and more realism. In the past few years a number of children's books have surfaced that address such delicate topics as incest and child abuse, topics that were once taboo and certainly not in the domain of the teacher. Today, however, teachers are being asked to be on the lookout for signs of possible physical and sexual abuse among their students and to identify these children to their school principal and nurse.

If teachers suspect they have such victims in their classes, they might want to read aloud to the class a book that deals with these topics. However, because of the sensitivity of these areas, teachers should use bibliotherapy only in consultation with the school psychologist. The reading aloud of a book that deals with these problems is not enough to help the victims. The book, however, may help these children recognize that they are not alone and that they are not "bad" or "evil"; it may also help prompt them to tell someone about their problem.

An even more controversial issue that society is grappling with that has entered the classroom deals with the treatment of acquired immune deficiency syndrome (AIDS) victims. In the 1990s we should see a number of children's books emerge that may help children cope better with this issue. (See bibliography for annotated references that will help in selecting literature that portrays life as it is.) Table 4-1 consists of a good sampling of books for bibliotherapy organized by theme.

Bibliotherapy: A Final Note

Bibliotherapy can be effective in helping students better understand themselves and their feelings. When students realize that other people have similar problems, they are able to cope better with their own. Bibliotherapy, as already stated, helps students seek solutions in a positive, intellectual, and logical manner.

TABLE 4-1   Some Books for Bibliotherapy, Organized by Theme

Theme	Title	Author	Level
Adoption	*Here's a Penny*	Carolyn Haywood	Upper primary
Aging and death	*The Granny Project*	Anne Fine	Intermediate
Child who is different	*A Girl Called Al*	Constance Greene	Upper intermediate
	Dinky Hocker Shoots Smack	M. E. Kerr	Upper intermediate
Childhood fears	*There's a Nightmare in My Closet*	Mercer Mayer	Preschool
Death	*Run Softly, Go Fast*	Barbara Wersba	Young adult
	The Dead Bird	Margaret Wise Brown	Preschool/kindergarten
	My Grandpa Died Today	Joan Fassler	Primary
	Charlotte's Web	E. B. White	Upper primary/ intermediate
	Annie and the Old One	Miska Miles	Intermediate
	A Taste of Blackberries	Doris Buchanan Smith	Primary
	The Tenth Good Thing about Barney	Judith Viorst	Preschool/lower primary
	Grandpa's Slide Show	Deborah Gould	Preschool/lower primary
	That Dog!	Nanette Newman	Lower primary
	When People Die	Joanne E. Bernstein and Steven V. Gullo	Primary
	Loss	Joanne Bernstein	Upper intermediate
Dealing with a younger sibling	*Tales of a Fourth-Grade Nothing*	Judy Blume	Upper primary/lower intermediate
	Nobody Asked Me If I Wanted a Baby Sister	Martha Alexander	Preschool
Dislike of name	*Sabrina*	Martha Alexander	Preschool/lower primary
Divorce	*A Month of Sundays*	Rose Blue	Upper primary/lower intermediate
	My Dad Lives in a Downtown Hotel	Peggy Mann	Upper primary/lower intermediate
	It's Not the End of the World	Judy Blume	Intermediate
	Just as Long as We're Together	Judy Blume	Upper intermediate
Divorce, loneliness, and the finding of self	*Dear Mr. Henshaw*	Beverly Cleary	Intermediate
Finding of self	*Then Again, Maybe I Won't*	Judy Blume	Upper intermediate/ young adult
	Are You There God? It's Me, Margaret	Judy Blume	Intermediate
	Nikki 108	Rose Blue	Upper intermediate
	The Soul Brothers and Sister Lou	Kristin Hunter	Young adult
First day of school	*Shawn Goes to School*	Petronella Breinberg	Preschool/lower primary
Hearing aid	*Keeping It Secret*	Penny Pollack	Intermediate
Illness (in a hospital)	*Elizabeth Gets Well*	Alfons Weber	Primary
Learning-disabled child	*Will the Real Gertrude*	Sheila Greenwald	Intermediate

TABLE 4-1 *Continued*

Theme	Title	Author	Level
	Hollings Please Stand Up?		
Moving	*Maggie Doesn't Want to Move*	Elizabeth Lee O'Donnell	Preschool/lower primary
New baby	*Confessions of an Only Child*	Norma Klein	Upper primary/ intermediate
	Peter's Chair	Ezra Jack Keats	Preschool
	My Mama Needs Me	Mildred Potts Walker	Preschool
Overcoming fear	*Frizzy the Fearful*	Marjorie W. Sharmat	Preschool
Prejudice	*Maple Street*	Nan Hayden Agle	Upper primary/ intermediate
Transformation of a loner	*Get Lost, Little Brother*	C. S. Adler	Intermediate
Youngest child	*Weezie Goes to School*	Sue Felt Kerr	Primary

Television and Reading for Appreciation

Television is one of the competitors for children's time and attention. However, studies show that television can actually be a positive force in encouraging students to read rather than a negative one. Those programs that have peers modeling proreading behavior seem to encourage children to read because children imitate the proreading modeling behavior. An analysis of the results of young children's watching "Sesame Street" found that a significant number of the children who watched "Sesame Street" entered school with prolearning and proreading attitudes, even though the attainment of these attitudes was not the objective of the program.[30]

It has been hypothesized that since children like to watch other children on television, "peer role modeling of reading behaviors could motivate and reinforce positive attitudes toward reading."[31] This substantiates what has been said earlier in this chapter regarding the need for the teacher to be a good role model by also reading while the children are reading and by using peer role modeling to stimulate students to read.

Television can act as a positive force by portraying segments in which children choose to read rather than engage in another activity, by showing peers not disturbing other peers when they are reading, by having a child interest another in reading, and by showing situations in which everyone is engaged in reading.[32]

The following scenario shows how one teacher uses television as a catalyst for reading.

[30] Pamela M. Almeida, "Children's Television and the Modeling of Proreading Behaviors," in *Television and Education*, Chester M. Pierce, ed. (Beverly Hills, Calif.: Sage Publications, 1978), pp. 56–61.

[31] Ibid., p. 59.

[32] Ibid., p. 60.

SCENARIO

Ms. Hart Uses Television to Stimulate Reading

Ms. Hart read some articles on the amount of time that nine- and ten-year-olds spent watching television, and she was amazed to learn that some spent as much as four to six hours a day,[33] and that the typical child spends from three to four hours a day watching television. She couldn't believe it, so she decided to see for herself. She Xeroxed a weekly television schedule and brought enough copies in for her fourth-grade students. She asked them to put a mark next to the shows that they watched regularly. She walked around the room and helped any child who needed assistance in reading something on the schedule. Ms. Hart realized that her students knew how to look things up in the television schedule because she had used television schedules for one of her skimming lessons. (Prior to the skimming lesson, she had presented a lesson on using different kinds of schedules, and television schedules were one of those used [see "Skimming" in Chapter 9].)

The results of her action research (informal research done in the regular classroom) were not surprising because they seemed to corroborate research findings, that is, that students spend a lot of time in front of the television set. She also found that children like situation comedy shows the best and that they like story-type shows second best.[34]

Ms. Hart knows also that the question of the influence of television viewing on children's reading skills has been debated since television was first introduced. The researches have not been definitive. Some suggest that "television viewing has a considerable negative impact on reading achievement only for children who watch for relatively many hours—more than 4 to 6 hours a day."[35] Television also seems to affect different groups of children in different ways. The reading achievement of children who come from high-socioeconomic-status homes decreased when they watched greater amounts of television, whereas the converse appeared to be true for those who come from low socioeconomic status homes; that is, heavier viewing for these children increased their reading achievement.[36]

Ms. Hart wants her students to spend more time reading, but she is a realist. She knows that her students have many other activities competing for their time and attention besides television. One way that she can compete effectively to have students read more is to try to integrate reading with television so that it is palatable and enjoyable. To do this, she has to learn as much as possible about the medium of television and then use it as an instructional tool (see Figure 4-11).

---

[33] Aletha H. Stein, "Mass Media and Young Children's Development," *71st Yearbook for the National Society for the Study of Education.* Part II, Ira J. Gorden, ed. (Chicago: University of Chicago Press, 1972), pp. 181–202; Kate Moody, "The Research on TV: A Disturbing Picture," *New York Times* Spring Survey of Education, Section 12, Sunday, April 20, 1980, p. 17; A. Adams and C. Harrison, "Using Television to Teach Specific Reading Skill," *Reading Teacher* 29 (October 1975): 46.

[34] Adams and Harrison, "Using Television," p. 48.

[35] Johannes W. J. Beentjes and Tom H. A. Van Der Voort, "Television's Impact on Children's Reading Skills: A Review of Research," *Reading Research Quarterly* 23 (Fall 1988): 401.

[36] Ibid.

© 1966 United Feature Syndicate, Inc.

Reprinted by permission of UFS, Inc.

FIGURE 4-11 Someone should introduce Lucy to a good book.

Television as Part of the Communicative Process

Communication
Exchange of ideas.

Ms. Hart felt that one of her first challenges was to make television part of the communicative process and to channel children's enjoyment of television into constructive instructional paths that would eventually lead to more reading. Television requires listening and viewing; communication requires interaction—an exchange of ideas. To make television part of the communication process, students must be actively involved and be able to react to what they are hearing and seeing. To do this, Ms. Hart and a number of her fellow teachers spent an afternoon brainstorming some ideas for using television in the classroom. They all agreed that television should be used as an instructional tool and that it should be brought into the classroom. Here are some of the suggestions that Ms. Hart and her colleagues came up with to make television part of the communicative process:

1. Use television in the classroom.

   a. Have children discuss the shows that they watch and why they watch the shows that they do.
   b. If videotapes and video cassettes are available, you might tape a favorite situation comedy and watch it together. A discussion should follow of the characters, plot, dialogue, and message that the writer is trying to convey.
   c. Watch some special educational program together. Prepare students for the program. Set purposes for the viewing. Follow up with a discussion.
   d. Listen to a tape recording of two different commercials that promote two different products. Then view a videotape of the same two commercials. Discuss which medium is more effective in getting its message across.

2. Correlate out-of-school television viewing with your language arts (listening, speaking, reading, and writing) program.

   a. Discuss the various commercials that appear on television and what makes them so memorable.

b. Analyze the most popular commercials to try to determine why they became so popular.

c. Discuss the propaganda tactics used in different commercials seen on television. (intermediate grade level)

d. Have students watch a number of television news shows at home, and have them read a number of newspapers. Then have them make a comparison/contrast between the two media concerning the coverage of news, sports, entertainment, weather, and so on. (intermediate-grade level)

e. Encourage students to write a script for their favorite television character.

f. Encourage children to role-play their favorite television characters in a given scenario.

g. Encourage students to present a puppet show based on their favorite television program or their favorite characters.

h. Have students watch a play or special television movie based on a book. Then have students read the book on which the television show is based. The students can compare the television production with the book.

i. Students can present character sketches to the class portraying the main character of a television show, and the rest of the class is challenged to figure out who the character is.

j. Some students could present a scene from a television show and then challenge the rest of the class to name the show.

Television as a Catalyst for Reading

Once Ms. Hart set her mind to doing something, she did it. Ms. Hart read everything she could on instructional television and, in particular, the use of television to teach reading. She was surprised to find that there were a number of projects in this area besides "Sesame Street" and "The Electric Company." ("Sesame Street," which was developed primarily as a preschool program rather than as a prereading program, particularly for high-risk urban children, became useful in teaching prereading and reading skills. "The Electric Company" was primarily concerned with literacy and was a basic reading program for seven- to ten-year-old children with reading problems.) As a matter of fact, she had just received a flyer in the mail and an educational guide to six television shows aimed at her students. The shows' themes were ones that the children in her class would be able to empathize with (see "Bibliotherapy" in this chapter), and they were being presented as after-school specials. The educational guide gave a synopsis of the television story, and then questions and activities were provided based on the story. The questions encouraged critical and creative thinking. Ms. Hart thought that it might be a good idea to have the media people in her school get permission to tape a few of the shows so that she could present them in the class during school time and then use them as a springboard for critical and creative thinking comprehension lessons. She also thought that she could use them as a means to encourage reading because she would have on hand books with similar themes, which she would introduce to her students. Ms. Hart found that the major networks also presented a number of shows based on popular children's books. She decided that it would be a good idea for her to skim the television guide every week to make sure that she didn't miss any. She wanted to prepare the students in her class for the program and have some of the books available for the children to read. She would then ask them to make a comparison between the television version and the book version.

The more Ms. Hart read, the more convinced she was that the only way to win the battle for children's time was to join forces with some of the competing factors rather than to fight them in nonproductive ways or to look upon them as "the enemies." She also realized from her readings that studies showed important findings that she could not ignore. For example, in one source it was found that differences existed in some ways between children who listened to a story and those who watched the same story on television. Although there were no differences in the conclusions that both groups of students reached concerning the story, the "television-viewing group rarely went beyond the 'picture language,' either to pay attention to the audio portion or to integrate their own real-life experiences with the television experiences."[37] It was also found that the younger the audience, the greater the difference. Ms. Hart appreciated that this could be a drawback for using television because the development and use of imagination were an important part of her instructional program. However, Ms. Hart had no intention of using television as a steady diet in this way. Also, she is continually encouraging the children in her class to be creative and she has worked hard to provide a nonthreatening environment in the class that fosters creativity and allows children to be risk takers. As a matter of fact, divergent thinking is emphasized in most of her reading lessons.

Ms. Hart is also aware from her reading that the language of books offers a wider vocabulary and more varied and complicated sentence patterns than television and that these are needed for children to learn to be better writers. Again, Ms. Hart feels that this is no problem because she is not going to use television as an end in itself. In her program, television will be the steppingstone to reading—it will be used as a stimulus and as a catalyst. Ms. Hart will emphasize the integrating of reading and writing, the "stretching" of her students' imagination, and the appreciation of reading by giving children time to read.

Ms. Hart also got some good suggestions on how to integrate television viewing with reading from reading what other teachers had done. For example, she learned about script reading or scripting, which consists of having students read a script before it is broadcast. In class they discuss the subject matter, main ideas, vocabulary, and issues. Another suggestion had to do with having students produce their own television shows to develop the ability to follow directions, read, and write. Ms. Hart liked the ideas and decided to use them.

[37] Moody, "The Research on TV," p. 17.

The more Ms. Hart read about using television to stimulate children to read, the more convinced she was that the idea was a good one. She learned that the increase in dramatizations of books for children actually increased the demands for these books at bookstores and libraries. She was excited about what some television stations had done to stimulate reading, and she wanted her local television station to do the same. She decided that she would try to get her station interested in a dramatization program that dramatizes the first half of a book and then stops in the middle and urges the viewing children to finish the rest of the book themselves.

Ms. Hart was also able to attend a workshop given by a public television station. At the workshop she gained some more insights into the potential uses of instructional television in the field of reading. She was delighted to learn that the workshop included parents as well as teachers (see Chapter 16 on parental involvement in schools) and that the television people see television as an instructional tool and not as an end in itself nor as something to supplant the teacher. The steps that instructional television uses in presenting a reading lesson are similar in many ways to those used in a directed reading lesson except that the medium is different (see Chapter 11). For example, the first step has to do with the preparation of the children, the second step has to do with setting the goals or helping the children to know what to expect, the third step is the viewing with the children of the program, and the last step is follow-up. The follow-up can consist of a variety of methods to check whether certain goals have been accomplished. For example, the teacher can ask questions that have to do with feelings or emotions, as well as questions that test comprehension, and can have students involved in a number of activities that reinforce the desired skills. The emphasis is on the integration of reading in all the other language arts areas.

The Newbery Medal and the Caldecott Medal

The Newbery Medal is given annually to the book published in the United States that has been voted "the most distinguished literature" for children. The Caldecott Medal is given for the book chosen to be the best picture book of the year. Tables 4-2 and 4-3 list the Newbery and Caldecott Medal books chosen since 1980.

Newbery Award books
The books that have received the Newbery Medal, which is given annually to the book in the United States that has been voted "the most distinguished literature" for children.

TABLE 4-2   Newbery Medal Awards

Title	Author	Year
A Gathering of Days: A New England Girl's Journal, 1830–32	Joan W. Blos	1980
Jacob I Have Loved	Katherine Paterson	1981
A Visit to William Blake's Inn: Poems for Innocent and Experienced Travelers	Nancy Willard	1982
Dicey's Song	Cynthia Voigt	1983
Dear Mr. Henshaw	Beverly Cleary	1984
The Hero and the Crown	Robin McKinley	1985

TABLE 4-2 *Continued*

Title	Author	Year
Sarah, Plain and Tall	Patricia MacLachlan	1986
The Whipping Boy	Sid Fleischman	1987
Lincoln: A Photobiography	Russell Freedman	1988
Joyful Noise: Poems for Two Voices	Paul Fleischman	1989
Number the Stars	Lois Lowry	1990
Maniac Magee	Jerry Spinelli	1991
Shiloh	Phyllis Reynolds Naylor	1992

Caldecott Award books
The books that have received the Caldecott Medal, which is given annually to the book in the United States that has been chosen as the best picture book of the year.

TABLE 4-3 Caldecott Medal Awards

Title	Author and Illustrator	Year
Ox-Cart Man	Donald Hall; Barbara Cooney (illus.)	1980
Fables	Arnold Lobel	1981
Jumanji	Chris Van Allsburg	1982
Shadow	Blaise Cendrars; Marcia Brown (illus.)	1983
The Glorious Flight: Across the Channel with Louis Blériot, July 25, 1909	Alice and Martin Provensen	1984
Saint George and the Dragon	adapted by Margaret Hodges; Tina Schart Hyman (illus.)	1985
Polar Express	Chris Van Allsburg	1986
Hey Al	Arthur Yorinks; Richard Egielski (illus.)	1987
Owl Moon	Jane Yolen; John Schoenherr (illus.)	1988
Song and Dance Man	Karen Ackerman; Stephen Gammell (illus.)	1989
Lon Po Po: A Red Riding Hood Story	Ed Young	1990
Black and White	David Macaulay	1991
Tuesday	David Wiesner	1992

Graphic Summary of Chapter

Here is a graphic summary of Chapter 4. If you have read the chapter, this graphic illustration should help you remember its main points. Under or beside each heading, you might want to jot down some of the information you recall, as well as some of the key concepts in this chapter. This can act as a good review. You can then check your key concepts against those that follow the graphic summary.

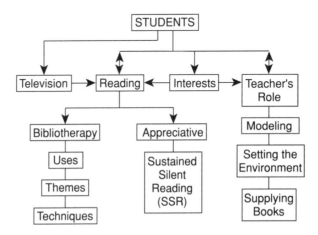

Key Concepts

- Good literature is the foundation of a good reading program.
- Good literature encountered early helps you on the path to lifelong reading.
- Appreciative reading is reading for pleasure and enjoyment that fits some mood, feeling, or interest.
- Reading helps reading.
- Many activities vie for children's time and attention.
- Teachers should provide time for reading for pleasure in their classrooms.
- Sustained Silent Reading (SSR) is independent silent reading.
- Teachers should create an environment in their classrooms that is conducive to reading.
- Teachers who are seen reading are good role models for their students.
- Big books lend themselves to interactive sessions with young children.
- Teachers should be aware of the criteria for selecting books for their students.
- Books chosen for a classroom library should present all groups of people in a positive light.
- Books can be a bridge to multicultural understanding.

- Children's interests should be taken into account when choosing books for a classroom library.
- Reading aloud to children can interest children in books.
- Humor is an important ingredient in children's books.
- Children should be exposed to various kinds of good literature.
- Readability formulas should be used with caution.
- Bibliotherapy is the use of books to help individuals cope better with their emotional and adjustment problems.
- Classroom teachers can use bibliotherapy as a means to interest students in books.
- Teachers must use bibliotherapy with caution in their classrooms.
- Teachers can use television as a catalyst for reading.

Suggestions for Thought Questions and Activities

1. Choose and read a book that you feel primary grade children would enjoy. Give your criteria for choosing the book. Explain how you would present this book to gain the attention and interest of your students. Do the same for the intermediate grades.
2. Choose and memorize the plot of a story that you feel primary grade children will find entertaining. Present the story in your own words using videotape. Do a critique of your presentation.
3. You teach an intermediate grade in an inner-city school with a large population of children who speak nonstandard English. What criteria would you use in choosing books for these children?
4. You have been appointed to a special school committee whose function it is to determine criteria for choosing books for your school. You have a limited budget. How would you determine the book-buying criteria? What factors would you take into consideration in determining your criteria?
5. You have been appointed to a committee whose responsibility it is to determine the books that children like to read. How would you go about doing this?
6. You have been invited to speak on bibliotherapy. What books would you choose to discuss in your talk?
7. Critically analyze the Newbery Award books for the past two decades. Look specifically at their portrayal of the following: the elderly, sexism, the culturally different child.
8. Brainstorm some ways you can use television as a catalyst for reading.

Selected Bibliography

Bernstein, Joanne E. *Books to Help Children Cope with Separation and Loss,* 2nd ed. New York: Bowker, 1983.

Burke, Eileen. *Literature for the Young Child,* 2nd ed. Boston: Allyn and Bacon, 1990.

Butler, Francelia. *Sharing Literature with Children: A Thematic Anthology.* Prospect Heights, Ill.: Waveland Press, 1990.

Cox, Susan, and Lee Galda. "Multicultural Literature: Mirrors and Windows on a Global Community." *The Reading Teacher* 43 (April 1990): 582–589.

Dreyer, Sharon S. *Bookfinder,* Vols. 3 and 4. Circle Pines, Minn.: American Guidance Service, 1989.

Hopkins, Lee Bennett, comp. *The Sky Is Full of Song.* New York: Harper & Row, 1983.

Jett-Simpson, Mary, ed. *Adventuring with Books: A Book List for Pre-K–Grade 6,* 9th ed. Urbana, Ill.: National Council of Teachers of English, 1989.

Keating, Charlotte Mathew. *Building Bridges of Understanding between Cultures.* Tucson, Ariz.: Palo Verde, 1971.

Moir, Hughes, Melissa Cain, and Leslie Prosak-Beres. *Collected Perspectives: Choosing and Using Books for the Classroom.* Boston: Christopher-Gordon, 1990.

Moss, Barbara. "Children's Nonfiction Trade Books: A Complement to Content Area Texts." *The Reading Teacher* 45 (September 1991): 26–32,

5

Emergent Literacy
Children's Early Literacy Development

SCENARIO: MELISSA'S EMERGENT LITERACY

At not quite three years of age, Melissa can point out letters and recognize her name in print. When she rides in a shopping cart at the food store, she points to many of the oversized letters and says, "Look, Mommy, that's an M" (M is her favorite letter). Just the other day she proudly showed her mother a paper with the letter M on it. Melissa also knows when they are close to her favorite toy store because she recognizes the letters and always points out the backward R. She can recognize the word STOP on the hexagonal sign and state many of the words on cereal boxes. Melissa, at not quite three, recognizes context-related words as well as environmental words, and she is beginning to gain the realization that groups of letters stand for words we say.

Almost from the day she was born, Melissa has been immersed in a world filled with storytelling, sharing, and books. For example, she "reads" and "writes" stories that she loves to tell to her Mommy and Daddy. She can retell her favorite stories, and when she is read a new story she can usually state what will happen or recite the predictable refrain. Often she will take the storybook from her parents and "read" aloud to them. All the words may not be intelligible, but there is no mistaking the intonation, expression, and "falsetto" voice she uses to imitate a storybook character. Melissa is on her way to becoming an excellent reader.

Of course, some people might look at Melissa's written renderings (Figure 5-1) and call them mere scribbling, and they might call her "storytelling" gibberish—but these activities are more than that. Melissa is engaged in an important aspect of literacy development: She has made the connection between reading and writing, and her attempts at reading and writing show that she is anxious to enter the world of script. The good news is that there are many children like Melissa; unfortunately, this is not the case for all (see "Individual Differences: Two Case Studies" in Chapter 2).

Today we talk about levels of literacy in the realization that there is no

Oct 1991

Melissas birthday hed a pink
birthday cake. Eric was crying because
he wanted cake; he didn't want to
sing "happy birthday." I didn't want him
to start crying. He's not crying right now.

FIGURE 5-1   Melissa (at her third birthday) says she is writing like a grown-up. As she writes her story, she tells it to her mother. Her mother writes it for her and then reads it aloud to Melissa.

specific point on a scale that separates the literate from the illiterate. Literacy should begin in early childhood and continue through senescence. Melissa is in the emergent literacy stage of the literacy continuum.

Emergent literacy is an important topic that demands our attention because of its relationship to reading. Young children who engage in many language activities, such as listening to stories and retelling stories, are gaining the literacy necessary for beginning reading.

    This chapter will help you gain a better understanding of emergent literacy and its relation to beginning reading.

KEY QUESTIONS

After you finish reading this chapter, you should be able to answer the following questions:

1. What is emergent literacy?
2. What is the relationship of emergent literacy to beginning reading?
3. What is phonemic awareness?
4. Why has the term *reading readiness* taken on such negative connotations?
5. What are viable literacy activities for young children?
6. What kinds of activities in kindergarten help prepare children for formal reading?
7. What are auditory and visual discrimination?
8. What are the roles of auditory and visual discrimination in reading?
9. What is memory span?
10. What are mixed and crossed dominance?
11. How can teachers help at-risk children?

KEY TERMS IN CHAPTER

You should pay special attention to the following key terms:

auditory discrimination	observation
auditory memory span	phoneme
classroom assessment	phonemic awareness
crossed dominance	proximodistal development
emergent literacy	readiness
emergent writing	reversals
laterality	visual discrimination
mixed dominance	

Acquisition of Reading

How children learn to read has been a topic of debate for years, and will probably persist into the next century. Researchers investigating the area of beginning reading claim that "we know very little about the transition from what has been termed emergent literacy to beginning reading."[1] Research suggests also that "reading skill may not be developed as quickly or as well in the primary grades as

[1] Connie Juel, "Beginning Reading," in *Handbook of Reading Research,* Vol. II, Rebecca Barr, Michael L. Kamil, Peter Mosenthal, and P. David Pearson, eds. (New York: Longman, 1991), p. 759.

© 1958 United Feature Syndicate, Inc.

Reprinted by permission of UFS, Inc.

FIGURE 5-2   Linus is not illiterate; he is in the process of developing literacy.

is believed."[2] And "we are just beginning to detect the dire consequences that a poor initial start with reading has on later development."[3]

Researchers feel that the most fruitful approach to gaining insights into how children learn to read is to focus on the child and what he or she does before formal reading begins (see Figure 5-2). "Insights about the world of print arise over time, often through interaction with storybooks in the home and printed materials in the environment."[4]

Young children who are exposed to extensive print begin to recognize the communicative function of print, which is certainly an important step in learning to read. Let's look more closely at this very important step, emergent literacy.

Defining Emergent Literacy

Emergent literacy That stage in literary development concerned with the young child's involvement in language and his or her attempts at reading and writing before coming to school or before conventional or formal reading and writing begin.

Agreement does not exist on the definition of emergent literacy. Many educators define emergent literacy as the "period between birth and the time when children learn to read and write conventionally."[5] Others define it as "the knowledge that the child acquires about language, reading, and writing before coming to school."[6] If one embraces the former definition, the question is: At what point would children be considered as reading and writing conventionally? (*Reading conventionally* usually means the child can decode the words on a printed page and understand what he or she is reading. *Writing conventionally* usually means the child can write something that makes sense and that others can read.) Some

2 Ibid.

3 Ibid.

4 Ibid., p. 761.

5 Elizabeth Sulzby and William Teale, "Emergent Literacy," in *Handbook of Reading Research,* Vol. II, Rebecca Barr, Michael L. Kamil, Peter Mosenthal, and P. David Pearson, eds. (New York: Longman, 1991), p. 728.

6 Lesley Mandel Morrow and Jeffrey K. Smith, "Introduction," in *Assessment for Instruction in Early Literacy,* Leslie Mandel Morrow and Jeffrey K. Smith, eds. (Englewood Cliffs, N.J.: Prentice Hall, 1990), p. 2.

children may be upper-graders who are involved in formal reading and writing programs but are not reading and writing in the conventional sense. Are they still in the emergent literacy continuum of literacy? Probably not, because this would violate the spirit of "emergent literacy, which deals with the earliest phases of literacy development."[7]

In this book, emergent literacy is defined as the stage in literacy development that is concerned with the young child's involvement in language and his or her attempts at reading and writing before coming to school or before conventional or formal reading and writing begin. On the basis of this definition, a child's scribblings and his or her attempts at telling a story from a storybook would be considered signs of emergent literacy whether these attempts at reading and writing take place in the home and community or in such school settings as Head Start, prekindergarten, or kindergarten.

Usually kindergarten acts as the bridge between emergent literacy and beginning reading. It is important to note, however, that kindergarten programs may differ not only among school districts but even within the same school district. Generally, in kindergarten, children continue to engage in such activities as listening to stories, retelling stories, and a host of other oral language activities, including learning about sound–letter and letter–sound correspondences. All these activities help them acquire the foundation for beginning reading. Some children, however, are already reading and writing when they come to school. Such children are ready to engage in a more formal reading program based on their needs. (See "Kindergarten: Establishing a Foundation for Formal Reading Instruction" later in this chapter.)

Proponents of the emergent literacy theory feel strongly that the kinds of language activities the young child is engaged in are legitimate reading activities, not merely precursors to reading. Regardless of whether these are precursors to reading or actual reading-to-learn activities, it makes sense that young children should be involved in innumerable language activities and that parents play an essential role in their children's literacy development (see Chapter 16, "Parents Are Partners in Learning"). In addition, when children come to school, teachers must present a program based on the individual differences of their students.

Special Note

In *A Practical Approach to Teaching Reading,* Second Edition, the emphasis is on children being engaged in those activities that will help them become good readers rather than on the exact labeling of the various literacy stages that they may be in or going through.

Storybook Reading and Emergent Literacy

The following remarks should sound familiar:

---

[7] Sulzby and Teale, "Emergent Literacy," p. 728.

"Read me a story, Mommy."

"Daddy, let me read the story to you."

One of the most pleasurable memories that children have is that of being read to. Reading with a parent is an interactive, socially rewarding activity that helps advance a child's literacy development (see "Reading Aloud to Children" in Chapter 3).

Children who are read to will feel more secure about "trying out reading" (Figure 5-3); that is, they will attempt to tell the story as if they were reading it by themselves. "Young children's independent, not-yet-conventional readings of books grow out of interactive readings and serve to advance children's literacy development."[8] Story reading exposes young children to the language they will be meeting in books and gives them opportunities to operate at their current level of ability without risk to their self-concepts. The children will "try out" reading on their own when they feel they can; the adults act as the scaffolding that safely guides them to the next level.

Emergent Writing

Emergent writing
Part of a child's emergent literacy; his or her preconventional writing.

Give a young child a crayon or a pencil and immediately he or she will begin to "write" (see Figure 5-4). The writing may be unintelligible to the onlooker, but

FIGURE 5-3 Melissa is "trying out reading."

[8] Sulzby and Teale, "Emergent Literacy," p. 731.

FIGURE 5-4   Melissa is "trying out writing."

the child can usually tell you what it "says." As with storybook reading, children write in preconventional or emergent forms (such as scribbling, drawing, non-phonetic letterings, and phonetic spelling) long before they write conventionally, and they develop into conventional writers through various stages in writing (see Figure 5-5).[9]

Figure 5-6 is a profile of a child's writing ranging from preschool to third grade.

Emergent Literacy – in Historical Perspective

Literacy is an ongoing, dynamic process that takes place all through life, and emergent literacy, as already stated, is that stage in the literacy continuum that deals with the young child's developing literacy. The term *emergent literacy,* itself, connotes an ongoing process. The idea of a "waiting period" in literacy development violates the spirit and essence of literacy as a developmental process. The term *reading readiness,* on the other hand, seems to suggest the existence of such a waiting period.

It is not surprising, then, that there has been a shift from the concept of reading readiness to that of emergent literacy. With this change, the term *reading*

[9] Ibid., p. 737.

FIGURE 5-5   These kindergarten children are writing their names.

readiness seems to have vanished from the professional literature. In professional journals and reading method books today, one would be hard pressed to find the term *readiness,* and especially *reading readiness.* Yet these terms pervaded the literature for decades, and a survey of many school districts shows that they are still used by many teachers, principals, and supervisors.

A number of educators have been so disenchanted with the term *readiness* and especially *reading readiness,* and with a number of the practices they have evoked, that they have probably said "good riddance" to their demise in the professional literature. The expunging of these terms, however, can cause a problem for many new teachers who have not encountered them in their reading courses but are now meeting them in their school systems.

The sections that follow should help readers gain an insight into the terms *readiness* and, in particular, *reading readiness,* so they can gain a perspective on what has taken place. An essential part of teacher empowerment is knowledge. The more knowledge teachers have, the better informed their decisions will be. Deleting or changing terms will not change practices; only teachers can change practices. Many good teachers subscribed to the developmental aspect of literacy before the label *emergent literacy* surfaced and replaced reading readiness.

Special Note
It's important to note that emergent literacy is a more encompassing concept than reading readiness. The term *reading readiness* has not usually been applied to the literacy activities children engaged in before coming to school.

2 yrs. 6 mos.

ME AND MOMMY
AND DADDY BOOK
BY. Jennifer
The BOOK CO.

4 yrs. 6 mos.

FIGURE 5-6 Profile of a child's writing ranging from preschool to third grade.

Continued

Figure 5-6 *Continued*

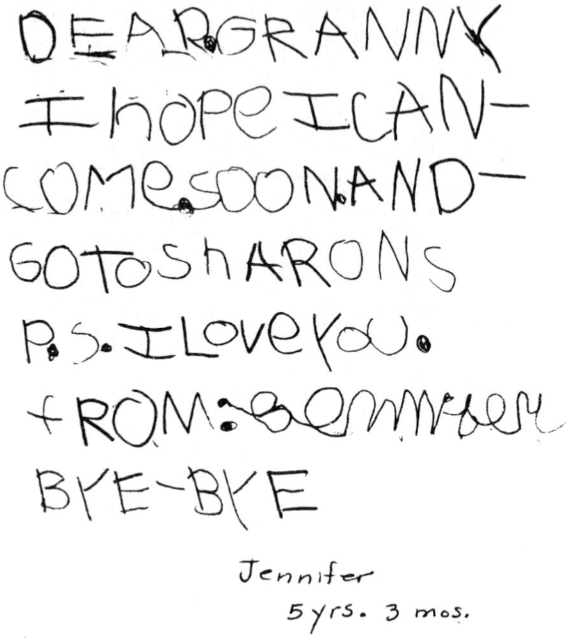

DEARGRANNY
IhopeICAN-
COMESOONAND-
GOTOShARONS
P.S. ILOVEYOU.
fROM: Jennifer
BYE-BYE

Jennifer
5 yrs. 3 mos.

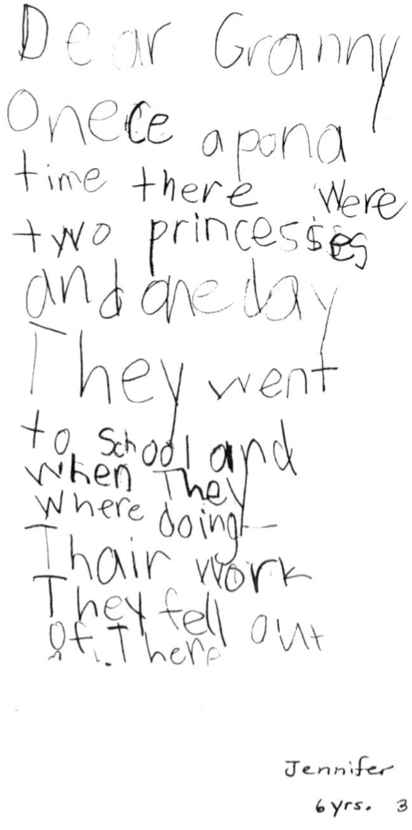

Dear Granny
Onece apona
time there were
two princesses
and one day
They went
to school and
when They
where doing
Thair work
They fell out
of there

Jennifer
6 yrs. 3 mos.

Figure 5-6 *Continued*

My Adventures on the Rainbow

I was playing inside with my friends Sally, Allissa, Shea and Kelly Jo because it was raining. All of a sudden a rainbow appeared. A strange voice said, "Follow the rainbow and your dream."

We went on red first. Just as we went about a mile we came upon a forest. A tree grabbed me and the others. They got away. When the tree let me down it didn't put me down like any decent tree would, it threw me down. When it threw me, I landed on a shiny thing. It was a key, but to what? I decided not to tell the others about it.

I saw them waiting at the end of the forest. We saw a sign that said "Welcome to Orange." Orange was very poor. I saw Munchkins begging. I gave them all my bread. They were so happy they told us the history of their land. They said that there was a pot of gold somewhere and they used to be the richest color.

We were on our way again when we fell down a deep hole and then we saw a sign that said "Welcome to Yellow, the Richest Color." Yellow was so sassy that we got out as quick as we could. When we were running we ran into a tree. There was a door in it. We went inside and the door closed. We found a map and a secret passageway. We took the map and went through the passageway. It was very dark and scary. Soon we saw a light pointing upward on a ladder. We climbed the ladder and when we came up we walked about half a mile when we saw a sign that said "Welcome to Green."

Well now that we're in green we've only got two more colors to go. We came to green which was the biggest color and we got lost. We decided to ask someone the way. We asked someone who looked like a nice man but as soon as we said one word, he kidnapped us! He took us to his hideout and tied us up. "Now where had I seen him? Oh, I remember, he was wanted for murder!" Well at least he went away to get some more people. I just thought of something. I had my brother's pocket knife! I cut my rope and Kelly Jo's, Sally's, Shea's and Allissa's. We left Allissa there to make big dolls that looked like us. We went to the police and they came to put the kidnapper in jail. We had to stay in green for another day because they had a feast in our honor. We got $50 and all the pizza we wanted. They showed us the way to blue.

Blue and indigo were having war. It was terrible. There were no bomb shelters or hospitals. Sally and Kelly Jo got wounded on their legs so

Continued

Figure 5-6   *Continued*

they couldn't walk. Shea and I went to get a blue building robot to build a big shelter for the wounded while Allissa took care of Kelly Jo and Sally. We asked a man why there was a war. He said it was all because a few blue dogs got into the Indigo people's gardens. We thought that was so stupid! I stood on the monument and told them that the blue people would keep their dogs tied up if the indigo people would stop the war. I was surprised that they agreed. They gave all of us $100 for stopping the war.

We went into Indigo and they gave us $100 again for stopping the war. Indigo was mostly forest. Soon a terrible ogre came and chased us into Violet. There was a beautiful castle that said leprechaun's castle. We tried to go in but it was locked. I thought about the key I found in Red. I took it out and tried it. It worked! When we got inside there were five tables. Each had a key. We took them. We decided to catch the leprechaun. We put a big net over the inside of the castle to catch him. After several tries we finally caught him. He said we had three wishes because we caught him. We wished to have as many wishes as we wanted. We also wished for a girl leprechaun and for him to show us the way to a pot of gold each. He took us to the end of Violet and undid a boat into the white ocean. We all jumped in the boat. Soon we landed on a rainbow colored island. On it were five vaults. We took out our keys and opened them. There were 10 zillion gold pieces in each pot! We also wished that we could take all the leprechauns, including the king, home with us so that we could have magical powers and live forever. When we got home, we became the richest people in the world. We had a palace and a magical fountain in the front courtyard. One night somebody stole our money! We looked everywhere. Then we asked the leprechaun king to tell us where the robber and the money were. He said the robber and the money were in the magic fountain's basement. When we went down, there he was! We captured him and we each got $5,000 for capturing him. When we got our money back, nobody ever stole it again. We were going to have life forever and we were going to make it be happy!

THE END

Jennifer
8 yrs. 7 mos.

What Is "Readiness"?

Starting School

George and Jim have been friends since they were two years old. They have spent practically every day of their lives together. Tomorrow, for the first time George will be entering a new world—the world of school—but Jim will not. Even though George and Jim are only one day apart in age, George is considered *ready* for school, but Jim is not. Why? The reason is very simple. George was born on November 30, and Jim was born on December 1. The cutoff date for school entry in George and Jim's school district is November 30.

According to the educators in George and Jim's school district, George is ready for school, whereas Jim is not. Readiness in George and Jim's school district is arbitrarily determined by a cutoff date.

If we were to survey various school districts across the country, we would find the same practice taking place, whereby chronological age rather than mental age is the determining factor for beginning school. Yet two children of similar chronological ages may be months and even years apart mentally, socially, and emotionally.

Webster's College Dictionary defines readiness as "the act of being prepared mentally or physically for some experience or action." This definition is not very helpful because we still have to determine what "being prepared" means.

Jerome Bruner, a noted psychologist, in his book *The Process of Education,* made the following pronouncement concerning the readiness of children that startled many in the educational community in the early 1960s:[10]

> *We begin with the hypothesis that any subject can be taught effectively in some intellectually honest form to any child at any stage of development. It is a bold hypothesis and an essential one in thinking about the nature of a curriculum. No evidence exists to contradict it; considerable evidence is being amassed that supports it.*

According to Bruner, any child is *ready* to learn if the teacher can properly structure the curriculum to suit the developmental level of the child. Readiness to learn is not a waiting period but is determined by how to present concepts to

---

[10] Jerome S. Bruner, *The Process of Education* (Cambridge, Mass.: Harvard University Press, 1963), p. 33.

children based on their developmental needs. Bruner's concept of readiness is not really as provocative as it sounds and not actually original. In 1936, Arthur Gates, a noted reading authority, stated that the important variable in beginning reading success was not mental age but rather the methods and materials by which the child was to be instructed.[11]

In the past, *readiness* has often been defined as follows: "the adequacy of existing capacity in relation to a given task."[12] There are a number of problems associated with this definition, which may have helped to cause the furor over use of this term in relation to beginning reading. First, this definition implies that educators can adequately determine "existing capacity" (see "Intelligence" in Chapter 2). The ability to determine one's "existing capacity" is difficult for all individuals and especially for young children. Also, this definition may cause teachers to create a "waiting period" for those students who they feel do not have the "capacity" for a task. In addition, it can become a self-fulfilling prophecy. If teachers feel that certain students do not have the ability to read, they may treat these students in a negative way and not expect them to be able to learn to read. These feelings could be picked up by the children, harming their self-concept.

Readiness
An ongoing, dynamic process, which teachers use to prepare students for various learning activities throughout the school day.

Not everyone, however, has defined readiness in such a narrow sense. Numerous educators have defined readiness as an ongoing, dynamic process, which teachers use to prepare students for various learning activities throughout the school day. For these educators, readiness for all learning including reading is an interaction of maturation, past experiences, and a desire to learn; it is a holistic concept. Readiness is never construed as an excuse for not engaging children in meaningful learning.

Reading Readiness—Not a Waiting Period
Today, as has already been stated throughout this text, we talk about levels of literacy and reading as a developmental process. Because we look at reading in this way, many people feel that the concept of reading readiness has become a moot point.

In a number of school districts across the country, however, reading readiness tests, which are a direct outgrowth of the reading readiness movement and are supposed to be designed to predict those children who are ready to read, are alive and vigorously supported by many administrators. Therefore, as stated earlier, it makes sense that we should have some understanding of reading readiness.

Those people who adhere to the purely maturational view of reading readiness—and there are not too many educators in the nineties who do—claim that children cannot read until they are ready. (They feel that reading readiness is dependent on one specific trait—namely, mental age.) They claim that maturation (internal growth) cannot be encouraged; children cannot be induced to read until they have a mental age of six and a half. The proponents of this view look upon reading as a waiting period rather than an ongoing process of literacy develop-

11 Joanne R. Nurss, "Assessment of Readiness," in *Reading Research: Advances in Theory and Practice,* T. G. Waller and G. E. MacKinnon, eds. (New York: Academic Press, 1979), p. 32.
12 Ibid.

ment. Mabel Morphett and Carlton Washburne, superintendent of schools in Winnetka, in the early 1930s claimed that their study showed that six and a half was the mental age necessary for learning to read, and it was not worthwhile to begin children at earlier ages.[13] For a number of decades this view was solidly held, but, as stated earlier, it is hardly held by any educators in the 1990s.

The use of mental age to defer reading is not a valid one. A child with a chronological age of ten and a mental age of six has an IQ (intelligence quotient) of 60. A child with an IQ of 60 will not progress in reading as a child of five with a mental age of six and a half, who has an IQ of 130. As has been pointed out, ". . . one cannot conclude that those children in Morphett and Washburne's study who had mental ages lower than six and a half and made slow progress would have made the same amount of progress as did the brighter children if only reading instruction had been delayed for the duller children until their mental ages had reached six and a half."[14]

The concept of delaying reading instruction until a child is ready is not a tenable one and is at variance with our view of literacy as an ongoing process. Also, to invoke the argument that a child should not be taught to read because he or she is not ready or that a child is not ready to read because he or she has not been successful in reading is ridiculous, because it is a circular argument.

Teachers are cautioned, therefore, "against delaying reading instruction to wait for cognitive maturation. Instead, . . . it would be both wiser and more efficient to provide all beginning readers with a variety of language games and activities designed to develop their linguistic awareness directly."[15] Even though IQ and general mental skills seem not to have much bearing on early reading achievement, early reading failure seems to result in a progressive diminution in IQ scores and general mental skills.[16]

Phonemic Awareness and Early Reading

In order to read, it is necessary to understand the pronunciation clues of written language. Children's phonemic awareness, which is "the ability to recognize that a spoken word consists of a sequence of individual sounds,"[17] is related to effi-

---

[13] Mabel V. Morphett and Carleton Washburne, "When Should Children Begin to Read?" *Elementary School Journal* 31 (March 1931): 503.

[14] Max Coltheart, "When Can Children Learn to Read?" in *Reading Research: Advances in Theory and Practice*, T. Gary Waller and G. E. Mackinnon, eds. (New York: Academic Press, 1979), p. 8.

[15] Marilyn Jager Adams, *Beginning to Read: Thinking and Learning about Print—A Summary*, Steven A. Stahl, Jean Osborn, and Fran Lehr, eds. (Urbana, Ill.: Center for the Study of Reading, 1990), p. 39.

[16] Ibid.

[17] Eileen W. Ball and Benita Blachman, "Does Phoneme Awareness Training in Kindergarten Make a Difference in Early Word Recognition and Developmental Spelling?" *Reading Research Quarterly* 26 (1) (1991): 51.

Phonemic awareness
The ability to recognize that a spoken word consists of a sequence of individual sounds.

Phoneme
Smallest unit of sound in a specific language system; a class of sounds.

cient decoding for children at a variety of ages . . . and decoding . . . is one of the essential elements of conventional reading."[18]

In phonemic awareness training, young children are helped to become aware of sounds in spoken words. They are usually explicitly taught to say the sounds of single phoneme items—for example, *a* or *i;* two-phoneme items—for example, *at* or *it;* and three-phoneme items—for example, *fat* or *fit*. The usual training consists of having children learn how to segment the target (chosen) word into phonemes.

Phonemic awareness training sessions seem to vary from trainer to trainer, and the emphasis is usually on a target word in isolation. The technique that follows also uses words in isolation, but it is combined with a story and children are encouraged to discuss the story. Teachers could use this technique with their kindergarten children to help them acquire phonemic awareness. It should be helpful for many children and especially helpful for those children who speak nonstandard English or who have limited English proficiency.

When the sessions begin, the teacher usually tells the children that words can be divided into sounds that can be heard. Then they are given an example of the special way to pronounce a word whereby the first phoneme is stressed by holding it longer than usual and the rest of the word is pronounced as usual. Examples are (/*bbbbat*/); (/*fffit*/); and (/*ssssat*/).

After the children are familiar with this way of pronouncing a word, the children are exposed to a short story that highlights one particular sound (phoneme). Before reading aloud the story to the children, the teacher introduces the story by showing them illustrations that have pictures of words with the target sound in beginning, medial, and final positions. The teacher and children discuss the events of the story, the characters, and so on. The teacher then tells the children she will read aloud the short story and they should listen carefully to find out which sound they hear very often in the story.

After the story is read, the teacher asks the children to state the sound they heard very often in the story. The teacher could also have the children repeat some of the sentences that contain the target sound.[19]

Studies show that phonemic awareness, whereby children have been trained to segment words into phonemes, is related to success in reading. However, "those studies that have also included instruction in the relations between sound segments and letters appear to have demonstrated a greater effect on reading and spelling."[20]

Many young children, such as Melissa (see the scenario at the beginning of this chapter), are gaining phonemic awareness, even though they are not receiving explicit training in this area, because their parents are giving them a rich background of literacy experiences that include storybook reading and retelling,

[18] Sulzby and Teale, "Emergent Literacy," p. 746.

[19] See Alfred Lie, "Effects of a Training Program for Simulating Skills in Word Analysis in First-Grade Children," *Reading Research Quarterly* 26 (3) (1991): 240–241.

[20] Ball and Blachman, "Does Phoneme Awareness Training Make a Difference?" p. 54.

language play, seeing parents read and write, and "trying out" reading and writing. When these children come to school, they will be ready to benefit from formal training in letter–sound relationships because they will have had the experiential background necessary to benefit from such training. Teachers will, however, have to be ever vigilant for those children who have not had these rich literacy experiences and should provide these children with the help they need (see the next section on "At-Risk Children and Early Reading Instruction").

At-Risk Children and Early Reading Instruction

Proponents of emergent literacy claim that listening to stories, retelling stories, and interacting with storytellers are legitimate reading activities rather than merely precursors to reading. We have already made the point that how these critical reading activities are labeled is not important. What is crucial is that all children, regardless of their backgrounds, are exposed to many reading and writing experiences so that they can make the connection between the spoken word and print.

When children come to school, teachers need to engulf them in many rich language experiences so that they can develop their linguistic awareness. These kinds of experiences are especially critical for at-risk children who come from educationally disadvantaged homes. Children who are at high risk when they come to school would be put at even greater risk if teachers were to delay their reading instruction to wait for their cognitive maturity. Rather than delaying instruction, it's a matter of building a foundation for these children so that they can benefit the most from reading instruction (see "Reading Intervention Programs" in Chapter 13).

Kindergarten: Establishing a Foundation for Formal Reading Instruction

As stated previously, phonemic awareness is necessary for children to be able to decode words, and phonemic awareness depends on children's having a strong exposure to print. Teachers cannot take for granted that all young children who begin school have been surrounded with books and have engaged in rich oral language experiences. Therefore, teachers in kindergarten usually involve children in many different types of linguistic activities to build their foundation for formal reading.

Most of the scenarios that follow are those that are directly related to beginning reading; however, it is important to state that even though most of the scenarios that are directly related to beginning reading take place in kindergarten, these types of activities are not limited to kindergarten. Some children will be involved in such activities at home, some in preschool, and some in first grade.

There are also some children, such as Jennifer (see "Teacher-Made or Classroom [Informal] Assessments" later in this chapter) who may not need many of the activities presented in the scenarios because they are already reading.

A good program at any literacy stage should be based on the needs of the individual child and determined by the kind of activities presented rather than by when the child is involved in the program.

Here are a number of very short scenarios. In which ones are the children involved in activities directly related to beginning reading?

SCENARIO 1

Seven Children, Kindergarten

Two children are building with large blocks, two others are molding clay, two are playing tenpins with a ball, and one is cutting out pictures of people from a magazine.

SCENARIO 2

Seven Children, Kindergarten

The seven children are seated in a semicircle around the teacher. The teacher says, "Listen carefully. I am going to make a sound, and then I want you to make the sound." The teacher says, "sss." Then she says, "I'll say, 'sss, sss' once more, and then I want you to say, 'sss.' " After the children have said, "sss" in unison, the teacher calls on individual children to produce the sound.

SCENARIO 3

Seven Children, Kindergarten

The children are seated in a semicircle around the teacher. The teacher tells the children that she will say a word. The children have to tell her the first sound they hear in the word. She says *fffat,* emphasizing the initial phoneme. The children are asked to state the first sound they hear. She says the word again, but this time she emphasizes the middle phoneme (*faaat*) and has the children say this phoneme. She does the same for the final phoneme; that is, she says *fattt.* She does this with a number of words that begin with different phonemes and uses the same technique with medial and final phonemes.

SCENARIO 4

Seven Children, Kindergarten

The children are seated in a semicircle around the teacher. The teacher tells the children that she will say a word. The teacher says *bbbat,* emphasizing the initial consonant. She has the children state the first sound they hear in the word. Then she puts the letter *b* on the chalkboard and tells them the letter *b* stands for the first sound they heard in *bat*. The teacher follows the same procedure for a number of other words; that is, she says a word, emphasizes a specific phoneme, and then places the letter that stands for the phoneme on the chalkboard.

SCENARIO 5

Seven Children, Kindergarten

The seven children are seated in a semicircle around the teacher. The teacher tells the children that she will say three words. Two of the words begin in the same way, and one does not. The children are asked to state the two words that begin in the same way. The teacher does this with a number of different sets of words.

SCENARIO 6

Seven Children, Kindergarten

The children are seated in a semicircle around the teacher. The teacher tells the children that she will hold up a letter, identify the letter, and say a word that begins with that letter. She then wants the children to look at the pictures she is holding to help them come up with other words that begin like that word. She holds up the letter *b* and says, "baby." The children are then challenged to come up with other words that begin like *baby*.

SCENARIO 7

Seven Children, Kindergarten

Seven children are seated in a semicircle around the teacher. The teacher tells the children that they will have to listen very carefully and pay attention because she is going to say some words, and then she will call on someone to repeat the words in exactly the same way that she had said them. The teacher says the following words very clearly and one second apart: *can, door, tree*. The teacher then calls on a child to repeat the words in the same order. The teacher continues in this way with word sets made up of three, four, and five words.

SCENARIO 8

Seven Children, Kindergarten

Seven children are seated in a semicircle around the teacher. Each child has a sheet in front of him or her. On the sheet of paper there are various uppercase and lowercase letters. The teacher tells the children to look carefully at the first letter and then to put a circle around all those letters that are the same as the first letter.

SCENARIO 9

Seven Children, Kindergarten

The seven children are seated in a semicircle around the teacher. The children have a number of letters in front of them. The teacher puts a letter on the board and names the letter. She asks the children to hold up the same letter. The children hold up the letter. This procedure continues for a number of letters. She then asks students to choose a letter, name it, and hold it up (Figure 5-7).

SCENARIO 10

Seven Children, Kindergarten

The seven children are standing in the center of the room. The teacher tells them to listen carefully because they are going to play "Simon Says." The teacher explains the game and its rules to the children. She also tells the children that the winner will be Simon for the next game. Many of the Simon Says instructions ask the children to discriminate between their right and left hands and feet.

FIGURE 5-7   These kindergarten children are learning their letters.

SCENARIO 11

Seven Children, Kindergarten

The children are seated in a semicircle around the teacher. Each child has a sheet of paper with geometric figures on it. The geometric figures are of different sizes. The teacher asks the children to look at all the figures on their sheet. Then she tells them to point to the one that is the largest. Next she asks them to point to the one that is the smallest. She asks them to point to the first figure, the last figure, and so on.

SCENARIO 12

Seven Children, Kindergarten

The seven children are seated in a semicircle around the teacher. The teacher holds up a picture. In the picture there are a number of children dressed in snowsuits. The teacher asks the children the following questions: What kind of day do you think it is? Where are the children going? What do you think they will do?

SCENARIO 13

Seven Children, Kindergarten

The seven children are seated in a semicircle around the teacher. The teacher shows the children a set of three pictures. She places the three pictures on a flannel board, which is in front of the children. The teacher tells the children that the pictures are out of order. She tells the children to look carefully at the pictures and then to arrange them in another way so that they make sense.

SCENARIO 14

Seven Children, Kindergarten

The seven children are seated in a semicircle around the teacher. The teacher tells the children to listen carefully because she is going to read them a short story. After she reads the short story, she is going to ask someone to retell the story in his or her own words. The teacher reads the short story to the children. After she finishes the story, she calls on someone to retell the story in his or her own words.

Activities Related to Beginning Reading

Let's look more closely at the kinds of activities presented in the fourteen scenarios. First, let's look at those that would not be considered related to beginning reading—that is, activities that are not directly related to the skills that will be necessary for formal reading. All of the activities except those in Scenario 1 would be considered related to beginning reading activities. In Scenario 1 the activities that the children are engaged in are good activities that help them to develop muscular coordination, and they are *indirectly* related to reading because they require eye coordination. However, these activities are too general and do not lead *directly* to reading; that is, they are not directly related to the skills that will be necessary for formal reading. For example, it is possible to be a good athlete and be unable to read; conversely, it is possible to be poorly coordinated and be a good reader. This does not mean that those activities that are not directly related to reading should be discarded or are unimportant. It does mean that teachers should recognize that children who spend their school days in only those activities that help to develop large or small muscle coordination are not involved in a program to help develop literacy.

Now, let's look at those activities that would fall into the province of early literacy development.

Speech Improvement

The activity in Scenario 2 is actually a speech sound production activity. In a speech sound production activity, the teacher's purpose is speech improvement. If children are having difficulty producing words correctly, this can affect the children's reading (see Chapters 1 and 2 and "Phonemic Awareness and Early Reading" in this chapter). A knowledgeable teacher determines which sounds are causing difficulty for the children and usually presents these sounds to the children in isolation. The children first listen to each individual sound and then imitate the sound. This speech sound production activity would be a prerequisite activity that is related to reading because of the interrelatedness of the language arts. If students have difficulty in hearing or producing certain sounds, this may affect their ability to make the proper letter–sound correspondences when they are reading. Teachers, however, should not confuse sound production activities with phonics. Sound production activities are not decoding activities.

Phonemic Awareness

Scenario 3 is related to Scenario 2, but it is not the same. In this scenario, the teacher is determining whether the children are aware of the sounds in spoken words. She wants to help them recognize that a spoken word consists of a sequence of individual sounds. As stated already, phonemic awareness is necessary for children to be able to make proper letter–sound relationships.

Sound–Letter Relationships

The activity in Scenario 4 is different from Scenario 3 in that the teacher in this scenario is concerned with children being able to recognize sound–letter relation-

ships. As stated previously in this chapter, studies have shown that explicit instruction in the relations between sounds and letters appears to have a greater
effect on reading and spelling than an emphasis on sounds alone. Knowledge of
sound–letter relations is necessary in order to make proper letter–sound relationships.

Auditory Discrimination

In Scenarios 5 and 6 the children are engaged in auditory discrimination activities.

Auditory discrimi-
nation
Ability to distin-
guish differences
and similarities
between sound
symbols.

Auditory discrimination, which is the ability to distinguish between
sounds, is essential for the acquisition of language and for learning to read. The
essence of what speech clinicians have learned concerning auditory discrimination is summarized as follows:

1. There is evidence that the more nearly alike two phonemes are in phonetic
   (relating to speech sounds) structure, the more likely they are to be misinterpreted.
2. Individuals differ in their ability to discriminate among sounds.
3. The ability to discriminate frequently matures as late as the end of the
   child's eighth year. A few individuals never develop this capacity to any
   great degree.
4. There is a strong positive relation between slow development of auditory
   discrimination and inaccurate pronunciation.
5. There is a positive relationship between poor discrimination and poor reading.
6. Although poor discrimination may be at the root of both speech and reading difficulties, it often affects only reading or speaking.
7. There is little if any relationship between the development of auditory discrimination and intelligence, as measured by most intelligence tests.[21]

For children who speak a nonstandard dialect of English or for whom English is a second language, it is well to bear in mind that the acquisition of speech
sounds for any given dialect or language is learned very early in life and is usually established by the time the child starts school. These children especially
need help in auditory discrimination if they are to learn standard English (see
Chapter 2).

Auditory memory
span
Amount of informa-
tion able to be
stored in short-term
memory for imme-
diate use or repro-
duction.

Memory Span

In Scenario 7 the children are involved in an auditory memory span activity.

Auditory memory span is essential for individuals who must judge whether
two or more sounds are similar or different. In order to make such comparisons,
the sounds must be kept in memory and retrieved for comparison. Auditory
memory span is defined as "the number of discrete elements grasped in a given

21 Joseph W. Wepman, "Auditory Discrimination, Speech and Reading," *Elementary School Journal*
60 (1960): 326.

moment of attention and organized into a unity for purposes of immediate reproduction or immediate use."[22]

A deficiency in memory span will hinder effective listening, which in turn
will affect reading (see Chapter 1). Reading requires concentration, which is
sustained attention. If a child cannot retain a certain amount of information or be
attentive, he or she will have difficulty with both decoding and comprehension
skills. Although the activity in Scenario 7 is a classic activity primarily designed
to improve memory span, the activities in many of the other scenarios could also
come under the umbrella of memory span. In many of the activities the children
are required to listen carefully, that is, to attend or concentrate. (See Chapter 9
for a digit-span scale for determining how well children are doing in memory
span.)

Visual Discrimination

Visual discrimination
The ability to
distinguish differ-
ences and similiari-
ties between written
symbols.

In Scenarios 8 and 9 the children are engaged in visual discrimination activities.
Visual discrimination is the ability to distinguish between written symbols. If
pupils have difficulty discriminating between and among letters, they will not be
able to read. Numerous studies have found that letter recognition and letter naming are the most effective single predictors of reading achievement.[23] In learning
to read, children need to be able to make fine discriminations; therefore, children
need activities involving letters or numbers rather than geometric figures or pictures. Also, transfer of learning is greater if the written symbols that children are
working with are similar to those that they will meet in reading.

Left–Right Orientation

In Scenario 10 the teacher is emphasizing directions that require the children to
differentiate between their left and right sides. In order to read English, children
must learn to read from left to right. A number of children, especially those who
are left-handed or who have crossed dominance, may read *saw* for *was* and *was*
for *saw* because they are reading from right to left.

**Proximodistal
development**
Muscular develop-
ment from the
midpoint of the
body to the extrem-
ities.

To understand better the left-handed child's problem in reading and writing,
we must refer to proximodistal development—development from the midpoint of
the body to the extremities. Right-handed children move their right hands from
left to right naturally. But for left-handed children, moving their left hand from
left to right goes against their natural inclination.

Try this simple experiment to illustrate the point: Bring both hands to the
center of your body. Now, move both hands out away from your body. The right
hand will follow a left-to-right path corresponding to the English pattern of writing; the left hand follows a right-to-left path. Ask some left-handed persons to
write a *t*. Observe carefully how they make the horizontal line. Most of them,
unless they have been well conditioned, will draw the line from right to left.

---

[22] Virgil A. Anderson, "Auditory Memory Span as Tested by Speech Sounds," *American Journal of
Psychology* 52 (1939): 95.

[23] Adams, *Beginning to Read,* p. 36.

Teaching reading is a complex task, and one of the things the child learns is to read from left to right. For right-handed people this follows physical developmental laws and is based on natural development. Teachers must recognize that reading from left to right is not natural for left-handed children and should be on the alert for possible reversal problems with them.

Reversals
Confusion of letters and words by inverting them; for example, *b = d, was = saw,* and vice versa.

Human perceptual-motor activity is usually initiated from one dominant side of the body, even though humans are bilateral, or two-sided. By the time children enter school, they usually show a fairly consistent preference for their right or left hand. There are also preferences in the use of eyes and feet; by the time children come to school they have usually also established these preferences. Such preferences concern *laterality* or sidedness. People are said to have a *dominant side* if their hand, eye, and foot preferences are similar. When people have a dominant hand on one side and a dominant eye on the other, they are said to have *crossed dominance.* Individuals who do not have a consistent preference for one eye, hand, or foot are said to have *mixed dominance.* It has been hypothesized that children who have crossed or mixed dominance may tend to have reversal difficulties in reading and writing, but studies done in this area have not been definitive. Children with crossed dominance can perhaps shift from a left-handed orientation to a right-handed one in writing, but this might cause difficulties for them.

Laterality
Sidedness.

Crossed dominance
The dominant hand on one side and the dominant eye on the other.

Mixed dominance
No consistent preference for an eye, hand, or foot.

A teacher can easily test whether a child has crossed or mixed dominance. To determine hand dominance, a teacher can observe which hand the child uses to throw a ball, write, or open a door. The teacher can tell which eye is dominant by observing which eye the child uses to look through a microscope, telescope, or an open cylinder formed by a roll of paper. Foot dominance can be easily determined by observing which foot the child uses to kick a ball or stamp on the floor with.

Teachers should be cautioned that crossed or mixed dominance in a child does not mean that the child will have a problem, although the possibility exists. The teacher should give special attention to those children who are having reversal problems by emphasizing left-to-right orientation for reading and writing.

Children's Early Literacy Development and Comprehension Skills

If children have difficulty in the area of cognitive development, they will have difficulty with reading because reading is a thinking act (see Chapters 1, 2, and 7). The activities in Scenarios 2–10 are prerequisite reading activities that are most closely related to the decoding aspect of reading. The activities in Scenarios 11–14 are prerequisite reading activities related to the comprehension aspect of reading. Both decoding and comprehension ability are needed to read. Let's look more closely at the kinds of activities presented in Scenarios 11–14. In Scenario 11 the activity has to do with concept development. Children need to know certain concepts in order to be able to comprehend what they read. As we have seen in previous chapters, the more advanced children are in language and concept development, the better readers they will be. The concepts of *smallest, largest, first,* and *last* are some of the concepts young children should be developing. In Scenarios 12 and 13 the children are engaged in thinking activities similar to those they will meet in print. The activity in Scenario 12 involves both inferential and creative thinking. These are high-order thinking skills, but the skills are presented at the children's readiness level; that is, the vocabulary being used is at the listening vocabulary of the children and pictures are being used rather than print. The activity in Scenario 14 involves a number of skills that are also necessary to be a good reader. To be able to retell a story in his or her own words, the child must be able to concentrate, that is, have sustained attention, comprehend the story, follow the order of the story, and have such command of the language that he or she can retell the story.

It is important to note again that many of the comprehension skills that children will be developing in the formal reading program are similar to those that they will have met in the early reading program; the only differences are in the level and manner of presentation. In the formal reading program, the children will be developing these comprehension skills mainly from oral language and reading print; in the early reading program, the children are developing these skills primarily from oral language and pictures. (See the section "Listening and Reading" in Chapter 1.) This book is based on the premise that children can and should be exposed to high-level comprehension skills at their readiness levels and that this should be done as early as possible. It is not too soon to encourage children to develop inferential, critical, and creative thinking at the early reading level.

Special Note

In Scenario 11 geometric figures are used to help children to develop the concepts of size and position. If, however, the purpose of the lesson is for the children to have practice in fine visual discrimination, which is necessary for the decoding of words, letters or numbers rather than geometric figures should be used. Also, words rather than pictures should be used for visual discrimination activities related to whole word recognition.

Sample Early Literacy Activities and Ideas for Activities

Here are some sample activities that teachers can use as a springboard to develop their own.

Auditory Discrimination Activities

1. Have children listen to various tapes that feature city, country, school, animal, and other kinds of sounds. Have children pick out sounds they hear.

2. Make a tape of many people talking at the same time. Have them try to pick out what the students are saying. Discuss how difficult it is to hear anything if there is a lot of noise or a lot of conversation at once.

3. Tape children's voices. Have students pick out who is talking.

4. Choose one child to be "it." The child who is "it" must turn his or her back to the class. The teacher then chooses four other children. The child who is "it" asks any questions that he or she wants to and each of the four children must answer the questions. The child who is "it" must guess who the four children are from their voices. The child who is "it" may ask three questions only.

5. Choose a book or poem that involves sounds. Some good books for this purpose are Peter Spier's *Crash! Bang! Boom!*, Margaret Wise Brown's *The Noisy Book*, Karla Kuskin's *Roar and More*, Valentine Teal's *The Little Woman Wanted Noise*, and June Behren's *What I Hear in My School*. Read a book such as *What I Hear in My School*. Then list the following on the board: a bell, two children whispering, children jumping rope, a ball bouncing, a xylophone, a guinea pig eating lettuce, a creaking gate, a guitar, and so on. Have children go down the list and make the characteristic sound of the animal or object. Put the children in groups of two or three and assign a specific object from the story to each group. Reread the story. Tell the children that whenever they hear the object mentioned in the story, they should make the sound characteristic of the object.

After working with general sounds, children should work with letters and sounds. Here are some sample activities:

1. Present three words to the children that have similar beginning consonant sounds and one that has a different beginning consonant sound. Have children state the word that has the different consonant sound. Example:

Listen carefully! I am going to say four words. Three begin with the same sound. Pick out the one that does not begin with the same sound.

book	baby	cat	bank
cake	man	cookie	candy
happy	home	hop	lamp

2. Present words to the children with similar initial beginning sounds and those with different consonant sounds. Have children state the words with the same consonant sounds. Example:

Listen carefully! I am going to say some words that begin like book and ball. Listen and try to pick out all those words that start like book and ball.

bath	coat	baby
bang	Bobby	hat
banana	candy	bicycle

3. The teacher can give the children three words. Two start with the same sound and one does not. Children have to state the two that start with the same sound.

happy	see	help
sun	cat	Sara
zebra	wet	zero

4. Tell children to listen carefully. Tell them that you are going to state three words that begin with the same sound. Only a person whose name begins with that sound can give a word that also starts with that sound.

Teachers can vary the auditory discrimination activities and present similar types of activities for final and medial consonant sounds. As children gain skill in differentiating among the various sounds, they can play such games as the "Sentence Fun Game," "I Spy," the "Matching Bingo Letter Game," and so on.

1. *Auditory Discrimination Sentence Fun.* State a sentence that repeats the initial sound at the beginning of almost every word. Challenge the children to add a word to the sentence that has the same beginning sound as most of the other words. Example:

Betty Benson bought bitter butter.

Children can also be challenged to make up their own sentences in which the beginning sound is the same in almost all the words.

2. *I Spy.* This game correlates the children's observational abilities with their abilities to match similar sounds. The teacher can initiate the game by saying, "I spy something in this room that begins like *darling.*" The child who gives a word that begins like *darling* then makes up an "I Spy" sentence.

To make the game more challenging, use beginning vowel sounds, final consonant sounds, and medial vowel sounds.

3. *Matching Sound to Letter Game.* The children have bingo-type cards that have consonant letters on them and a number of free spaces. The teacher states a word that either begins or ends with a certain letter. If a child has the initial or final consonant that has been specified by the teacher, the child covers the letter with a colored tab having the appropriate consonant letter on it. The first child who fills a row across, down, or diagonally wins. The teacher repeats each word so that the card can be checked for correctness. Note that a letter may appear more than once on the card. Make sure children have tabs with duplicate letters. The game can continue until a child fills a card.

SAMPLE CARD

b	FREE	h	n	p
l	w	FREE	s	r
m	d	z	f	FREE
t	r	g	FREE	f
v	g	s	p	n

4. *Categories and Initial Sounds.* This game correlates children's ability to classify with their ability to match similar sounds. The teacher can initiate the game, and then the children can be the leaders. The teacher says, "I am thinking of a color that begins like the word *part.*" (*pink, purple*) The child who gives the color becomes the leader. Examples:

I am thinking of a wild animal that begins like wall. (wolf)

I am thinking of a boy's name that begins like dark. (Don)

I am thinking of a pet that begins like cake. (cat)

Visual Discrimination Activities

1. Children have a card with nine different letters on it. The teacher holds up a letter. If the children have that letter on their card, they raise their hand, and the teacher gives them a square with that letter on it to place over the same letter on the card.

2. This is played in the same way as No. 1, but words rather than letters are used.

Concentration and Following Directions Activities

1. Tell your children that they are going to build a story together. Everyone must listen very carefully to what everyone else has said. No one can interrupt anyone else, and each person will have a turn to add something to the story. Before you begin, make sure everyone knows when it's his or her turn. Having the children sit in a circle facing one another is helpful.

2. Tell children that they will have to listen very carefully in order to be able to follow the directions. Tell them that they have to do everything in order and correctly. Examples:

> Stand up; jump up and down three times; clap your hands four times.
>
> Stand up; hop three times on your right foot; hop six times on your left foot.
>
> Go to the front chalkboard, and put the number 5 on the chalkboard; clap your hands four times.

The teacher can either increase or decrease the number of directions according to the ability levels of the students.

3. Tell children to listen carefully because you are going to tell them to do some things. In order to do them correctly, they will have to listen carefully. For some they will have to do nothing. Examples:

> If the sun is cold, jump up and down three times.
>
> If the rain is wet, touch the toes of your left foot with your left hand.
>
> If you have a name that begins like Melissa, hop on your right foot three times.
>
> If a rooster lays eggs, say the nursery rhyme "Mary Had a Little Lamb."
>
> If ice melts in the sun, count to ten.

Listening Comprehension Activities

1. The teacher reads a description of a familiar television character, and the students determine who the character is and the name of the television show.

2. The teacher reads a list of words such as *cookies, milk, eggs,* and *apples,* and the children state what they all have in common; that is, the children state the category (food). (The categories can be more specific or more general, based on the ability levels of the students.)

3. The teacher tells the children to listen carefully because he or she is going to tell them a short story. One of the sentences in the story is out of order. They have to listen carefully to find the sentence that is out of order. Example:

> Jennifer decided to have a party.
>
> She sent out invitations for her party.
>
> The party was fun. (out of order)
>
> Lots of children came to the party.

4. The teacher reads a short paragraph in which a sentence that has nothing to do with the paragraph is inserted. The children are asked if they noticed anything funny about the paragraph that was just read. If so, what was it?

5. The children are told to listen carefully because they are going to recite a nursery rhyme, but the nursery rhyme will have a word or words from other nursery rhymes. The children have to state what word or words do not belong and then correctly recite the nursery rhyme. Example:

Hickory, dickory, dock,
Jack and Jill ran up the clock,
   The clock struck one,
   Jack and Jill ran down,
Hickory, dickory, dock.
(Jack and Jill should be *the mouse.*)

6. The teacher reads a story such as "What I Hear in My School" by June Behrens. The children are told to listen carefully because they will have to retell the story and tell all the things that are heard in school.

7. The children are told to listen carefully. The teacher will say something, and then the children will have to tell who is talking. Examples:

What would you like to order? (waiter or waitress)

Move to the back. (bus driver)

Open your mouth wide. (dentist)

This needle won't hurt. (doctor)

Dinner is ready. (mother or father)

Open your books to page 30. (teacher)

The children can make up their own statements and challenge the other children to tell who is talking.

8. The teacher reads a short story. Before getting to the end of the story, he or she asks the children to tell what they think happens or how the story ends.

9. The teacher reads a short story to the children. Then the teacher asks the children to make up another adventure for one of the characters in the story.

Teacher-Made Classroom (Informal) Assessments

Classroom assessment
Teacher-made tools or instruments to assess students' strengths and weaknesses; also called informal assessment.

Observation
A technique that helps teachers collect data about students' behavior.

When children first come to school, teachers must assess the skills the children possess and develop a program based on each child's needs. Teachers usually use published as well as teacher-made instruments and observations to make their assessments. Probably the most beneficial assessments come from observation and teacher-made techniques or instruments (see Chapter 13). Let's look at the kind of observations Jennifer and Tom's kindergarten teacher, Mrs. Hamilton, can make when they first enter school:

Jennifer

Continually raises hand to answer questions.

Speaks in sentences.

Speaks clearly and seems to have a very rich vocabulary.

Brings book to school with her and tells teacher she can read it.

Reads words under pictures.

Is able to retell a short story in her own words.

Asks teacher when she can read more books.

Tells teacher that she can write lots of words.

Writes her name and a sentence for the teacher.

Tom

Has difficulty sitting still.

Doesn't recognize letters.

Doesn't speak clearly.

Answers questions with one- or two-word answers.

Doesn't remember what happened in a short story that was just read aloud.

Doesn't raise hand to answer questions.

From observing Jennifer and Tom, the teacher has learned a great deal about them. The essential factor is to utilize what she has learned.

Fortunately for both Jennifer and Tom, Mrs. Hamilton is a very astute person who believes in recognizing the individual differences of her children. After observing both children, she met with their parents to learn more about their backgrounds.

She learned that Jennifer has always been precocious for her age. At two and one-half she was able to pick out the letters of the alphabet; at three and one-half she was able to read and write her name, as well as a number of words; at four she was able to read a number of story books. She could tell what had happened in the story, relate details, and summarize the whole story. She could make up her own endings for stories, and she could even make up her own stories. Jennifer is a gifted child. She delights in the world around her because every day is a day of wonder and discovery. Jennifer is curious and excited about learning.

Mrs. Hamilton learned that Tom has always been slower in development than other children of comparable age. Tom was slow in lifting his head, he was slow in sitting, he was slow in walking, and he was slow in talking. Tom at five still does not speak too well. Tom has difficulty sitting still for long periods of time. He likes to run and play. He appears to be a happy child, and he has many friends, with whom he enjoys playing.

Tom and Jennifer are at different levels on the literacy continuum; therefore, the kinds of programs they need are significantly different. Jennifer's program should be one that takes account of her advanced maturation, rich past experiences, and desire to learn. It is one that should initiate her into more advanced reading skills while making sure that she acquires needed decoding skills. Tom, on the other hand, needs to be involved in an extensive early literacy program that emphasizes print material.

Commentary

All the children in Tom and Jennifer's class are very fortunate to have Mrs. Hamilton as their teacher because she is aware of the studies in the reading field and this awareness helps her make good judgments. She knows there is voluminous evidence available to support the relationship between young children's letter naming and their later reading achievement and general school achievement.[24] From observation, she soon learned which children knew their alphabet letters and numbers, and she used this information to develop a program based on each student's present literacy level.

Young Children's Retelling: An Assessment Technique

Read a story aloud to a child. What happens? Usually, the child makes many comments, asks questions, and then at the end of the story wants to "read" it himself or herself. Astute teachers can learn a great deal about their children's literacy development by listening carefully to the kinds of questions and comments the children make, as well as to how well they can retell a story after they have heard it once or a few times.

In working with kindergarten or younger children, it's a good idea to use a story that can be told in one sitting, that is at their interest and concentration levels, that does not have too many characters, that does not have subplots, and that has some kind of sequence or repetitive refrain.

The teacher can have children first retell the story using the pictures and then advance to retelling the story without any aids. In evaluating a young child's ability to do the retelling, the teacher could use the following checklist:

Checklist for Retelling a Story

	Yes	Somewhat	No
1. The child remembers the names of the characters in the story.			
2. The child follows the sequence of the story.			
3. The child presents the plot correctly.			
4. The child can give details about the characters.			

The more advanced the children are in their language and literacy development, the more detail they will usually include in the retelling of the story.

---

[24] Adams, *Beginning to Read,* p. 10; Daniel J. Walsh, Gary Glen Price, and Mark G. Gillingham, "The Critical but Transitory Importance of Letter Naming," *Reading Research Quarterly* 23 (Winter 1988): 110.

Early Literacy Diagnostic Assessment Related to Beginning Reading

This section presents informal diagnostic assessments related to beginning reading that teachers can use to assess their students' early literacy development. Again, as stated previously in this chapter, it would be a misuse of these tests if teachers were to use them to delay instruction for children who do not do well on the tests. Remember, our purpose is diagnosis to determine a student's needs. If a child does poorly on the auditory and visual discrimination parts of the assessment, that child needs *more* rather than less exposure to print and related activities. Delaying a child's entrance into a formal reading program will ensure failure for that child rather than success.

Diagnostic Early Literacy Assessment

Student's Name: _____

Grade: _____

Teacher: _____

Part 1

Listening (organic)	Observation Dates

Symptoms
 1. The child is absent due to ear infection.
 2. The child speaks very softly.
 3. The child speaks very loudly.
 4. The child speaks in a monotone.
 5. The child complains of noises in head.
 6. The child turns head to one side to hear.
 7. The child reads lips while listening.
 8. The child asks to have things repeated.
 9. The child cups hand behind ear to listen.

Part 2

Auditory Discrimination (samples)	Yes	No

 1. The child can state whether the following sets of words are similar or different:

   Tim   Tom
   bit   bet

Part 2 (continued)

Auditory Discrimination (samples)	Yes	No

none none		
fan van		
saw saw		
down pawn		

2. The child can state which words from the following
   sets of words begin with the same sound:

boy book can		
dog bag down		
sand some came		
pet bat pat		
mine name mat		

3. The child can state which word from the following
   sets of words begins with a different sound:

fan fall pat		
big pat ball		
car can sat		
put bat bet		
girl get cat		

4. The child can state which words from the following
   sets of words end with the same sound.

ball sell fat		
cook sand lake		
man rag sun		
tag car dog		
set tap lip		

5. The child can state which word from the following
   sets of words ends with a different sound:

same band mend		
set bad hat		
pass sink bank		
gang trick block		
make miss less		

6. The child will look at a group of pictures and state
   the name of the object that begins like
   baby.
   sun.
   damp.

Diagnostic Early Literacy Assessment   *Continued*

Part 2 (continued)

Auditory Discrimination (samples)	Yes	No

time.
fun.

	Yes	No

7. The child can state another word that begins like
   four.
   Tom.
   pan.
   some.
   down.

	Yes	No

8. The child can state the two words that rhyme from
the following sets of words:

man	mop	tan
pet	wet	bat
look	make	book
way	wall	ball

	Yes	No

9. The child can state the one word that does not rhyme
from the following sets of words:

fat	hen	cat
cook	harm	farm
pail	mail	milk
get	girl	set

	Yes	No

10. The child can state another word that rhymes with
   look.
   fat.
   tan.
   bake.

	Yes	No

Part 3

Memory Span	Yes	No

1. The child has difficulty in repeating sets of digits in
proper order:
a. forward
b. backward

	Yes	No

2. The child has difficulty in following given sets of
directions.

	Yes	No

Part 4

Visual Discrimination	Yes	No

The child is able to do the following visual
discrimination activities:

1. Following are a number of letters. Choose the letter
   that is different from the first one in the line:
   Example: B   B   <u>P</u>   B   B
   a. L   V   L   L   L   L
   b. c   c   c   c   s   c
   c. d   d   d   d   d   b
   d. e   e   e   o   e   e

2. Following are a number of letters. Choose the letter
   that is the same as the first one in the line.
   Example: M   N   S   L   <u>M</u>   B
   a. R   B   P   Q   R   D
   b. Q   O   B   D   C   Q
   c. O   C   Q   R   O   Q
   d. P   B   O   R   P   B

3. Following are a number of words. Draw a circle
   around the word that is the same as the first word:
   Example: tall tell late let (tall) tale
   a. saw was son wet sat saw
   b. big bag gag age big bat
   c. last lass sale last less sell
   d. otter other rather other rotten otter

4. Following are numbers. Draw a circle around the
   number that is different from the first number:
   Example: 4   4   4 (6) 4   4
   a. 9   9   9   9   6   9
   b. 7   7   7   7   4   7
   c. 3   3   3   3   7   3
   d. 6   6   6   9   6   6

5. Following are groups of letters. Draw a circle
   around the letter group that is the same as the first in the line:
   Example: AMN   OAM   MNA (AMN) NMO
   a. STX   OAS   STO   STX   OXS
   b. ROL   LOR   NOR   MOR   ROL
   c. BEM   MEB   EMB   BEM   LEB
   d. SAQ   SAQ   OBC   LAQ   REQ

Diagnostic Early Literacy Assessment *Continued*

Part 5

Speech and Language Development	Yes	No

Speech (general): The child's speech is
 1. distinct.
 2. inaudible.
 3. monotonous.
 4. expressive.

Nonverbal communication: The child
 1. uses facial expressions effectively.
 2. uses hands effectively.
 3. uses body movements effectively.

Vocabulary (general): The child's vocabulary is
 1. meager.
 2. rich.
 3. accurate.
 4. incorrect.

Sentences
 1. The child uses incomplete sentences.
 2. The child uses simplistic sentences.
 3. The child uses involved sentences.
 4. The child uses standard English.
 5. The child uses a variation of English.
 6. English is not the dominant language for the child.

The child engages in conversation freely.
The child respects other persons when he or she
  is speaking.

The child enters into class discussions.

The child can describe in his or her own words
  an event that has occurred.

Part 6

Left–Right Orientation	Yes	No

 1. The child can differentiate between his or her left and
    right hands.
 2. The child moves his or her eyes from left to right when looking
    at a picture book.

Part 7

Comprehension	Yes	No
1. The child is able to listen to a short story and retell it in his or her own words.		
2. The child is able to listen to a story and pick out anything in the story that does not make sense.		
3. The child is able to listen to a story and answer some literal questions on the story.		
4. The child can look at a sequence of pictures and choose the one that is out of order.		
5. The child can look at a picture and answer some inference questions about the picture.		
6. The child uses words correctly.		

Graphic Summary of Chapter

Here is a graphic summary of Chapter 5. If you have read the chapter, this graphic illustration should help you remember its main points. Under or beside each heading, you might want to jot down some of the information you recall, as well as some of the key concepts in this chapter. This can act as a good review. You can then check your key concepts against those that follow the graphic summary.

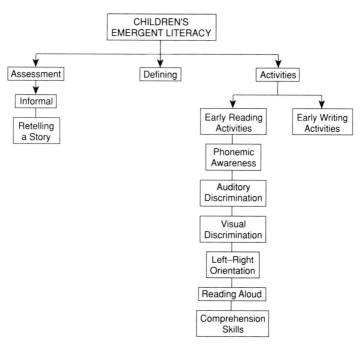

Key Concepts

- One of the most fruitful ways to gain insights into how children learn to read is to focus on what children do before formal reading begins.
- Young children who are exposed to extensive print materials begin to learn the communicative function of print.
- Emergent literacy is the stage of literacy that is concerned with the young child's involvement in language and his or her attempts at reading and writing before coming to school or before conventional or formal reading and writing begin.
- Children who are read to will feel more free about "trying out" reading.
- Readiness is an ongoing, dynamic process, which teachers use to prepare students for various activities throughout the school day.
- Readiness is an interaction of maturation, past experiences, and a desire to learn.
- Phonemic awareness is the ability to recognize that a spoken word is made up of a sequence of individual sounds.
- Children's phonemic awareness is a prerequisite for efficient decoding.
- Training in phonemic awareness combined with sound–letter correspondences seems to have a beneficial effect on young children's beginning reading and spelling.
- Auditory discrimination is the ability to distinguish between sounds.
- Auditory memory span is necessary in order to determine whether two or more sounds are similar or different.
- Visual discrimination is the ability to differentiate between written symbols.
- In order to read English, children must learn to read from left to right.
- If children have difficulty in cognitive development, they will have difficulty in reading.
- The early literacy level is not too soon to help children develop higher level thinking.
- When children first come to school, teachers must assess the skills they have and develop a program based on their needs.

Suggestions for Thought Questions and Activities

1. You have been selected to serve on a committee that is reviewing the kindergarten early reading program in your school system. What are some of the factors that you would want to look at? Discuss each factor, and explain why you feel it would be important to look at each.
2. You have been selected to present a talk on your philosophy of early reading programs. What will you say?

3. The administrator in your school building has asked you to serve on a committee to determine ways of assessing children's early literacy. You do not feel that formal reading readiness or early reading tests should be used. Explain your position and defend it.
4. Develop some activities related to beginning reading.
5. You have been asked to explain emergent literacy. What will you say?
6. Discuss phonemic awareness and its place in the early reading program. Develop some activities that can be used to develop children's phonemic awareness.

Selected Bibliography

Adams, Marilyn Jager. *Beginning to Read: Thinking and Learning about Print—A Summary,* Steven A. Stahl, Jean Osborn, and Fran Lehr, eds. Urbana, Ill.: Center for the Study of Reading, 1990.

Ball, Eileen W., and Benita A. Blachman. "Does Phoneme Segmentation Training in Kindergarten Make a Difference in Early Word Recognition and Developmental Spelling?" *Reading Research Quarterly* 26 (1) (1991): 49–66.

McGee, Lea M., and Donald J. Richgels. *Literacy's Beginnings: Supporting Young Readers and Writers.* Boston: Allyn and Bacon, 1990.

Morrow, Lesley Mandel, and Jeffrey K. Smith. *Assessment for Instruction in Early Literacy.* Boston: Allyn and Bacon, 1990.

Sulzby, Elizabeth, and William Teale. "Emergent Literacy." In *Handbook of Reading Research,* Vol. II, Rebecca Barr, Michael L. Kamil, Peter Mosenthal, and P. David Pearson, eds. New York: Longman, 1991.

6

Word Recognition

SCENARIO: UNLOCKING THE MYSTERY

Professor Johnson has been teaching reading for a number of years at a state college. He believes strongly that he must be a good role model for his students, so he teaches his students in the way he would like for them to teach their students.

Whenever he has to introduce a new topic to his students, he racks his brain to come up with a motivating technique that will arouse their interest and direct their attention to the topic at hand. Word recognition is the topic he is about to introduce to his students.

Word recognition is an area that seems to cause a great amount of heat among reading people; regardless of one's position in the controversy, however, it is an especially important area, and students must have the skills at their fingertips. Professor Johnson has conveyed to his students that reading is a thinking act; without comprehension there is no reading. In other words, even though a child can read all the words on a page, if he or she doesn't understand what is being read, there is no reading. In order to gain comprehension, however, students must first unlock the written code. Dr. Johnson does not feel that children gain knowledge of the written code through osmosis.

After a great deal of thought, Dr. Johnson decides to initiate his students into the topic by directly involving them in a number of activities that will give them some insight into what young children go through when they are learning to read.

Professor Johnson begins by placing the following sentence on the board and asking his students to read it.

Hye fom Bre tuw bup raf.

Needless to say, his students are perplexed. The words he has written are pseudowords—that is, nonsense words. Dr. Johnson tells his students that, in fact, this is what the English written code looks like to many children. Actually, it's amazing that so many children learn to break the code as well as they do in a relatively short period of time.

Next Dr. Johnson places a sentence on the board that is composed of regular English words except for one nonsense word:

My slan is late again, today.

He asks his students to read this sentence to themselves silently and then to try to analyze what they did when they met the unfamiliar word *slan*.

By this time Professor Johnson has achieved his objective of capturing his students' attention. He tells them that he would like to help them understand what word recognition entails and learn about the various word recognition strategies that individuals use to decode words. And that is exactly what he does, as will be discussed throughout this chapter.

This chapter concentrates on helping you gain a better understanding of word recognition strategies and presents a developmental sequence of phonic skills.

KEY QUESTIONS

After you finish reading this chapter, you should be able to answer the following questions:

1. What is the place of word recognition in the reading program?
2. How do individuals attain word recognition?
3. What strategies help students pronounce words?
4. What strategies help students figure out word meanings?
5. What is the place of phonics in the word recognition program?
6. What is explicit (synthetic) phonics instruction?
7. What is implicit (analytic) phonics instruction?
8. What skills are included in a developmental sequence of phonics instruction?
9. What are consonant and vowel digraphs?
10. What are diphthongs and consonant blends (clusters)?
11. What are phonograms?
12. What are some phonic generalizations?
13. What is the relationship of syllabication to phonics?
14. What are some syllabication generalizations?
15. What should students know about accenting?
16. What is the relationship between linguistics and phonics?

KEY TERMS IN CHAPTER

You should pay special attention to the following key terms:

consonant
consonant blends (clusters)

consonant clusters (blends)
consonant digraph

context
diacritical marks
diphthongs
explicit (synthetic) phonics instruction
implicit (analytic) phonics instruction
linguistics
phonemics
phonetics
phonic analysis
phonics
phonic synthesis

phonogram (graphemic base)
phonology
schwa
silent consonants
structural analysis
structural synthesis
syllable
vowel
vowel digraph
whole word or "look and say"
word recognition

The Transition from Emergent Literacy to Beginning Reading

Beginning reading is that stage in the literacy continuum that follows emergent literacy; it is the child's involvement in a formal reading program. This involvement, as stated in Chapter 5, can begin in either kindergarten or first grade. For most children it begins in grade 1.

The question is: How do children go from context-related words (words on cereal boxes, for example) and environmental words (STOP, for example) to reading the same words in running text? A number of theories and stage models of reading have been put forth to explain how children learn to read. Although the stage models may use different terminology and disagree on when and how long a stage lasts, "they all assign great importance to the child learning to decode words."[1] In addition, investigators claim that "they paint a remarkably similar picture of beginning reading. After the child discovers that print itself carries meaning, the process of identifying or remembering specific printed words appears to involve at least two qualitatively different stages."[2]

In the first stage, called the *selective-cue stage,* the child identifies words in a random fashion by using either environmental or other special features clues. In other words, the child recognizes a word because of its placement on a page or its particular appearance. The child uses very little in the way of graphic clues.[3]

The second stage, referred to as the *spelling-sound stage,* is the one in which the child uses graphic clues to the maximum extent.[4] This chapter is concerned primarily with this second stage in the child's literacy development.

---

[1] Connie Juel, "Beginning Reading," in *Handbook of Reading Research,* Vol. II, Rebecca Barr, Michael L. Kamil, Peter Mosenthal, and P. David Pearson, eds. (New York: Longman, 1991), p. 766.

[2] Ibid., p. 767.

[3] Ibid.

[4] Ibid.

Defining Word Recognition

Word recognition
A twofold process that includes both the identification of printed symbols by some method so that the word can be pronounced and the association of meaning with the word after it has been properly pronounced.

Few people would refute the statement that word recognition is the foundation of the reading process. Although it is possible to have adequate word recognition but still have a problem in reading comprehension, it is not possible to have good reading comprehension if one has word recognition problems.

In this book word recognition is looked upon as a twofold process that includes both the identification of printed symbols by some method so that the word can be pronounced and the attachment or association of meaning with the printed symbols.

Word recognition is essential to reading, but "the ultimate purpose of reading is comprehension."[5] The quicker and more skillful students become in word recognition, the better are their chances for becoming good readers.

Special Note

Some reading authorities differentiate between word identification and word recognition. For them, *word identification* refers to the figuring out of unknown words only, whereas *word recognition* refers to words an individual has met previously. In this book, however, *word recognition* refers to the figuring out of any written or printed word.

Word Recognition Strategies

Good teachers want to do what is best for their students. In order to do what is best for elementary grade children, teachers must be aware of the different word recognition strategies and the purpose for each. For example, teachers must recognize that helping pupils become proficient in phonics will not help them to be good readers unless they have also developed a stock of vocabulary and have adequate concept development.

Teachers not only should be aware of the different strategies for figuring out word pronunciations and meanings but also should recognize that some strategies work better than others with specific children. This advice, however, should not prevent teachers from trying to help children become proficient in using all the strategies or helping them to determine which strategy or strategies are best to use in a specific situation. Usually, a combination of strategies is used in word recognition.

[5] Keith E. Stanovich, "Word Recognition: Changing Perspectives," in *Handbook of Reading Research*, Vol. II, Rebecca Barr, Michael L. Kamil, Peter Mosenthal, and P. David Pearson, eds. (New York: Longman, 1991), p. 418.

Word Recognition Strategies for Pronunciation

When we read, we are intent on getting the message and appear to do so automatically and in one step. We don't notice the individual letters, groups of letters, or even every word. If we are good readers, this is what should be taking place. It isn't until we stumble on an unfamiliar word that we become aware of the individual letters that are grouped together to form a word. The reason we stop reading is because the word we have stumbled on has interfered with our getting the message. The question is: Do you remember what you did when a word interfered with your understanding of what you were reading? To understand better the concept that word recognition is a twofold process, that there are a number of strategies that can be used to figure out how to pronounce a word as well as strategies that can be used to determine the meaning of a word, and that these strategies are not necessarily the same, we will be involved in a number of exercises involving nonsense and actual words.

Read the following sentence:

My slan is late again, today.

You should have stumbled on the nonsense word *slan*. Imagine that you do not know that *slan* is a nonsense word. Let's look at the kinds of strategies we could and could *not* use to help us to gain the pronunciation of a word *independently.*

Strategy 1: Phonic analysis and synthesis.

Definition: Phonics is a decoding technique that depends on students' being able to make the proper grapheme (letter)–phoneme (sound) correspondences (Figure 6-1). *Analysis* has to do with the breaking down of something into its component parts. *Synthesis* has to do with the building up of the parts of something usually into a whole. (In this chapter, a sequential development of phonic skills will be presented.)

© Copyright 1975, United Feature Syndicate, Inc.

Reprinted by permission of UFS, Inc.

FIGURE 6-1   Charlie Brown may have difficulty decoding the unfamiliar Russian names, but the pronunciation of these names is not crucial to his understanding the story.

Phonic analysis
The breaking down
of a word into its
component parts.

Phonic synthesis
The building up of
the component
parts of a word into
a whole.

**Whole word or
"look and say"**
A word recognition
technique in which
a child's attention is
directed to a word
and then the word
is said.

Analysis: Break down *slan* into the blend *sl* and the phonogram *an*. We have met the blend *sl* before in such words as *slip* and *slap*. We have met the phonogram *an* before in such words as *can* and *man*. We, therefore, know the pronunciations of *sl* and *an*.

Synthesis: Blend together the *sl* and the *an*.

Using this technique, we should be able to pronounce *slan*.

Strategy 2: Whole word or "look and say" method.

Definition: The whole word or sight method has to do with having the teacher or any other individual direct a student's attention to a word and then saying the word. The student must make an association between the oral word and the written word, and he or she shows this by actually saying the word.

The whole word method is often referred to as the "look and say" method because this strategy is dependent on the teacher's getting the attention of the child and directing him or her to the word. When the child is looking at the word, the teacher says the word and then asks the child to say the word. For this method to be effective, the child *must look at the word while pronouncing it* so that the association is made between the spoken and written word. The whole word strategy is usually used when children are beginning to learn to read and later on with those words that do not readily lend themselves to decoding (see the section "Learning Phonics"). This technique is a useful word recognition strategy that helps us to learn to pronounce words, but it will not help us to figure out the pronunciation of unfamiliar words independently.

Strategy 3: Ask someone to pronounce the word for you.

This could be done, but it would be similar to the whole word method, and it would not help us to figure out the word independently.

Strategy 4: Context clues

Definition: By *context* we mean the words surrounding a word that can shed light on its meaning. Context clues are clues that are given in the form of definitions, examples, comparisons or contrasts, explanations, and so on, which help us figure out word meanings. (For more on context, see Chapter 8.)

This is a word recognition technique, but it is not one that helps us to figure out the pronunciation of words. It is one that is used for helping us to gain the meaning of a word.

Strategy 5: Structural analysis and synthesis (word parts).

Structural analysis
A technique for breaking a word into its pronunciation units; the breaking down of a word into word parts such as prefixes, suffixes, roots, and combining forms.

Structural synthesis
A technique for building up of word parts into a whole.

Definition: Structural analysis and synthesis have to do with the breaking down (analysis) of words into word parts and the building up (synthesis) of word parts into words. Word parts are prefixes, suffixes, roots (bases), and combining forms (see Chapter 8, "Vocabulary Expansion").

Structural analysis is most often used in conjunction with phonic analysis. Knowledge of word parts such as prefixes, suffixes, and roots helps us to isolate the root of a word. After the root of a word is isolated, phonic analysis is applied. If the word parts are familiar ones, then we can blend them together to come up with the pronunciation of the word. Structural analysis is a helpful word recognition technique that can aid with the pronunciation of words, but it will not help us to figure out the pronunciation of *slan* unless we apply phonic analysis to *slan* because *slan* as a nonsense word is an unfamiliar root (base) word.

Structural analysis is helpful in figuring out the pronunciation of an unfamiliar word if the word is composed of familiar word parts such as prefixes, suffixes, and roots. The technique we would use is similar to that used with phonic analysis and synthesis. For example, let's see how we would go about figuring out how to pronounce the italicized word in the following sentence using structural analysis and synthesis.

That is not *replaceable.*

Structural analysis: Break down the word into its parts to isolate the root.

re   place   able

If we had met *re* before and if we had met *able* before, we should know how to pronounce them. After we have isolated *place,* we may recognize it as a familiar word and know how to pronounce it.

Structural synthesis: Blend together *re, place,* and *able.*

If *place* is not a familiar root word for us, then we could apply phonic analysis to it and after that blend it together with the prefix *re* and the suffix *able.*

Strategy 6: Look up the pronunciation in the dictionary.

This is a viable method, but you may not have a dictionary handy, and by the time you look up the pronunciation of the word, you may have lost the trend of what you were reading.

Let's list those techniques that can help us to figure out the pronunciation of words:

1. Phonic analysis and synthesis
2. Whole word or "look and say"

3. Asking someone
4. Structural analysis and synthesis
5. Looking up the pronunciation in the dictionary

Notice that of all the techniques, phonic analysis and synthesis do give you a great amount of power in figuring out the pronunciation of words *independently.*

Word Recognition Strategies for Word Meaning

Being able to pronounce a word is important, but it does not guarantee that we will know the meaning of the word. As stated previously, word recognition is a twofold process; the first part involves correct pronunciation, and the second part involves meaning. After we have pronounced the word, we have to associate the word with one in our listening vocabulary in order to determine the meaning of the word; that is, we have to have heard the word before and know what the word means. Obviously, the larger our stock of listening vocabulary, the better able we will be to decipher the word. As *slan* is a nonsense word, we would not have heard the word before, and we cannot associate any meaning with it. Even though we can pronounce a word such as *misanthropic,* it doesn't mean that we can associate any meaning with it. If we have never heard the word before, it would not be in our listening vocabulary; therefore, the pronunciation would not act as a stimulus and trigger an association with a word that we have stored in our memory bank. Let's see the techniques that we can use to help us unlock words that we have never heard of or met before.

Strategy 1: Context

Context
The words surrounding a particular word that can shed light on its meaning.

By context we mean the words surrounding a particular word that can help shed light on its meaning. (Context clues are especially important in determining the meanings of words, and because of its importance, special emphasis is given to this area in Chapter 8 on "Vocabulary Expansion.") Read the following sentence:

Even though my *trank* was rather long, I wouldn't take out one word.

From the context of the sentence you know that the nonsense word *trank* must somehow refer to a sentence, paragraph, paper, or report of some sort. Even though you had never met *trank* before, the context of the sentence did throw light on it. You know from the word order or position of the word (syntax) that *trank* must be a noun, and words such as *word* and *long* give you meaning (semantic) clues to the word itself. There are times, however, when context is not too helpful so that other strategies must be used.

Strategy 2: Structural analysis and synthesis for word meaning

Read the following sentence:

We asked the *misanthrope* to leave.

From the position of the word *misanthrope* in the sentence, we know that it is a noun; however, there is not enough information to help us figure out the meaning of *misanthrope*. Structural analysis would be very useful in situations where there are insufficient context clues, and the word consists of a number of word parts.

Analysis: Break down *misanthrope* into its word parts. *Mis* means either "wrong" or "hate," and *anthropo* means "mankind" or "humankind."

Synthesis: Put together the word parts. It doesn't make sense to say "wrong mankind," so it must be *hate* and *mankind*. As *misanthrope* is a noun, the meaning of *misanthrope* would have to be "hater of mankind."

Structural analysis is a powerful tool, but it is dependent on your having at your fingertips knowledge of word parts and their meanings. If you do not have these at hand, you obviously need another strategy. (More will be said about structural analysis in Chapter 8, which is about vocabulary expansion.)

Strategy 3: Ask someone the meaning of the word. This may be the most convenient if someone is available who knows the meaning of the word.

Strategy 4: Look up the meaning in the dictionary. If you cannot figure out the word independently rather quickly so that your train of thought is not completely broken, the dictionary is a valuable tool for word meanings.

Let's list those techniques that can help us figure out the meaning of words:

1. Context of a sentence
2. Structural analysis and synthesis
3. Asking someone
4. Looking up the meaning in the dictionary

There are times when it is possible for context clues to help with the correction of mispronounced words that are in the listening vocabulary of the reader but not yet in his or her reading vocabulary. Here is such an example. A child is asked to read the following sentence:

The thief stole the car.

The child reads the sentence as follows:

The *thife* stole the car.

The child then self-corrects himself and rereads the sentence correctly. What has taken place? The first pronunciation of *thief* was obtained from graphic clues. As the student continued to read, the context of the sentence indicated to the student that the mispronounced word should be *thief* rather than *thife*. Because *thief* was in the listening vocabulary of the child, he was able to self-correct his mispronunciation. In this case, the context clues helped the reader to correct his mispronunciation of *thief*.

It is important to state that the child would not have been able to self-correct his mispronunciation if the word *thief* had not been in his listening vocabulary and if he had not heard it correctly pronounced.

Teachers should stress to their students that phonics usually only gives an approximation of the way a word is pronounced. Often readers must rely on sentence meaning and their familiarity with the spoken word to be able to pronounce it correctly.

Special Notes

1. Many foreign students who are learning English as another language or students who speak nonstandard English may pronounce a number of words incorrectly because they have heard them pronounced that way, but they may know the meaning of the word. The teacher must be careful to determine the cause of the child's mispronunciation: Is the mispronunciation due to a pronunciation problem or a comprehension problem?
2. Configuration has not been presented as a viable word recognition strategy because of its limited value. Configuration, which has to do with the shape or outline or a word (can father night), cannot be used to figure out unfamiliar words. Configuration is supposed to help the children remember the word because of its shape. It may be useful in a few limited cases where the shape of the word is unique. Time, however, would better be spent on students learning more useful cues, such as semantic, syntactic, and graphic ones.

The Importance of Decoding in Reading

As we have seen, students who have difficulty in listening will have problems in oral language as well as in reading. Because reading involves the process of interpreting printed symbols that are based on arbitrary speech sounds, it depends on a foundation of previously learned speech symbols. Usually, beginning readers have a substantial oral vocabulary before they begin to read, when they learn that each word they speak or listen to has a printed symbol. Students who become effective readers must be able to automatically decode written symbols that represent speech sounds. Inability to do this will prevent readers from bringing to or getting any message from the printed page.

Defining Phonics

Phonics
The study of the relationships between letter symbols of a written language and the sounds they represent.

Phonics, the study of relationships between the letter symbols (graphemes) of a written language and the sounds (phonemes) they represent, is a pedagogical term that describes one method used in teaching word recognition in reading. Phonics is used in the classroom as an aid to decoding words. It helps students gain independence and reliance in reading, but it is only one aspect of the reading process.

Learning Phonics

Phonics instruction is important in the early grades, but it must be taught in conjunction with meaning and the emphasis should not be on the stating of generalizations but on children's being able to internalize them so that they can become proficient readers as quickly as possible. According to an extensive analysis of program comparison research projects on beginning reading instruction, "the approaches that, one way or another, included systematic phonics instruction consistently exceeded the straight basal programs in word recognition achievement scores. The approaches that included both systematic phonics and considerable emphasis on connected reading and meaning surpassed the basal alone approaches on virtually all outcome scores."[6] In addition, "there appeared to be no basis for the widely held belief that systematic phonics instruction is only useful for brighter students."[7] A recent longitudinal study in which first-graders received training sessions in word analysis suggests that "students of lower ability profited the most from the phonological training"[8] (see "Phonemic Awareness and Early Reading" in Chapter 5).

Teachers, however, must be aware that some children may have difficulty learning to make the proper grapheme–phoneme correspondences, and that these children will benefit from another method. In other words, teachers must take the individual differences of their children into account. Teachers are again cautioned that phonics is but one part of word recognition, which itself is but one part of the reading process.

In teaching phonics, the material should be interesting and related as closely as possible to the phonics skills the children are learning. This is not as simple as it sounds because the books that have attempted to teach phonics have often been stilted and uninteresting.

One of the best ways for teachers to understand how children learn phonic

---

[6] Marilyn Jager Adams, *Beginning to Read: Thinking and Learning about Print — A Summary,* Steven A. Stahl, Jean Osborn, and Fran Lehr, eds. (Urbana, Ill.: Center for the Study of Reading, 1990), p. 9.

[7] Ibid., pp. 9–10.

[8] Alfred Lie, "Effects of a Training Program for Stimulating Skills in Word Analysis in First-Grade Children," *Reading Research Quarterly* 26 (1991): 234.

word attack skills is to experience the phenomenon themselves. To simulate this experience, teachers must know the steps involved. First the child usually learns a few sight words. Then, when the child learns that some words look and/or sound alike, the mastering of phonic word attack skills has begun.

Learning to decode words is not a simple task. In the scenario at the beginning of this chapter, Professor Johnson uses nonsense words to heighten his students' consciousness of the difficulty. He also presents his students with various nonsense words made up of unfamiliar symbols, which he pairs with pictures (see Figure 6-2). He then follows through with a number of exercises so that his students learn the importance of auditory and visual discrimination in decoding words.

Explicit versus Implicit Phonics Instruction

Before presenting a developmental sequence of phonics instruction, it is important to explain the differences between explicit and implicit phonics instruction.

Explicit phonics instruction Each sound associated with a letter in the word is pronounced in isolation, and then the sounds are blended together; also known as **synthetic phonics.**

In explicit phonics, each sound associated with a letter in the word is pronounced in isolation and then the sounds are blended together. A problem with this method is that it is very difficult to produce pure speech sounds in isolation. As a result, what usually takes place in the classroom is the following. The teacher shows the children the word *cat,* points to the letter *c,* and says that it stands for the sound *cuh.* The teacher then points to the letter *a* in the word *cat* and says it stands for the sound *ah* and then points to the letter *t* and says it stands for the sound *tuh.* The children are then told to blend *cuh ah tuh* together to get *cat.* Even though *cuh ah tuh* does not sound like *cat,* children are supposedly able to recognize the word *cat* from this method. (See "Phonemic Awareness and Early Reading" in Chapter 5.)

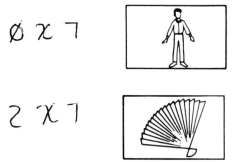

FIGURE 6-2   The pairing of nonsense words composed of unfamiliar symbols with pictorial representations.

Implicit phonics instruction
Does not present sounds associated with letters in isolation. Children listen to words that begin with a particular sound; then they state another word that begins with the same sound; also known as **analytic phonics.**

Implicit phonics instruction, on the other hand, does not present sounds associated with letters in isolation. The children are presented with a list of words that all begin with the same initial consonant, such as the following:

girl   game   get

The children are helped to recognize that all the words begin with the same letter *g*. Then they are told to listen carefully to the beginning sound of each word. The teacher pronounces each word and tells the children that the letter *g* stands for the sound at the beginning of the words *girl, game, get.* The children are then often asked to look around the room for other words that begin like *game* or with the letter *g*. (Usually, the teacher has pictures of items around the room that begin with the letter *g*.)

It appears that many teachers use a combination of both explicit and implicit phonics. The important thing to remember is that any method that helps children unlock words as quickly as possible should be used and that phonics gives children the power and independence they need to pronounce unfamiliar words. The key, of course, is for children to overlearn words after they have sounded them out a number of times so that the words will become part of their sight vocabulary.

Special Note

Some writers use the terms *synthetic phonics* to refer to explicit phonics instruction and *analytic phonics* to refer to implicit phonics instruction.

A Developmental Sequence of Phonics Instruction

Although the teaching of phonics will vary according to the needs of the students, in a developmental sequence certain skills are usually taught before others.[9] Also, as stated earlier in this chapter, it is best for phonic skills to be taught in relation to what the children are reading; therefore, teachers should try to choose stories that emphasize the specific skills they are teaching. The teaching of the skills in relation to connected text gives students reinforcement because they can immediately apply what they have learned. It gives students the power to be more independent readers.

Regardless of what approach teachers use in teaching reading, they should be proficient in phonics so that they can properly diagnose the needs of their students in this area. The following outline of the developmental sequence of phonics instruction should help teachers to achieve this goal. Each area listed will be defined, and examples for each skill will be presented.

---

[9] For ease of reading, I have omitted the slashes that are often used to enclose phonemic symbols.

1. Auditory discrimination
2. Visual discrimination
3. Consonants:[10]

   a. Initial consonants
   b. Final consonants
   c. Consonant clusters (blends) (*bl, st, str*)
   d. Initial consonant blends (clusters); final consonant blends (clusters)
   e. Initial consonant digraphs (*th, ch, sh*)
   f. Final consonant digraphs (*ng, gh*)
   g. Silent consonants (*kn, pn, wr*)

4. Vowel sounds:

   a. Long vowel sounds
   b. Short vowel sounds
   c. Effect of final *e* on vowel
   d. Double vowels:

      (1) Digraphs
      (2) Diphthongs

   e. Vowel controlled by *r*

5. Special letters and sounds
6. Phonograms
7. Syllabication:

   a. Meaning of syllable
   b. Generalizations:

      (1) Double consonant vc/cv
      (2) Vowel-consonant-vowel v/cv
      (3) Consonant with special *le* c/cle or v/cle

   c. Syllable phonics:

      (1) Open syllable
      (2) Closed syllable

   d. Accent

Auditory and Visual Discrimination

As has already been stated, unless children are able to hear sounds correctly, they will not be able to say them correctly, read them, or write them. Not only must children be able to differentiate between auditory sounds and visual symbols in

[10] Consonants are usually taught before vowel sounds.

order to be ready for reading, they must also learn that the sounds they hear have written symbols.

Since they must have good auditory and visual discrimination, these samples of exercises should help in determining such discrimination.

Visual Discrimination

Visual discrimination is the ability to detect similarities and differences in written symbols.

___

Sample Exercises

Directions: Circle the letter that is like the first letter.

b	s	g	p	b	d
g	d	b	c	q	g
d	b	c	d	p	o
M	N	M	W	K	F
W	M	N	H	W	U

Directions: Circle the word that is like the first word.

can	cap	car	man	can	tan
beat	bear	meat	seat	beet	beat
camp	came	lamp	camp	damp	cent

Directions: Circle the group of numbers that is like the first group of numbers.

3916	6391	3961	3619	3916
5827	5278	5827	5872	5728
9638	9683	9386	9368	9638

Auditory Discrimination

Auditory discrimination is the ability to detect similarities and differences in sound symbols.

___

Sample Exercises

Directions: Listen carefully. Which pair of words is the same?

see	seem	car	car
cap	can	bell	ball
bite	pipe	grow	grow
bun	but	blew	blew

Sample Exercises   *Continued*

Directions: Listen carefully. Give me another word that rhymes with

tall _____   cat _____

pan _____   hay _____

sell _____   men _____

Directions: Listen carefully. Give me another word that begins like

bath _____

sit _____

hop _____

fan _____

Consonants

Consonant
One of a class of speech sounds; a letter representing a consonant; any letter of the English alphabet except *a, e, i, o,* and *u.*

Initial Consonants

Initial consonants are single consonants (one speech sound represented by one letter) at the beginning of a word. For example: *b* (*baby*), *c* (*can*), *m* (*map*), *p* (*pet*), *r* (*red*), *t* (*top*), *z* (*zoo*).

Presentation

The instructional technique used here is generally an implicit one. Teachers state a number of words beginning with the same initial consonant. They ask the children to listen to words such as *ball, book,* and *bee.* They should write the words on the board. Then they should ask how *ball, book,* and *bee* are similar. They all have the same beginning letter, *b.* They all start with the same sound. Teachers can then give a list of words that begin with *b* and ask students to state some others that start with *b,* like *big, bench,* and *balloon.*

For variety, the children can be given a series of words that begin with the same initial consonant and be told to match these words with those in a second column that start with the same letter by drawing a line from one to the other. For example:

```
ball        said
said        not
not         make
make        ball
```

Substitution of Initial Consonants   After children have learned to recognize and are able to state single consonants, they are ready to substitute those in already learned words to generate new words. The new words must be in their listening vocabulary; that is, they must have heard the word and know its meaning in order to be able to *read* it. For example, children have learned the consonant letter *c* and they also know the word *man*. They should then be able to substitute *c* for *m* and come up with the word *can*.

Special Notes

1. Letters do not *have* sounds; they are merely representations of them. However, the concept of "the letter that stands for the sound" may be confusing for some children; therefore, many teachers say "the sound of the letter" when teaching children letter–sound correspondences, even though this usage is not linguistically correct. Our purpose is not to teach linguistic principles to children but to help them see and hear patterns in words so they can decode them as quickly as possible when they meet the words in connected text.
2. According to research, "the most critical factor beneath fluent word reading is the ability to recognize letters, spelling patterns, and whole words, effortlessly, automatically, and visually. Moreover, the goal of all reading instruction — comprehension — depends critically on this ability."[11]

Final Consonants and Substitution of Final Consonants

Final consonants are similar to the list given for initial consonants, except that they appear at the end of the word. Examples of the most frequent single consonants are: *b* (*rob*), *d* (*road*), *g* (*pig*), *k* (*brook*), *l* (*tool*), *m* (*mom*), *n* (*hen*), *p* (*top*), *r* (*car*), *s-z* (*has*), *t* (*hot*).

Some teachers teach final consonants at the same time that they teach initial consonants. This approach is preferable, for teachers are working with a particular sound that they want the children to "overlearn"; that is, they want students to be able to recognize and state the sound–letter combination over an extended period of time. Emphasizing the initial and final consonants in words gives the children extra practice in both the particular sound and the letter that represents the sound being studied. As the children have learned that the letter *Gg* stands for a certain sound and can recognize this sound in *girl, go, game, get,* and so on, they should also be given words such as *pig, log, leg, tag,* and so on, to see whether they can recognize the same sound at the end of the word.

In order to gain skill in the substitution of final consonants, the children are given a list of words that they can already decode and recognize, such as *bat, pet, let, tan.* Then they are asked to substitute the final letter *g* in all the words to make new words. For example, *bat* would become *bag, pet* would become *peg, let* would become *leg,* and *tan* would become *tag.* Pupils can also be asked to substitute other consonants to make new words — for example, *d* for *g* in *bag* to make *bad,* and *d* in *let* to make *led.*

---

[11] Adams, *Beginning to Read*, p. 14.

Consonant Clusters (Blends)

Consonant clusters (blends)
A combination of consonant sounds blended together so that the identity of each sound is retained.

Consonant clusters are simply a way of combining the consonant sounds of a language. Clusters are a blend of sounds. (In some basal reader series, the term *consonant cluster* has replaced the term *consonant blend;* however, *consonant blends* is the term teachers usually use.)

Initial Consonant Blends (Clusters)

Consonant blends (clusters)
Same as consonant clusters. A combination of consonant sounds blended together so that the identity of each sound is retained.

Consonant blends (clusters) are a combination of sounds, not letters. They are two or more consonant sounds blended together so that the identity of each sound is retained. For example: *bl (blame), pl (play), cr (crack), tr (try), sk (skate), sl (sled), sm (smile), sn (snow), sp (spot), sw (swim), scr (scream), str (stream), spr (spread), spl (splash)*.

Consonant blends are generally introduced in the first grade at the primer level in basal readers and are then developed throughout the primary grades. The teaching of the initial consonant blends depends on the readiness levels of the children, who may be at the stage where they can benefit from added instruction in order to help them more readily decode words. The children must be able to recognize, sound, and substitute initial consonants in words before proceeding to blends. They should be given a list of sight words that have blends, such as *spin, snow, play,* and *stop,* and should be asked to say these words and then tell what sounds they hear at the beginning of the words. They should also be asked to say a list of words such as *go, get, me,* and *mother* and then to tell what the difference is between the two groups of words. The children should be able to discern that in the group consisting of *play, stop,* and *spin,* they were able to hear two consonant sounds rather than one. Thus, the concept of a blend is introduced. The teacher should then give the children exercises similar to those presented in the section on initial consonants. For example, the pupils could be given a list of words that they may not necessarily know as sight words:

1	2	3	4
black	big	mother	happy
ball	play	great	broom
blue	draw	farm	track
chain	down	spin	grow

Teachers would tell the children to underline only those words they pronounce, such as *black, play, spin,* and *broom.*

This exercise can also be used to see how well children listen, follow directions, and recognize blends. For example, the teacher can instruct the children to *listen carefully* and not to do anything until he or she has completed the sentence. Then, the teacher can say, "Put a circle around *black* and a cross on *blue.* Put a circle around *draw* and a line under *play.* Put a line under *great* and a circle around *spin.* Put a cross on *track* and a circle around *broom.*"

Final consonant blends are usually taught after initial consonant blends, using similar techniques.

Initial Consonant Digraphs

Consonant digraph
Two consonants that represent one speech sound.

Consonant digraphs consist of two consonants that represent one speech sound. For example, *ch* (*chair*), *sh* (*show*), *th* (*thank*), *ph* (*phone*).

Final Consonant Digraphs

Examples of final consonant digraphs are: *th* (*booth*), *ng* (*sing*), *sh* (*mash*), *ch* (*cinch*), *gh* (*rough*). *Note:* It is possible to have a digraph represent one of the sounds in a cluster. In the word *cinch,* *nch* represents a cluster (blend) because *nch* represents a blend of *two* sounds. The letter *n* represents a sound, and the digraph *ch* represents another sound.

Silent Consonants

Silent consonants
Two adjacent consonants, one of which is silent — for example, *kn* (*know*), *pn* (*pneumonia*).

Silent consonants refer to a pair of consonants of which one is silent. Examples are: *kn* (*know*), *gh* (*ghost*), *wr* (*wreck*). These are analogous to consonant digraphs, for the two consonants represent one speech sound.

Vowel Sounds

Vowel
One of a class of speech sounds; a letter representing a vowel; *a, e, i, o, u,* and sometimes *y* in the English alphabet.

Working with vowel sounds is more difficult than working with consonants because of the inconsistency of vowel sounds. There are exceptions for almost every vowel generalization. Most children have met many of the vowel generalizations in sight words and have learned to pronounce the words properly before they are able to state the generalization. Vowel generalizations are generally introduced at some time in the first grade and are usually taught throughout the primary grades. Again, the discussion of when to teach vowel generalizations would depend on the readiness level of the pupils in the class. The purpose of teaching vowel generalizations is to help students become more proficient in analyzing words so that they can be more effective independent readers.

The emphasis, however, should not be on the stating of generalizations or on children's knowledge of specialized terminology. It should be on children's being able to recognize certain word patterns. In other words, the children's attention should be on the spelling and sound structures of the word patterns they are learning.[12] (See the section on phonograms later in this chapter.)

Should long or short vowels be taught first?[13] As the long vowel sound is the name of the vowel, children might have less difficulty in hearing this sound. Therefore, it would be better to start with long vowel sounds even though there are more words with short vowel sounds.

[12] Ibid., p. 80.

[13] Although some linguists frown at the use of the terms *long* and *short vowels,* because they claim there are only gradations of vowel sounds, it is helpful to use these terms in the teaching of phonics.

Whichever kind of vowel is taught first, it is important that the teacher use the children's background of experiences to help them acquire new skills.

Teachers should familiarize children with the schwa sound, represented by (ə) of the phonetic alphabet. The schwa is important in phonics instruction because it frequently appears in the unstressed (unaccented) syllables of words with more than one syllable. (See the section on "Special Letters and Sounds.")

Long Vowel Sounds—a e i o u (and Sometimes) y

In the teaching of this concept, attention should be drawn to the sound element. A number of sight words illustrating the long vowel sound can be placed on the board:

āpe	bē	gō
āge	hē	nō
Āpril	ēven	ōpen
āte	mē	

The children are told to listen to the words as they are sounded. Can they hear the name of any of the vowels in the words? If they can, they can tell which ones they hear. After they correctly state the vowel they heard, "saying its name," it is explained that these vowels are called long vowels and they are marked, for example, ā.

A list of words containing long vowels should be read to the children, and the students should then say which vowel is long in each word. They can be given a list of words and asked to mark all the vowels that are long after everyone has said the words aloud. For example:

āble	gāme	hāte	mōst
boy	get	hid	nāme
cāke	girl	hīde	nō
come	gō	man	nōte
father	hat	mē	pet

After children have had practice in recognizing long vowel sounds in spoken words, the teacher presents written exercises in which the children work independently at marking the long vowel sound. The words in these exercises should all be sight vocabulary words—those the children have already met and are able to recognize.

Y represents a long vowel sound when it occurs at the end of a word or syllable and when all the other letters in the word or syllable are consonants—for example, *by, cry, baby, deny.* Note that *y* in these words represents different vowel sounds. It stands for a long *i* sound in one-syllable words containing no other vowels. (See the section on "Special Letters and Sounds.")

Short Vowel Sounds

As the children have already had practice in long vowel sounds, a list of words with short vowel sounds can next be placed on the board and each one pronounced:

not	get	man
got	let	can
pin	put	mad
tin	cut	cap
met	hat	had

The list containing long vowels can be presented so that children can hear the differences between long and short vowel sounds. The children's attention should also be brought to the *position* of the short vowel in such words as the following:

fat	man	net	got
mat	mad	get	not
cat	can	let	
hat		pet	

Children should be helped to notice the vowel generalization—*a single vowel in the middle of a word or syllable is usually short.* As this concept is usually introduced in the first grade, the presentation of the term *syllable* should be deferred. The concept of closed syllable is reviewed in the intermediate grades in conjunction with syllabication.

Words like *gō, nō, mē,* and *hē* should also be noticed. The vowels are all long; there is only one vowel in the word; and *a vowel at the end of a one-vowel word (or syllable) usually has the long sound.*

Special Note

In phonics, the term *generalization* is preferred to the term *rule* because the latter is a more prescriptive term and implies great consistency. In working with children, however, the term *rule* is easier for them to use and understand than *generalization.* The terms are used interchangeably in this chapter.

The Effect of the Final e

Words that the children know as sight words should be listed on the board and sounded:

note	cake	cute
made	take	mile

The children are asked to listen to the vowel sound, and it is stressed that in each of the sounded words the first vowel stands for a long sound. The children are then asked to notice what all the words have in common: All of the words have two vowels; one of the vowels is an *e,* which is always at the end of the word, and this *e* always has a consonant preceding it; the first vowel is long, and the final *e* is silent. The teacher then lists the following words on the board:

hat	cap	tub
kit	Tim	rob
can	not	hug
tap	cut	hop

The students read the words and tell what the vowel is and what kind of vowel sound the word has. The teacher then asks the children to put an *e* at the end of each of the words, so that the word list becomes the following:

hate	cape	tube
kite	time	robe
cane	note	huge
tape	cute	hope

The pupils are asked to read the words aloud. If they need help, the teacher reads the word. Again they are asked to notice what all of the words have in common and what happened to the words when the final *e* was added to each of them.

The teacher, through observation and discussion, helps children develop the silent (final) *e* rule, which states that *in words or syllables containing two vowels, separated by a consonant, one of which is a final* e, *the first vowel is usually long and the final* e *is silent.*[14]

Some practice exercises include a list of words to which children are instructed to add a final *e* to make a new word. The children then use both words in a sentence to show that they understand the difference in meaning between them. Another exercise shows their ability to recognize differences between words:

Directions   Put in the correct word.

1. He _____ himself. (cut, cute)

2. She is _____. (cut, cute)

3. I _____ you like my pet. (hop, hope)

4. I like to _____ on my foot. (hop, hope)

5. My friend's name is _____. (Tim, time)

6. What _____ is it? (Tim, time)

---

[14] When we say that a letter is silent, we mean that it does not add a sound to the syllable; however, it is just as important as any other letter in the syllable. It signals information about other letters, and it helps us to determine the sound represented by other letters.

Double Vowels

Vowel digraph
Two vowels that represent one speech sound.

Digraphs   *Two vowels adjacent to one another in a word (or syllable) stand for a single vowel sound and are called vowel digraphs; for example, ea, oa, ai, ei, oe, ie* in words like *beat, boat, hail, receive, believe.* In first grade children usually learn the rule that when two vowels appear together, the first is usually long and the second is silent. This usually does hold true for a number of vowel combinations such as *ai, oa, ea, ay,* and *ee;* however, there are exceptions to this rule, such as *ae, uy, eo, ew.* These digraphs are sounded as a single sound, but not with the long sound of the first. Some examples are *sew, buy, yeoman, Caesar.* Note that in the word *believe,* it is the *second* vowel that is long. Some vowel digraphs combine to form one sound that is not the long sound of either vowel. For example, in the words *neighbor, weigh,* and *freight,* the digraph *ei* is sounded as a long *a,* and in the word *sew* the digraph *ew* is sounded as a long *o,* with the *w* acting as a vowel. Note that in the word *rough,* the digraph *ou* is not sounded as a long vowel.

Obviously, the teacher should spend time on those vowel combinations that are the most useful. These are *ea, oa, ai, ay,* and *ee.*

Diphthongs
Blends of vowel sounds beginning with the first and gliding to the second. The vowel blends are represented by two adjacent vowels, for example, *oi.* For syllabication purposes, diphthongs are considered to be one vowel sound.

Diphthongs   *Diphthongs are blends of vowel sounds beginning with the first and gliding to the second.* The vowel blends are represented by two adjacent vowels. Examples include *ou, oi, oy, ow.* Some of these diphthongs can be confusing to children because the *ou* in *house* is a diphthong, but the *ou* in *rough* is not a diphthong but a digraph. Note that in the word *how* the *w* acts as a vowel in the diphthong *ow.* (Even though a diphthong is a *blend* of two vowel sounds, for syllabication purposes you should consider it as one vowel sound.)

Vowel Controlled by r

A vowel followed by *r* in the same syllable is controlled by the *r.* As a result, the preceding vowel does not have its usual vowel sound. Examples are *car, fir, or, hurt, perch.* If a vowel is followed by *r,* but the *r* begins another syllable, the vowel is not influenced by the *r.* Examples: ī · rāte̸, tī · rāde̸.

Review of Vowel Generalizations

1. A long vowel is one that sounds like the name of the vowel.
2. A single vowel followed by a consonant in a word or syllable usually has a short vowel sound.
3. A single vowel at the end of a word or syllable usually has a long vowel sound.
4. A vowel digraph consists of two adjacent vowels with one vowel sound. Many times the first vowel is long and the second is silent. There are exceptions, such as *believe,* in which the two vowels form a single sound where the first vowel is not long, and *weigh,* in which the two vowels form a single sound but neither vowel is long.

5. In words or syllables containing two vowels separated by a consonant, and one vowel is a final *e*, the first vowel is usually long and the final *e* is silent, as in *bāké*.

6. A vowel followed by *r* is controlled by the consonant *r*.

7. When *y* is at the end of a word containing no other vowels, the *y* represents the long sound of *i*, as in *my, sky*.

8. Diphthongs are blends of vowel sounds beginning with the first and gliding to the second, as in *boy, boil, house*.

Review Exercise

Clues to Vowel Sounds   Here are five clues that will help in determining which vowel sound you would expect to hear in a one-syllable word:

1. A single vowel letter at the beginning or in the middle is a clue to a short vowel sound—as in *hat, let, it, hot,* and *cup*.

2. A single vowel letter at the end of a word is a clue to a long vowel sound—as in *we, by,* and *go*.

3. Two vowel letters together are a clue to a long vowel sound—as in *rain, day, dream, feel,* and *boat*.

4. Two vowel letters separated by a consonant, and one vowel is a final *e*, are a clue to a long vowel sound—as in *age, ice, bone,* and *cube*.

5. A vowel letter followed by *r* in the same syllable is a clue to a vowel sound that is controlled by the *r*—as in *far, bird, her, horn, care,* and *hair*.

In the blank before each word, write the number of the statement in the list that would help you determine the vowel sound in the word.

____ she	____ grave	____ curb
____ pin	____ plot	____ up
____ oak	____ drain	____ pain
____ lung	____ harsh	____ coax
____ mane	____ whine	____ charm
____ hurt	____ freak	____ plead
____ bean	____ ate	____ flag

Special Note
Generalizations should not be taught unless enough cases warrant their teaching. Research on phoneme–grapheme relationships has been done with enumerated specific rule generalizations and the percentage of time that words followed the rule. Some investigators have claimed that a rule should not be taught unless it

holds true at least 75 percent of the time.[15] However, the decision should depend on the words. There are some frequently used words that may conform to a rule pattern, whereas a number of less frequently used words may not conform to the same rule generalization. The percentage of these latter words that conform to a rule pattern may not be as high as 50 percent, even though the most often used words almost always conform to the same pattern. For example, the "silent (final) *e*" rule, which is usually taught in the early primary grades, only has 63 percent applicability.[16] This 63 percent includes many frequently used words that conform to the same rule pattern. Therefore, the rule should be taught as a phonic generalization.

In addition, other evidence suggests that Clymer's research concerning utility "cannot be calculated accurately with the procedures used by Clymer and others who replicated his study."[17]

Special Letters and Sounds

Y

As already mentioned, *y* is used as both a consonant and a vowel. When *y* is at the beginning of a word or syllable, it is a consonant. Examples are *yes, yet, young, your, canyon, graveyard.* (In the words *canyon* and *graveyard*, *y* begins the second syllable; therefore, it is a consonant.)

When *y* acts as a vowel, it represents the short *i* sound, the long *i* sound, or the long *e* sound. *Y* usually represents the short *i* sound when it is in the middle of a word or syllable that has no vowel letter. Examples are *hymn, gym, synonym, cymbal. Y* usually represents the long *i* sound when it is at the end of a single-syllable word that has no vowel letter. Examples are *by, try, why, dry, fly. Y* usually represents the long *e* sound when it is at the end of a multisyllabic word. Examples are *baby, candy, daddy, family.*

C *and* G

Some words beginning with *c* or *g* can cause problems because the letters *c* and *g* each stand for both a hard and a soft sound. The letter *g* in *gym, George, gentle,* and *generation* stands for a soft *g* sound. A soft *g* sounds like *j* in *Jack, jail,* and *justice.* The initial letter *c* in *cease, center, cent,* and *cite* stands for a soft *c* sound. A soft *c* sounds like *s* in *so, same,* and *sew.* The initial letter *g* in *go, get, game, gone,* and *garden* stands for a hard *g* sound. The initial letter *c* in *cat, came, cook, call,* and *carry* stands for a hard *c* sound. A hard *c* sounds like *k* in *key, king, kite, kettle.* Note that the letter *c* represents a sound that is either like the *s* in *see* or like the *k* in *kitten.*

---

[15] Theodore Clymer, "The Utility of Phonic Generalizations in the Primary Grades," *The Reading Teacher* 16 (January 1963): 252–58; and Lillie Smith Davis, "The Applicability of Phonic Generalizations to Selected Spelling Programs," *Elementary English* 49 (May 1972): 706–12.

[16] Davis, "Phonic Generalizations," p. 709.

[17] Patrick Groff, "The Maturing of Phonics Instruction," *The Reading Teacher* 39 (May 1986): 921.

Q

The letter *q* is always followed by the letter *u* in the English language. The *qu* combination represents either one speech sound or a blend of two sounds. At the beginning of a word, *qu* almost always represents a blend of two sounds, *kw*. Examples are *queen, quilt, quiet, queer, quack*. When *qu* appears at the end of a word in the *que* combination, it represents one sound, *k*. Examples are *unique, antique, clique*.

The Schwa (ə)

Schwa
The sound often found in the un-stressed (unac-cented) syllables of words with more than one syllable. The schwa sound is represented by an upside-down e (ə) in the phonetic (speech) alphabet. A syllable ending in *le* preceded by a consonant is usually the final syllable in a word and contains the schwa sound.

The *schwa* sound is symbolized by an upside down *e* (ə) in the phonetic (speech) alphabet. The schwa sound frequently appears in the unstressed (unaccented) syllables of words with more than one syllable. The schwa, which usually sounds like the short *u* in *but*, is represented by a number of different vowels. Examples are believe (bə·lēve'), police (pə·lēs'), divide (də·vīde'), robust (rō'·bəst), Roman (rō'·mən). In the examples the italicized vowels represent the schwa sound. Although the spelling of the unstressed syllable in each word is different, the sound remains the same for the different vowels. (Note: The pronunciations presented here come from *Webster's New Collegiate Dictionary*, but it should not be inferred that these are the only pronunciations for these words. Pronunciations may vary from dictionary to dictionary and from region to region.)

Phonograms (Graphemic Bases)

Phonogram (gra-phemic base)
A succession of graphemes that occurs with the same phonetic value in a number of words (*ight, ake, at et*, and so on); word family.

Phonograms (graphemic bases), which are a succession of graphemes that occurs with the same phonetic value in a number of words, are helpful in both unlocking and building words.[18] Some examples of phonograms are *an, and, old, et, at, ate, eat, ap, ash, ump, ook, ad, ock, ame, ill, ink,* and so on. All phonograms begin with a vowel, and words that contain the same phonogram rhyme—for example, *bake, cake, rake, lake, take, make, fake,* and so on. (Phonograms may also be referred to as *word families*.)

1. Children can build many words using phonograms in the following manner:

   a. Present children with the following phonograms.

   _____et _____an _____ill _____old

   b. Have the children add different single consonants, consonant digraphs, and blends to the beginning of the phonograms to see how many words they can make.

2. Children can use phonograms to unlock words in the following manner:

---

[18] See Adams, *Beginning to Read*, pp. 84–85, for researches that are very supportive of this technique.

a. The child meets the unfamiliar word *tank*.

b. The child recognizes *ank* as a phonogram he has met in *bank*.

c. The child substitutes *t* for *b*.

d. The child blends *t* and *ank* to get *tank*.

3. Children can be encouraged to write funny rhyming poems using phonograms. Here is a rhyming poem using the phonogram *at* that a teacher and children wrote together after reading *The Cat in the Hat*.

I have a fat cat.
He has a big hat.
He is afraid of Mr. Rat,
Who sleeps on his mat.

My cat fell into his hat.
The hat fell on the mat.
"Help, help!" screamed the cat.
"Help, help!" screamed the rat.

Away rolled the hat.
Away rolled the mat.
Bump, bump right into a bat.
"Help, help!" screamed the bat.

Away rolled the hat.
Away rolled the mat.
Away rolled the bat.
Right into a gnat.

"Help, help!" screamed the cat.
"Help, help!" screamed the rat.
"Help, help!" screamed the bat.
"Help, help!" screamed the gnat.

Soon the cat, the rat,
The bat, and the gnat
Were together in the hat
Right on top of the mat.

There they all sat
The cat, the rat, the bat,
And the gnat
Until they became fat.

4. Here is a lesson plan on the phonogram *at*.

Lesson Plan: Early Primary Grades

Objectives

1. The students will be able to recognize words containing *at*.
2. The students will be able to state eight words that end in *at*, which have different initial consonants.
3. The students will be able to read eight words that contain *at*.

Preliminary Preparation

Drawing paper, crayons
Chairs arranged in a semicircle near the chalkboard

Introduction

"Yesterday we talked about and played a game with a word family. What family did these words belong to?"

"Yes, the *ake* family. Who can give me some words belonging to that family?"

"Yes, *make, lake, take, cake,* and *rake*. Very good. Today we're going to meet words that belong to another family, and I am going to tell you a funny story about this family. Listen carefully to this story because you are going to help me tell the story, create an ending for it, and then draw some special pictures about it."

Development

Once, a long time ago, there lived a cheerful and friendly animal called Kippa Kappa. He lived in outer space in a village called Kippa Kump, near the earth's moon. Although Kippa Kappa was cheerful and friendly, he was very lonely because he had no friends. One day Kippa Kappa told his mother and father that he was leaving Kippa Kump in order to travel to other villages in search of friends.

Kippa Kappa started on his journey. He walked and walked. Soon he became tired and hungry. He stopped and, lo and behold, he saw his favorite moon food growing. What do you think Kippa Kappa's favorite moon food is? In case you don't know, moon food is very different from earth food. On the moon, words are eaten as food. Kippa Kappa's favorite moon food is a word with *at* in it. How many children can help Kippa Kappa pick some of his favorite food? Let's see. Kippa Kappa picked a *bat* and ate it. Does that have an *at* in it?

Yes, but Kippa Kappa is still very hungry, so he picked a *fat* and a *mat* and ate them. "Um mm, these are good," said Kippa Kappa. In order to satisfy his hunger, Kippa Kappa must eat eight delicious foods with *at* in them. How many has he already picked?

Yes, he's picked three. How many more does he need?

Yes, he now needs five more. Let's list the three on the board, and then let's help Kippa Kappa find five more moon goodies to eat.

Have the children think of other initial consonants that they can use with *at*. As they state the words, list them on the board, for example, *cat, hat, pat, rat, sat,* and so on. Give the children word clues if they have difficulty thinking of some of the words.

Lesson Plan: Early Primary Grades   *Continued*

Now ask the children how they think the story will end. Tell the group that the end depends on them, and let them supply the ending.

Finally, tell the children to draw a picture of one of Kippa Kappa's favorite foods and label it. The children can also draw a picture of Kippa Kappa and write a sentence about eating a word containing *at*.

Summary

"What have we done today?" Have each child tell the name of the *at* word he or she drew a picture of, and hang the *at* chart made by the children in the reading area as a reference. Discuss the next word family the children will learn.

Syllabication – Intermediate Grades

Syllable
A vowel or a group of letters containing one vowel sound, for example, *blo*.

A syllable is a vowel or a group of letters containing one vowel sound. Syllabication of words is the process of breaking known and unknown multisyllabic words into single syllables. This is important in word recognition because in order to be able to pronounce the multisyllabic word, a child must first be able to syllabicate it. Knowledge of syllabication is also helpful in spelling and writing. In attacking multisyllabic words, the pupil must first analyze the word, determine the syllabic units, apply phonic analysis to the syllables, and then blend them into a whole word. For multisyllabic words the result will almost always be an approximation of the pronunciation. As for one-syllable words, the correct pronunciation will depend on the student's having heard the spoken word and whether it makes sense in what is being read. Usually, students will have more success in applying phonics to monosyllabic words than to multisyllabic ones because the blending of the syllables into a whole word often changes the pronunciation from the syllable by syllable pronunciation. (See "Accenting Words" in this chapter.)

Syllabication Generalizations

Because a multisyllabic word must be syllabicated before applying phonic analysis, syllabication generalizations will be given first. The vowel generalizations that the students have learned since first grade should be reviewed because these same generalizations will be used in the application of phonic analysis.

Generalization 1: Vowel followed by two consonants and a vowel (vc/cv). If the first vowel in a word is followed by two consonants and a vowel, the word is divided between the two consonants.

Examples: but/ter   can/dy   com/ment

Generalization 2: Vowel followed by a single consonant and a vowel (v/cv). If the first vowel is followed by one consonant and a vowel, the consonant usually goes with the second syllable.

Examples: be/gin   ti/ger   fe/ver   pu/pil

An exception to the v/cv syllabication rule exists. If the letter *x* is between two vowels, the *x* goes with the first vowel rather than with the second one.

Examples: ex/it   ex/act   ox/en

Generalization 3: Vowel or consonant followed by a consonant plus *le* (v/cle) or (vc/cle). If a consonant comes just before *le* in a word of more than one syllable, the consonant goes with *le* to form the last syllable.

Examples: sam/ple   can/dle   an/kle   bun/dle   pur/ple   daz/zle   bea/gle
   ca/ble

Generalization 4: Compound words. Compound words are divided between the two words.

Examples: girl/friend   base/ball

Generalization 5: Prefixes and suffixes. Prefixes and suffixes usually stand as whole units.

Examples: re/turn   kind/ly

Phonics Applied to Syllabicated Syllables

After the word has been divided into syllables, the student must determine how to pronounce the individual syllables. The pronunciation is determined by whether the syllable is open or closed, and whether it contains a vowel digraph or diphthong.

Open syllable — one that contains one vowel and ends in a vowel. The vowel is usually sounded as long, as in *go*.

Closed syllable — one that contains one vowel and ends in a consonant. The vowel is usually sounded as short, as in *mat*.

Application of Vowel Generalization to Syllabication
Generalization 1 — Double Consonant Generalization (vc/cv)

The closed-syllable vowel generalization would apply to a syllable that contains one vowel and ends in a consonant. The vowel sound is usually short.

Examples: căn/dy   ăs/sĕt

Application of Vowel Generalization Syllabication
Generalization 2 — Vowel Consonant Vowel Generalization (v/cv)

The open-syllable generalization would apply to a syllable that contains one vowel and ends in a vowel. The vowel sound is usually long.

Examples: bē/gin   tī/ger   ō/ver   fā/tal   dē/tour

Application of Vowel Generalization to Syllabication
Generalization 3 – Special Consonant le Generalization
(v/cle) or (vc/cle)

If the syllable is closed as in the first syllable of *săd/dle* and *căn/dle*, then the vowel sound is usually short in the first syllable, for it ends in a consonant. If the syllable is open as in the first syllable of *fā/ble* and *bū/gle*, then the vowel sound is usually long in the first syllable, for it ends in a vowel. The letter combinations containing *le*—such as *cle, ble, gle, tle,* and so on—usually stand as the final syllable. The final syllable is not accented; it is always an unstressed syllable containing the schwa sound.

    Examples: sĭm/pəl   fā/bəl   săd/dəl   ăp/pəl   bū/gəl

Syllabication Review Activity

Here are three clues that will help you:

1. can dy, mit ten: vowel followed by two consonants and a vowel.
2. o pen, bea con, la dy: vowel followed by a single consonant and a vowel.
3. bu gle, rum ble, strug gle: final *le* preceded by a consonant.

    Look at each word below and decide where the first syllable ends. Draw a line between the first and second syllable of the word. Put the number of the clue listed above on the line to show how you know where the first syllable ends. The first three words are done for you.

garbage __1__	able ____	master ____
handle __3__	collar ____	pronounce ____
pupil __2__	nimble ____	giggle ____
hobby ____	mirror ____	maple ____
bacon ____	eager ____	pepper ____
elbow ____	pilot ____	shuffle ____
wrinkle ____	snuggle ____	lazy ____
tiger ____	person ____	bundle ____
baby ____	reason ____	corner ____
table ____	acorn ____	after ____
borrow ____	cargo ____	nature ____
tailor ____	rifle ____	captain ____
purpose ____	simple ____	amble ____
tangle ____	notice ____	iron ____

Accenting Words

Accenting is taught in conjunction with syllabication in the intermediate grades. To pronounce words of more than one syllable, pupils should syllabicate the word, apply phonic analysis, and then blend the syllables into one word. To blend the syllables into one word correctly, pupils should know something about accenting and how accents affect vowel sounds. They should know that unaccented syllables are usually softened, and if the syllable of a multisyllable word is an unstressed syllable, it will often contain the schwa sound. (Stressed syllables never contain the schwa sound.) Note: When syllables are blended together, the pronunciation may not be exactly the same as the syllable-by-syllable pronunciation.

Example: (kĭt) (tĕn) kĭt'ʃən); (bē) (lĭēvĕ) (bə·lĭēvĕ')

There may be differences between pronunciation of homographs (words that are spelled the same but have different meanings) owing to a difference in accent.

Example: con'duct (noun); con duct' (verb)

Procedures for Teaching Accenting A number of two-syllable words are placed on the board and syllabicated:

pi/lot	a/ble	ap/ple	va/cant
den/tist	rea/son	help/ful	bot/tle
sub/due	wi/zard	wis/dom	tai/lor
lo/cal	col/lar	jour/nal	

The teacher explains that even though students are able to syllabicate the individual words and are able to apply the proper phonic analysis, in order to be able to pronounce the words correctly, they still must know something about accenting the words.

Students are asked to listen while the teacher pronounces each word, to determine which syllable is stressed. The teacher then asks individual students to volunteer to pronounce the words and explains that the syllable that is sounded with more stress in a two-syllable word is called the accented syllable. The teacher explains that the accent mark (') is used to show which syllable is stressed—that is, spoken with greater intensity or loudness. This mark usually comes right after and slightly above the accented syllable. (Some dictionaries such as *Webster's Third New International Dictionary* have the accent mark come before the syllable that is stressed.) The teacher further explains that the dictionary has a key to pronunciation of words and that the marks that show how to **Diacritical marks** pronounce words are called *diacritical marks*. The most frequent diacritical **Marks that show** marks are the breve (˘) and the macron (‾), which pupils have already met as the **how to pronounce** symbols for the short and long vowel sounds. The accent (') is also in the class of **words.** diacritical marks.

A list of words correctly syllabicated are put on the board:

pi' lot	a' ble	ap' ple	pro' gram
rea' son	help' ful	bot' tle	jour' nal
wis' dom	tai' lor	lo' cal	den' tist

Syllabication and vowel generalizations are then reviewed. The two-syllable words in the preceding list are all accented on the first syllable. Another group of words in which the second syllable is stressed are then listed:

ap point′	pro ceed′	as tound′
sub due′	pa rade′	po lite′
re ceive′	com plain′	pro vide′

Students are again asked to listen while each word is pronounced to determine which syllable is being stressed and to see if they notice any similarity among all the second syllables. They should notice that all stressed second syllables have two vowels. From their observations they should be able to state the following generalization: *In two-syllable words the first syllable is usually stressed, except when the second syllable contains two vowels.*

In three-syllable words it is usually the first or second syllable that is accented as in *an′ ces tor, cap′ i tal, ho ri′ zon.*

These skills for decoding words are useful for all children, including those who speak nonstandard English. However, for those speaking nonstandard English or a foreign language, the teacher must be especially certain to utilize the aural–oral approach before attempting to teach reading. (See sections in Chapter 2 on nonstandard English.) Obviously, the child must have the words that are to be decoded in both his or her hearing and speaking vocabularies in order to make the proper grapheme (letter)–phoneme (sound) associations.

Children who speak nonstandard English or a foreign language will need more practice in auditory discrimination and sound production education, as was discussed in previous chapters, before being able to read. This approach will facilitate the acquisition of phonic and word attack skills that will help these children to become proficient and independent readers. As was stated earlier, individual differences will determine when an approach is preferable with a given child or group. Teachers must be cautioned against attempting to teach such skills to all children, for not all are able to learn phonic or syllabication rules. Students at low ability levels usually have difficulty with syllabication and accenting.

Linguistics and Phonics

Linguistics
The scientific study of language.

Linguistics, the scientific study of language, is not a new science. However, its influence on reading instruction and in particular on beginning reading was not pronounced until the 1960s. Although there are many branches of linguistics, only those subdivisions that directly relate to the area of phonics will be discussed.

Phonology
Branch of linguistics dealing with the analysis of sound systems of language.

Phonology, which is a branch of descriptive linguistics, is the study of the sound system of language and consists of the related studies of phonetics and phonemics. Phonology is the division that is the most closely related to the area of phonics.

Phonetics
The study of the nature of speech sounds.

Since the terms *phonics, phonetics,* and *phonemics* are often confused, definitions of the three follow.

Phonics involves the study of relationships between the letter symbols (graphemes) of a written language and the sounds (phonemes) they represent. It is a method used in teaching word recognition in reading; that is, it belongs in the area of pedagogy. By now you should be very familiar with this term.

Phonetics, a branch of linguistics, is the study of the nature of speech sounds. According to Betts, phonetics includes the following:

1. How speech sounds are produced by tongue, teeth, vocal bands, and other parts of the speech mechanism.
2. The perception of speech sounds by the hearing mechanism.
3. The variant pronunciation and varying usage of speech sounds in different regions of a country or of the world.
4. The system of speech symbols—their symbolic nature—for communication of messages.

"Applied" phonetics includes the following:

1. Correction of defective speech.
2. Teaching a "standard" speech in a given region.
3. Devising symbols to represent speech sounds; for example, one pronunciation of *call* is transcribed via the phonetic symbols [kol]; *hat* as [hat].[19]

Phonemics
Deals with the problem of discovering which phonemes are part of the conscious repertoire of sounds made by speakers of a language or dialect.

Phonemics "deals with the problems of discovering which phonemes are part of the conscious repertoire of sounds made by speakers of a language or dialect."[20] "The phonemic system is that group of phonemes used by speakers of a language to put their utterances together."[21] A *phoneme* is the smallest unit of sound that a speaker uses to distinguish one utterance from another.

Both phonemics and phonetics are more concerned with the analysis of the sound system of language than with pedagogy.

Linguists' Definition of Vowels and Consonants

Phonemes are classified into consonants and vowels and then are further divided into *voiced* or *voiceless* sounds. All vowels are voiced.

Whether a sound is voiced or voiceless can be determined by placing your hand over your larynx (Adam's apple) and making the sound. For example, for the sound [b] vibrations can be felt, whereas for the sound [p] no vibrations can be felt.[22]

---

[19] Emmett Albert Betts, "Confusion of Terms," *The Reading Teacher* (February 1973): 454–455.

[20] Burt Liebert, *Linguistics and the New English Teacher* (New York: Macmillan, 1971), p. 82.

[21] Ibid., p. 84.

[22] Ibid., p. 76.

Phonemes are also categorized "according to the point of articulation, the place in the oral cavity where the speech stream is modified."[23] Vowel sounds can be produced when "the air stream passes comparatively freely through the oral cavity, being modified mainly by the position of the tongue." Consonants result when, in speaking, the outgoing breath stream is either partially or completely obstructed by the organs of speech.

A phoneme is a class of sounds, not a distinct and separate sound. There are a number of variations within any phoneme, and each variation is called an *allophone*. However, persons speaking their native language are not aware of these differences.

Recording of Phonemic Symbols and Phonetic Symbols

As many of the phonemes of the language are written with letters of the alphabet, in order to distinguish between letters and representation of sounds, specific brackets are used.

Phonemic symbols are written between slashes (//), whereas phonetic symbols are written within square brackets ([ ]).

For example, the letter *b* stands for the second letter of our alphabet and is part of the graphemic (written) system of English, but the symbol [b] stands for a sound, part of the phonetic (spoken) system of language, and the phonemic symbol /b/ stands for the sound that belongs to a particular language.

Special Note

Because confusion often exists between the terms *grapheme–phoneme* relationship and *phoneme–grapheme* relationship, these terms will also be discussed. *Grapheme–phoneme* relationship refers to letter-sound relationship; it is the decoding process used in reading, in which sound symbols are related to their written symbols. *Phoneme–grapheme relationship* refers to the sound–letter relationship in which written symbols are related to their sound symbols. In a *grapheme–phoneme relationship* you start with the written symbol, and in a *phoneme–grapheme relationship* you begin with the sound symbol.

Diagnostic Word Recognition Assessment

Student's Name: _____

Grade: _____

Teacher: _____

---

[23] Ibid., p. 78.

Diagnostic Word Recognition Assessment *Continued*

Auditory Discrimination	Yes	No

1. The student is able to listen to a set of words and state
which pair are the same:

Ted	Ted		
cap	cap		
bud	but		
out	out		
shell	shall		
bit	bet		
send	sand		

2. The student is able to listen to a word and state another
word that begins like
boy.
ran.
mine.
pencil.

3. The student is able to listen to a word and give another that
ends like
clock.
hat.
card.
plant.

4. The child can state another word that rhymes with
look.
fat.
tan.
bake.

5. The child can give the letter that stands for the first sound
heard in
bury.
mother.
zone.
curb.
label.
jewel.
yell.

Continued

Diagnostic Word Recognition Assessment *Continued*

	Yes	No
Auditory Discrimination		

6. The child can give the two letters that stand for the first two
sounds heard in

plan.		
twin.		
stone.		
swan.		
float.		
snag.		
cry.		
glove.		

7. The child can give the two letters that stand for the first
sound heard in

chair.		
shame.		
thumb.		
phone.		

8. The child can give the letter that stands for the last sound
heard in

plan.		
mom.		
rug.		
hare.		
buzz.		
lake.		

	Yes	No
Visual Discrimination		

The student is able to do the following visual
discrimination activities:

1. Following are a number of letters. Choose the letter that is
different from the first one in the line:

Example: E E *D* E E

a. U	R	U	U	U	U			
b. P	P	P	P	P	D			
c. d	d	d	b	d	d			
d. p	p	p	p	d	p			

2. Following are a number of words. Choose the word that is the same as the first
word.

Diagnostic Word Recognition Assessment   *Continued*

Visual Discrimination	*Yes*	*No*
Example: big bag get *big* beg bug		
a. won now own won was war		
b. saw son saw son sow sun		
c. fun far fat fan fin fun		
d. noon none nine noon neon name		

Word Analysis Test—Auditory	*Yes*	*No*

1. The student is able to state the number of syllables in each word.

("Listen carefully. Each of the words I am going to pronounce has one or more than one syllable. Tell me the number of syllables you hear in each word.")

a. vocabulary (5)		
b. bicycle (3)		
c. baby (2)		
d. reached (1)		
e. mother (2)		

2. The student is able to state the vowel sound heard in each word.

("Listen carefully. Tell me the vowel sound you hear in each word.")

a. bake (ā) f. use (ū)		
b. coat (ō) g. leap(ē)		
c. pit (ĭ) h. neck (ĕ)		
d. hen (ĕ) i. pine (ī)		
e. bat (ă) j. lip (ĭ)		

Word Analysis Test—Visual	*Yes*	*No*

The student is able to pronounce the following nonsense words.

("Can you pronounce the following nonsense words?")

a. l o a p (lōáp)		
b. h a k e (hāké)		
c. c h i n e (chīné)		
d. p h a t (fāt)		
e. l i p o (līpō)		

Diagnostic Checklist for Word Recognition Skills

Student's Name: _____

Grade: _____

Teacher: _____

	Yes	No	Sometimes

1. The student uses
   a. context clues.
   b. picture clues (graphs, maps, charts).			

2. The student asks someone to state the words.			
3. The student uses the dictionary to try to unlock unknown words.			

4. The student uses phonic analysis by recognizing
   a. consonants.
      (1) single consonants: initial, final
      (2) consonant blends (clusters) (br, sl, cl, st, and so on)
      (3) consonant digraphs (th, sh, ph, ch, and so on)
      (4) silent consonants (kn, gn, pn)			

b. vowels.
      (1) short vowels (cot, can, get, and so on)
      (2) long vowels (go, we, no, and so on)
      (3) final silent e (bake, tale, role)
      (4) vowel digraphs (ea, oa, ee, ai, and so on)
      (5) diphthongs (oi, oy)
   c. the effect of r on the preceding vowel.
   d. special letters and sounds (y, c, g, q).
   e. known phonograms or graphemic bases (a succession of graphemes that occurs with the same phonetic value in a number of words [ight, id, at, ad, ack]).			

5. The student is able to apply the following syllabication rules to words: a. vowel consonant/consonant vowel rule (vc/cv) (but/ter, can/dy).			

Diagnostic Checklist for Word Recognition Skills   *Continued*

	Yes	No	Sometimes
b. vowel/consonant vowel rule (v/cv) (na/tive, ca/bin).			
c. special consonant *le* rule (vc/cle) or (v/cle) (ca/ble, can/dle).			

Graphic Summary of Chapter

Here is a graphic summary of Chapter 6. If you have read the chapter, this graphic illustration should help you remember its main points. Under or beside each heading, you might want to jot down some of the information you recall, as well as some of the key concepts in this chapter. This can act as a good review. You can then check your key concepts against those that follow the graphic summary.

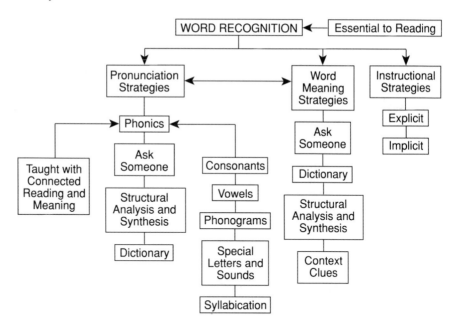

Key Concepts

- Word recognition is the foundation of the reading process.
- Word recognition is a twofold process that includes both the identification of printed symbols by some method and the attachment or association of meaning to the printed symbols.

- There are a variety of pronunciation strategies.
- There are a variety of word meaning strategies.
- Phonics is a decoding technique that depends on grapheme–phoneme correspondences.
- Phonics should be taught in conjunction with connected text and meaning, and the emphasis should not be on stating generalizations.
- Phonics usually gives only an approximation of the way a word is pronounced.
- In phonics instruction the material should be related as much as possible to the phonics skills being taught.
- Teachers usually use both explicit and implicit phonics instruction.
- Phonograms are a particularly helpful way of unlocking and building words.

Suggestions for Thought Questions and Activities

1. You have been appointed to a special primary grade reading committee. Your task is to help teachers to gain a better understanding of the role that phonics plays in the word recognition process. How would you go about doing this?
2. You have been asked to give a workshop on creative activities that would enhance the teaching of phonics. What are some activities that you would present as samples of these?
3. The administration in your school district has asked you to present a demonstration lesson in the area of word recognition. What kind of lesson would you prepare for a primary grade level?
4. You have a child in your class who seems to have a great amount of difficulty retaining information. He needs extensive practice in order to overlearn his letters and words. You need to develop some activities that would be fun and that would help this child to overlearn his initial consonants. What kind of activities would you develop to help this primary grader recognize and name initial consonants?
5. Present a lesson that would help primary grade students understand the concept of open and closed syllables. How would you be able to determine whether your lesson has been successful?
6. Present a lesson that would help intermediate grade level students with accenting. What kind of accenting rules would you help them to learn? What should students know about accenting and word meanings?

Selected Bibliography

Adams, Marilyn Jager. *Beginning to Read: Thinking and Learning about Print.* Cambridge, Mass.: MIT Press, 1990.
"Beginning to Read: A Critique by Literacy Professionals and a Response by Marilyn Jager Adams." *The Reading Teacher* 44 (February 1991): 370–395.

Chall, Jeanne S. *Learning to Read: The Great Debate,* 2nd ed. New York: McGraw-Hill, 1983.

Ehri, Linnea C., and Claudia Robbins. "Beginners Need Some Decoding Skill to Read Words by Analogy." *Reading Research Quarterly* 27 (1992): 12–26.

Stahl, Steven A. "Saying the 'P' Word: Nine Guidelines for Exemplary Phonics Instruction." *The Reading Teacher* 45 (April 1992): 618–625.

Stanovich, Keith E. "Word Recognition: Changing Perspectives." In *Handbook of Reading Research,* Vol. II. Rebecca Barr, Michael L. Kamil, Peter Mosenthal, and P. David Pearson, eds. New York: Longman, 1991, pp. 418–452.

Wilson, Robert M., and MaryAnne Hall. *Programmed Word Attack for Teachers,* 5th ed. Columbus, Ohio: Merrill, 1990.

7

Reading Comprehension

SCENARIO: GAINING READING COMPREHENSION – ONE SCHOOL'S EFFORTS

When Mr. Lear became principal of a kindergarten to sixth-grade school, he told his teachers that at first he considered turning down the position because he loved being a classroom teacher. He said that he was sure that they, too, know that almost nothing can compare with the warm glow you get when you see the look in a child's eyes that says, "I understand."

Mr. Lear told his teachers that he decided to become a principal because he felt he could have a greater impact that way. He hoped he was correct.

Mr. Lear was determined to make a difference. He initiated a weekly seminar meeting for his teachers to keep them informed of new trends and to discuss important curriculum issues and how these issues affected what the teachers were doing in their classes.

The focus of the past few weeks has been on reading comprehension and the strategies teachers use to help their students gain an understanding of what they are reading. Mr. Lear started the discussion by sharing with his teachers the report on reading from the National Assessment of Educational Progress (NAEP). He said that there was both good and bad news. The good news is that the performance gap of black and Hispanic students is narrowing in relation to whites,[1] and "the results across the three ages (9, 13, and 17) show tremendous growth in reading comprehension as the students move through school."[2] The bad news, however, is that there is still a disparity between minority and white students, that the performance overall for white students did not change significantly over the seventeen-year period from 1971 to 1988, and that the gains that were made were at the literal comprehension level. No gains were evident at the higher levels of reading ability defined by adept and advanced skills and strategies."[3] Mr. Lear stated further that a major conclusion of the report is that "until our students are exposed—through schools, individuals at home, and their own initiative—to more varied and intensive reading experiences, the reading

---

[1] Ina V. S. Mullis and Lynn B. Jenkins, *The Reading Report Card, 1971–1988.* National Assessment of Educational Progress (Princeton, N.J.: Educational Testing Service, 1990), p. 15.

[2] Ibid., p. 35.

[3] Ibid.

proficiency of American students is unlikely to change dramatically for the better."[4]

Mr. Lear said that the nation was up in arms about students' poor showing in many content areas and that this poor showing may well be directly related to their comprehension problems. At that point, Mr. Lear asked some teachers to volunteer to research the topic under discussion and to report their findings to the rest of the faculty.

Miss Smith and Mr. Brown volunteered. Each chose a specific aspect of comprehension to research and report to the rest of the faculty.

Miss Smith discussed how relatively new research on comprehension is, and how the research by Dolores Durkin at the end of the 1970s "about the complete lack of reading comprehension in middle-grade classrooms"[5] shocked the educational community. It seemed almost incomprehensible "that there was nothing 'instructive' about our classrooms. Instead instruction consisted primarily of giving students opportunities to demonstrate, by answering questions, completing workbook pages, or taking tests, whether they could perform the various comprehension tasks that form the basis of school reading curricula."[6] Her research played a major role in stimulating others to investigate what would make instruction "instructive" (see Chapter 3).

Mr. Brown discussed comprehension strategies and how teachers can help their students gain the most from their reading.

After both Miss Smith and Mr. Brown had presented their reports, Mr. Lear asked all his teachers to evaluate the kinds of techniques they used to teach comprehension; then, at their next meeting, they would share what they did and see how they could apply the research findings in their teaching.

Mr. Lear is a good principal. He realizes the importance of having an informed faculty, and one way to ensure this is to make sure that he himself is knowledgeable about what is taking place in the educational arena. He especially tries to keep abreast of what is taking place in the field of reading because he recognizes the importance of reading comprehension and its effect on students' achievement in all content areas. He feels his weekly meetings are accomplishing his objective of having an informed faculty who are on the cutting edge of what is taking place in the educational arena.

This chapter will help teachers gain a better understanding of reading comprehension and of the most effective strategies for helping students gain needed comprehension skills. The premise in this chapter is similar to Mr. Lear's; that is, the more teachers know about reading comprehension, the better able they will be to implement a good reading comprehension program in their classrooms. Knowledge is an essential element of empowerment.

---

[4] Ibid., p. 37.

[5] P. David Pearson and Linda Fielding, "Comprehension Instruction," in *Handbook of Reading Research*, Vol. II, Rebecca Barr, Michael L. Kamil, Peter Mosenthal, and P. David Pearson, eds. (New York: Longman, 1991), p. 815.

[6] Ibid.

KEY QUESTIONS

After you finish reading this chapter, you should be able to answer the following questions:

1. What is comprehension?
2. How is reading comprehension defined?
3. What are some characteristics of good comprehenders?
4. What are some reading comprehension strategies?
5. What are reading comprehension taxonomies?
6. How is reading comprehension categorized in this textbook?
7. What are some questioning strategies to enhance comprehension?
8. What is the role of metacognition in questioning?
9. What are some direct reading instructional methods, activities, or strategies teachers can use to help students gain comprehension?
10. What is the Directed Thinking–Reading Activity
11. What is literature webbing?
12. What is the role of critical thinking in first grade?
13. What is the role of pictures in comprehension?
14. How can teachers help students with their content textbooks?
15. What are some important comprehension skills?

KEY TERMS IN CHAPTER

You should pay special attention to the following key terms:

analogies
bias
categorizing
central idea
comprehension
creative reading
critical reading
Directed Reading–Thinking Activity
  (DRTA)
divergent thinking
fact
finding inconsistencies
inference

interpretation
literal comprehension
literature webbing
main idea
opinions
propaganda
Question Answer Relationships
  (QARs)
reading comprehension
reading comprehension taxonomy
schema theory
supporting details
topic sentence

What Is Comprehension?

Comprehension
Understanding; the ability to get the meaning of something.

Comprehension refers to understanding, the ability to get the meaning of something. Because comprehension is a construct—that is, something that cannot be observed or measured directly—we can only infer that someone understands from the overt behavior of the person. *Webster's Third International Dictionary* defines *comprehension* as "the act or action of grasping (as an act or process) with the intellect," and *intellect* is defined as "the capacity for rational or intelligent thought especially when highly developed." Obviously, the more intelligent an individual is, the more able he or she would be to comprehend, as was discussed in Chapter 2. What may not be so obvious is that persons who have difficulty understanding may have this difficulty because they have not had certain experiences that require higher levels of thinking; they may not have learned how to do high-level thinking. Such people will have difficulty in all the language arts areas, because listening, speaking, reading, and writing all require reasoning ability (Figure 7-1). (See Chapter 1 for a discussion of the relationship of reading to the other language arts.)

In 1917, Edward Thorndike wrote the following paragraph, which still seems significant today:

> *Understanding a paragraph is like solving a problem in mathematics. It consists in selecting the right elements of the situation and putting them together in the right relations, and also with the right amount of weight or influence or force for each. The mind is assailed as it were by every word in the paragraph. It must select, repress, soften, emphasize, correlate and organize, all under the influence of the right mental set or purpose or demand.*[7]

Thorndike stresses further that the reading of text material requires an active mind and thought. "It thus appears that reading an explanatory or argumentative paragraph in his [the student's] text-books on geography or history or civics, and (though to a lesser degree) reading a narrative or description, involves the

Reprinted by permission of UFS, Inc.

FIGURE 7-1   Without understanding, there is no reading.

[7] Edward L. Thorndike, "Reading as Reasoning: A Study of Mistakes in Paragraph Reading," *Journal of Educational Psychology* 8 (6) (June 1917): 329.

same sort of organization and analytic action of ideas as occur in thinking of supposedly higher sorts."[8]

What Is Reading Comprehension?

Reading comprehension
A complex intellectual process involving a number of abilities. The two major abilities involve word meanings and reasoning with verbal concepts.

Reading comprehension is a complex intellectual process involving a number of abilities. The two major abilities involve word meanings and verbal reasoning. Without word meanings and verbal reasoning, there would be no reading comprehension; without reading comprehension, there would be no reading. Most people would agree with these statements, but there is disagreement when we ask, "How does an individual achieve comprehension while reading?" In 1917 Edward Thorndike put forth his statement that "reading is a very elaborate procedure, involving a weighing of each of many elements in a sentence, their organization in the proper relations one to another, the selection of certain of their connotations and the rejection of others, and the cooperation of many forces to determine final response."[9] He stated further that even the act of answering simple questions includes all the features characteristic of typical reasonings. Today investigators are still exploring reading comprehension in attempts to understand it better, and through the years many have expounded and expanded upon Thorndike's theories.

For more than a quarter of a century, research into the process of understanding has been influenced by the fields of psycholinguistics and cognitive psychology. As a result, terms such as *surface structure, deep structure, microstructure, macrostructure, semantic networks, schemata, story grammar, story structure,* and so on have invaded the literature. The studies that have been done are not conclusive; that is, from the studies it is not possible to say that if a reader were to follow certain prescribed rules, he or she would most assuredly have better comprehension.

Reading Comprehension Taxonomies

Reading comprehension taxonomy
A hierarchy of reading comprehension skills ranging from the more simplistic to the more complex ones; a classification of these skills.

A number of reading comprehension taxonomies exist, and many appear similar to one another. This is not surprising. Usually the people who develop a new taxonomy do so because they are unhappy with an existing one for some reason and want to improve upon it. As a result, they may change category headings but keep similar descriptions of the categories, or they may change the order of the hierarchy, and so on. Most of the existing taxonomies are adaptations in one way or another of Bloom's taxonomy of educational objectives in the cognitive domain, which is concerned with the thinking that students should achieve in any discipline. Bloom's taxonomy is based on an ordered set of objectives ranging

[8] Ibid., p. 331.

[9] Thorndike, "Reading as Reasoning," p. 323.

from the more simplistic skills to the more complex ones. Bloom's objectives are cumulative in that each one includes the one preceding it. And most of the taxonomies that have been evolved are also cumulative.

Of the many persons who have tried to categorize reading comprehension, one attempt that is often referred to is Barrett's *Taxonomy of Reading Comprehension.* Barrett's taxonomy consists of four levels: literal comprehension, inferential comprehension, evaluation, and appreciation. In this text, an adaptation of Nila Banton Smith's model is used, which at first glance may appear to be similar to Barrett's. The differences become obvious when we look at the skills subsumed under each of the first three levels. In the model used in this book, literal questions are those that require a low-level type of thinking; skills such as finding the main idea of a paragraph would not be included under the literal level. However, in Barrett's taxonomy, "recognition or recall of main ideas" is included in his literal level. Finding the main idea of a paragraph is not easy even if the idea is directly stated in the paragraph; students must do more than a low-level type of thinking to determine that something stated in the paragraph is the main idea. In other words, any time that a student must interpret what he or she is reading, the student is required to do reasoning that goes beyond merely recalling what is in the text.

Also, in this text, appreciation is not in the hierarchy because appreciation has a hierarchy of its own. It is possible for us to appreciate something we have read or that is read to us at any level of the hierarchy, even though, of course, we would probably have the highest appreciation at the level at which we had the greatest understanding of what we read or heard. (See "What Is Reading for Appreciation?" in Chapter 4.)

Categorizing Reading Comprehension

Comprehension involves thinking. As there are various levels in the hierarchy of thinking, so are there various levels of comprehension. Higher levels of comprehension would obviously include higher levels of thinking. The following model adapted from Nila Banton Smith divides the comprehension skills into four categories:[10] (1) literal comprehension, (2) interpretation, (3) critical reading, and (4) creative reading. The categories are cumulative in that each builds on the others.

Special Note
In this text an adaptation of Nila Banton Smith's model is used. In her original model, she presented literal-level reading skills as requiring no thinking. In the model used in this book, literal-type questions do require thinking, even though it is just a low-level type of thinking.

---

[10] Nila Banton Smith, "The Many Faces of Reading Comprehension," *The Reading Teacher* 23 (December 1969): 249–259, 291.

Literal compre-hension
The ability to obtain a low-level type of understand-ing by using only information that is explicitly stated.

Literal Comprehension   Literal comprehension represents the ability to obtain a low-level type of understanding by using only information explicitly stated. This category requires a lower level of thinking skills than the other three levels. Answers to literal questions simply demand that the pupil recall from memory what the book says.

Although literal-type questions are considered to involve a low-level type of thinking, it should *not* be construed that reading for details to gain facts that are explicitly stated is unimportant in content-area courses. A fund of knowledge is important and necessary; it is the foundation for high-level thinking. If, how-ever, teachers ask only literal questions, students will not graduate to higher lev-els of thinking. (See "Questioning Strategies to Enhance Comprehension" in this chapter.)

Interpretation
A reading level that demands a higher level of thinking ability because the material it involves is not directly stated in the text but only suggested or implied.

Interpretation   Interpretation, the next step in the hierarchy, demands a higher level of thinking ability because questions in the category of interpretation are concerned with answers that are not directly stated in the text but are suggested or implied (see Figure 7-2). To answer questions at the interpretive level, readers must have problem-solving ability and be able to work at various levels of ab-straction. Obviously, children who are slow learners will have difficulty working at this level as well as in the next two categories (see Chapter 15).

The interpretive level is the one at which the most confusion exists when it comes to categorizing skills. The confusion concerns the term *inference*. The definition of inference is: Something derived by reasoning; something that is not directly stated but suggested in the statement; a logical conclusion that is drawn from statements; a deduction; an induction. From the definition we can see that inference is a broad reasoning skill involving analysis and synthesis and that there are many different kinds of inferences. All of the reading skills in interpre-tation rely on the reader's ability to "infer" the answer in one way or another. However, by grouping all the interpretive reading skills under inference, "some of the most distinctive and desirable skills would become smothered and ob-scured."[11]

Some of the reading skills that are usually found in interpretation are as follows:

Determining word meanings from context
Finding main ideas
"Reading between the lines" or drawing inferences[12]
Drawing conclusions
Making generalizations
Recognizing cause-and-effect reasoning
Recognizing analogies

[11] Ibid., pp. 255–256.

[12] Although, as already stated, all the interpretive skills depend on the ability of the reader to infer meanings, the specific skill of "reading between the lines" is the one that teachers usually refer to when they are teaching *inference*.

Critical reading
A high-level reading skill that involves evaluation; making a personal judgment on the accuracy, value, and truthfulness of what is read.

Critical Reading   Critical reading is at a higher level than the other two categories because it involves evaluation, the making of a personal judgment on the accuracy, value, and truthfulness of what is read. To be able to make judgments, a reader must be able to collect, interpret, apply, analyze, and synthesize the information. Critical reading includes such skills as the ability to differentiate between fact and opinion, the ability to differentiate between fantasy and reality, and the ability to discern propaganda techniques. Critical reading is related to critical listening because they both require critical thinking.

Creative reading
Uses divergent thinking skills to go beyond the literal comprehension, interpretation, and critical reading levels.

Creative Reading   Creative reading uses divergent thinking skills to go beyond the literal comprehension, interpretation, and critical reading levels. In creative reading, the reader tries to come up with new or alternative solutions to those presented by the writer. (A special section, "Using Divergent Thinking," is presented in this chapter.)

Special Note

It is at the interpretive level and above that studies suggest students are in the most need of help.[13] Students appear to have difficulty reading analytically and performing well on challenging reading assignments.[14]

Questioning Strategies to Enhance Comprehension

All children need help in developing higher level reading comprehension skills. If teachers persist in asking only literal comprehension questions that demand a simple convergent answer, higher level skills will not be developed.

Unfortunately, much of what goes on in school is at the literal comprehension level. Teachers usually ask questions that require a literal response, and children who answer this type of question are generally seen as being excellent

Reprinted by permission of UFS, Inc.

FIGURE 7-2   Sally can work on a literal level only.

[13] Ina V. S. Mullis, Eugene H. Owen, and Gary W. Phillips, *America's Challenge: Accelerating Academic Achievement,* National Assessment of Educational Progress (Princeton, N.J.: Educational Testing Service, 1990).

[14] Ibid., p. 9.

students. It is to be hoped that this perception will change now that many reading task forces across the country are emphasizing the teaching of higher level comprehension skills.

The kinds of questions the teacher asks will determine the kinds of answers he or she will receive. Rather than asking a question that calls for a literal response, the teacher must learn to construct questions that call for higher levels of thinking. This process should begin as early as kindergarten and first grade. For example, the children are looking at a picture in which a few children are dressed in hats, snow pants, jackets, scarves, and so on. After asking the children what kind of clothes the children in the picture are wearing, the teacher should try to elicit from his or her students the answers to the following questions: "What kind of day do you think it is?" "What do you think the children are going to do?"

These very simple inference questions are geared to the readiness and cognitive development level of the children. As the children progress to higher levels of thinking, they should be confronted with more complex interpretation or inference problems. It is important that the teacher work with the children according to their individual readiness levels. The teacher should expect all the children to be able to perform but should avoid putting them in situations that frustrate rather than stimulate them (see Figure 7-3).

Critical reading skills are essential for good readers. Teachers can use primary graders' love of folktales to begin to develop some critical reading skills. For example, after the children have read "The Little Red Hen" (see Chapter 12 for an adapted version of "The Little Red Hen"), the teacher can ask such questions as the following:

1. Should the Little Red Hen have shared the bread with the other animals? Explain.
2. Would you have shared the bread with the other animals? Explain.
3. Do you think animals can talk?
4. Do you feel sorry for the other animals? Explain.
5. Do you think this story is true? Explain.

Creative reading questions are probably the most ignored by teachers. To help children in this area, teachers need to learn how to ask questions that require divergent rather than convergent answers. A teacher who focuses only on the author's meaning or intent and does not go beyond the text will not be encouraging creative reading. Some questions that should stimulate divergent thinking on the part of the reader would be the following:

1. After reading "The Little Red Hen," try to come up with another ending for the story.
2. Try to add another animal to the story of "The Little Red Hen."
3. Try to add another part to the story of "The Little Red Hen."

Divergent answers, of course, require more time than convergent answers. Also, there is no one correct answer.

Following are a short reading selection and examples of the four different types of comprehension questions. These are being presented so that the teacher can have practice in recognizing the different types of questions at the four levels.

One day in the summer, some of my friends and I decided to go on an overnight hiking trip. We all started out fresh and full of energy. About halfway to our destination, when the sun was almost directly overhead, one-third of my friends decided to return home. The remaining four of us, however, continued on our hike. Our plan was to reach our destination by sunset. About six hours later as the four of us, exhausted and famished, were slowly edging ourselves in the direction of the setting sun, we saw a sight that astonished us. There, at the camping site, were our friends who had claimed that they were returning home. It seems that they did indeed go home, but only to pick up a car and drive out to the campsite.

The following are the four different types of comprehension questions:

Literal comprehension: What season of the year was it in the story? What kind of trip were the people going on?

Interpretation: What time of day was it when some of the people decided to return home? How many persons were there when they first started out on the trip? In what direction were the hikers heading when they saw a sight that astonished them? At what time did the sun set?

Critical reading: How do you think the hikers felt when they reached their destination? Do you feel that the persons who went home did the right thing by driving back to the site rather than hiking? Explain.

Creative reading: What do you think the exhausted hikers did and said when they saw the two who had supposedly gone home?

Metacognition and Questioning

Question Answer Relationships (QARs)
Helps students distinguish between "what they have in their heads" and information that is in the text.

The more children understand what they do when they are in the act of answering questions, the better question solvers they can be. Raphael has designed an instructional strategy, Question Answer Relationships (QARs), that teachers can use to help their students gain insights into how they go about reading text and answering questions. It helps students "realize the need to consider both information in the text and information from their own knowledge background."[15]

In the QAR technique, students learn to distinguish between information that "they have in their heads" and information that is in the text. The steps that can help children gain facility in QAR are presented in the following paragraphs. Note that the amount of time children spend in the steps is determined by the individual differences of the students.

[15] Taffy E. Raphael, "Teaching Question Answer Relationships, Revisited," *The Reading Teacher* 39 (February 1986): 517.

Reprinted by permission of UFS, Inc.

FIGURE 7-3 Does this complaint sound familiar?

Step 1   Students gain help in understanding differences between what is in their heads and what is in the text. The children are asked to read a passage, and the teacher asks questions that guide them to gain the needed understandings. Here is a short sample:

> Mike and his father went to the ball game.
> They were lucky to get tickets for the game.
> They saw many people they knew.
> At the game Mike and his father ate hot dogs.
> They also drank soda.

The students are then asked the following questions:

1. Where did Mike and his father go? (To the ball game)
2. Where did they see the people? (At the ball game)

The children are helped to see that the first answer is directly stated, whereas the second is not; it is "in their heads."

Step 2   The "In the Book" category is divided into two parts. The first deals with information that is directly stated in a single sentence in the passage, and the second deals with the piecing together of the answer from different parts of the passage. (Raphael calls this step "Think and Search" or "Putting It Together."[16])
The children are then given practice in doing this.

Step 3   This would be similar to Step 2 except that now the "In My Head" category is divided into two parts, "Author and You" and "On My Own."[17] The teacher helps students recognize whether the question is text-dependent or independent. For example, the answer to the first question would require the student to read the text to be able to answer it, even though the answer would come from the student's background of experiences. However, the student can answer the second without reading the passage.

1. How else do you think the cat could have escaped?
2. How would you feel if you were lost?

The QAR approach can be very useful in introducing children to inferential reasoning; it helps children understand better what information is directly stated and what is implied. Teachers can modify the QAR approach to suit their students' needs. (See "Questioning as a Diagnostic Technique" in Chapter 13.)

[16] Ibid., p. 518.
[17] Ibid.

Reading Comprehension Instruction

A major factor in reading success appears to be time spent in reading, whether it is direct instructional time or time spent reading independently. Independent reading is reading students do on their own in or outside of school. Unfortunately, a number of children do not spend time reading on their own because of other competing activities. See "Time Spent in Reading" in Chapter 3; also see Chapter 4.) Therefore, teachers must plan for students to have time to read independently as well as provide direct instruction in reading.

Direct instruction requires teachers to directly present strategies to help their students comprehend the material being read (see "Direct Reading Instruction Strategies" in Chapter 3); this is done in addition to asking children questions before, during, and after they read. "Direct instruction in comprehension means explaining the steps in a thought process that gives birth to comprehension."[18] Obviously, teachers themselves must be good problem solvers and thinkers in order to help their students become better comprehenders.

There are various methods, activities, and strategies that can be used with direct instruction; some are less structured than others. The instructional pattern that teachers use to help students gain comprehension will vary depending on the concept being taught, the uniqueness of the learners, and the ability of the teacher. (See "Direct Reading Instruction Strategies" in Chapter 3.)

The Directed Reading–Thinking Activity

In the 1980s the basal reader series were revised in terms of both the kinds of reading matter included in the readers and their approach. They began to include more literature-based material and whole pieces of literature to try to appease their critics and also started to present more questions before, during, and after silent and oral reading that require higher level thinking. In addition, their Directed or Guided Reading Approach appears to be modeled more on the Directed Reading–Thinking Activity advocated by Russell Stauffer, whereby teachers encourage students to make predictions about what they read. This is good news (see "Basal Reader Programs" in Chapter 11).

Directed Reading–Thinking Activity (DRTA) Requires teachers to nurture the inquiry process and students to be active participants and questioners; includes prediction and verification.

The Directed Reading–Thinking Activity (DRTA) can be an especially effective approach in the hands of good teachers, whether they use a basal reader series or trade books (library books). DRTA requires that students be active participants. "The reading–thinking process must begin in the mind of the reader. He must raise the questions and to him belongs the challenge and the responsibility of a judgment. The teacher keeps the process active and changes the amount of data to be processed."[19] Here is an outline of the process:[20]

[18] Richard C. Anderson, Elfrieda H. Hiebert, Judith A. Scott, and Ian A. G. Wilkinson. *Becoming a Nation of Readers: The Report of the Commission on Reading* (Washington, D.C.: National Institute of Education, 1985), p. 72.

[19] Russell G. Stauffer, *Directing the Reading–Thinking Process* (New York: Harper & Row, 1975), p. 37.

[20] Ibid.

I. Pupil actions:

    A. Predict (set purposes).

    B. Read (process ideas).

    C. Prove (test answers).

II. Teacher actions:

    A. What do you think? (activate thought)

    B. Why do you think so? (agitate thought)

    C. Prove it. (require evidence)

The DRTA is not as teacher-directed as the one used by basal reader series, and even though there are a number of sequential steps in the DRTA, they are not as delineated as in a basal reader series. The DRTA requires teachers who know how to encourage students to ask questions that stimulate higher level thinking; it requires teachers who are masters in nurturing the inquiry process.

Modeling (Thinking Out Loud) Strategy

Many good teachers have probably used this approach but may not have been aware of it. Often when a teacher has students who have difficulty understanding something that is being explained, the teacher may "model" the skill for the children. That is, the teacher "thinks aloud" or verbalizes his or her thoughts to give the students insight into the process. The teacher literally states out loud exactly the steps that he or she goes through to solve the problem or gain an understanding of a concept. Many basal reader series are including modeling as part of their instructional plans. (A number of the scenarios presented in this book include modeling strategies. For an example, see "Scenario: Mrs. Johnson Uses a Modeling Strategy" in Chapter 3.)

Literature Webbing with Predictable Books in the Early Grades

Success breeds success! If children have good experiences in reading at an early age, these experiences will help instill good attitudes about reading in the children. Predictable books appear to be one way to provide these.[21] (See "Instilling a Love for Reading in the Early Grades with Big Books" in Chapter 4.) Literature webbing is a story map or graphic illustration that teachers can use as one approach to guide them in using predictable trade books with their children.

Literature webbing
A story map technique to help guide children in using predictable trade books.

The literature webbing strategy lesson (LWSL), which is an adaptation by Reutzel and Fawson of Watson and Crowley's Story Schema Lessons to "provide support for early readers,"[22] includes a six-step process. The teacher's preliminary preparation includes reading the text and excerpting a number of samples

---

[21] D. Ray Reutzel and Parker C. Fawson, "Using a Literature Webbing Strategy Lesson with Predictable Books," *The Reading Teacher* 43 (December 1989): 208.

[22] Ibid., p. 209.

from it that are large enough so that children can make predictions about them. (The excerpts may be accompanied by enlarged illustrations if this procedure is used early in the year.) After the excerpts are chosen, the title of the book is placed in the center of the board with various web strands projecting from the title. (There are three more strands than needed for the number of excerpts. These strands, which are used for discussion purposes, are personal responses to the book, other books we've read like this one, and language extension activities.) Then the children follow these six steps.[23]

1. Sample the book by reading the randomly ordered illustrations and text excerpts that are placed on the chalk tray below the literature web.
2. Predict the pattern or order of the book by placing the excerpts in clockwise order around the literature web.
3. Read the predictable book straight through. (It may be a big book or a number of copies of the normal-sized text.)
4. Confirm or correct their predictions.
5. Discuss the remaining three strands that are on the board for discussion purposes.
6. Participate in independent or supported reading activities.

Scenarios: Comprehension Strategies

Read the following scenarios. In which scenario do you feel students will gain the most understanding from what they are reading?

SCENARIO 1

Mr. Moore, a sixth-grade teacher, is meeting with a reading group that has been working with trade books. Each time they meet, Mr. Moore goes over the material that the students were asked to read the previous time. Today is no different. He begins by asking if anyone had any problems reading the chapter. When no one says anything, he immediately begins to ask the students questions about the chapter. After they answer the questions, Mr. Moore gives them their next reading assignment.

SCENARIO 2

Mr. Jones also teaches a sixth grade, and his students are also reading trade books. However, Mr. Jones's approach to teaching reading is quite different from Mr. Moore's. Here is what Mr. Jones does.

He begins his reading lesson by asking a student to summarize what he or she has read so far in his or her book. He then tells the students to try to make

[23] Ibid.

SCENARIO 2   *Continued*

predictions about what they think will happen in the next chapter based on what they already know. He asks them to write these predictions. Next he introduces the vocabulary for the new chapter and discusses with the students some background information about the setting in which the new chapter takes place. He then presents them with a provocative question that brings a quizzical look to their faces. He looks at his students and tells them to read the first two pages to answer his question.

While the students read silently, Mr. Jones observes them. He looks around the room to see what the other students are doing and then reiterates his provocative question. Four of the students raise their hands. He calls on one. After she gives her answer, Mr. Jones asks if the others agree. A lively discussion ensues. Throughout the lesson, Mr. Jones asks questions at various levels of difficulty and encourages students to do the same. He also challenges them to find evidence to support their positions. He keeps asking them what they think the author's purpose is in doing what he does or in presenting characters the way he does. He also asks them what the key ideas of the chapter are. When students have difficulty answering some questions, he models for them how he goes about getting the answer. He constantly prods his students to ask themselves whether what they are saying makes sense based on what they know.

Toward the end of the lesson, he has his students summarize the chapter they have read and then asks them to try to think of how they would resolve the conflicts in the book. He would like them to write how they would end the novel before they meet on Monday, when they will read the last chapter. At that time they will compare their endings to the author's and discuss which they like better and why. In addition, they will construct a graphic illustration of the main plot and subplots in the book so they can see how these all relate to one another.

Commentary

Both Mr. Moore and Mr. Jones are attempting to use certain approaches to help students gain comprehension of what they are reading. From observing the two teachers, we see that Mr. Moore depends primarily on questions for students to demonstrate understanding of text material. Mr. Jones, however, combines questions with a number of other valuable instructive strategies. Let's look more closely at what Mr. Jones does.

Mr. Jones prepares his students for the chapter they are going to read by drawing relationships between what they are going to read and the students' background knowledge and experiences. Because the novel they are reading has its setting in the South at the time of the Civil War, he helps them relate this to what they have been studying. He has also previewed the material beforehand and culled all those words that he feels might cause difficulty for his students, and he goes over these with them. He then presents them with a provocative question to get their attention. In addition, he asks them to make some predictions about what they expect to happen based on what they have already read. Mr. Jones uses a modeling strategy and guides his students through the reading with questions before, during, and after. He also has them generate their own questions about the material they are reading.

On the basis of the latest reading comprehension research, Mr. Jones is using strategies that should help his students gain comprehension skill. It appears that "students of a variety of ages and abilities benefit when teachers take the time to help them either recall or build knowledge of text structure by paying systematic attention to it."[24] This "systematic attention" can be in the form of questions to help guide students through the material, a summary, or a visual representation, among a host of other techniques.[25] In addition, researchers suggest that especially for inferential comprehension, helping relate students' background knowledge to the material they are reading improves students' comprehension. "This may involve invoking appropriate knowledge structures before reading, making and verifying predictions before and during reading, or answering inferential questions during or after reading."[26]

Teacher's Checklist of Reading Comprehension Instruction

Here is a checklist that teachers can use when preparing a reading lesson to determine whether they are using techniques that will help ensure that their students are actively engaged in learning.

The teacher:

1. relates reading material to students' background knowledge.
2. has students make predictions about material to be read.
3. asks questions before reading.
4. asks questions during reading.
5. asks questions at the end of reading.
6. encourages students to ask questions about material.
7. asks interpretive questions.
8. asks critical thinking questions.
9. asks creative thinking questions.
10. has students verify predictions.
11. has students find evidence from material to support answers.
12. uses visual representations to show relationships of main plot and subplots.
13. asks students to summarize materials.
14. models (thinks aloud) the steps he or she goes through to gain understanding.
15. knows when to intervene to benefit comprehension.

[24] Pearson and Fielding, "Comprehension Instruction," p. 846.

[25] Ibid., pp. 846–847.

[26] Ibid., p. 847.

First Grade Is Not Too Soon to Teach Critical Thinking

MS. MASON TEACHES CRITICAL THINKING IN FIRST GRADE

Ms. Mason is a first-grade teacher who believes strongly that the early primary grades are not too soon to teach her students higher order thinking skills. She uses her children's love of folk and fairy tales to help them develop skill in critical thinking—passing personal judgment on the accuracy, truthfulness, and value of something. Around Ms. Mason's classroom you can find picture scenes from stories such as "Cinderella," "Jack and the Beanstalk," "Sleeping Beauty," Rumpelstiltskin," and "Goldilocks and the Three Bears."

Ms. Mason introduces her lesson on helping children differentiate between reality and fantasy, a critical thinking skill, by asking students about some of the folk and fairy tales they have been reading. After the children name stories, she asks them to look at a few pictures from tales they have read. She calls on children to tell about each of the pictures. The children state that the first shows Cinderella's coach turning back into a pumpkin; the second picture shows Rumpelstiltskin spinning straw into gold; and the third shows the prince awakening Sleeping Beauty, who has been asleep for a hundred years. She tells the children that today they will discuss what all the pictures have in common.

Ms. Mason continues by saying, "I know many of you watch television. What are some of the shows you've seen lately?" After children name a number of shows, the teacher asks whether they think it is really possible for Superman to do the things he does. Also, the teacher asks the children whether they think Superman can really fly. "What do many of the shows that portray animals talking, persons flying, or people changing into different forms or shapes have in common with the fairy tales we've been reading? Let's look again at the pictures I brought in. If I told you that I had a spinning wheel that could change straw into gold, would you believe me?" "No, of course not." "If I told you that I knew someone who had been asleep for one hundred years, and that the kiss of a handsome young man had awakened her, would you believe me? If I told you that I knew a charming little house in which three bears lived and that the three bears slept in beds and lived just like we do, would you believe me?" "No, of course not." "Can someone tell me what all these pictures have that is the same?" "Yes, that is very good. None of them could really happen. What about many of the cartoon shows that we watch on television and such shows as 'Superman'? Do these people really exist?" "No, of course not."

"When something is not real, we say that it is a fantasy. Fairy tales are all fantasies. Most of the cartoons—'Superman,' and others like these—are fantasies. Fantasy is make-believe. We've played pretend games. Who can give me some examples? Yes, we've made-believe that we were lots of famous people. When you make-believe, it's not real. Let's make up some fantasies."

After the children share their fantasy statements with one another, Ms. Mason asks them to create some statements that are not fantasy but based on

Continued

SCENARIO   *Continued*

reality. She models for them how to do this. She then passes out a sheet of paper to each child. The sheet has statements such as these: *The moon has a face. A rug can turn into a flying carpet. Bears can talk. People can fly. Mr. Toad can drive a car. Bears sleep in beds. Bears eat at a table. People can fly to the moon in a spaceship.* The children must state whether the statements are based on fantasy or reality. Ms. Mason again models for her children how she goes about determining this. She then goes over the answers with the children and helps them pull the main points of the lesson together.

What Is the Role of Pictures in Comprehension?

Although educators have debated the "picture question" for a long time, there is very little research in this area. According to the studies that exist, the effect seems to be that pictures neither hurt nor help comprehension of text material.[27]

Some educators have stated that the pictures detract from the text material, but "the research provides no arguments against the presence of text-compatible illustrations."[28] On the other hand, illustrations help to make books more attractive and instill positive attitudes toward them. Certainly, pictures are of prime importance in young children's books (see Figure 7-4). It seems reasonable that "parent–child discussions of pictures are key to the appreciation of language and literature that grows from picture book reading"[29] (see Chapter 16).

Comprehension and Reading Content Textbooks

One problem with many of the comprehension studies done at the lower grade levels is that they deal primarily with simple stories rather than with more complex material or the kinds of material elementary children would meet in content books. As a result, some children may do well in a reading group but have difficulty in reading their content textbooks.

Elementary teachers should make a concerted effort to help their students gain the skills they need to read their content textbooks and not take for granted that their students will be able to transfer what they learn in the reading lesson to the content-area textbook.

Teachers can help their students by directly teaching any comprehension skills or strategy that they feel their students need. This should be done using relevant content material—that is, content material the students are actually reading at the time.

---

[27] Marilyn Jager Adams, *Beginning to Read: Thinking and Learning about Print—A Summary,* Steven A. Stahl, Jean Osborn, and Fran Lehr, eds. (Urbana, Ill.: Center for the Study of Reading, 1990), p. 68.

[28] Ibid.

[29] Ibid., p. 69.

FIGURE 7-4 This child likes books with lots of pictures.

The studies that deal with the recall or retention of material and text structure have relevance for the reading of both stories and content material. What seems significant from many of the studies is that attention to text structure appears to help students recall important text ideas. It follows logically, then, that techniques such as outlining and noting top-level structure (the way in which the information in the passage is organized) would be helpful to students reading content material.[30] For example, one study in particular trained students to identify main ideas and organizational patterns and found that the quantity and quality of students' recall was enhanced by this procedure.[31] Another study found that poor comprehenders of text material have a processing deficiency; that is, they "do not spontaneously organize paragraph details around main ideas of a passage. . . ."[32] Good comprehenders, on the other hand, engage in meaningful

[30] Barbara M. Taylor, "Children's Memory for Expository Text after Reading," *Reading Research Quarterly* 15 (3) (1980): 399–411.

[31] B. J. Bartlett, "Top-Level Structure as an Organizational Strategy for Recall of Classroom Text," Unpublished doctoral dissertation, Arizona State University, 1978.

[32] John P. Richards and Catherine W. Hatcher, "Interspersed Meaningful Learning Questions as Semantic Cues for Poor Comprehenders," *Reading Research Quarterly* 13 (4) (1977–1978): 551–552.

learning by assimilating new material to concepts already existing in their cognitive structures;[33] that is, good comprehenders relate their new knowledge to what they already know. They also seem to know what information to attend to and what to ignore; they have good strategies for processing information. A recent study with high school students that also has relevance for students in lower grades suggests that, as the passage difficulty increases, good comprehenders appear to use more types of strategies and to use them more often than poor comprehenders do.[34]

Special Note
If the elementary grade level students are not in a self-contained classroom where the teacher teaches all subjects including reading, the teacher of reading and the content-area teachers should meet regularly to discuss how to help their students gain the most from their content textbooks.

Good Comprehenders: A Summary

Although it is difficult to state definitively how persons achieve comprehension while reading, from the discussion in this chapter and in others, we can see that good comprehenders are good strategic readers, who have certain characteristics. It appears that "expert readers use rapid decoding, large vocabularies, phonemic awareness, knowledge about text features, and a variety of strategies to aid comprehension and memory."[35] Novice readers and unskilled older readers, conversely, "often focus on decoding single words, fail to adjust their reading for different texts or purposes, and seldom look ahead or back in text to monitor and improve instruction."[36]

The rest of this chapter presents information about the kinds of skills that good comprehenders should have and suggests ways to help students acquire these needed and important skills.

Schema theory
Deals with relations between prior knowledge and comprehension.

Special Note
Schema theory deals with the relations between prior knowledge and comprehension. "According to schema theory, the reader's background knowledge serves as scaffolding to aid in encoding information from the text."[37] From this we can see

33 Ibid., p. 552.

34 Sharon Benge Kletzien, "Strategy Use by Good and Poor Comprehenders Reading Expository Text of Differing Levels," *Reading Research Quarterly* 26 (1) (1991): 67–86.

35 Scott G. Paris, Barbara A. Wasik, and Julianne C. Turner, "The Development of Strategic Readers," in *The Handbook of Reading Research*, Vol. II, Rebecca Barr, Michael L. Kamil, Peter Mosenthal, and P. David Pearson, eds. (New York: Longman, 1991), p. 609.

36 Ibid.

37 Steven Stahl, Michael G. Jacobson, Charlotte E. Davis, and Robin L. Davis, "Prior Knowledge and Difficult Vocabulary in the Comprehension of Unfamiliar Text," *Reading Research Quarterly* 24 (Winter 1989): 29.

that a person with more background knowledge will comprehend better than one with less and that the preparation of readers for what they will be reading "by actively building topic knowledge prior to reading will facilitate learning from text."[38]

Some Important Comprehension Skills

This section presents some comprehension skills that need special emphasis. Teachers should teach those skills directly and in relation to what children are reading. It is also a good idea for the teacher to explain to the students why they are learning the skill and how it can help them be better readers. The more children understand why they are doing what they are doing, the better learners they should become. In addition, all teachers should have these comprehension skills at their fingertips and help students attain them regardless of the program or approach they are using to teach reading.

Special Note
A special section on context clues appears in the vocabulary chapter.

Main Idea of a Paragraph

Main idea
The central thought of a paragraph. All the sentences in the paragraph develop the main idea. The term *central idea* is usually used when referring to a group of paragraphs, an article, or a story.

The main idea is probably the skill with which teachers and students spend the most time; this is good. It is, however, a skill that seems to cause a great amount of difficulty for students. Students especially find constructing or inventing the main idea more difficult than selecting the main idea ; that is, students have more difficulty coming up with the main idea themselves than with choosing one from a given list. In fact, the main idea construction process is much more difficult.[39] Even if the main idea is directly stated, this process is a difficult one. (See "Reading Comprehension Taxonomies" earlier in this chapter.)

Because of the difficulty of the main idea construction task, sufficient "think time" must be allotted. In addition, research has demonstrated "that if readers' prior knowledge for the text topic is not sufficient, the difficulty of main idea construction is compounded."[40]

Confusion in finding the main idea may exist because it seems to mean different things to different people. One researcher investigating the literature found that "educators have increasingly given attention to main idea comprehension, but with no concomitant increase in the clarity of what is meant by main or

[38] Ibid., p. 30.

[39] Peter P. Afflerbach, "The Influence of Prior Knowledge on Expert Readers' Main Idea Construction Strategies," *Reading Research Quarterly* 25 (Winter 1990): 44.

[40] Ibid.

important ideas. The exact nature of main ideas and the teaching practices intended to help students grasp main ideas vary considerably."[41]

Even though the concept of main idea is nebulous to some researchers and the "notion that different readers can (and should) construct identical main ideas for the same text has been questioned,"[42] the teaching of main idea is a very important skill for reading, writing, and studying that can and should be taught. It is possible that the skepticism concerning the ability to teach main idea may result from "the failure to teach students to transfer their main idea skills to texts other than those found in their readers."[43] Some studies have found that "students who have been taught to identify main ideas using only contrived texts such as those found in basal reader skills lessons will have difficulty transferring their main idea skills to naturally occurring texts."[44]

In reading and writing, finding the main idea is very useful. In reading, the main idea helps you to remember and understand what you have read. In writing, the main idea gives unity and order to your paragraph. (See "Summarizing as a Mode of Learning" in Chapter 10.)

The main idea of a paragraph is the central thought of the paragraph. It is what the paragraph is about. Without a main idea, the paragraph would just be a confusion of sentences. All the sentences in the paragraph should develop the main idea.

Finding the Main Idea of a Paragraph

To find the main idea of a paragraph, you must find what common element the sentences share. Some textbook writers place the main idea at the beginning of a paragraph and may actually put the topic of the paragraph in bold print in order to emphasize it, but in literature this is not a common practice. In some paragraphs the main idea is not directly stated but implied. That is, the main idea is indirectly stated, and you have to find it from the clues given by the author.

Although there is no foolproof method for finding the main idea, there is a widely used procedure that has proved to be helpful. In order to use this procedure, you should know that a paragraph is always written about *something* or *someone*. The something or someone is the topic of the paragraph. The writer is interested in telling his or her readers something about the topic of the paragraph. To find the main idea of a paragraph, you must determine what the topic of the paragraph is and what the author is trying to say about the topic that is special or unique. Once you have found these two things, you should have the main idea. This procedure is useful in finding the main idea of various types of paragraphs.

---

41 James W. Cunningham and David W. Moore, "The Confused World of Main Idea," *Teaching Main Idea Comprehension,* James F. Baumann, ed. (Newark, Del.: International Reading Association, 1986), p. 2.

42 Afflerbach, "The Influence of Prior Knowledge," p. 45.

43 Victoria Chou Hare, Mitchell Rabinowitz, and Karen Magnus Schieble, "Text Effects on Main Idea Comprehension," *Reading Research Quarterly* 24 (Winter 1989): 72.

44 Ibid.

Reread the preceding paragraph and state its main idea. *Answer:* A procedure helpful in finding the main idea of a paragraph is described.

Now read the following paragraph. After you have read the passage, choose the statement that *best* states the main idea.

> Frank Yano looked like an old man, but he was only thirty. Born to parents who were alcoholics, Frank himself started drinking when he was only eight. He actually had tasted alcohol earlier, but it wasn't until he was eight or nine that he became a habitual drinker. His whole life since then has been dedicated to seeking the bottle.

1. Frank Yano looks old, but he's not.
2. Frank Yano enjoys being an alcoholic.
3. Frank Yano was a child alcoholic.
4. Frank Yano has been an alcoholic since childhood.
5. Frank Yano would like to change his life of drinking, but he can't.
6. Frank Yano's parents helped him become an alcoholic.

Answer: #4

Numbers 1 and 3 are too specific because each relates to only one detail in the paragraph. Numbers 2 and 5 are not found in the paragraph; that is, no clues are given about Frank Yano's wanting to change his life or about his enjoying his life as an alcoholic. Number 6 is also too specific to be the main idea because it relates to only one detail. Number 4 is the answer because what is special about Frank Yano is that he has been an alcoholic since early childhood. All the details in the paragraph support this main idea.

Special Note

The main idea of a paragraph is a general statement of the content of the paragraph. You must be careful, however, that your main idea statement is not so general that it suggests information that is not given in the paragraph.

Textbook authors usually see to it that their paragraphs have clear-cut main ideas. The main ideas of paragraphs in other books may be less obvious. The literary author is usually more concerned with writing expressively than with explicitly stating the main ideas. The main idea may be indirectly given. If the main idea is indirectly given, the steps presented earlier are especially helpful. Let's look again at the steps involved in finding the main idea.

1. Find the topic of the paragraph.
2. Find what is special about the topic. To do this, gather clues from the paragraph, find out what all the clues have in common, and make a general statement about the clues.

Special Notes

Topic sentence
The sentence that states what the paragraph will be about by naming the topic.

Supporting details
Additional information that supports, explains, or illustrates the main idea. Some of the ways that supporting details may be arranged are as cause and effect, examples, sequence of events, descriptions, definitions, comparisons, or contrasts.

1. The topic sentence is usually the first sentence in a paragraph, and it states what the paragraph will be about by naming the topic. From the topic sentence you can usually anticipate certain events. You can usually determine that the following sentences will supply supporting details as examples, contrasts, similarities, sequence of events, cause-and-effect situations, and so on to support the main idea.
2. The main idea can be developed in many different ways. Whatever technique is used to develop the main idea, it must support and add meaning to the main idea.
3. A topic sentence may or may not contain the main idea.
4. It is possible for any sentence in the paragraph to be the topic sentence.
5. Some paragraphs may not have a topic sentence.
6. Do not confuse the topic sentence with the main idea. The topic sentence usually anticipates both the main idea and the development of the main idea.
7. Even though the topic sentence is stated explicitly (fully and clearly) in a paragraph, the main idea may not be stated explicitly.

Practice Activities

1. Here is a paragraph that you can use with your primary grade level students for practice.

   Sharon was sad. She felt like crying. She still couldn't believe it. Her best friend, Jane, had moved away. Her best friend had left her. What will she do?

   Ask your students what the topic of the paragraph is or about whom or what the paragraph is written.

   Answer: Sharon

   Ask your students what the writer is saying that is special about Sharon?

   Answer: Sharon is sad because her best friend moved away.

2. Here is another paragraph that you can use for practice with your upper primary grade or intermediate grade level students.

   Jim and his friends planned to go on a camping trip. For weeks, he and his friends talked about nothing else. They planned every detail of the trip. They studied maps and read books on camping. Everything was set. Everything, that is, except for asking their parents to let them go. Jim and his friends had planned everything. They had not planned on their parents' refusal. However, that is what happened. Jim's and his friends' parents did not allow them to go.

   Ask your students what the topic of the paragraph is or about whom or what the paragraph is written.

Answer: Jim and his friends' plans to go camping

Ask your students what the writer is saying that is special about Jim and his friends' plans to go camping.

Answer: Jim and his friends' plans to go camping are blocked by their parents.

3. Have the students state the topics of a number of paragraphs and then compare them to the main idea of each paragraph.
4. Have the students read paragraphs that have sentences in them that do not help to develop the main idea of the paragraph. Have students pick out those sentences that do not belong.
5. Have students write paragraphs and then challenge one another to state the main idea of each paragraph. Students should check each of their paragraphs to make sure all the sentences develop the main idea.
6. Give the students a paragraph that has its sentences out of order. Have them organize the sentences into a logical paragraph. Then have them state its main idea.

Visual Representations and Main Idea

It is difficult to read a textbook, magazine, or newspaper without finding a variety of visual representations in the form of graphs, diagrams, and charts. The sprinkling of these representations gives relief from print; a graphic representation is worth a thousand words. Graphs, diagrams, and charts grab your attention and pack a great amount of information in a small space. For these reasons, *USA Today* uses pictorial representations every day in each section of its newspaper.

Writers use visual representations to convey information, and each one, like a paragraph, has a main idea. To understand the charts, diagrams, and graphs, you must be able to get the main idea of them. Not surprisingly, the technique we use to do this is similar to that for finding the main idea of a paragraph. It would probably be a good idea for content-area teachers to model how they go about constructing the main idea of various visual representations in their specific subject. Figure 7-5 is a visual representation from *USA Today.* [45] Here is how one teacher helps his students get the main idea of it.

1. The teacher tells his students that he first looks at the visual representation to determine its topic. He tells them that writers usually give clues to the topic of their graph or chart, and some writers may actually state it for their readers. He then asks them to write about what they think the topic is, and says that he will do the same.

He tells his students that for this example, the writer has made it very easy for them because he has stated the topic. Therefore the topic is: *Top fruits and vegetables people buy specifically for health reasons.*

---

[45] *USA Today* "Snapshots," Life Section, June 12, 1991, p. 10.

USA SNAPSHOTS®

A look at statistics that shape our lives

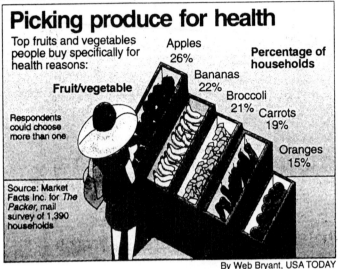

Picking produce for health

Top fruits and vegetables people buy specifically for health reasons:

Fruit/vegetable

Respondents could choose more than one

Apples 26%

Bananas 22%

Broccoli 21% Carrots 19%

Oranges 15%

Percentage of households

Source: Market Facts Inc. for *The Packer,* mail survey of 1,390 households

By Web Bryant, USA TODAY

USA Today "Snapshots," Life Section, June 12, 1991, p. 10.

FIGURE 7-5   A visual representation.

2. Next, he tells his students to look at the graph a little more closely to figure out what is special about the topic. He will also do the same.

He tells them that he sees the writer is showing the percentage of households that is buying each of the top fruits and vegetables. Therefore, the main idea would be: *The greatest percentage of households buys apples specifically for health reasons over other top fruits and vegetables.*

Finding the Central Idea of a Group of Paragraphs

Central idea
The central thought of a group of paragraphs, an article, or a story. All the paragraphs develop the central idea of a group of paragraphs, an article, or a story.

We generally use the term *central idea* rather than *main idea* when we refer to a *group* of paragraphs, a story, or an article. However, the procedure for finding the main idea and that for finding the central idea are the same.

The central idea of a story is the central thought of the story. All the paragraphs of the story should develop the central idea. To find the central idea of a story, students must find what common element the paragraphs in the story share. The introductory paragraph is usually helpful because it either contains or anticipates what the central idea is and how it will be developed. The procedure for finding the central idea of a story is similar to that for finding the main idea of a paragraph.

It is important to help your students recognize that the title of a story and the central idea are not necessarily the same. The ability to state the title of a story is related to the skill of finding the central idea. However, many times the title merely gives the topic of the story. The central idea is usually more fully stated than the title.

Practice Activities

1. Here is a story you can use with your primary grade level students.

   Directions   Read the story. Write the central idea of the story. Then write a title for the story that gives readers an idea of what the story is about.

   > There was once a beautiful princess who was very sad. She was so sad that she couldn't eat. Every day the princess grew thinner and thinner. The king and queen were sad, too. They were sad because the princess was getting thinner and thinner.
   > "We must do something," said the queen to the king.
   > "Yes, but what can we do?" asked the king.
   > "We must speak to the wise men," said the queen.
   > "You are right," agreed the king.
   > The wise men were called to appear before the king and queen. The wise men told the king and queen that they had to find out why the princess was sad. Once the princess stopped being sad, she would eat. Once she started eating, she would stop growing thinner and thinner.
   > "That is wise," said both the king and queen together.
   > With that, the wise men left.
   > The king and queen went to the princess. "Why are you sad?" asked both the king and queen together.
   > "I am sad because I have no one to play with," said the princess.
   > "But everyone is your friend," said the queen.
   > "I don't want grown-up friends. I want someone my own age," answered the princess.
   > "If we find you someone to play with, will you stop being sad?" asked the king.
   > "If you stop being sad, will you start eating again?" asked the queen.
   > The princess answered, "Yes" to both questions.
   > The king and queen called all their helpers. They told their helpers to find someone for the princess to play with. The helpers went into the village. They found a little girl the same age as the princess. They brought the little girl to the princess. The princess liked the little girl. The princess stopped being sad. She started to eat. She stopped growing thinner and thinner.

   Answers

   Central idea: A sad princess cannot eat until she has a friend of her own age to play with.

   Sample title: "The Sad Princess" or "The Princess Who Became Thinner and Thinner"

2. Here is a story you can use with your upper intermediate grade level students.

Directions   Read carefully the following short story to determine the central idea of the story. Finding the central idea of a story is similar to finding the main idea of a paragraph. (To find the central idea of the story, find the topic of the story and what is special about the topic.) Note that in this tale there are actually two topics. State the two topics, and then state the central idea for each. After you have done this, try to write a symbolic central idea or a saying that would relate to both topics. Then choose a title for the story that best fits your central idea statement.

Once upon a time the king of a large and rich country gathered together his army to take a faraway little country.

The king and his soldiers marched all morning long and then went into camp in the forest.

When they fed the horses they gave them some peas to eat. One of the Monkeys living in the forest saw the peas and jumped down to get some of them. He filled his mouth and hands with them, and up into the tree he went again, and sat down to eat the peas.

As he sat there eating the peas, one pea fell from his hand to the ground. At once the greedy Monkey dropped all the peas he had in his hands, and ran down to hunt for the lost pea. But he could not find that one pea. He climbed up into his tree again, and sat still looking very glum. "To get more, I threw away what I had," he said to himself.

The king had watched the Monkey, and he said to himself: "I will not be like this foolish Monkey, who lost much to gain a little. I will go back to my own country and enjoy what I now have."

So he and his men marched back home.

Answers:

Topics: A monkey; the king of a large rich country

Literal level central idea: A monkey lost all the peas he had because he tried to get one more, and the king of a large rich country didn't risk everything by trying to take over a small country.

Symbolic level central idea that applies to both topics: It's foolish to risk a lot to gain a little or if you are greedy, you may lose everything.

Sample title: "Being Greedy Can Cost You Everything"

Drawing Inferences

Inference Understanding that is not derived from a direct statement but from an indirect suggestion in what is stated; understanding that is implied.

Many times writers do not directly state what they mean but present ideas in a more indirect, roundabout way. That is why inference is called the ability to "read between the lines." *Inference* is defined as *understanding that is not derived from a direct statement but from an indirect suggestion in what is stated.* Readers draw inferences from writings; authors make implications or imply meanings.

The ability to draw inferences is especially important in reading fiction, but it is necessary for nonfiction, also. Authors rely on inferences to make their stories more interesting and enjoyable. Mystery writers find inference essential to the maintenance of suspense in their stories. For example, Sherlock Holmes and Perry Mason mysteries are based on the ability of the characters to uncover evidence in the form of clues that are not obvious to the others around them.

Nonfiction writers, especially textbook writers, usually present information in a more straightforward manner than fiction writers do, but even text material includes implied meanings that readers must deduce or infer. For example, when students read about the actions and decisions of some important persons in history, students can deduce something about the characters of the men or women. When people read about a region such as the North Pole, they can deduce the kind of clothing people there have to wear, as well as the kind of life they probably have to lead. Readers can also draw inferences about conditions in a region by reading information about the way of life in the region.

Inference is an important process that authors rely on. Good readers must be alert to the ways that authors encourage inference.

Implied Statements   As has been said already, writers count on inference to make their writing more interesting and enjoyable. Rather than directly stating something, they present it indirectly. To understand the writing, the reader must be alert and be able to detect the clues that the author gives. For example, in the sentence *Things are always popping and alive when the twins, Herb and Jack, are around,* readers are given some clues to Herb's and Jack's personalities. From the statement readers could make the inference that the twins are lively and lots of fun to have around.

Readers must be careful, however, that they do not read more into some statements than is intended. For example, read the following statements, and put a circle around the correct answer.

Example: Mary got out of bed and looked out of the window. She saw that the ground had some white on it. What season of the year was it? (a) winter, (b) summer, (c) spring, (d) fall, (e) can't tell.

The answer is "(e) can't tell." Many people choose "(a) winter" for the answer. However, the answer is (e) because the "something white" could be anything; there isn't enough evidence to choose (a). Even if the something white was snow, in some parts of the world, including the United States, it can snow in the spring or fall.

In *A Study in Scarlet,* Holmes, upon meeting Watson for the first time, tells Watson that he knows that Watson has been in Afghanistan. Watson is incredulous. He feels that someone must have told Holmes. Following is what Holmes says:

> *Nothing of the sort. I knew you came from Afghanistan. From long habit the train of thought ran so swiftly through my mind that I arrived at the conclusion without*

being conscious of intermediate steps. There were such steps, however. The train of reasoning ran: "Here is a gentleman of medical type but with the air of a military man. Clearly an army doctor then. He has just come from the tropics, for his face is dark, and that is not the natural tint of his skin, for his wrists are fair. He has undergone hardship and sickness, as his haggard face says clearly. His left arm has been injured. He holds it in a stiff and unnatural manner. Where in the tropics could an English army doctor have seen such hardship and get his arm wounded? Clearly, in Afghanistan." I then remarked that you came from Afghanistan, and you were astonished.

Holmes is able to correctly identify Watson's former residence. The information is all there, but it is not obvious. It is implied, and Holmes through deduction is able to make the proper inferences. (See "Metacognition and Questioning" earlier in this chapter for a technique that helps students gain an insight into information that is in the text and information that is implied.)

Practice Activities

1. Here is an exercise you can use with your primary grade level students for practice.

   Directions   Read the short story. Answer the questions that follow the story.

   > Zip, the cat, and Zap, the rat, wear special clothing on the moon. They must wear this clothing all the time that they are outside. If they did not wear the special clothing, they would dry out and jump too high. One day, Zip was running after Zap. Zap ran outside. He jumped up and down. Zip ran outside, too. He jumped up, but he didn't come down. Zap turned around. When he did, he saw Zip soaring away into space. "Oh, no!" screamed Zap. "Come back, come back." Zip, however, just floated away.

   > 1. Who was wearing outdoor clothing? How do you know?
   > 2. Why did Zip float away?
   > 3. Is Zip a boy cat or a girl cat? Explain.

   Answers

   > 1. Zap was wearing the special clothing because he didn't float away when he jumped up. When Zip jumped up, he floated away.
   > 2. He wasn't wearing the special clothing.
   > 3. A boy. The pronoun *he* is used to refer to Zip.

2. Here is an exercise you can use with your intermediate grade level students for practice.

   Directions   Read the short story carefully. Read each of the statements below the story. For each of the statements, see if there is enough information in the story to write *true* or *false*. If there is not enough information in the story to write *true* or *false*, write *can't tell*.

John and Jim became friends in kindergarten. When Jim came to school the first day, he was frightened. Jim cried. John saw Jim crying. He said, "Come sit by me." John took Jim's hand. He led Jim to his table. Jim stopped crying. From then on, whenever you saw John, you would know that Jim was close by. In fourth grade something happened. Whenever you saw John, you no longer saw Jim.

1. John and Jim are about the same age.
2. John and Jim have been friends for about six years.
3. Jim isn't too bright.
4. John is smarter than Jim.
5. John and Jim had a fight in fourth grade.
6. John made new friends in fourth grade.
7. John was kind to Jim in kindergarten.
8. John and Jim were close friends in the early grades.
9. John and Jim have been friends for about four years.
10. John and Jim knew each other before kindergarten.

Answers (1) true, (2) false, (3) can't tell, (4) can't tell, (5) can't tell, (6) can't tell, (7) true, (8) true, (9) true, (10) can't tell.

Categorizing

Categorizing
A thinking skill involving the ability to classify items into general and specific categories.

The ability to divide items into categories is a very important thinking skill and necessary for concept development (see Chapter 8). As students advance through the grades, they should be developing the skill of categorizing; that is, students should be able to differentiate and group items into more complex categories; they should be able to proceed from more generalized classifications to more specialized classifications.

You should help your students to recognize that every time they put things into groups such as pets, farm animals, wild animals, cities, states, countries, capitals, fruits, vegetables, colors, and so on, they are using the skill of categorizing. When they categorize things, they are classifying things. To be able to classify things, they must know what belongs together and what does not belong together. You can help your students to classify or categorize things into more general or more specific categories. For example, the category of food is more general than the categories of fruits, vegetables, or nuts. The category of animals is more general than the categories of pets, wild animals, or tame animals. The category of pets is less general than the category of animals but more general than the categories of dogs or cats.

The ability to classify or organize information is a skill that usually differentiates a good comprehender from a poor one. As stated earlier in this chapter, it was found that the ability to note the organizational structure of the text, as well as outlining, enhances the quantity and quality of a student's recall. (See "How to Study" in Chapter 9 and "Outlining" in Chapter 10.)

Practice Activities

Here are some exercises you can use with your primary grade level students for practice.

1. *Directions* First read the list of words. Then group them in at least seven different ways.

scarf	watch	shoes	sweater	pants
socks	bracelet	coat	earrings	slip
cap	stockings	gloves	blouse	tights
shirt	vest	slippers	hat	mittens
dress	jeans	gown	skirt	boots

2. *Directions* Read each word. This word has lots of things that belong to its group. Read the words in the word list. Choose a word from the word list that would belong to the group. All words from the word list are used as answers. The first is done for you.

Word List coat, green, circle, milk, Terry, checkers, cat, ten

1. Foods   _____milk_____

2. Colors   _____

3. Clothing   _____

4. Animals   _____

5. Shapes   _____

6. Numbers   _____

7. Games   _____

8. Names   _____

Here is an exercise you can use with your upper intermediate grade level students for practice.

Directions First read the words in each set to see what they have in common; then circle the word in each set that does not belong. You may use the dictionary to look up unfamiliar words.

1. Indiana, Connecticut, Seattle, Maine
2. large, huge, immense, heavy
3. trumpet, bell, bray, chirp
4. devil, warlock, wizard, witch
5. occult, mysterious, weary, secret
6. dachshund, Siamese, poodle, Schnauzer
7. spiders, ticks, flies, scorpions
8. frogs, snakes, turtles, lizards

   9. Albany, Harrisburg, San Francisco, Nashville
   10. stove, coal, oil, wood

Understanding Analogies

Analogies
Relationships
between words or
ideas.

Working with analogies, or word relationships, requires high-level thinking skills. Students must have a good stock of vocabulary and the ability to see relationships. Students who have difficulty in classification will usually have difficulty working with analogies.

Some primary grade level children can begin to be exposed to simple analogies based on relationships with which they are familiar.[46] Analogies are relationships between words or ideas. In order to be able to make the best use of analogies or to complete an analogy statement or proportion, the children must know the meanings of the words and the relationship of the pair of words. For example: *Sad is to happy as good is to* _____. Many primary grade level children know the meanings of *sad* and *happy* and that *sad* is the opposite of *happy;* they would, therefore, be able to complete the analogy statement or proportion with the correct word—*bad.*

Some of the relationships that words may have to one another are similar meanings, opposite meanings, classification, going from particular to general, going from general to particular, degree of intensity, specialized labels, characteristics, cause–effect, effect–cause, function, whole–part, ratio, and many more. The preceding relationships do not have to be memorized. Tell your students that they will gain clues to these from the pairs making up the analogies; that is, the words express the relationship. For example: *"pretty is to beautiful"*—the relationship is degree of intensity (the state of being stronger, greater, or more than); *"hot is to cold"*—the relationship is one of opposites; and *"car is to vehicle"*—the relationship is classification.

Analogy Activities

It would probably be a good idea for you to review the word lists of the presented analogy exercises to determine whether your students are familiar with the vocabulary. You can encourage students to use dictionaries to look up any unfamiliar words.

The analogy activities can be done in small groups or with the entire class orally as well as individually. If children work individually on the analogy activities, it would help to go over the answers together in a group so that interaction and discussion can further enhance vocabulary development.

Special Notes

   1. In the primary grades the term *word relationships* should be used with the students rather than *analogies.* You might want to introduce the term *anal-*

---

[46] See Sister Josephine, C.S.J., "An Analogy Test for Preschool Children," *Education* (December 1965): 235–237.

ogy to some of your highly able upper primary grade level children and intermediate grade level children. Highly able children especially enjoy working with analogies.

2. In introducing some of the relationships that pairs of words can have to one another, you should, of course, use words that are in your student's listening vocabulary. The list of some possible relationships that was presented earlier is presented as an aid for you, the teacher.

Picture Relationships

Primary grade level children can be exposed to analogy activities using pictures. An example of such an activity is shown in Figure 7-6.

Teacher Instructions   Present the picture sets shown in Figure 7-6 to your children. Tell them that the sets of pictures belong together in some way. Each set has

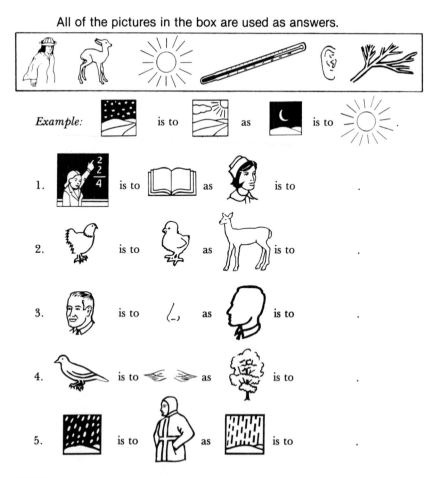

FIGURE 7-6   A picture analogy activity.

a missing picture. Have them look at the first pair of pictures in the set. Tell them to try to figure out how they belong together. Then have them choose a picture from the large box that would *best* complete the second pair in the set. Have them draw a line from the picture in the large box to the empty space. Tell them that all pictures are used as answers. Do the example with the children.

Word Relationships

Upper primary grade level children can be exposed to activities such as the following:

Directions   Here are sets of words that have a certain relationship to one another. Each set has a missing word that you have to supply. Look at the first pair of words. Try to figure out what the relationship is. Then choose a word from the word list that *best* completes the second pair in the set. (All words are used as answers.) The first is done for you.

Word List   sentence, wolf, bed, story, knee, smell.

1. *Sit* is to *chair* as *lie* is to _____*bed*_____.

2. *Mouth* is to *taste* as *nose* is to _____.

3. *Water* is to *shark* as *land* is to _____.

4. *Arm* is to *leg* as *elbow* is to _____.

5. *Sentence* is to *word* as *paragraph* is to _____.

6. *Sentence* is to *paragraph* as *paragraph* is to _____.

Answers   (1) bed, (2) smell, (3) wolf, (4) knee, (5) sentence, (6) story

Completing Analogies

Intermediate grade level children can be exposed to activities such as the following:

Directions   Find the relationship between a pair of words, and then complete each analogy with the best word from the word list. There are more words given in the word list than you need. The first is done for you. You may use the dictionary to look up unfamiliar words.

Word List   hen, male, female, big, bother, assist, water, face, spice, warm, hot, cold, hospital, nurse, ram, animal, drake, fowl, deer, nickel, quarter, self, dollar, another, book, fig, fruit, dessert, grape, meat, solid, food, bandage, mouth, low

1. *Up* is to *down* as *high* is to _____low_____.

2. *Minister* is to *church* as *doctor* is to

_____.

3. *Pretty* is to *beautiful* as *cool* is to _____.

4. *Juice* is to *liquid* as *beef* is to _____.

5. *Mare* is to *horse* as *doe* is to _____.

6. *Chicken* is to *rooster* as *duck* is to _____.

7. *Cent* is to *dime* as *dime* is to _____.

8. *Prune* is to *plum* as *raisin* is to _____.

9. *Car* is to *vehicle* as *pepper* is to _____.

10. *Frighten* is to *scare* as *annoy* is to _____.

11. *Torn* is to *ripped* as *aid* is to _____.

12. *Biography* is to *another* as *autobiography* is to

_____.

13. *Wrist* is to *arm* as *nose* is to _____.

Answers   (1) low, (2) hospital, (3) cold, (4) solid, (5) deer, (6) drake, (7) dollar, (8) grape, (9) spice, (10) bother, (11) assist, (12) self, (13) face.

Finding Inconsistencies

Finding inconsistencies
Finding statements that do not make sense.

Good thinkers are logical; that is, they are able to reason correctly. Finding inconsistencies refers to statements that do not make sense—they are illogical; they are not in accord with the given information.

Good readers are alert readers. You should help your students to recognize that everything that they read is not necessarily true or correct. If they read something that does not make sense, even if it is a textbook written by an authority in the field, they should question it. For example, if in their science book they found the statement "Humans drink about 1,000 quarts of fluid in a week," should they believe it? Reread it. Does it make sense? Of course not. Think about it. Why doesn't it make sense? *Answer:* There are only seven days in a week. Even if someone drank four quarts of liquid a day (which is a large amount), that person would still have had only 28 quarts of fluid. The "1,000" is an obvious error. The author probably meant to say 10 quarts.

Here is another example you can use with your children. Have them read the following statement. Then ask them to underline the word in the sentence that does not make sense.

Sample   For weeks, the hunters tried to trap the lion. Finally, they had the lion cornered. Then the tame lion attacked the hunters.

Answer   *Tame* should be underlined. The writer probably meant to use the word *wild*.

Distinguishing between Fact and Opinion

Opinions
Based on attitudes or feelings; they can vary from person to person, but cannot be conclusively proved right or wrong.

Fact
Something that exists and can be proved true.

The ability to differentiate between facts and opinions is a very important skill that students need to develop. Often opinions are presented as though they are facts (see Figure 7-7). Opinions are not facts. They are based on attitudes or feelings. Opinions can vary from individual to individual; they cannot be conclusively proved right or wrong. Facts, on the other hand, do not change from person to person. Facts are things that exist and can be proved true. *Examples* of facts: Albany is the capital of New York. Twelve inches equals a foot. A meter equals 39.37 inches. *Examples of opinions:* That is a pretty dress. He is very smart. It's important to visit museums.

It is important to help your students as early as possible to determine whether information is factual or not. You can present a picture to your children and ask them if they like it. After a number of children have given their opinions, discuss with them how different children had different feelings about the picture. Tell them that they were giving their opinions about the picture, and opinions may change from person to person. Next ask them to tell you their names. Call on a few children to name the same person in the class. Discuss with them how everyone agreed on the person's name. Tell them that it's a fact that Jennifer

© 1971 United Feature Syndicate, Inc.

Reprinted by permission of UFS, Inc.

FIGURE 7-7 Charlie Brown is being dogmatic. On matters of opinion, you can't be sure.

Smith's name is Jennifer Smith. Tell them that something that is a fact does not change from person to person. Facts can be proved true. Present the following statements to them. Ask them which is an opinion and which is a fact.

Statements

Jennifer is pretty. (opinion)
Arithmetic is a school subject. (true)
The United States of America is a country. (true)
Baseball is fun. (opinion)
Ice cream tastes good. (opinion)

Help your students to understand that not everyone thinks that Jennifer is pretty, not everyone likes baseball, and not everyone likes the taste of ice cream.

Practice Activities

1. Here is an example of a fact or opinion activity that you could use with your primary grade children.

Directions   Read each sentence *carefully*. Figure out if the statement is true or if the statement is an opinion. Remember that if it's an opinion, then it can change from person to person. If the statement is true, it can't change. In front of each sentence, put the letter *O* if it's an opinion. Put the letter *F* if it's a fact.

_____ **1.** Television is fun to watch.

_____ **2.** Game shows are better than talk shows.

_____ **3.** A person can't fly like a bird.

_____ **4.** Jogging is good for you.

_____ **5.** Air is needed to live.

Answers   (1) O, (2) O, (3) F, (4) O, (5) F.

2. Here is an example of a fact or opinion activity that you can use with intermediate grade level students.

Directions   Read each sentence *carefully*. Determine whether the sentence is expressing a fact or an opinion. In front of each sentence put the letter *F* if it's a fact or the letter *O* if it's an opinion. (Remember that facts do not change from person to person as opinions do.)

_____ **1.** A citrus fruit has more Vitamin C than a chocolate bar.

_____ **2.** Reading is better than watching television.

_____ **3.** An opinion is what someone believes or the way someone

feels.

_____   **4.** Fat people are all cheerful.

_____   **5.** History tells us about past events.

_____   **6.** A hippopotamus has very thick skin.

_____   **7.** Soda is better than water.

_____   **8.** Not all birds can fly.

_____   **9.** The museum is a good place to visit.

_____   **10.** You can depend on his word.

Answers   (1) F, (2) O, (3) F, (4) O, (5) F, (6) F, (7) O, (8) F, (9) O, (10) O.

Detecting Propaganda Techniques and Bias

Students should be helped to detect the presence of propaganda or bias in what they read.

Propaganda
Any systematic, widespread, deliberate indoctrination or plan for indoctrination.

Propaganda is defined as *any systematic, widespread, deliberate indoctrination* (the act of causing one to be impressed and eventually filled with some view) *or plan for indoctrination.* The term *propaganda* connotes deception or distortion. In other words, people who use propaganda are trying to influence individuals by using deceptive methods.

Bias
A mental leaning, a partiality, a prejudice, or a slanting of something.

Bias refers to a *mental leaning, a partiality, a prejudice,* or a *slanting of something.*

From the two definitions, you can see that persons interested in propagandizing something have a certain bias. They use propaganda techniques to distort information to indoctrinate people with their own views or biases.

1. *Name calling:* Accusing or denouncing an individual by using a widely disapproved label such as Red, Fascist, miser, reactionary, radical, and so on.
2. *Glittering generalities:* Seeking acceptance of ideas by resorting to terms generally accepted, such as freedom, American, Christian, red-blooded, democratic, businesslike, and so on.
3. *Bandwagon:* Seeking acceptance through appealing to pluralities. For example, an advertisement states: *"Most* people prefer Dazzles. They know what's good! Do you?" In the "bandwagon" approach, you go along because everyone else is doing so.
4. *Card stacking:* Seeking acceptance by presenting or building on half-truths. Only favorable facts are presented, whereas anything unfavorable is deliberately omitted, and vice versa.
5. *Transfer:* Seeking acceptance by citing respected sources of authority, prestige, or reverence such as the home, the Constitution, the flag, the Church, and so on, in such a way as to make it appear that they approve the proposal. For example, in an advertisement, it is stated: "Our forefathers ate

hearty breakfasts. Our country is built on strength. Our forefathers would want you to be strong. Eat Product X for strength. Product X will give you a hearty breakfast."

6. *Plain folks:* Seeking acceptance through establishing someone as "just one of the boys." *Example:* A presidential candidate is photographed milking cows, kissing babies, wearing work clothes, and so on.

7. *Testimonial:* Seeking acceptance by using testimonials from famous people to build confidence in a product. For example, in TV commercials, actors, athletes, and famous personalities are used to endorse a product.

Practice Activity

Here is a sample activity for upper elementary grade level children on detecting propaganda techniques.

Directions   Read each of the following sentences *carefully.* Each sentence uses a propaganda technique. After reading each sentence, determine what propaganda technique is being used. Put your answer in the space provided.

1. Don't be the last kid on your block to get Frizzles.

   _____

2. Chocos are good for you. Eat them with a glass of milk, and you'll get all the nourishment you need for breakfast. _____

3. A well-known actor says, "I've been driving an FBA car for some time, and I'm happy with it. I wouldn't drive any other car." _____

4. A political candidate says to a group of people, "Folks, it's good to be here with you. There's nothing I enjoy better than visiting with you hard-working people. I know what it's like because I've worked hard all my life just like you."

   _____

5. Be in. Wear Jeano's jeans. _____

6. I wouldn't listen to a stooge like him. _____

7. She's so democratic. _____

8. The Constitution states that everyone has a right to protect himself or herself. Join our club. We believe in self-protection, too.

   _____

9. This is a fantastic deal! For only a few cents down and a dollar a month, you can own this Brazzle. _____

10. Only troublemakers would talk that way. _____

Answers   (1) bandwagon, (2) card stacking, (3) testimonial, (4) plain folks, (5) bandwagon, (6) name calling, (7) glittering generalities, (8) transfer, (9) card stacking, (10) name calling

Using Divergent Thinking

Divergent thinking
The many different ways to solve problems or to look at things.

Divergent thinking has to do with the many different ways of looking at things. Good divergent thinkers are able to look beyond the obvious and come up with new or alternate solutions. Students should be encouraged to try to solve problems in many different ways and try to be intelligent risk-takers or make educated guesses.

You should help your students to recognize that divergent thinking requires that they go beyond the obvious and that they look for alternate ways to solve problems. In this chapter, examples of questions to stimulate divergent thinking are given. An activity that would help children to be more divergent follows. Ask your students to state the many different uses of a brick.

Answers

A brick can be used to build a wall.
A brick can be used as a weapon.
A brick can be used as a bed warmer.
A brick can be used to write with.
A brick can be carved out and used as an ashtray.
A brick can be used as a paperweight.
And so on . . .

If they stated only uses that included building, they were not being very divergent. To be divergent, they had to go beyond the obvious uses of a brick.

Practice Activities

1. Here is an example of a divergent thinking activity that could be used with primary grade level children:

Directions   Read the story. Answer the questions on it.

Zeres lives in the forest. He is a troll. Only animals in the forest can see trolls. Forest trolls usually come out at night and sleep during the day. Zeres is a special kind of troll. He likes to play with children. Children are not supposed to be able to see trolls. No humans are supposed to be able to see trolls. This, however, does not stop Zeres. Every day when the other trolls are asleep, Zeres sneaks out. He skips through the forest in search of children. When he sees a child, he claps his hands, jumps up and down three times, and screams with glee. The children Zeres meets can see him. They like to play with Zeres. He knows lots of places. Sometimes they go to the tops of mountains. Sometimes they go to deserts. Sometimes they go on a ship. Sometimes they fly to another land. The children love Zeres. He is their best friend.

1. Describe Zeres. Tell what you think he looks like.
2. Make up an adventure that Zeres has with some children.

2. Here is an activity that can be used with intermediate grade level children:

Directions   Read the story. Answer the questions on it.

"If I can only get through the first day, I'll be fine," thought Terry. "This is my fifth school in four years. We never seem to stay long enough for me to make friends. I wonder what it would be like to be a kid who has a normal home life? Well, I'll probably never know. I better pull myself together and get going. If I'm late I'll be even more conspicuous. Since it's the beginning of the term, I may be able to slip into the classroom and become invisible. I've been able to do that for so long now that I sometimes feel that maybe I am invisible. I always seem to be looking in and watching others. Sometimes I feel like yelling, 'Hey, everybody look at me, look at me; I'm alive! I'm not invisible!' I know I won't do that. Boy, my hands are so cold and my heart is racing so fast—well, here goes. I wish myself luck! Who knows, maybe it'll turn out all right."

1. What do you think is Terry's problem?
2. Describe what you think will happen to Terry at school.

Diagnostic Checklist for Selected Reading Comprehension Skills

Student's Name: _____

Grade: _____

Teacher: _____

	Yes	No	Sometimes
1. The student is able to state the meaning of a word in context.			
2. The student is able to give the meaning of a phrase or a clause in a sentence.			
3. The student is able to give variations of meanings for homographs (words spelled the same but with more than one meaning—for example, *train, mean, saw, sole,* and so on).			

Diagnostic Checklist *Continued*

	Yes	No	Sometimes
4. The student is able to give the meaning of a sentence in a paragraph.			
5. The student is able to recall information that is explicitly stated in the passage. (literal questions)			
6. The student is able to state the main idea of a paragraph.			
7. The student is able to state details to support the main idea of a paragraph.			
8. The student is able to group items that belong together.			
9. The student is able to answer a question that requires "reading between the lines."			
10. The student is able to draw a conclusion from what is read.			
11. The student can complete analogy proportions.			
12. The student can hypothesize the author's purpose for writing the selection.			
13. The student can differentiate between fact and opinion.			
14. The student can differentiate between fantasy and reality.			
15. The student can detect bias in a story.			
16. The student can detect various propaganda tactics that are used in a story.			
17. The student can go beyond the text to come up with alternate solutions or ways to end a story or solve a problem in the selection.			
18. The student shows that he or she enjoys reading by voluntarily choosing to read.			

Graphic Summary of Chapter

On the following page is a graphic summary of Chapter 7. If you have read the chapter, this graphic illustration should help you remember its main points. Under or beside each heading, you might want to jot down some of the information you recall, as well as some of the key concepts in this chapter. This can act as a good review. You can then check your key concepts against those that follow the graphic summary.

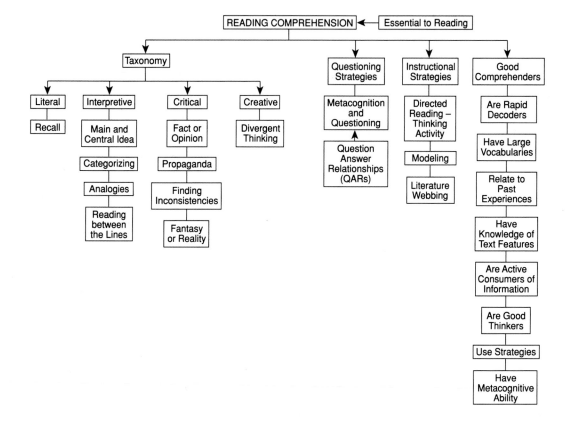

Key Concepts

- Comprehension is a construct that cannot be directly observed or measured.
- Reading comprehension is a complex intellectual process.
- Good comprehenders are active consumers of information.
- Good comprehenders are able to relate present information and experiences to past information and experiences.
- Comprehension involves various levels of thinking.
- The literal, interpretive, critical, and creative comprehension skills are a hierarchy of reading/thinking skills ranging from lowest to highest.
- Literal thinking comprehension skills are based on recall.
- Interpretive reading comprehension skills are based on information that is not directly stated.
- Critical reading comprehension skills are based on making a personal judgment on the truthfulness, accuracy, and value of something.
- The creative reading comprehension skills are based on divergent thinking.
- Divergent thinking deals with going beyond the obvious.

- Teachers must learn to ask questions that go beyond the literal level.
- Strategies such as Question Answer Relationships (QARs) help students gain insight into how they go about reading text and answering questions.
- Teachers should provide direct instruction to help their students gain understanding.
- Teachers should use various methods and strategies to help students gain understanding of what they are reading.
- Literature webbing is a technique that can guide teachers in using predictable books with children.
- Main idea is an essential skill that is not easy to acquire.

Suggestions for Thought Questions and Activities

1. State the four levels of comprehension presented in this chapter. State one skill for each level, and then prepare an activity for each skill at each level (primary grades).
2. Do the same as above for intermediate grades.
3. You have just been appointed to a special reading curriculum committee at your school. The committee is charged with developing a dynamic reading comprehension program. What suggestions would you make to the committee on how to proceed?
4. Prepare some activities for primary grade level students in the area of categorizing.
5. Prepare some activities for intermediate grade level students in the area of propaganda.
6. Explain the relationship between thinking and comprehension.
7. You have been appointed to a reading committee to help to revamp the primary grade level reading comprehension program. There is a person on the committee who feels that primary grade level children are too young to be exposed to skills such as categorizing and analogies. You hold an opposing view. How do you convince this person? What arguments do you use?
8. Prepare a lesson using one of the strategies presented in this chapter. Videotape your lesson and then critique it.
9. Observe a teacher teaching a reading comprehension lesson. Note the strategies she or he uses to help students understand what they are reading.

Selected Bibliography

Afflerbach, Peter P. "The Influence of Prior Knowledge on Expert Readers' Main Idea Construction Strategies." *Reading Research Quarterly* 25 (Winter 1990): 31–46.
Baumann, James F., ed. *Teaching Main Idea Comprehension,* Newark, Del.: International Reading Association, 1986.
Paris, Scott G., Barbara A. Wasik, and Julianne G. Turner. "The Development of Strategic

Readers." In *Handbook of Reading Research,* Vol. II, Rebecca Barr, Michael L. Kamil, Peter Mosenthal, and P. David Pearson, eds. New York: Longman, 1991, pp. 609–640.

Pearson, David P., and Linda Fielding. "Comprehension Instruction." In *Handbook of Reading Research,* Vol. II, Rebecca Barr, Michael L. Kamil, Peter Mosenthal, and P. David Pearson, eds. New York: Longman, 1991, pp. 815–860.

Stauffer, Russell. *Teaching Reading as a Thinking Process.* New York: Harper & Row, 1969.

Wendler, David, S. Jay Samuels, and Vienna Moore. "The Comprehension Instruction of Award Winning Teachers, Teachers with Master's Degrees and Other Teachers." *Reading Research Quarterly* 24 (Fall 1989): 382–397.

8

Vocabulary Expansion

SCENARIO: MRS. HILL TEACHES VOCABULARY AGGRESSIVELY

Mrs. Hill teaches in a large inner-city school, a school that has special drills to teach children how to slither like a snake to survive a gang attack of bullets. Mrs. Hill teaches here from choice, much to the surprise and often the dismay of her family and friends.

In the school where Mrs. Hill teaches, fourth grade is a transitional one for many children — it's the grade level at which many children seem to cease being children. Many have already lost their innocence, and this loss is most noticeable in their eyes and in the way they walk and talk. It's very sad, but Mrs. Hill knows from personal experience that feeling sorry doesn't help.

Mrs. Hill recognizes that the only way these children will be able to survive and make it in the economic world is to gain the best education they possibly can. She knows, too, that one of the children's major lacks is a good vocabulary. This is not surprising considering that many of these children come from one-parent homes where there are many siblings and where books are noticeably missing. Mrs. Hill has been so successful with her students' progress that a well-known magazine published a story explaining how she makes a difference.

She explained to the reporter that good vocabulary and good reading go hand in hand. Unless readers know the meaning of words, they will have difficulty in understanding what they are reading. She stressed that just knowing the meanings of the words will not ensure that individuals will be able to state the meanings of sentences, nor does knowing the meanings of sentences ensure that readers can give the meanings of whole paragraphs, and so forth. Not knowing the meanings of words, however, considerably lessens the individual's chances of being able to read well. Without an understanding of words, comprehension is impossible.

Mrs. Hill told the reporter that on the basis of what she knows about the importance of having a good vocabulary, she has a very aggressive reading and vocabulary program in her class. She said that she believes strongly that many of her students' problems stem from lack of vocabulary and, consequently, of the concepts they need to be successful in school. As children advance in their concept development, their vocabulary must also advance because the two are interrelated. In other words, children who are deficient in vocabulary will

237

usually be deficient in concept development. Earlier studies have suggested that "vocabulary is a key variable in reading comprehension and is a major feature of most tests of academic aptitude."[1] Investigators continue to confirm earlier findings: "Numerous researchers have noted that poor readers have smaller vocabularies than good readers. Indeed, vocabulary knowledge is one of the best single predictors of reading comprehension."[2]

Mrs. Hill told the reporter that most teachers are aware of the importance of building sight vocabulary and word attack skills, and these are a large part of the beginning reading program. However, the development of a larger meaning vocabulary is often neglected, especially, she said, in inner-city schools. Often teachers in inner-city schools spend more time on the decoding aspect of word recognition than on building word meanings.

Some teachers may feel that students will learn the words incidentally if they are exposed to them once or twice. Mrs. Hill does not believe this is true. Therefore, she takes a very aggressive approach to teaching vocabulary. This aggressive approach incorporates direct teaching of vocabulary with the use of many motivating techniques to attract her students' attention and direct them to the desired goals.

This chapter should give you some insights into the kinds of things that Mrs. Hill does to help her students expand their vocabulary. In addition, readers of this text will also learn about the techniques and strategies that all teachers can use to help both their primary and intermediate grade level students to expand their vocabulary.

KEY QUESTIONS

After you finish reading this chapter, you should be able to answer the following questions:

1. How is concept development related to language and reading?
2. What is a concept?
3. How are concepts acquired?
4. What should teachers know about vocabulary development and individual differences?
5. What is a vocabulary consciousness?
6. What is the teacher's role in vocabulary development?
7. Which vocabulary words should teachers choose for study?

[1] Walter M. MacGinitie, "Language Development," in *Encyclopedia of Educational Research*, 4th ed. (London: Collier-Macmillan, 1969), p. 693.

[2] Meredyth Daneman, "Individual Differences in Reading Skills," in *Handbook of Reading Research*, Vol. II, Rebecca Barr, Michael L. Kamil, Peter Mosenthal, and P. David Pearson, eds. (New York: Longman, 1991), p. 524.

8. What is the relationship of semantic mapping to vocabulary development?
9. What are the levels of word meaning knowledge?
10. What are some examples of context clues that students should know about?
11. How does knowledge of context clues help students figure out homographs and other words?
12. What is the connotative meaning of words?
13. What is the role of the dictionary in vocabulary expansion?
14. How can knowledge of word parts help students expand their vocabulary?
15. What is the role of vocabulary development in a reading lesson?

KEY TERMS IN CHAPTER

You should pay special attention to the following key terms:

accommodation	equilibrium
affixes	example
antonyms	homographs
assimilation	homonyms
cognitive development	homophones
combining forms	prefix
comparison	root
compound word	schemata
concept	semantic clue
connotative meaning	semantic mapping (graphic organizer)
context clue	suffix
contrast	synonyms
denotative meaning	syntax
derivatives	vocabulary consciousness

Language Development, Concept Development, and Reading

Language development depends on the interrelationships of such factors as intelligence, home environment, cultural differences, gender differences, and so on. The factors that influence language development also influence concept development, and students who are more advanced in language development also tend to be better readers than those who are not as advanced. For example, in Chapter 2 (see "Individual Differences: Two Case Studies") a scenario presents a student who has had many advantages because of her home environment, and you probably had little difficulty making predictions about how well you feel she would do in school. Her family reads, so she reads. The more she reads, the better reader she becomes; the better reader she becomes, the more information she gains; the more information she acquires, the better prepared she is for reading her textbooks, and so on. Yes, it appears that success breeds success. The importance of a student's home background in determining school success is enormous. However, teachers cannot change their students' home environment or lift them from one socioeconomic class to another.

Teachers, nevertheless, must be able to help all students, regardless of socioeconomic class, attain the concepts they need in order to gain the most from their textbooks. It's not an easy task, but it can be done. To accomplish this goal, teachers must know as much as possible about how concepts are acquired, as well as what a concept is.

What Is a Concept?

Read the following statements. Do they sound familiar? They should, because teachers every day in almost every classroom probably make statements similar to these:

"We're working with the concept of _____."

"Students don't understand the concept of _____."

"Jerome's concept on _____ is erroneous."

"I'm teaching the concept of _____."

Teachers use the term *concept* very often, but is it understood? Unless it is, teachers would usually have difficulty helping students correct or acquire certain concepts.

Is *Julia Smith* a concept? Is *animal* a concept? Is *my pet canary, Sheshe,* a concept? Is *New York* a concept? Is *war* a concept? What about *peace?* (If you said *animal, war,* and *peace* are concepts, you are correct.) Stop reading for a moment, and state how you would define *concept.*

Concept
A group of stimuli with common characteristcs.

A concept is a group of stimuli with common characteristics. These stimuli may be persons, objects, or events. Terms such as *peace, game, book, poem, human, animal, pet, teacher, coach,* and so forth are concepts. All these concepts refer to classes or categories of stimuli. Particular stimuli, such as Ms. Smith; Mr. Johnson; the Korean War; Miss Green, the lawyer; Stephen King, the writer; the Rose Bowl; and Emily Dickinson's poem "There Is No Frigate Like a Book" are not concepts.

Concepts are needed to reduce the complexity of the world. When children learn that their shaggy pets are called dogs, they tend to label all other similar four-footed animals as "dogs." This is because young children overgeneralize: They tend to group all animals together, and have not yet perceived the differences between and among various animals. Unless children learn to discern differences, the class of words that they deal with will become exceptionally unwieldy and unmanageable. However, if children group each object in a class by itself, this too will bring about difficulties in coping with environmental stimuli because it is such an unwieldy method (see Figure 8-1).

Piaget and Concept Development

Cognitive development
Refers to development of thinking.

Concept development is closely related to cognitive (thinking) development. The renowned Swiss psychologist Jean Piaget has written on children's cognitive development in terms of their ability to organize (which requires conceptualization), classify, and adapt to their environments.

Schemata
These structured designs are the cognitive arrangements by which the mind is able to categorize incoming stimuli.

According to Piaget,[3] the mind is capable of intellectual exercise because of its ability to categorize incoming stimuli adequately. *Schemata* (structured designs) are the cognitive arrangements by which this takes place. As children develop and take in more and more information, it is necessary to have some way to categorize all the new information. This is done by means of schemata, and, as children develop, their ability to categorize grows, too. That is, children should be able to differentiate, to become less dependent on sensory stimuli, and to gain more and more complex schemata. Children should be able to categorize a cat as distinct from a mouse or a rabbit. They should be able to group *cat, dog,* and *cow* together as animals. Piaget calls the processes that bring about these changes in children's thinking *assimilation* and *accommodation*.

Assimilation
A continuous process that helps the individual to integrate new incoming stimuli to existing concepts— Piaget's cognitive development.

Assimilation does not change an individual's concept but allows it to grow. It is a continuous process that helps the individual to integrate new, incoming stimuli into existing schemata or concepts. For example, when children tend to label all similar four-footed animals as dogs, the children are assimilating. They have assimilated all four-footed animals into their existing schemata.

If the child meets stimuli that cannot fit into the existing schema, then the

FIGMENTS   **BY DALE HALE**

Reprinted by permission of Dale Hale.

FIGURE 8-1 Language development and concept development are closely related. Not understanding that words may have different meanings, the child incorrectly interprets adult speech.

[3] Jean Piaget, *The Origins of Intelligence in Children* (New York: International Universities Press, 1952).

Accommodation
The individual's developing of new categories rather than integrating them into existing ones—Piaget's cognitive development.

alternative is either to construct a new category or to change the existing category. When a new schema or concept is developed or when an existing schema is changed, this is called accommodation.

Although both assimilation and accommodation are important processes that the child must attain in order to develop adequate cognition, a balance between the two processes is necessary. If children overassimilate, they will have categories that are too large to handle. Similarly, if they overaccommodate, they will have too many categories, as we have already seen. Piaget calls the balance between the two *equilibrium.* A person having equilibrium would be able to see similarities between stimuli and thus properly assimilate them and would also be able to determine when new schemata are needed for adequate accommodation of a surplus of categories.

Equilibrium
According to Piaget, a balance between assimilation and accomodation in cognitive development.

Instructional Implications

Concepts are necessary to help students acquire increasing amounts of knowledge. For example, in school, as one proceeds through the grades, learning becomes more abstract and is expressed in words, using verbal stimuli as labels for concepts. Many teachers take for granted that those spoken concept labels are understood by their students, but this is not always so. Many times these concepts are learned either incompletely or incorrectly. Here is an example that illustrates incomplete concepts for *tourist* and *immigrant:*[4]

All tourists may be obviously American whereas all immigrants may be obviously Mexican. The tourists may be well dressed, the immigrants poorly dressed, and so on. If the natural environment is like a grand concept-formation experiment, it may take a child a long time to attain the concepts *tourist* and *immigrant;* indeed, the environment may not be as informative as the usual experimenter since the child may not always be informed, or reliably informed, as to the correctness of his guesses. No wonder a child might form the concept that a tourist is a well-dressed person who drives a station wagon with out-of-state license plates!

When children come to school, the teacher must assess their concept-development level, then help them to add the attributes necessary and relevant for the development of particular concepts and to delete all those concepts that are faulty or irrelevant.

The Acquisition of Concepts

The first step in acquiring concepts concerns vocabulary. Teachers must help their students to expand vocabulary and to be more precise in their use of language so that they can distinguish subtle differences in word meanings (see Fig-

[4] John Carroll, "Words, Meanings and Concepts" in *Thought & Language: Language and Reading,* Maryanne Wolf et al., eds. (Cambridge, Mass.: *Harvard Educational Review,* 1980), p. 42.

Berry's World

"I'm collecting for those more than 100 poor helpless <u>lame ducks</u> in Washington that I heard about."

Reprinted by permission of NEA, Inc.

FIGURE 8-2   This child needs help in concept development.

ure 8-2). Vocabulary development, as already stated, is closely related to concept development because concepts are based on word meanings. Without vocabulary, there would be no concepts because there would be no basis for the development of concepts.

The second step in acquiring concepts involves reading to gather data—that is, specific information about the concept to be learned. While reading, students must notice the way that the specific information is related—that is, how it is organized. This is important because it enables students to categorize those items that belong together and those that do not. Concepts are formed when the data are organized into categories. For more information on concept development, see the sections on outlining in Chapter 10 and the section on categorizing in Chapter 7.

Vocabulary Development and Individual Differences

For a vocabulary program to be successful, teachers must recognize that individual differences exist with respect to the number and the kinds of words their students possess. For example, when kindergarten and first-grade children come to school, the words in their listening vocabulary will vary depending on their home environment. Some children come to school with a rich and varied vocabulary, whereas others have a more limited and narrower vocabulary. Some children may come to school with a rich and varied vocabulary that they use with their peers and at home, but it may not be one that is useful to them in school. For example, some children may possess a large lexicon of street vocabulary and expressions, while others may speak a dialect of English that contains its own special expressions and vocabulary (see Figure 8-3).

When children first come to school, teachers should recognize that these young children's listening vocabulary is larger than their speaking vocabulary and obviously larger than their reading and writing vocabularies. However, as children go through the grades, it is possible for a student's reading vocabulary to include words that may not be in his or her listening vocabulary; that is, the student may have gained the meaning of the word from context clues rather than from having heard it. As a result, the student may be able to "read" the word, but he or she may not be able to pronounce it. It seems apparent, then, that those students who are good readers and who read frequently will have a larger vocabulary than those who do not spend time reading (see Figure 8-4).

Teachers can learn a great deal about students' reading habits by observing the vocabulary they use in writing. Some students can pronounce a word cor-

Reprinted by permission of UFS, Inc.

FIGURE 8-3   Some children come to school with a rich lexicon of "street" words.

Reprinted by permission of UFS, Inc.

FIGURE 8-4 Good writing is hard work; however, those people who read a lot have a larger pool of words from which to choose.

rectly but still use it incorrectly. Others are unable to pronounce a word correctly but can use it correctly in writing. The latter, as already stated, have acquired their vocabulary through reading, and they may greatly surprise their teachers with their written productions.

Although most persons' speaking vocabulary tends to be more limited than their reading or writing vocabularies, there are some students who can express themselves better orally. Teachers should recognize that not all students who are verbal are good writers, and, conversely, not all good writers are good orators.

In helping children to expand their vocabularies, teachers will need to assess their students' stock of words so that they can build a program based on their needs. Students who have a good vocabulary, who are curious about words, and who are interested in increasing their stock of words will need a program different from those students who are weak in vocabulary and who rely primarily on overworked words or clichés. The former group of students has developed a vocabulary consciousness, whereas the latter has not.

Vocabulary Consciousness

Vocabulary consciousness
An awareness that words may have different meanings based on their context and a desire to increase one's vocabulary.

When students recognize the power of words and their ability to have different meanings based on surrounding words, they are building a vocabulary consciousness. This vocabulary consciousness grows and matures when students independently search out word meanings. Teachers can help awaken and advance this awareness in students by helping them acquire tools in addition to the dictionary to expand their vocabulary.

Vocabulary consciousness grows when students do the following:

1. Become aware of words they do not know.
2. Have a desire to unlock the meanings of unfamiliar words.
3. Become interested in gaining insight into the strategies for recognizing words and for expanding vocabulary.
4. Try to determine the meaning of words from the context and from their knowledge of word parts.
5. Learn the most used combining forms.
6. Jot down words they do not know and look them up later in the dictionary.
7. Keep a notebook handy to write down words they have missed in their vocabulary exercises.
8. Learn to break down words into word parts to learn their meanings.
9. Maintain interest in wanting to expand their vocabulary.

The Teacher's Role in Vocabulary Development

Teachers need to help students recognize how knowledge of word meanings is essential for precision and clarity in language. Also, they need to help their students gain strategies for vocabulary expansion. Several methods exist. One way for a teacher to show students that he or she feels vocabulary study is important is to devote time to it. Another is to be a good role model—that is, to use a good vocabulary oneself. For example, when a teacher is presenting information, discussing something, or merely conversing with students, he or she could use an unfamiliar word and pair this word with a synonym. If students hear the word often enough, many will get its meaning. Another tactic teachers can use is to challenge students to use more descriptive words in their writing and in their oral reports. One of the most important roles of the teacher in vocabulary development is, of course, to expose the children to lots of books. A good literature program is an excellent way to help children expand their vocabulary. (We have already discussed this in other chapters; more will be said about this later in the chapter, as well as in other chapters.)

In addition, it is important that teachers, rather than relying only on incidental methods, *directly* teach students strategies for developing their vocabulary.

Teachers and students should plan to set aside time during the week for vocabulary study. (More will be said about this in upcoming sections in this chapter.)

Acquainting Students with Vocabulary Aids in Textbooks

Teachers should help acquaint students with the many aids that textbook writers provide for their readers. At the beginning of the term teachers should spend time with students to discuss the various techniques used in their textbooks to help students acquire vocabulary; nothing should be taken for granted. Most textbook writers use a combination of aids such as the following: context clues, marginal notes, footnotes, parenthetical explanations, illustrations, glossaries, pronunciation keys, word lists, italicized words, bold print, and so on. Teachers should familiarize students with each of the aids to make sure that students can use them effectively.

Choosing Vocabulary Words for Study

Teacher judgment plays an essential role in determining which words will be selected for special emphasis, as well as the number of words, the kind, and the method of presentation. Teachers should choose for study those words that students will need to gain key concepts in the areas that they are studying. Also, they should present students with the most common combining forms; that is, the combining forms from which a great number of words are derived. It is just not possible to state specifically all those words that students at each grade level will need because of the individual differences of the students. Using a number of techniques, teachers will have to assess the vocabulary ability of students to determine the type of vocabulary program they should present as well as the type of words their students need.

One technique a teacher can use is word lists containing those words that persons at various levels will meet most frequently in reading and also will require in writing. Disadvantages exist, however. Word lists are usually given to assess students' word-recognition vocabularies, and these require individual administration, a process that is quite time consuming. Also, it is possible for a student to be able to pronounce a word correctly because he or she has excellent word-analysis skills but not know its meaning. Conversely, a student may not be able to pronounce the word but may know its meaning when it is said aloud. Another problem with word lists is determining which ones to use.[5]

Written vocabulary tests are probably more effective than word lists because they are not as time consuming, and they give teachers a good gauge of a student's meaning vocabulary. Teachers need to recognize, however, that a stu-

---

[5] See Mary Monteith, "A Whole Word List Catalog," *Reading Teacher* 29 (May 1976): 844–846.

dent who has decoding problems will obviously have difficulty taking the vocabulary test. Again, it is possible that the student may know the meaning of the word when it is said aloud but not be able to figure out the pronunciation of the written word. Such students will need help in building their decoding skills rather than in building a meaning vocabulary. This point is being stressed so that language arts teachers will recognize that differences exist between a student's listening and reading vocabularies, and that a good vocabulary expansion program takes these factors into account.

A good technique that teachers could use in choosing words for vocabulary study is to peruse their students' reading assignments to select all those words that they feel are necessary for students to understand what they are reading. Even if these words are defined in their books, it would be a good idea for the teacher to present these words before their students read them in print. If students have met a number of key words beforehand, they will be reinforced when they meet the words in their reading, and this recognition will help to improve their reading comprehension. Teachers should especially be on the lookout for words with multiple meanings that are used frequently in everyday language because such words can cause difficulty for students.

Vocabulary Development in the Reading Lesson

Vocabulary development is an exceedingly important part of most reading lessons regardless of the approach or program teachers use in their classrooms. At the beginning of the reading lesson, teachers usually prepare students for what they are going to read by presenting the new words to them and reviewing some previously learned words.

The techniques that the latest literature-based basal reader series use to develop concepts and present their vocabulary do not vary much from the strategies of teachers who use trade books. Here are some of the strategies good teachers employ:

1. They develop concepts by relating present information to past information and by building on students' knowledge base to help them gain topic information.
2. They present each new word in the context of a sentence related to the material they are reading and challenge students to figure out the meaning using context clues and/or word parts (see the sections on context clues and word parts in this chapter).
3. They use questioning strategies that challenge students to demonstrate they understand the meanings of the words and how they are used. For example, the teacher could ask how certain words are alike, or which vocabulary words refer to a specific job, person, and so on. (See the sample lesson from a language-based basal reader in the "Basal Reader Programs" section of Chapter 11 for an example of the vocabulary strategies used in its series to present new words to students.)

Vocabulary Development and Semantic Mapping
(Graphic Organizer)

Semantic mapping (graphic organizer)
A graphic representation used to illustrate concepts and relationships among concepts such as classes, properties, and examples.

Semantic mapping is a technique that is becoming more and more popular because it seems to help students gain the concepts they need to comprehend their reading material better. Semantic mapping stresses word meanings and categorizing—two major elements for concept development. (See "The Acquisition of Concepts" earlier in this chapter.)

There is no one set pattern for semantic mapping; however, a few steps are usually followed. First, the teacher chooses a word or topic that is germane to what the students are reading about or studying. The word is put in a central position on the chalkboard. Next the children are asked to brainstorm as many words as they can think of that are related to the word on the board. The children's words are put on the board in categories. Then the teacher asks the students to work by themselves and write on a sheet of paper as many words as they can generate that are related to the central word. The teacher also suggests that they group their words. The teacher then encourages the students to share their lists with the class. As the children do this, the teacher writes the words in categories on the chalkboard. (This procedure does not usually take too long because there are generally many duplications.) In addition, the teacher adds words to the list.

After all the words are recorded on the chalkboard, the teacher asks the children to suggest labels for the various groups of words on the board. Finally, the teacher and children discuss the listed words and how they are labeled, paying special attention to all new words.[6]

Here is a scenario that illustrates how one teacher uses semantic mapping in her first-grade class.

Mrs. Smith's class will begin a new unit on various types of animals. She has broken the unit into a number of manageable parts and has perused the children's textbook, as well as some other materials they will be reading. From the readings, she has chosen a few terms related to the topic and based on the level and needs of her students. One of the terms she has chosen is *farm animals*. She would like to determine the background information that her students have on this concept. (She knows that relating past information or experiences to present information or experiences is necessary for comprehension.) She does not want to take anything for granted. As she would like them to write stories about farm animals, a semantic mapping exercise would be very helpful.

Mrs. Smith explains to the children that before they begin the new unit, she would like to go over some key words with them. She puts FARM ANIMALS in upper-case letters in the center of the board and asks the children to state all the words that they can think of related to farm animals.

6 Adapted from Dale D. Johnson, Susan P. Pittleman, and Joan E. Heimlich, "Semantic Mapping," *The Reading Teacher* 39 (April 1986): 780.

Mrs. Smith writes the words in categories on the board as the children state them. Here is what the chalkboard looks like at this point:

stable	helpful
coop	friendly
	noisy
	cute

FARM ANIMALS

seeds	horse	chicken
hay	cow	duck
grain	pig	

Next, the children are told to list on a sheet of paper any other words they can think of related to farm animals and to group the words so that those things that belong together are together. (The children have worked with categorizing before.)

After a while, Mrs. Smith asks the children to share their lists and then to add labels to the lists of words on the board. A finished semantic map is shown in Figure 8-5.

Mrs. Smith and her students discuss the words and how they are grouped. She pays particular attention to the words she added and any other she feels some children may not know. They also discuss how the words can be categorized in a number of different ways. In addition, the teacher makes sure the children note that the words *pet, stable,* and *pen* have different meanings based on their position in the sentence. (See also "Semantic Mapping (Graphic Organizer) and Notetaking" in Chapter 10.)

Levels of Word Meaning Knowledge

All of us usually have three levels of word meaning knowledge: unknown, acquainted, and established.[7] Words at the unknown level are obviously unfamiliar words, words whose meanings we do not know. Words with which we are acquainted are those that we have met at one time or another, but we cannot easily figure out their meanings (see Figure 8-6). Often, we may be able to determine their meanings after a great amount of effort. Words at our established level are those for which we can very easily state meanings.

---

[7] See Michael F. Graves, Wayne H. Slater, and Thomas G. White, "Teaching Content Area Vocabulary," in *Content Area Reading and Learning,* Diane Lapp, James Flood, and Nancy Farnan, eds. (Englewood Cliffs, N.J.: Prentice-Hall, 1989), pp. 216–217.

FIGURE 8-5   A finished semantic map.

© 1963, United Feature Syndicate, Inc.
Reprinted by permission of UFS, Inc.

FIGURE 8-6   Lack of word meanings can be painful.

Throughout the term, teachers should help their students expand their vocabulary to increase their established level of word meaning knowledge. Teachers need to do this by using direct instruction in vocabulary rather than depending completely on incidental learning. Often incidental learning of vocabulary increases our acquaintance level, but it does not ensure that the words will become part of our established level of word knowledge. Words that are at our established level are those that we have usually overlearned. In other words, we have made a concerted effort to learn the meanings of the words and have continued practice beyond the point at which we thought we needed the practice.

Vocabulary Learning: A Special Note

The studies done on the acquisition of word meanings have not been conclusive. That is, one cannot point to a specific technique or strategy and say that it is the best way to promote vocabulary learning. "And, indeed a variety of positions has been taken by different researchers."[8] However, "none of these positions is espoused to the exclusion of others, but the degree of emphasis among various researchers is quite different."[9]

Some researchers' feelings that students can learn vocabulary from context "has led to a laissez-faire view of instruction."[10] Rather than instruction in vocabulary, this group has advocated wide reading. Another group also believes in context as a strong factor in vocabulary learning, but this group recommends giving students instruction in gaining word meaning from context. Another group prefers the dictionary over context, and still another group feels that "no matter what context contributes, direct instruction can play an important role in vocabulary development."[11]

In this book, direct instruction using a combination of strategies is advocated to promote vocabulary expansion. The rest of this chapter is primarily concerned with techniques that help students expand their vocabulary and stir their vocabulary consciousness.

Gaining Word Meanings through Context

In 1918, Chief Justice Oliver Wendell Holmes said the following concerning a word:

[8] Isabel Beck and Margaret McKeown, "Conditions of Vocabulary Acquisition," in *Handbook of Reading Research,* Vol. II, Rebecca Barr, Michael L. Kamil, Peter Mosenthal, and P. David Pearson, eds. (New York: Longman, 1991), p. 809.

[9] Ibid.

[10] Ibid.

[11] Ibid.

A word is not a crystal, transparent and unchanged; it is the skin of a living thought and may vary greatly in color and content according to the circumstances and the time in which it is used.

Syntax
Refers to word order or position of the word in a sentence.

Semantic clue
Meaning clue.

Because many words have more than one meaning, the meaning of a particular word is determined by the position (syntax) of the word in a sentence and from meaning (semantic) clues of the surrounding words. By *context,* we mean the words surrounding a word that can shed light on its meaning.

Although investigators do not agree on the best way to help students derive word meanings, common sense dictates that students learn unfamiliar words best when the new word is presented in a meaningful, familiar context so that the learner can see how the word is used, as well as when the word is used. The student can then assimilate the new information into his or her existing schemata or categories. The ability to relate the word to what is already known aids the learner in retaining the word's meaning.[12]

Teachers should make a concerted effort to help students learn the various types of context clues that writers and speakers use. One way to do this is for teachers to present their students with many written and oral sentences and then to challenge them to determine the meanings of some of the key words in the sentences. Teachers should try to elicit from their students how they figured out the word meanings. After a discussion of the various tactics that the students used, teachers could share with their students information about context clues. The sections that follow should help teachers to become more adept in directly teaching context clues to their students.

Context Clues

Context clue
An item of information from the surrounding words of a particular word in the form of a synonym, antonym, example, definition, description, explanation, and so on, that helps shed light on the particular word.

A context clue is the specific item of information that helps the reader to figure out the meaning of a particular word. Context clues can be in the form of definitions, descriptions, comparisons, contrasts, examples, and so forth. The following examples display different kinds of context clues that writers frequently use.

1. Context Clues (Definition, Description, and Explanation)

If a writer or speaker wants to ascertain that the reader or listener will get the meaning of a key word, he or she will define, explain, or describe the word in the same sentence or in a following one. For example, in the preceding sections, the words *context* and *context clue* have been defined because they are key words in the sections. In the following example the writer or speaker actually gives us the **definition** of a word. You should help students to recognize that sentences such as this are generally found in textbooks.

[12] Joan Gipe, "Investigating Techniques for Teaching Word Meanings," *Reading Research Quarterly* 14 (4) (1978–1979): 624–644.

Example   The pictures in your mind formed by the words in the poem are called *imagery.*

In the next example, notice how the writer **describes** the word that he wants the reader to know.

Example   Andrew is a *frugal* young man who spends money wisely and never spends more than he has.

Now notice how the next writer uses **explanation** to help readers understand the term *jealous.*

Example   Barry was *jealous* because his girlfriend was going out with someone else.

Special Notes

a. The word *or* may be used by the writer when he or she uses another word or words with a similar meaning.

  Example: Andrew felt ill after he had eaten rancid, or spoiled, butter.

b. The words *that is* and their abbreviation *i.e.* usually signal that an explanation will follow.

  Example: No human being is immortal, that is, can live forever. *Or,* No human being is immortal, i.e., can live forever.

2. Context Clues (Example and Comparison/Contrast)

Example
Something representative of a whole or a group.

Many times authors or speakers help us get the meaning of a word by giving us **examples** illustrating the use of the word. An example is something representative of a whole or a group. It can be a particular single item, incident, fact, or situation that typifies the whole. In the following sentence notice how the examples that the writer gives in her sentence help us determine the meaning of the word *illuminated.*

Example   The lantern *illuminated* the cave so well that we were able to see the formations and even spiders crawling on the rocks.

From the sentence you can determine that *illuminated* means "lit up."

Comparison
A demonstration of the similarities between persons, ideas, things, and so on.

Another technique writers employ that can help us gain the meaning of a word is **comparison.** Comparison usually shows the similarities between persons, ideas, things, and so on. For example, in the following sentence notice how we can determine the meaning of *passive* through the writer's comparison of Paul to a bear in winter.

Example   Paul is as *passive* as a bear sleeping away the winter.

From the sentence you can determine that *passive* means "inactive."

Contrast is another method writers use that can help the reader to figure out word meanings. Contrast is usually used to show the differences between persons, ideas, things, and so on. In the following sentence we can determine the meaning of *optimist* because we know that *optimist* is somehow the opposite of one "who is gloomy and expects the worst."

Contrast
A demonstration of the differences between persons, ideas, things, and so on.

Example   My sister Marie is an *optimist,* but her boyfriend is one who is always gloomy and expects the worst to happen.

From the sentence you can determine that *optimist* means "one who expects the best" or "one who is cheerful."

Special Notes

a. The writer may use the words *for example* or the abbreviation *e.g.* to signal that examples are to follow.

Example: Condiments, e.g., pepper, salt, and mustard, make food taste better.

From the examples of condiments we can determine that *condiments* are seasonings.

b. Many times such words as *but, yet, although, however,* and *rather than* signal that a contrast is being used.

Example: My father thought he owned an *authentic* antique chest, but he was told recently that it was a fake.

From the sentence the reader can tell that *authentic* is the opposite of *fake;* therefore, *authentic* means "not false but genuine or real."

Synonyms
Words similar in meaning.

3. Context Clues (an Emphasis on Synonyms)

Often a word can be defined by another, more familiar word having basically the same meaning. For example, *void* is defined as *empty,* and *corpulent* is defined as *fat.* The pairs *void* and *empty* and *corpulent* and *fat* are **synonyms**. Synonyms are different words that have the same or nearly the same meaning. Writers use synonyms to make their writing clearer and more expressive (see Figure 8-7).

Example   Ms. Green had told her *constituents* to *trust* her; however, from the returns of the election, we can see that the *voters* obviously did not have *faith* in her.

4. Context Clues (an Emphasis on Antonyms)

Antonyms
Words opposite in meaning to each other.

Antonyms, which are words opposite in meaning to each other, are used often by writers and, like synonyms, are an effective strategy to teach word meanings. In an earlier section, it was also stated that authors use contrast to help make their sentences clearer and more informative. Antonyms are used to show contrast.

BORN LOSER

Reprinted by permission of NEA, Inc.

FIGURE 8-7   Hattie makes good use of synonyms.

Example   Have you ever noticed how whenever Frank is *despondent,* his supposed friend Jordan is *lighthearted?*

Context Clues and Homographs

Homographs
Words that are spelled the same but have different meanings.

Many words that are spelled the same have different meanings (see Figure 8-8). These words are called *homographs.* The meaning of a homograph is determined by the way the word is used in the sentence. For example, the term *run* has many different meanings. (One dictionary gives 134 meanings for *run.*) In the listed sentences, notice how *run's* placement in the sentence and context clues help readers figure out the meaning of each use.

1. Walk, don't *run.*
2. I have a *run* in my stocking.
3. Senator Jones said that he would not *run* for another term.
4. The trucker finished his *run* to Detroit.

THE BORN LOSER   **by Art Sansom**

Reprinted by permission of NEA, Inc.

FIGURE 8-8   When words have more than one meaning, people may get the wrong meaning.

5. She is going to *run* in a ten-mile race.
6. The play had a *run* of two years.

In Sentence 1 *run* means "go quickly by moving the legs more rapidly than at a walk."

In Sentence 2 *run* means "a tear or to cause stitches to unravel."

In Sentence 3 *run* means "be or campaign as a candidate for election."

In Sentence 4 *run* means "route."

In Sentence 5 *run* means "take part in a race."

In Sentence 6 *run* means "continuous course of performances."

From these examples, we can see that the way the word is used in the sentence will determine its meaning. As already stated, words that are spelled the same but have different meanings are called *homographs*. Some homographs are spelled the same but do not sound the same. For example, *refuse* means "trash," but it also means "to decline to accept." In the first sentence, *refuse* (ref′ use) meaning "trash" is pronounced differently from *refuse* (re fuse′) meaning "to decline to accept" in the second sentence. In reading, we can determine the meaning of *refuse* from context clues. For example:

1. During the garbage strike there were tons of uncollected *refuse* on the streets of the city.
2. I *refuse* to go along with you.

Special Note

Homonyms
Words that sound alike, are spelled differently, and have different meanings.

Homophones
Same as homonyms; words that sound alike, are spelled differently, and have different meanings.

Confusion may exist among the terms *homonym, homophone,* and *homograph* because some authors are using the more scientific or linguistic definition for the terms, and others are using the more traditional definition. *Homonyms* have traditionally been defined as words that sound alike, are spelled differently, and have different meanings—for example, *red, read*. However, many linguists use the term *homophone* rather than homonym for this meaning. Linguists generally use the term *homonym* for words that are spelled the same, pronounced the same, but have different meanings—for example, *bat* (the mouselike winged mammal) and *bat* (the name for a club used to hit a ball). *Bat* (baseball bat) and *bat* (animal) would traditionally be considered a homograph (words that are spelled the same but have different meanings), but linguists usually define *homographs* as words that are spelled the same but have *different pronunciations* and *different meanings*—for example, *lead* (dense metal) and *lead* (verb).

The Dictionary and Vocabulary Expansion

Even though the dictionary is a necessary tool and one with which all students should be familiar, it should not be used as a crutch. Every time students meet a word whose meaning is unknown to them, they should first try to use their knowledge of combining forms and context clues to unlock the meaning. If these techniques do not help and the word is essential for understanding the passage, then they should look up the meaning.

Teachers should tell their students that difficulties exist concerning pronunciation because people in different parts of the United States often pronounce words differently. As a result, pronunciation of a word as given in the dictionary may not be in accord with their region's pronunciation of it.

Teachers should also help their students to recognize that different dictionaries may use different pronunciation keys and to be on the lookout for this. The pronunciation key is composed of words with diacritical marks. To know how to pronounce a word in a particular dictionary, students must familiarize themselves with the pronunciation key in that dictionary. For example, look at the way that five different dictionaries present a few similar words in Table 8-1.

If your students had no knowledge of the pronunciation key of the specific dictionary, they would have had difficulty in pronouncing the word. Pronunciation guides are generally found at the beginning of dictionaries. Many dictionaries also have a simplified pronunciation key at the bottom of every page. (See upcoming sections and Chapter 9 for more on the dictionary.)

Defining Word Part Terms

Compound word
Separate words that combine to form a new word, for example, *grandfather, stepdaughter, sunlight.*

Prefix
A letter or a sequence of letters added to the beginning of a root word that changes its meaning.

Suffix
A letter or sequence of letters added to the end of a root word.

Affixes
Prefixes and suffixes.

Root
Smallest unit of a word that can exist and retain its basic meaning.

To help students use word parts as an aid to increasing vocabulary, we should define some terms. There are a great number of words in our language that combine with other words to form new words—for example, *grandfather* and *chairperson* (compound words). You may also combine a root (base) word with a letter or a group of letters, either at the beginning (prefix) or end (suffix) of the root word, to form a new, related word—for example, *replay* and *played. Affix* is a term used to refer to either a prefix or a suffix.

In the words *replay* and *played, play* is a root or base, *re* is a prefix, and *ed* is a suffix. A *root* is the smallest unit of a word that can exist and retain its basic meaning. It cannot be subdivided any further. *Replay* is not a root word because it can be subdivided to *play. Play* is a root word because it cannot be divided further and still retain a meaning related to the root word.

Derivatives are combinations of root words with either prefixes or suffixes or both. *Combining forms* are usually defined as roots borrowed from another language that join together or that join with a prefix, a suffix, or both a prefix and a suffix to form a word. Many times the English combining form elements are derived from Greek and Latin roots. In some vocabulary books, in which the major emphasis is on vocabulary expansion rather than on the naming of word parts, *combining forms* are defined in a more general sense to include any word part that can join with another word or word part to form a word or a new word.[13]

---

[13] Dorothy Rubin, *Gaining Word Power,* 3rd ed. (New York: Macmillan, 1993); Dorothy Rubin, *Vocabulary Expansion,* 2nd ed. (New York: Macmillan, 1991).

TABLE 8-1   Comparison of the Pronunciation of Three Words in Five Different Dictionaries

Word	Webster's New Twentieth Century Dictionary	Webster's Third New International Dictionary	Random House Dictionary of the English Language	The American Heritage Dictionary of the English Language	Funk & Wagnall's Standard College Dictionary
1. coupon	c̣ou'pon	'k(y)ü ˌpän	ko͞o' pon	ko͞o' pŏn	ko͞o' pon
2. courage	c̣ôur' āg̣e	'kər ij	kûr'ij	kûr'ĭj	kûr'ij
3. covet	c̣ŏv' et	'kəvət	kuv'it	kŭv'ĭt	kuv'it

Derivatives
Combinations of root words with either prefixes or suffixes or both.

More will be said about word parts in upcoming sections. Special emphasis is given to the use of word parts for vocabulary expansion in the upcoming section dealing with intermediate grade level vocabulary skills.

Primary Grade Level Vocabulary Skills

During or by the end of the *kindergarten–primary years* the child . . .

Has such concepts as *over, under, big, little, the one before, the middle one, on top of, next to, start, stop, go,* and so on.

Recognizes that words may have more than one meaning.

Has acquired the concept of antonyms.

Has acquired the concept of synonyms.

Is beginning to learn the meaning of some figures of speech.

Is increasing his or her vocabulary from literature.

Is acquiring a vocabulary consciousness by not only recognizing that some words have more than one meaning, but also by asking for or looking up the meanings of words that he or she does not know.

Is acquiring the ability to classify objects.

Is acquiring skill in recognizing word associations.

Is acquiring skill in recognizing and working with some word relationships (analogies).

Shows that he or she enjoys using new words by incorporating them in his or her oral and written expression.

Is able to solve word riddles.

Is able to figure out word meanings from context clues.

Is able to look up a word in the dictionary.

Is beginning to build words using word parts.

Vocabulary of the Senses

All children usually enjoy words that appeal to the senses. Young children especially enjoy the words that they can almost taste and feel when they say them because of their sounds. As preschoolers, they savored many words by repeating them very slowly over and over again; the sounds of the words were fun to say. Now, as primary grade students, teachers can take advantage of children's delight in words that appeal to the senses by helping them develop a vocabulary of the senses.

A technique a teacher can use is to ask children to give a word for various animal sounds. For example, a cow "moos," a cat "meows," a dog "barks," or "bays," a sheep "baas," a chick "peeps," and a bull "bellows." Then a word can be given for the sounds of nature. For example, the wind "howls," the brook "babbles," the trees "rustle," and so on. This technique can be continued for the sense of sight, of touch, and so on.

Vocabulary of Sounds Activities

Activity 1   The students look at a number of pictures such as a teakettle, a bell, a cow, a rooster, a trumpet, an airplane getting ready for take off, and so on. Then they give the characteristic sound of each.

Activity 2   The children are given a number of phrases with a blank for each phrase. A list of words is written on the board. The teacher states each word. The children must choose a word from the word list that *best* describes the sound of the object in the phrase.

Vocabulary of Feelings Activities

Activity 1   The students look at pictures showing persons with different expressions and in different moods. The children are asked to state words that describe the person's mood or the way they think the person is feeling.

Here are examples of words to describe persons in pictures:

sad	tired
glad	stern
happy	mean
worried	disappointed
confused	cheerful

Activity 2   The students role-play a certain mood, and other students have to guess what the mood is.

Activity 3   The students look through magazines and cut out pictures of persons expressing different moods.

Developing Vocabulary from Literature

By listening to or reading literature, children can increase their vocabulary.[14] For example, Margaret Wise Brown helps children gain the concept of *dead* in *The Dead Bird.*

> *The bird was dead when the children found it. But it had not been dead for long—it was still warm and its eyes were closed.*
>
> > *The children felt with their fingers for the quick beat of the bird's heart in its breast. But there was no heart beating. That was how they knew it was dead. And even as they held it, it began to get cold, and the limp body grew stiff, so they couldn't bend its legs and the head didn't flop when they moved it. That was the way animals got when they had been dead for some time—cold dead and stone still with no heart beating.*

Clyde Bulla in *The Poppy Seeds* helps children understand what a *spring* is.

> *It was a spring of clear cold water. It came from the foot of the mountain, ran a little way, and disappeared among the rocks. They heard the spring running over the rocks, but they never stopped for a drink of the cold, fresh water.*

Phyllis McGinley in *The Horse Who Lived Upstairs* helps children gain a better understanding of the term *stall.*

> *So every night, when Joey came home, he stepped out from the shafts of the wagon, and into an elevator, and up he went to his stall on the fourth floor of the big brick building. It was a fine stall and Joey was very comfortable there. He had plenty of oats to eat and plenty of fresh straw to lie on. He even had a window to look out of.*

Building Vocabulary Using Word Parts

It is not too soon to begin in the primary grades to help children to learn about word parts such as prefixes, suffixes, and roots in order to expand their vocabulary. (See "Defining Word Part Terms.") Here are some activities using word parts that can be used with primary grade level children.

Compound Words

Activity 1: Building Compound Words and Making Silly Sentences The children are told that compounds are words that combine with other words to make new words. Two lists of words are given to the children. The children are

---

[14] For a bibliography of excellent books that help children gain understandings of terms, see Dorothy Cohen, "Word Meaning and the Literary Experience in Early Childhood," *Elementary English* 46 (November 1969): 914–925.

told to combine words from both lists to make a new word. After they have combined the words to make a new word, they should make up a silly sentence. For example: *cat* and *fish* are combined to form the compound word *catfish*. The children make up a silly sentence such as "Did you ever see a cat fish?"

Activity 2: Fishy Compounds   The children are told that the answer to each of the riddles is a compound word for different kinds of fish.

> *Examples:* I'm a fish that comes out at night. (starfish)
>   I'm a fish that can fight in battles. (swordfish)

If children work individually on the compound word activities, it would be a good idea to go over the answers together in a group so that interaction and discussion can further enhance vocabulary development and also clear up any confusion.

Building Words Using Prefixes, Suffixes, and Roots

Prefixes	Roots	Suffixes
re – again, back	happy	er – one who
un – not	play	y – having, full of
pre – before	turn	ful – full of
dis – not	mind	able – can do, able
	charge	less – without
	dirt	ly – like
	paint	
	agree	

Activity 1   Challenge your students to make as many words as they can using the word parts. Have them put some of the words into sentences. Have them add root words to the list. Examples are *unhappy, player, playful, replay, return, turnable, returnable, turner, minder, remind, reminder, mindful, mindless, recharge, chargeable, rechargeable, dirty, dirtless, repaint, painter, disagree, agreeable, preheat, heater.*

Activity 2   Put each prefix and suffix on a separate slip of paper. Put all of them into a paper bag. Have each child pull out one slip of paper and make a word using the word part. The child supplies his or her own root word.

Activity 3   Put a number of root words on a slip of paper, and put each into a paper bag. Have each child pull out a slip of paper and make another word using the root word.

Fun with Words

Here are samples of some fun activities that your primary grade children should enjoy:

Word Riddles

Directions   See how many of the word riddles you can solve.

1. I shine on a clear night. Take away one of my letters, and I'll become black.

   _____   _____

2. I'm one of your bones. Add one letter to me, and you'll have a bed for a baby.

   _____   _____

3. I'm a color. Take away one of my letters, and I'll become part of your face.

   _____   _____

4. I'm a fruit. Take away one of my letters, and you can cook on me.

   _____   _____

Answers   (1) star – tar, (2) rib – crib, (3) brown – brow, (4) orange – range.

Word Square Puzzle

Directions   Below is a Hunting Square. If you follow the directions carefully, you will track down the animal that escaped from the zoo.

```
A  F  A  R  M  S
P  L  G  O  G  R
S  T  R  E  E  T
S  T  O  P  I  T
R  O  C  D  I  P
B  A  K  E  S  C
```

Directions   (1) Each clue, hidden in the square, helps you find a letter. Read each carefully. (2) Put the letters together to hunt down the animal.

Clues

1. Go to the end of street. _____

2. Look in the center of pit. _____

3. Look at the top of rock. _____

4. Look at the end of tree. _____

5. Look in the middle of farms. _____

Answer   (1) T, (2) I, (3) G, (4) E, (5) R = TIGER.

Word Riddle Puzzle

Directions   Each sentence below gives you a clue to a letter. Put the letters together, and you will have the answer to this riddle: "What has lots of eyes but doesn't see?"

_____   **1.** Its first letter is in *lap* but not in *late*.

_____   **2.** Its second letter is in *boat* but not in *beat*.

_____   **3.** Its third letter is in *note* but not in *honey*.

_____   **4.** Its fourth letter is in *band* but not in *bend*.

_____   **5.** Its fifth letter is in *feet* but not in *fame*.

_____   **6.** Its sixth letter is in *grow* but not in *grew*.

Answer   (1) P, (2) O, (3) T, (4) A, (5) T, (6) O = POTATO.

Word Puzzle

Directions   Here are seven clues for seven words. Each word is a three-letter word, and the middle letter of the word starts with the next letter of the alphabet. The first is done for you.

1. I'm a high card in a deck of cards.   a   c   e

2. You do this to numbers.   ___ d ___

3. I'm an insect.   ___ e ___

4. I'm the opposite of *on*.   ___ f ___

5. I tell how old you are.   ___ g ___

6. I'm the opposite of *he*.   ___ h ___

7. I have a sharp point.   ___ i ___

Answers   (1) ace, (2) add, (3) bee, (4) off, (5) age, (6) she, (7) pin.

The Dictionary as a Tool in Vocabulary Expansion

Although children use picture dictionaries in the early primary grades more as an aid to writing than in vocabulary expansion, if young readers discover the wonders of the dictionary they can enrich their vocabulary. Primary grade picture dictionaries consist of words that are generally in the children's listening, speaking, and reading vocabularies. They consist of alphabetized lists of words with pictures and can serve as the children's first reference tool, helping them to unlock words on their own and making them more independent and self-reliant. The children can also learn multiple meanings from a picture dictionary, when they see the word *saw* presented with two pictures that represent a tool and the act of seeing.

Vocabulary Lesson Plan (Upper Primary Grades)

Here is a lesson plan on homographs that teachers could use with their upper primary grade children.

Lesson Plan: Upper Primary Grade Level

Objectives

1. The students will be able to use context clues to figure out the meanings of words that are spelled the same but have different meanings (homographs).
2. The students will be able to make up word riddles using homographs.

Preliminary Preparation

Five sets of pictures showing that the following homographs are spelled the same but have different meanings: *train, block, slip, plant, bark.*

Five sentences on the chalkboard with blanks in each sentence.

1. I _____ my father _____ the tree in the woods. (saw)

2. In the _____ our flowers look very pretty near our _____. (spring)

3. My mother says that I _____ help her _____ some vegetables from her garden. (can)

4. Don't you _____ when you change a flat _____? (tire)

Continued

Lesson Plan: Upper Primary Grade Level *Continued*

5. After we drank the water in the _____, we did not feel

_____. (well)

Introduction

"We've been working with building our vocabulary. What are some of the new words we've learned?" "Yes, good. Who can put one of these words in a sentence?" "Good. Today we're going to learn some more new words, but these words are special, and we'll see why soon." The teacher holds up two pictures and says, "Look at these two pictures. What do you see in the pictures?" "Very good! The first picture is one of a *train,* and the second picture shows a boy trying to *train* his dog. Both pictures have something in common. Do you know what it is? Today we will work with homographs. When you figure out the answer to my question, you will know what homographs are."

Development

"Let's look again at the two pictures. Who can tell me what the two pictures have that is the same?" "Very good! They both have the word *train* in them. Let's look at a few other sets of pictures." The teacher holds up two pictures. One is a picture of a building block; the other, of a street block. The children are asked to tell what they see in the two pictures. The teacher follows this procedure for three more sets of pictures depicting the words *slip, plant,* and *bark.* The teacher then asks the children to try to state what each set of pictures has in common. The children should recognize that each set of pictures is different but that the word telling what each picture in the set is about is the same. The teacher then tells them that words that are spelled the same but have different meanings are called *homographs.* The teacher has the children read each of the five sentences on the board and asks them to fill in the blanks with one word that fits all the blanks in each sentence.

After the children have supplied the correct words, give them the following riddle: I can make things brighter; I am part of a camera; and plants develop from me. What am I? *Hint:* One word fits all three things. (bulb)

Ask the children to use their dictionaries to try to make up their own riddles to challenge their classmates.

Summary

Ask children what they have just learned about homographs. Elicit from the children that homographs are words that are spelled the same but have different meanings. Tell children to be on the alert for such words in their reading. Tell them that tomorrow they will work with more homographs and that they will start making a homograph riddle book.

Diagnostic Checklist (Primary Grades)

Student's Name: _____

Grade: _____

Teacher: _____

	Yes	No	Sometimes
1. The child shows that he or she is developing a vocabulary consciousness by recognizing that some words have more than one meaning.			
2. The child uses context clues to figure out word meanings.			
3. The child can state the opposite of words such as *stop, tall, fat, long, happy, big.*			
4. The child can state the synonym of words such as *big, heavy, thin, mean, fast, hit.*			
5. The child can state different meanings for homographs (words that are spelled the same but have different meanings based on their use in a sentence). *Examples:* I did not *state* what *state* I live in. Do not *roll* the *roll* on the floor. *Train* your dog not to bark when it hears a *train.*			
6. The child is developing a vocabulary of the senses by being able to state words that describe various sounds, smells, sights, tastes, and touches.			
7. The child is expanding his or her vocabulary by combining two words to form compound words such as *grandfather, bedroom, cupcake, backyard, toothpick, buttercup, mailman.*			
8. The child is expanding his or her vocabulary by combining roots of words with prefixes and suffixes. Examples are *return, friendly, unhappy, disagree, dirty, precook, unfriendly.*			
9. The child is able to give the answer to a number of word riddles.			
10. The child is able to make up a number of word riddles.			
11. The child is able to classify various objects such as fruits, animals, colors, pets, and so on.			
12. The child is able to give words that are associated with certain objects and ideas. Example: hospital — *nurse, doctor, beds, sick persons, medicine,* and so on.			
13. The child is able to complete some analogy proportions such as *Happy* is to *sad* as *tall* is to _____.			
14. The child shows that he or she is developing a vocabulary consciousness by using the dictionary to look up unknown words.			

Intermediate Grade Level Vocabulary Skills

During or by the end of the *intermediate years,* the child . . .

Is using words with more than one meaning correctly.

Is able to use synonyms and antonyms effectively in speaking and writing.

Is able to use context clues to figure out word meanings.

Is able to use word parts to figure out the meanings of words.

Is able to work with analogies.

Is able to solve word riddles.

Is able to build words, using word parts.

Shows that he or she has acquired a vocabulary consciousness not only by recognizing that some words have more than one meaning, but also by asking for or looking up the meanings of words he or she does not know.

Is acquiring skill in dealing with the connotative meaning of words.

Is increasing his or her vocabulary.

Is able to categorize things into more general or more specific categories.

Shows that he or she enjoys using new words by incorporating them in his or her oral and written expression.

In the intermediate grades, students should be guided to a mastery of vocabulary. If they are fascinated by words, they generally want to know the longest word in the dictionary, and many enjoy pronouncing funny or nonsense-sounding words such as *supercalifragilisticexpialidocious.*

Understanding the Connotative Meanings of Words

Teachers need to help students recognize that the author's purpose for writing will greatly influence what he or she has to say and how he or she says it. Just as our past experiences influence our feelings about what we read, so will the author's past experiences influence what he or she writes. Teachers must alert students to the fact that writers can sway unsuspecting or uncritical readers. One of the best defenses against this is to have a good understanding of the connotative meanings of words.

Denotative meaning
The direct, specific meaning of the word.

Connotative meaning
Includes all emotional associations of the word. It is based on an individual's background of experiences.

Many words have connotative meanings. They have meanings beyond the denotative meanings, which are the direct, specific meanings. When we speak or write, we often rely more on the connotative meanings of words than on their denotative meanings to express our true position. The connotative meaning includes all emotional senses associated with the word; it is the suggestive meaning of the word based on the individual's past experiences. The connotative use of a word, therefore, requires an understanding of more than a simple definition. Teachers must help students recognize that when they respect a word's connotative meanings, they will use the word precisely and effectively.

Here is what one sixth-grade teacher does to help students better understand the connotative meanings of words. Mrs. Adams has her students read the following two sentences written by two different writers about the same person:

Writer A: Mrs. Davis is a very trusting person.
Writer B: Mrs. Davis is very credulous.

She then asks them to look up the meanings of *trusting* and *credulous* in the dictionary. The students find that both words have a similar denotative meaning: "ready to believe or have faith in." Next, Mrs. Adams asks her students if they feel the two sentences mean the same. The students feel they do not mean the same. She asks them what is different about the sentences. The students state that they feel the one with the word *trusting* seems more positive than the other one. The one describing Mrs. Adams as *credulous* seems negative.

Mrs. Adams compliments the students and says she agrees with them. She says further that if you refer to someone as *trusting,* you are saying he or she has the admirable trait of believing the best of someone or something. If you refer to the same person as *credulous,* you are saying that he or she lacks judgment, that he or she foolishly believes anything. Although both words have the same denotative meaning, in their very different connotative senses one is complimentary and the other is belittling or insulting. Connotative meanings are obviously vital to saying the right thing the right way.

Mrs. Adams tells students that some words often have different overtones or associations for different people. For example, the term *mother* can bring forth images of apple pie, warmth, love, and kindness to one person, whereas for another it can mean beatings, hurt, shame, fear, and disillusionment. She also states that some words lend themselves more readily to emotional overtones or associations than others. For example, the term *home* can bring forth good or bad associations based on the past experiences of an individual. However, the term *dwelling,* which has the same specific definition as *home,* does not have the emotional overtones that *home* does.

She then tells them that a number of words have substitutes that more aptly express a particular meaning and puts the following sentences on the board:

1. The <u>conservative</u> man saves his money.
2. The <u>miserly</u> man saves his money.
3. The <u>economical</u> man saves his money.

She then asks the students to tell her what is different about the sentences. They state that sentence 1 is more or less neutral; it probably does not evoke any emotional response; whereas in sentence 2, the term *miserly* is a negative term. Mrs. Adams agrees. She says further that the derogatory term *miserly* is considered a pejorative term because it has strong negative overtones. She then questions them about sentence 3. Everyone agrees that the term *economical* is a positive term.

Mrs. Adams then challenges her students to generate some other adjectives with positive and negative overtones in place of *economical* and *miserly.* Her students had no difficulty stating such adjectives as *stingy* and *cheap* for *miserly* and *thrifty* and *prudent* for *economical.*

Building Vocabulary Using Word Parts

Combining forms Usually defined as roots borrowed from another language that join together or that join with a prefix, a suffix, or both to form a word, for example, *aqua/naut.*

Vocabulary expansion instruction depends on the ability levels of students, their past experiences, and their interests. If they are curious about sea life and have an aquarium in the classroom, this could stimulate interest in such combining forms as *aqua,* meaning "water," and *mare,* meaning "sea." The combining form *aqua* could generate such terms as *aquaplane, aqueduct,* and *aquanaut.* As *mare* means "sea," students could be given the term *aquamarine* to define. Knowing the combining forms *aqua* and *mare,* many will probably respond with "sea water." The English term actually means bluish-green. The students can be challenged as to why the English definition of aquamarine is bluish-green.

A terrarium can stimulate discussion of words made up of the combining form *terra.*

When discussing the prefix *bi,* children should be encouraged to generate other words that also contain *bi,* such as *bicycle, binary, bilateral,* and so on. Other suggestions follow.

Write the words *biped* and *quadruped* in a column on the board, along with their meanings. These words should elicit guesses for groups of animals. The teacher could ask such questions as, "What do you think an animal that has eight arms or legs would be called?" "What about an animal with six feet?" And so on. When the animals are listed on the board, the children can be asked to look them up in the dictionary so that they can classify them.

The students can also try to discover the combining forms of the Roman calendar.[15]

Martius	Sextilis
Aprilis	September
Maius	October
Junius	November
Quintilis	December

Students should discover that the last six months were named for the positions they occupy.

Another set of words made from combining forms describing many-sided geometric figures (polygons) are as follows:

3 sides	trigon
4 sides	tetragon
5 sides	pentagon

[15] See Loraine Dun, "Increase Vocabulary with the Word Elements, Mono through Deca," *Elementary English* 47 (January 1970): 49–55.

    6 sides   hexagon
    7 sides   septagon
    8 sides   octagon

When presenting the combining forms *cardio, tele, graph,* and *gram,* place the following vocabulary words on the board:

    cardiograph   telegraph
    cardiogram   telegram

After students know that *cardio* means "heart" and *tele* means "from a distance," ask them to try to determine the meaning of *graph,* as used in *cardiograph* and *telegraph.* Have them try to figure out the meaning of *gram,* as used in *telegram* and *cardiogram.* Once students are able to define *graph* as an instrument or machine, and *gram* as a message, they will hardly ever confuse a cardiograph with a cardiogram.

When students are exposed to such activities, they become more sensitive to their language. They come to realize that words are human-made, that language is living and changing, and that as people develop new concepts, they need new words to identify them. The words *astronaut* and *aquanaut* are good examples of words that came into being because of space and undersea exploration.

Children come to see the power of combining forms when they realize that by knowing a few combining forms they can unlock the meanings of many words. For example, by knowing a few combining forms, students can define correctly many terms used in the metric system, as well as other words.

deca:	ten
deci:	tenth
cent, centi:	hundred, hundredth
milli:	thousand, thousandth
decameter:	10 meters
decimeter:	1/10 meter
centimeter:	1/100 meter
millimeter:	1/1,000 meter
decade:	period of 10 years
century:	period of 100 years
centennial:	one hundredth year anniversary
millennium:	period of 1,000 years
million:	a thousand thousands

(*Centi, milli, deci* are usually used to designate "part of.")

You should caution your students that many times the literal definitions of the prefixes, suffixes, or combining forms may not be exactly the same as the dictionary meaning. For example, *automobile.*

Sample exercises that teachers should find helpful for stimulating interest in learning new words through word parts follow:

Building Vocabulary Activity (Combining Forms)

Directions   Master some useful combining forms. From the words on each line, figure out the meaning of the combining form or forms. Write the meaning. Think of other words with the same combining form or forms.

1. geo – geology, geography

_____

2. anni, annu, enni – annual, biannual, biennial, anniversary

_____

3. bio – biology, biography

_____

4. scope – microscope, telescope

_____

5. cent, centi – century, bicentennial, centennial, centimeter

_____

6. auto – autograph, autobiography

_____

7. graph – autograph, biography

_____

8. ped, pod – pedestrian, pedal, biped, apodal

_____

9. dic, dict – dictation, diction, dictator

_____

10. spect – spectacle, spectator, inspect

_____

Answers   (1) earth, (2) year, (3) life, (4) a means for seeing, (5) hundred, hundredth, (6) self, (7) something written, (8) foot, (9) say, (10) see.

Building Vocabulary Activity (Combining Forms, Prefixes, and Suffixes)

Directions   Choose a word from the word list that *best* fits the blank in each sentence. Use the word parts and their meanings to help you.

Word Parts and Meanings: grat = pleasing; in = not; con = with, together; ous = full of, having; jud, judi, judic = judge; pre = before

Word List: gratuity, ingrate, gratuitous, gratitude, congratulated, gratified, judicious, prejudiced.

1. It _____ her to have her friend wear her gift.

2. _____ persons are usually not interested in looking at all the evidence.

3. Everyone _____ him when he made the final point that won the game.

4. The decision was a(n) _____ one, and it was bound to be hailed as a step forward in bettering employer–employee relations.

5. We couldn't believe our ears when we were told that our _____ was not enough.

6. As I am not used to receiving _____ services, I insisted on paying something.

7. The _____ that the parents felt toward the doctor who had saved their child's life could not be put into words.

8. What a(n) _____ he is to behave in such a manner after we did so much for him.

Answers   (1) gratified, (2) Prejudiced, (3) congratulated, (4) judicious, (5) gratuity, (6) gratuitous, (7) gratitude, (8) ingrate.

Building Vocabulary Activity (Compound Words): Silly Compounds

Directions   Below are seven clues for seven compound words. Each of the words has a head in it. Find the word and write it in the blank.

1. The first head is combined with a pain. _____

2. The second head is combined with something that makes things bright. _____

3. The third head is combined with something you can hang things on. _____

4. The fourth head is combined with money. _____

5. The fifth head is combined with an antonym of *weak*. _____

6. The sixth head is combined with a thoroughfare. _____

7. The seventh head is combined with a person who searches for someone.

_____

Answers: (1) headache, (2) headlight, (3) headline, (4) headquarters, (5) head-strong, (6) headway, (7) headhunter.

Fun with Words

Here are samples of some activities that your intermediate grade students should enjoy:

Word Riddles

Directions   See how many of the word riddles you can solve.

1. I'm what you eat from; if you take away one of my letters, I'll never be on

   time.

   _____   _____

2. I absorb moisture; remove two of my letters, and I'm what you need if your

   car gets stuck.

   _____   _____

3. I'm found in a shell, and I'm good to eat; if you add one letter to me, I can

   fasten things.

   _____   _____

4. I'm what a worker likes to get if he or she does a good job; remove one of my

   letters, and I become something a worker likes even more.

   _____   _____

5. I'm a resting place for wild animals; add three letters to me, and I become a

   young, unmarried woman.

   _____   _____

6. We are persons with mysterious power; add one letter to us, and you will know our power.

_____ _____

Answers (1) plate—late, (2) towel—tow, (3) clam—clamp, (4) praise—raise, (5) den—maiden, (6) Magi—magic.

Word Puzzles

Directions Below are ten clues for ten words. After you guess the first word, each word begins with the last letter of the preceding word.

1. a male animal _____

2. a long, slimy, snakelike fish _____

3. the king of beasts _____

4. a bad dream _____

5. a tree _____

6. a representation of an area _____

7. part of your hand _____

8. a large, impressive residence _____

9. a fruit _____

10. a huge animal _____

Answers (1) sire, (2) eel, (3) lion, (4) nightmare, (5) elm, (6) map, (7) palm, (8) mansion, (9) nectarine, (10) elephant.

Word Puzzles

Directions Following are clues to eight words. Each new word adds one letter and uses all the letters of the word preceding it. To form the new word, you can rearrange the letters in any way. Insert your answer in the blank.

1. an indefinite article _____

2. like; the same as _____

3. the ocean _____

4. a mammal that lives in the ocean _____

5. a contract giving someone the use of something _____

6. to be agreeable _____

7. slipped away; passed _____

8. fell back into illness after almost recovering _____

Answers: (1) a, (2) as, (3) sea, (4) seal, (5) lease, (6) please, (7) elapsed, (8) relapsed.

Rhyming Word Puzzles

Directions   The answers for the following clues are two rhyming words. Insert your answer in the blank.

1. a frightening bird _____

2. incorrect melody _____

3. dual difficulty _____

4. large acting crew _____

Answers   (1) scary canary, (2) wrong song, (3) double trouble, (4) vast cast.

The Dictionary as a Tool in Vocabulary Expansion

In the intermediate grades dictionaries serve more varied purposes, and there is emphasis on vocabulary expansion. Children delight in learning new words. If properly encouraged by the teacher, vocabulary expansion can become an exciting hunting expedition, where the unexplored terrain is the vast territory of words.

At any grade level teachers can show by their actions that they value the dictionary as an important tool. If a word seems to need clarification, students should be asked to look it up in the dictionary. Although at times it may seem more expedient simply to supply the meaning, students should be encouraged to look it up for themselves. If the pupil discovers the meaning of the word on his or her own, he or she will be more apt to remember it.

In order to build a larger meaning vocabulary, the teacher could use a number of motivating techniques to stimulate vocabulary expansion. Each pupil can be encouraged to keep a paper bag attached to his or her desk, in which he or she puts index cards with words on one side and the meaning of the word he or she has looked up on the other. Sometime during the day students can be encouraged to challenge one another, with one student calling out the meanings of a word and another student supplying the word. This technique should make the dictionary one of the students' most treasured possessions.

A most ingenious technique used by two teachers to stimulate interest in the dictionary involved the "Land of Dictionopolis."[16] Students as citizens of Dictionopolis have a responsibility for learning a number of new words from a variety of areas. The classroom is set up with five booths, which are operated on a rotating basis by students in the classroom. They may choose any three words from any of the *five* booths. Once a word is chosen, it is the pupil's on loan, and he or she must take a contract on the word. It is now no longer available to any other pupil. At the end of the week the child must fulfill his or her contract. If he or she is successful, the word becomes his or hers. If not, the word must be returned to the booth. (See Chapter 9 for more on the dictionary.)

Vocabulary Lesson Plan (Upper Intermediate Grades)

Here is a lesson plan on word parts that teachers could use with their upper intermediate grade children.

Lesson Plan: Upper Intermediate Grade Level

Objectives

1. The students will be able to use word parts to form a number of words.
2. The students will be able to use word parts to figure out the meanings of words.

Preliminary Preparation

A chart is available with these word parts:

  bi
  ped, pod
  a
  anni, annu

The following sentences are on the board:

1. Humans are *bipeds.*
2. The snake is an *apodal* animal.
3. My father's company has its *annual* picnic in the spring.
4. I get an allowance *biweekly.*
5. The *pedestrian* was almost hit by a car.

Introduction

The teacher looks at the students and says, "Many animals other than humans are bipeds. Today I saw such an animal having a battle with an apodal animal. The

---

[16] Joan Joy and Marilyn Potter, "Dictionopolis," *Elementary English* (April 1964): 351–361.

Continued

Lesson Plan: Upper Intermediate Grade Level   *Continued*

amazing and unusual thing was that this was taking place right on Main Street, and the pedestrians completely ignored it."

He then says, "Does anyone understand why I said that what I saw was *amazing* and *unusual?* Did anyone understand what I said?" "I didn't think that too many of you would. Why didn't you understand what I was saying?" "Yes, because you didn't know the meanings of some key words in the sentences, and there weren't enough context clues to help you figure them out. We've been working with context clues, so we all know how important they are in helping us. Today, we're going to learn how word parts can give us even more power in figuring out words."

Development

"We've worked with prefixes. Who can tell me what they are?" "Yes, good, a letter or a group of letters added to the beginning of the root or base of a word. What is a suffix?" "Yes, a letter or a group of letters added to the end of a root or base. Today we're going to learn the meanings of a number of word parts and see how they will help us to figure out many unfamiliar things. We'll see also who can tell us the meaning of the sentence I stated at the beginning of this lesson. Here is a chart with some word parts without their meanings. I want everyone to study them for a few minutes."

bi
ped, pod
a
anni, annu

"Now that you've spent a few moments studying the words, can anyone give me a word that has *bi* in it?" "Yes, of course, *bicycle*. Any others?" If there is no response the teacher puts the words *biannual, biennial, biped,* and *binary* on the board. The teacher reminds the children that they have worked with the binary system in math. He asks them what base this system deals with. (base two) The children answer that *bi* means "two." The teacher asks what *ped, pod* means? He asks them what you call a person who walks or goes on foot. (a pedestrian) He asks them for the meaning of *ped.* The children say, "Foot." The teacher follows the same procedure for *a* and *anni, annu.* After the children know the meanings of all of these word parts, the teacher asks them to try to give the meanings of the underlined words in each of the sentences on the board.

1. Humans are <u>bipeds</u>.
2. The snake is an <u>apodal</u> animal.
3. My father's company has its <u>annual</u> picnic in the spring.
4. I get an allowance <u>biweekly</u>.
5. The <u>pedestrian</u> was almost hit by a car.

The teacher goes over the meanings of the underlined word with the students. He then restates the sentence that he said at the beginning of the lesson and calls on someone to explain what was amazing and unusual.

Lesson Plan: Upper Intermediate Grade Level   *Continued*

Summary

The teacher pulls the main points of the lesson together. He tells the children how knowledge of word parts can help them figure out many unknown words. He also tells them that tomorrow they will be able to understand what the following sentence means: "Did you know that on this universe there aren't any persons who are omnipotent or omniscient, but some potentates think that they are."

Diagnostic Checklist (Intermediate Grades)

Student's Name: _____

Grade: _____

Teacher: _____

	Yes	No	Sometimes
1. The student recognizes that many words have more than one meaning.			
2. The student uses context clues to figure out the meanings.			
3. The student can give synonyms for words such as *similar, secluded, passive, brief, old, cryptic, anxious.*			
4. The student can give antonyms for words such as *prior, most, less, best, optimist, rash, humble, content.*			
5. The student can state different meanings for homographs (words that are spelled the same but have different meanings based on their use in a sentence). Examples:			

It is against the law to *litter* the streets.
The man was placed on the *litter* in the ambulance.
My dog gave birth to a *litter* of puppies.

	Yes	No	Sometimes
6. The student is able to use word parts to figure out word meanings.			
7. The student is able to use word parts to build words.			
8. The student is able to complete analogy statements or proportions.			
9. The student is able to give the connotative meaning of a number of words.			
10. The student is able to work with word categories.			

Continued

Diagnostic Checklist (Intermediate Grades)   *Continued*

	Yes	No	Sometimes
11. The student is able to answer a number of word riddles.			
12. The student is able to make up a number of word riddles.			
13. The student uses the dictionary to find word meanings.			

Vocabulary Expansion in Content Areas

Unless students know word meanings, they will not be able to understand what they are reading. No one would dispute this statement. However, many teachers may not recognize that a student's problem in a content area may be that he or she does not have the prerequisite vocabulary to understand the concepts that are being presented.

Using word parts to help students expand vocabulary in the content areas is a viable approach (see previous sections). Another approach that the teacher can use is to select words directly from students' content areas. Each week the teacher could choose a certain number of words from various subject matter books and highlight these words as the words of the week. Each word would be pronounced, put into a sentence, and defined. During the week students can use these words to make up word riddles and challenge their classmates to answer the riddles. The words would become part of the week's spelling words, and students would be asked to put the words into sentences that show the students understand the meaning of the words, or the teacher could present the words in sentences to the students and ask them to define the word as used in the sentence.

Graphic Summary of Chapter

On the following page is a graphic summary of Chapter 8. If you have read the chapter, this graphic illustration should help you remember its main points. Under or beside each heading, you might want to jot down some of the information you recall, as well as some of the key concepts in this chapter. This can act as a good review. You can then check your key concepts against those that follow the graphic summary.

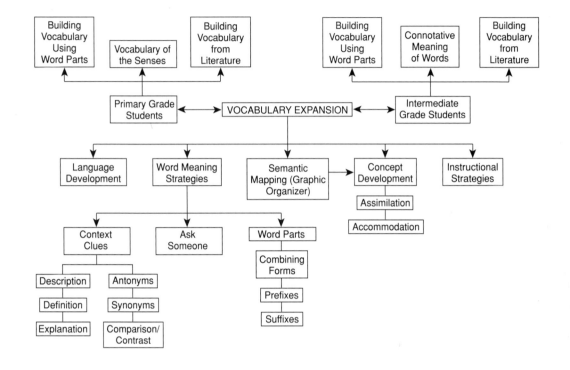

Key Concepts

- Knowledge of word meanings is essential for comprehension.
- Language development, concept development, and vocabulary are all inter-related.
- A concept is a group of stimuli with common characteristics.
- Assimilation helps individuals integrate new, incoming stimuli into existing schemata or concepts.
- Accommodation takes place when a new schema or concept is developed or when an existing schema is changed.
- Vocabulary and ability to categorize are necessary for concept development.
- Teachers should directly teach vocabulary in their classrooms.
- Individual differences exist among the amount and kind of words students possess.
- Teachers should acquaint students with textbook aids.
- Teacher judgment plays an essential role in selecting words for study.
- Vocabulary development is an important part of a reading lesson regardless of the reading program in use.

- Semantic mapping stresses word meanings and categorizing, which are the two major elements for concept development.
- The three levels of word meaning knowledge are unknown, acquainted, and established.
- Vocabulary consciousness grows when students independently search out word meanings.
- The connotative meaning of a word includes all the emotional senses associated with the word.
- Context refers to the words surrounding a word that can shed light on its meaning.
- A context clue is the specific item of information that helps a reader figure out the meaning of a particular word.
- There are a number of context clues that help students figure out word meanings in connected text.
- Knowledge of word parts is a viable method to help students figure out word meanings and expand vocabulary.
- Dictionaries are necessary tools but should not be used as a crutch; that is, students should first try to use their knowledge of combining forms and context clues to unlock an unfamiliar word.
- Young children especially enjoy words that appeal to the senses.
- Listening to literature helps children increase their vocabulary.
- Teachers should challenge their students with "fun with words" activities.
- Students' problems in a content area may occur because they do not have the prerequisite vocabulary.

Suggestions for Thought Questions and Activities

1. You have been put on a committee to develop a vocabulary expansion program for primary grade level students. What kinds of activities would you recommend?
2. You have been asked to generate a number of activities for intermediate grade level students in the area of vocabulary development. What kinds of activities would you develop?
3. A number of children in your first-grade class are weak in concept development. How would this affect their vocabulary development? What can you do to help them to acquire the concepts that they need?
4. You are interested in developing a vocabulary expansion program using combining forms. How would you go about doing this? What kinds of activities would you develop for intermediate grade level students?
5. How important is vocabulary development? Explain.

Selected Bibliography

Beck, Isabel, and Margaret McKeown. "Conditions of Vocabulary Acquisition." In *Handbook of Reading Research,* Vol. II, Rebecca Barr, Michael L. Kamil, Peter Mosenthal, and P. David Pearson, eds. New York: Longman, 1991, pp. 789–814.

Jenkins, Joseph R., Barbara Matlock, and Timothy A. Slocum. "Two Approaches to Vocabulary Instruction: The Teaching of Individual Word Meanings and Practice in Deriving Word Meanings from Context." *Reading Research Quarterly* 24 (Spring 1989): 215–235.

Rubin, Dorothy. *Vocabulary Expansion,* 2nd ed. New York: Macmillan, 1991.

Rubin, Dorothy. *Gaining Word Power,* 3rd ed. New York: Macmillan, 1993.

Stahl, Steven, and Barbara A. Kapinus. "Possible Sentences: Predicting Word Meanings to Teach Content Area Vocabulary." *The Reading Teacher* 45 (September 1991): 36–43.

9

Reading and Study Skills I
An Emphasis on Content-Area Reading

SCENARIO: MR. BROWN KNOWS ELEMENTARY CHILDREN NEED STUDY SKILLS

Mr. Brown teaches social studies and science in sixth grade. When he first meets his students, he has them fill out a checklist to learn as much as he can about their work habits (see Table 9-1). He uses the information he gathers to guide him in developing a program for his students that is based on their needs.

Mr. Brown is interested in helping his students attain content concepts, but he knows that his students will not be able to gain the necessary concepts unless they have good reading and study skills. Fortunately for his students, not only does Mr. Brown have a strong social studies and science background, but he is also very well versed in reading and study skills.

Therefore, at the beginning of every year, he provides special instruction in study techniques, and throughout the term he helps his students attain any special strategies they need to get the most from their content textbooks. The strategies include insights into the organization of the material and the tactics that the students should use to gain the most from what is being taught or read.

Mr. Brown gives meaningful and challenging homework because studies show that extra studying helps children at all levels of ability, and homework can boost the time spent studying. Effective homework assignments do not just supplement the classroom lessons; they also teach students to be independent learners. In addition, "generally, students who reported receiving and completing homework tended to read more proficiently than their classmates who either did not have homework assigned or did not do their homework."[1]

---

[1] Judith A. Langer, Arthur N. Applebee, Ina V. S. Mullis, and Mary A. Foertsch, *Learning to Read in Our Nation's Schools: Instruction and Achievement in 1988 at Grades 4, 8, and 12*, National Assessment of Educational Progress (Princeton, N.J.: Educational Testing Service, June 1990), p. 16.

Mr. Brown is a good teacher. He realizes that many students will not become good strategic readers without direct help or intervention. He also knows that he must get his students interested in what they are learning because in the end they are the ones who have to know how to use the strategies and also must want to use them when they are studying.

This chapter and the next are concerned with helping you to gain the information and skills that are necessary for you to help your students to become better readers and consequently better learners.

KEY QUESTIONS

After you finish reading this chapter, you should be able to answer the following questions:

1. What does studying require, and what is the key to building good study habits?
2. What is SQ3R?
3. What is the role of concentration in studying?
4. How do attitudes influence our studying?
5. What is skimming?
6. What role does skimming play in study techniques?
7. What are the purposes of maps, charts, and graphs?
8. What are examples of some reference books that can help students?
9. What should students know about the dictionary?
10. How can teachers help students organize their time better?

KEY TERMS IN CHAPTER

You should pay special attention to the following key terms:

concentration   skimming
dictionary   SQ3R
overlearning   study procedures
recite or recall   survey

The Importance of Acquiring Good Study Habits

Do the following statements sound familiar?

"I reread the chapter ten times, but I don't remember a thing."

"I reread it a lot too, but I don't understand it."

"I can't study unless I have the TV or radio on."

"I like to relax when I study."

"I don't need to study."

"I don't know how to study."

And so it goes . . .

Many students do poorly in school because they have never learned how to study. Elementary school teachers usually do not spend time in helping children to acquire study skills because they themselves may lack the skills,[2] and because they often feel that this is the job of high school teachers, and many high school teachers do not spend time in this area because they make the assumption that their students have already acquired the study skills they need. As a result, many students may go through the grades without ever having been helped to acquire study skills. This is a mistake. Children should be helped to acquire good study habits as soon as possible before they develop either poor study habits or erroneous concepts concerning studying. Children should be helped to learn that, with good study habits, they could spend less time in studying and learn more.

Building Good Study Habits

Study procedures (1) Build good habits, (2) devise a system that works for you, (3) keep at it, (4) maintain a certain degree of tension, and (5) concentrate.

Although there is no simple formula of study that will apply to all students, educational psychologists have found that some procedures help all students. The key is in building good habits, in devising a system that works, and in keeping at it.

A person cannot relax and study at the same time. Studying requires a certain amount of tension, concentration, and effort in a specific direction. Of course, the amount of tension varies with different individuals. The point is that studying is hard work, and students who are not prepared to make a proper effort are wasting their time (Figure 9-1).

Teachers at all grade levels throughout the school year should help students acquire the study skills they need to succeed in school. The amount of study skills information given will, of course, depend on the individual differences of the students and their grade level. The primary grades are not too soon to begin children on the path to good study habits. However, teachers need to provide different kinds of information to children in the primary grades than in the intermediate grades, where students are reading more for information than for learning to read. Teachers need to recognize, also, that even highly able students may not have good study habits.

---

[2] Eunice N. Askov, Karlyn Kamm, and Roger Klumb, "Study Skill Mastery among Elementary Teachers," *The Reading Teacher* 30 (February 1977): 485–488.

FIGURE 9-1   Jennifer knows studying is hard work.

A good study skills program requires continuous assessment of students' study habits to determine the kinds of help students need. One way teachers can gain information about their students' study habits is to present them with a questionnaire such as the one in Table 9-1. It is important that students know the

TABLE 9-1   Study Habits Questionnaire

Name _____

Grade _____

Subject _____

This questionnaire will not be used to determine your grade in this course. Please try to answer the questions as honestly as you can. If you do not want to give your name, you do not have to do so.

1. How much time do you usually spend a week in studying?
2. How much time do you expect to spend in studying this course?
3. Where do you study?
4. Do you have the radio on when you study?
5. Do you have the television on when you study?
6. Would you like help in gaining study skills?
7. Do you use any special technique when you study? If so, please explain.

purposes of the questionnaire and that they cooperate; otherwise they will answer in the expected direction—that is, in the way they think the teacher wants them to answer.

Steps in Building Good Study Habits

1. The first step in building good study habits is to determine *when to study.* Some students study only just before an announced test. Some may even stay up until all hours and cram. All of us have probably done this once or twice. However, if this is a student's normal way of doing things, he or she will not do well in school. Cramming does not bring about sustained learning. It can be justified only as a last resort. To be a good student, the student must plan his or her study time and spread it out over a period of time. Students must be helped to realize that a regular plan will prevent confusion and help them to retain what they are studying. Even in the elementary grades, students should be helped to plan an overall time schedule in which they allow for social and physical activities. It is to be hoped that their time schedule also allows for some recreational reading. (See Chapter 4 entitled "Teaching for the Love of Books: Children's Literature.") Students must recognize that a rhythm of activities is important. It does not matter whether they study in the evening, before or after dinner, or right after class during free periods. The important thing is for the student to follow a schedule and spread out the studying over the week. (See "Organizing a Weekly Schedule.")

2. The second step in building good study habits is to determine *where to study.* Some students are able to study well in a school or public library, but there are others who cannot. Most elementary school students study at home. Regardless of where the student studies, he or she should choose a place that is comfortable and convenient, has enough light, and is *free from distractions.* Consistency is important.

To help children to establish a comfortable, convenient, and suitable place for study at home, the teacher and the children can design such a place at school in the classroom. A special area in the classroom can be set aside as a study area. The area should be one that is as free from distractions as possible, comfortable, and well lighted. Students should be free to go to this area whenever they wish to study. If a student is in this area, other students should recognize this as "off bounds"; that is, other students should respect the student's desire to study and not interrupt or bother the student.

Teachers must recognize that there are some students in class who may not have a place at home to study. There may be many children in the house and not enough rooms, so that the only place to study may be the kitchen. This place, however, is not very good because it usually has too many distractions. Teachers should be aware of the home situations of their students and try to help them as much as possible without embarrassing them. One thing the teacher could do would be to discuss the possibility of the student's studying at the library or at a friend's house. If these are not feasible and if the student does not have to ride a school bus to school, the teacher might make some arrangements whereby the student can study in the school. A teacher must be sensitive to the fact that students who do not have a place to do homework or study at home are actually being penalized twice—once because they do not have a place to study and twice because they will probably be penalized for not doing the homework, and they also will probably not do well in school.

Overlearning
Helps persons retain information over a long period of time; occurs when individuals continue to practice even after they think they have learned the material.

3. The third step in building good study habits is to determine the *amount of time* to spend in studying. You must help students to recognize that the amount of time they spend in studying will depend on the subject and how well they know it. It is unrealistic to set up a hard-and-fast rule about the amount of time to study in a specific subject because the amount of time will vary. In some subjects a student may need to spend a lot of time studying because he or she is weak in that area, whereas in others the student may only have to spend a short time studying. You should help students to understand the concept of *overlearning* because some students feel that if they know something, they do not have to study it at all. In order to overlearn something, students must recognize that they need to practice it even after they feel that they know it. *Overlearning* is not undesirable like *overcooking* the roast. Overlearning helps persons retain information over a long period of time and happens when individuals continue to practice even after they think they have learned the material.

Organizing a Weekly Schedule

Many elementary school students today are pressured with an overload of activities that compete for their time and attention. Some claim that they do not have the time to just relax. On the other hand, there are children who are spending as many as four, five, or six hours a day in front of a television set. It could be that many children feel overburdened because they are not making effective use of their time.

The elementary grades are not too soon to help children recognize the importance of being a good planner. Teachers can begin at the intermediate grade level to help their children recognize that they are old enough to start setting short- and long-range goals for themselves and to plan a realistic weekly schedule. Here is what one teacher does with his fifth-grade class.

SCENARIO

Mr. Jones Helps Students Plan Their Activities

Mr. Jones first has his students keep a log of all their activities for a week. After the week is over, the students discuss what they learned about themselves from their weekly log. Mr. Jones tells them that good students are good planners and that it would be a good idea to try to organize a weekly schedule that would help them accomplish their short- and long-term goals realistically. He then shows them a transparency that displays a student's weekly schedule and asks them if they would like to try to develop their own schedules. The children all say, "Yes."

Continued

SCENARIO   *Continued*

Mr. Jones first brainstorms with his students the kinds of items they should include in their weekly plan. Next he tells them that they will develop a weekly schedule together but that each student will fill in the schedule based on his or her needs. After Mr. Jones guides the children in developing their individual plan, he suggests that the students try to follow their plan for a week to see how effective it is. He tells them to remember that the schedule is only a guide or tool to help them make more effective use of their time; they should use it as such and not become a slave to it. He also shares with them that their individual schedules would probably vary somewhat from week to week based on their activities and homework assignments.

At the beginning of each week, he would give each student a blank schedule and for homework have them fill it out. Then, throughout the school year, Mr. Jones would spend a few minutes discussing their schedules and how effective they were. He would continually remind them that the schedules are only guides and are not to be used as ends in themselves.

What follows are some items that Mr. Jones and his students included in their weekly schedule to make it a realistic one.

1. *Sleep:* It is not possible to function well over an extended period of time without adequate sleep. Even though the amount may vary from child to child, children should get at least eight hours of sleep a night.
2. *Meal time:* Students cannot do well without adequate nourishment. Young children are growing and need good, well-balanced meals and the time to eat them.
3. *School time:* The children are in school five days a week from 8:30 A.M. to 2:45 P.M. This should be included.
4. *Travel time:* Many children ride a school bus or are driven by their parents or other adults to and from school. This time must also be included.
5. *Physical activity time:* Students need to allow time for daily physical exercise. If children are in special physical activities such as baseball or football, then these activities should also be included.
6. *Special activities:* A number of children have special music, dance, art, or other kinds of practice or activities after school. These should also be included.
7. *Study time:* Children must include adequate time to do all their homework assignments and to study for tests.
8. *Leisure time:* Everyone needs time just to mull things over, listen to music, watch a TV show, go to a movie, read a book, magazine, or newspaper, go out with friends, or do whatever else will make a person relax—it may be just to do nothing.
9. *Miscellaneous things:* Students must also include such mundane things as taking care of their personal needs, shopping for clothing, going to the dentist or orthodontist, and so forth.

Student Achievement and Homework

Studies show that the investment of significant amounts of time in homework is related to students' success in school. "Extra studying helps children at all levels of ability and homework can boost the time spent studying."[3] The National Assessment of Educational Progress in a summary of findings states that "homework gives students experience in following directions, making judgments, working through problems alone, and developing responsibility and self-discipline."[4] However, the report found that teachers are not requiring students to do much homework.

The topic of homework and its effect on students' achievement has been making headlines in the 1990s and will probably make more. Some state legislators feel so strongly about the issue that they are talking about passing legislation mandating homework.

Making homework obligatory for all students all the time is not feasible. Teachers are the ones who must decide whether homework is necessary or not. If they do give homework, they must make sure they give meaningful and challenging homework to their students based on their students' ability levels and show them they feel that the homework is important by going over it in class.

The homework should supplement the work students are doing in class and provide the added practice students need to overlearn the material. In addition, teachers should prepare students for the homework and provide direct help based on the needs of their students.

How to Study

After you have helped students to attain positive attitudes toward their learning tasks and helped them to recognize that they must exert effort to study (see Figure 9-2), find a suitable place to study, and spend time in studying, you must still help

©1968 United Feature Syndicate, Inc.

Reprinted by permission of UFS, Inc.

FIGURE 9-2   Linus has a lot to learn about studying.

[3] Ina V. S. Mullis, Eugene H. Owen, and Gary W. Phillips, *America's Challenge: Accelerating Academic Achievement,* National Assessment of Educational Progress (Princeton, N.J.: Educational Testing Service, 1990), p. 74.

[4] Ibid.

SQ3R
A widely used study technique that involves five steps; survey, question, read, recite or recall, and review.

Survey
To gain an overview of the text material.

them learn *how to study.* There are a number of study techniques, but SQ3R[5] will be presented rather than some of the others because it is a widely used study technique developed by a well-known psychologist that has proved helpful to many students. Here are the five steps in this technique:

1. *Survey:* First students should get an *overall* sense of their learning task before proceeding to details. They should skim the whole assignment to obtain some idea(s) about the material and how it is organized.
2. *Question:* Students should check section headings and change these to questions to set their purposes for reading.
3. *Read:* Students should read to answer the questions that they have formulated for themselves. While reading, they should notice how the paragraphs are organized because this will help them to remember the answer.

Recite or recall
The process of finding the answer to a question in one's memory without rereading the text or notes.

4. *Recite or recall: This step is very important.* Without referring to their book, students should try to answer the questions that they have formulated for themselves. (Writing down key ideas will provide necessary notes for future review. See the section on notetaking in Chapter 10.)
5. *Review:* Students should take a few moments to review the major headings and subheadings of what they have just finished studying. Also, it's a good idea for students to relate what they have just finished studying to what they have previously studied on the same topic before starting to study a new assignment. (How well they are able to combine or incorporate the new learning with their previous learning will determine how well they will remember the new material.)

Make sure students understand that they can survey a reading assignment to determine its organization and to obtain some ideas about it, but they cannot study unfamiliar material by skimming or reading rapidly. Help your students to recognize that a key factor in remembering information is recall or recitation and not the immediate rereading of their assignment. The time they spend answering the questions that they have formulated is crucial in learning.

Here is an example of how you can help your students to adapt the SQ3R technique to suit their personal needs.

Example: Assignment — Reading a Chapter in a Textbook

Step 1. Students quickly look over the entire chapter to get an overview of the whole chapter and to see the organization and relationships. In doing this it's a good idea for students to read quickly the first sentence of each paragraph because textbook writers generally put the topic sentence at the beginning of the paragraph. (Students should notice section headings and author's margin notes.)

Step 2. Students should choose a part of the chapter to study. (The amount

---

[5] Adapted from Francis P. Robinson, *Effective Study,* 4th ed. (New York: Harper & Row, 1970).

of material they choose will depend on their concentration ability and their prior knowledge in the area; see the section on "Concentration" in this chapter.)

Step 3. Students should look over the first part of the chapter that they have chosen to study and formulate questions on it. (Most textbooks have section headings that are very helpful for formulating questions.)

Step 4. Students should read the material to answer their questions. While reading, they should keep in mind the way that the author has organized his or her details.

Step 5. Students should attempt to answer questions formulated before reading.

Step 6. Students should go on to the next section of their chapter and follow the same steps. After they have finished their whole assignment, they should review or go over *all* that they have studied. (When they review, they should go back to the beginning of the chapter, look at each section heading, and try to recall the main idea of each paragraph in the section.)

Activities

Here are some sample activities to give your students practice in using the SQ3R technique.

1. Choose a selection that your students have not read before, and have them do the following:
   a. Survey the selection to determine what it's about.
   b. Use the given six questions to set purposes for reading.
   c. Read the selection carefully.
   d. Without looking back at the selection, try to answer the questions. (Prepare six questions that can be used to set purposes for reading.)

2. Choose another selection that your students have not read before, and have them formulate questions that could help them in studying.

Concentration

Concentration
Sustained attention; it is important for both studying and listening to lectures.

You need to help your students to recognize that even though they are acquiring some good study habits, they may still have difficulty studying because they cannot *concentrate*. Concentration is necessary not only for studying but also for listening in class. Concentration is sustained attention. If you are not feeling well, if you are hungry or tired, if you are in a room that is too hot or cold, if your chair is uncomfortable, if the lighting is poor or if there is a glare, if there are visual or auditory distractions, you will not be able to concentrate. The following disturbing words from Dick Gregory's autobiography aptly illustrate what has just been discussed:

The teacher thought I was stupid. Couldn't spell, couldn't read, couldn't do arithmetic. Just stupid. Teachers were never interested in finding out that you couldn't concentrate because you were so hungry, because you hadn't had any breakfast. All you could think about was noontime, would it ever come? Maybe you could sneak into the cloakroom and steal a bite of some kid's lunch out of a coat pocket. A bite of something. Paste. You can't really make a meal out of paste, or put it on bread for a sandwich, but sometimes I'd scoop a few spoonfuls out of the big paste jar in the back of the room. Pregnant people get strange tastes. I was pregnant with poverty. [6]

Skill in concentration can be developed, and teachers should plan to have their students spend time in this area, which is essential for both reading and listening skills.

Concentration demands a mental set or attitude, a determination that you will block everything out except what you are reading or listening to. For example, how many times have you looked up a phone number in the yellow pages of your telephone directory and forgotten the number almost immediately? How many times have you had to look up the *same* number that you had dialed a number of times? Probably very often. The reason you did not remember is that you did not *concentrate*. In order to remember information, you must concentrate. Concentration demands active involvement; it is hard work. You must help your students to recognize that it is a contradiction to say that you will concentrate and relax at the same time. Concentration demands wide-awake and alert individuals. It also demands persons who have a positive frame of mind toward their work. Teachers need to have a good affective environment in their classrooms and be encouraging because the student's attitude or mental set toward what he or she is doing will greatly influence how well he or she will do. Obviously, if students are not interested in the lecture or reading assignment, they will not be able to concentrate. Teachers should, therefore, try to make the lectures and assignments as interesting as possible.

Teachers should also help their students recognize that they cannot listen to the radio or watch television and study at the same time; the combination of these activities tends to overload the brain's central processing capacity—that is, individuals' ability to take in information.

Researchers have found that human central processing resources are limited and that extra demands on attention such as watching TV or having the television on when students are involved in tasks that require concentration, such as reading or studying, may interfere with their getting the most from their primary task. [7] This certainly makes sense, and it should not be surprising that the researchers found that background television has adverse effects on activities such as reading comprehension, complex problem solving, and creative thinking. [8]

[6] Dick Gregory, *Nigger: An Autobiography* (New York: Dutton, 1964), p. 44.

[7] Blake Armstrong and Bradley S. Greenberg, "Background Television as an Inhibitor of Cognitive Processing," *Human Communication Research* 16 (Spring 1990): 375.

[8] Ibid.

It is, of course, necessary to help your students understand that paying attention does not guarantee that they will comprehend what they have read or heard, but it is an important first step. Without concentration, there is no hope of their understanding the information. The following types of activities will help your students to develop their concentration ability.

In Activity 1, the words that are presented are those that are not related to one another, so that the listener must concentrate very hard in order to be able to repeat them immediately. This activity can be done each day or a few times during the week. Children enjoy this activity and are delighted when they find that they are able to pay attention for longer periods of time and are, therefore, able to repeat more and more of the words.

Activity 1: Word Concentration (Listening)

Directions   In this activity, just two persons are needed — a speaker and a listener. It can also be done with teams. The speaker says, "Listen carefully. I am going to say some words and when I am through, I want you to repeat them exactly the way I have said them. The words have to be in the same order as I have said them. I will state the words only once and at a rate of one per second. Remember — listen carefully and do not say them until I am finished. I'll start with two words, and then I'll keep adding one word. Let's do one together."

Example   The speaker says, "Train, nail." The listener repeats, "Train, nail." If the words are repeated correctly, the speaker says, "Good."

Set 1: can/dog . . . red/map . . .

Set 2: mail/milk/book . . . cake/pen/sad . . .

Set 3: sad/none/in/may . . . chair/help/two/six . . .

Set 4: name/sail/bike/pen/man . . . worm/boat/sick/has/more . . .

Set 5: chair/name/key/same/hop/note   . . .   leg/rope/teach/dance/dog/hair . . .

Set 6: witch/rob/sleep/some/read/check/nuts . . . ball/ape/mind/sleep/dog/king/hair . . .

Set 7: spoon/mate/can/man/all/book/sad/show . . . love/rode/room/all/door/can/girl/pad . . .

Set 8: boat/lamp/paint/long/dock/teach/knife/win/chair . . . draw/food/pat/car/sand/pan/size/spring/farm . . .

Digit-span exercises based on a graduated level of difficulty are helpful in developing concentration ability. The instructions for the digits are similar to those in Activity 1 for words; however, in place of words, the term *digit* is inserted; and instead of saying the digits, they are written. Activity 2 is an example.

Activity 2: Digit-Span Concentration (Listening)

Directions   The speaker says, "Listen carefully. I am going to say some numbers and when I am through, I want you to write them exactly the way I have said them. I will state the numbers only once and at a rate of one per second. All right, let's begin. Remember, listen carefully and do not write them until I am finished giving you the whole sequence."

Following is a list of numerals at a span from 2 to 9. There are three sets of numerals in each span sequence. These could be given at one-week intervals so that the students can see whether they are making progress in increasing their digit span.

Numbers for Digits Forward

Span

(2) 85
     62
     94
(3) 374
     195
     837
(4) 7295
     4962
     6384
(5) 58274
     39481
     72583
(6) 362915
     725816
     817492
(7) 8514739
     7281594
     7359628
(8) 16952738
     95184726
     14793582
(9) 739584162
     581926374
     726938415

Digit-Span Scale   The following paragraph presents a scale that should help in determining how well your children are doing.

On the average, two-and-one-half-year-olds are able to repeat two digits in order, and three-year-olds are able to repeat three digits in order. Children from about the age of four and one-half to about seven years of age are able to repeat four digits in order. Seven- to ten-year-olds are usually able to repeat five digits in order. Ten- to fourteen-year-olds are usually able to repeat six digits in order.

Fourteen-year-olds to more able adults usually can repeat seven, eight, and nine digits in order. (*Digits* refer to numbers. One-syllable words may be substituted for digits.)

Activity 3: Adding Word Concentration Activity (Listening)

Directions   The teacher says, "I'm going to say two sets of words. The second set has all the words from Set 1, but it also has a new word. You have to write what the new word is. *Example:* Set 1: pen, dog, tall. Set 2: tall, dog, pen, snow. (The new word is *snow.*)"

        Set 1: stamp, week, red
        Set 2: week, stamp, red, (smoke)
        Set 1: child, help, dark, nice
        Set 2: child, (grow), help, nice, dark
        Set 1: sun, spoon, mouth, five, bet
        Set 2: spoon, mouth, five, (game), bet, sun
        Set 1: wild, rose, bread, couch, pill, cup
        Set 2: rose, bread, couch, pill, (crumb), cup, wild
        Set 1: pin, fat, net, pine, wind, swing, dog
        Set 2: fat, net, pine, wind, (damp), swing, pin, dog
        Set 1: green, school, twelve, tiny, camp, drape, arm, bulb
        Set 2: school, tiny, bulb, green, camp, (blame), arm, drape, twelve

Activity 4: Missing Word Concentration Activity (Listening)

Directions   The teacher says, "I am going to say two sets of words. The second set is the same as the first set except one word from the first set is missing. You have to write the word that is missing. *Example:* Set 1: car, book, step. Set 2: step, car. (The missing word is *book.*)"

        Set 1: (nice), sell, den
        Set 2: den, sell
        Set 1: can, net, (place), tire
        Set 2: tire, net, can
        Set 1: cake, cord, (sink), horse
        Set 2: cord, cake, horse
        Set 1: fire, sing, (ship), twine, sleep
        Set 2: twine, sing, sleep, fire
        Set 1: drink, camp, lamp, (house), cat, trunk
        Set 2: trunk, camp, drink, lamp, cat
        Set 1: big, sweet, tree, milk, (chin), dress, leaf
        Set 2: sweet, leaf, dress, milk, tree, big
        Set 1: pants, hole, nice, six, trail, doll, (wish), mice
        Set 2: hole, doll, nice, pants, six, mice, trail
        Set 1: dream, snow, limb, hair, cake, toy, (frame), desk, fish
        Set 2: fish, limb, snow, hair, cake, toy, desk, dream

Following Directions

Being able to follow directions is an important skill that we use all our lives. Scarcely a day goes by without the need to obey directions. Cooking, baking, taking medication, driving, traveling, repairing, building, planning, taking examinations, doing assignments, filling out applications, and a hundred other common activities require the ability to follow directions.

You can help your students to be better at following directions through practice and by having them heed the following pointers.

1. Read the directions *carefully*. Do *not* skim directions. Do not take anything for granted and, therefore, skip reading a part of the directions.
2. If you do not understand any directions, do not hesitate to ask your teacher and/or another student.
3. Concentrate! People who follow directions well have the ability to concentrate well.
4. Follow the directions that *are* given, not the ones that you think ought to be given.
5. Reread directions if you need to, and refer to them as you follow them.
6. Remember that some directions should be followed step by step.
7. Practice following directions. Try this activity, which will give you experience in following directions.

Activity

Directions   Read carefully the entire list of directions that follows before doing anything. You have four minutes to complete this activity.

1. Put your name in the upper right-hand corner of this paper.
2. Put your address under your name.
3. Put your telephone number in the upper left-hand corner of this paper.
4. Add 9370 and 5641.
5. Subtract 453 from 671.
6. Raise your hand and say, "I'm the first."
7. Draw two squares, one triangle, and three circles.
8. Write the opposite of *hot*.
9. Stand up and stamp your foot.
10. Give three meanings for *spring*.
11. Write the numbers from 1 to 10 backwards.
12. Write the even numbers from 1 to 20.
13. Write the odd numbers from 1 to 21.
14. Write seven words that rhyme with *fat*.
15. Call out, "I have followed directions."
16. If you have read the directions carefully, you should have done nothing until now. Do only directions 1 and 2.

Answer The directions stated that you should read the entire list of directions carefully *before doing anything*. You should have done only directions 1 and 2. When you take timed tests, you usually do *not* read the directions as carefully as you should.

Here are some sample activities in following directions.

Activity 1

Directions Read each numbered instruction *once* only, and then carry out the instructions on the boxed material. (This activity requires a great amount of concentration.)

```
1  7  3  4  play  dog  man  M  N  O  P  Q  35  32  63  15
10  stop  under  big
```

Instructions

1. If there are two numbers that added together equal 7 and a word that rhymes with *may,* put a line under the rhyming word.
2. If there is a word that means the same as *large,* a word opposite to *go,* and a word that rhymes with *fan,* put a circle around the three words.
3. If there are two numbers that added together equal 8, two numbers that added together equal 67, and a word the opposite of *over,* underline the two numbers that added together equal 8.
4. If there are five consecutive letters, four words that each contain a different vowel, and at least four odd numbers, put a cross on the five consecutive letters.
5. If there are six words, three even numbers, two numbers that added together equal 45, and three numbers that added together equal 16, do nothing.
6. If there are two numbers that added together equal 25, two numbers that added together equal 95, and three numbers that added together equal 79, put a circle around the three numbers that added together equal 79.

Activity 2

Directions Read each numbered instruction *once* only, and then carry it out on the circles given on page 300.

Instructions

1. If arrows in each of the three circles are pointing N, NE, S, and SE, put a circle around S in circle B.
2. If arrows in each of the circles B and C are pointing W, S, and SW, put a circle around SW in circle A.

3. If the arrows in circle C are pointing in the same directions as all the arrows in circle A, put a circle around S in circle A.
4. If arrows in each of the three circles are pointing in three directions that are similar in each of the three circles, put a circle around N in circle C.
5. If the arrows in circles A, B, and C are not pointing in at least one direction in each circle, put a circle around NW in circle B.

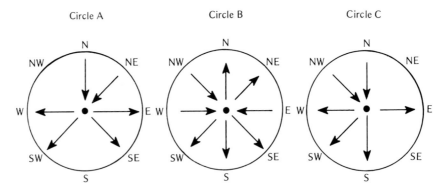

Here is a lesson plan that primary grade teachers can use with their children to help them gain ability in following directions.

Lesson Plan: Primary Grade Level

Objective

Students will show that they are gaining skill in concentration by following given directions correctly.

Preliminary Preparation
Graph paper, story

Introduction
"We've been talking about how important it is to be able to listen carefully to directions. Who can tell us some of the things that we have said?" "Very good. Yes, if we are lost and someone gives us directions, we have to be able to listen carefully so that we can remember the directions. What did we call it when we paid attention very carefully?" "Yes, good. We called it 'concentration,' and we said that we all needed to learn how to pay attention for longer periods of time or to concentrate." "Let's listen to this story." The teacher reads the following story:

> The phone rings in the Stewart house. Jane picks up the phone. "Hello," she says. "Hello," says Mrs. Brown, "is your mother home?" "No," answers Jane. "Would you give her a message for me, please?" "Yes," says Jane. "Please tell your mother that we are meeting at Mrs. Drake's house, not Mrs. Crane's. Also tell her to bring paper plates, not the cups. Do you have that, Jane? Should I repeat it for you?" "Oh, no," says Jane, "I'll remember."

Lesson Plan: Primary Grade Level   *Continued*

> When Jane's mother came home, Jane said, "Mom, Mrs. Brown phoned. She told me to tell you that they are meeting at Mrs. Crane's house and that you should bring paper cups."
>
> "Oh dear," says Mrs. Stewart. "I don't have any paper cups. I'll have to go out to buy some. Also, Mrs. Crane's house is so far away. Oh well, . . ."

Ask the children what Jane should have done to help her remember the message.

1. Write down the message.
2. Ask that it be repeated.
3. Repeat the message herself.

Tell the children that another reason that Jane did not remember the message was because she was not concentrating. Then tell the children that today they will be involved in some activities to help to make them better concentrators.

Development

"Children, you will have to listen very carefully because I will be giving you some directions to follow. In order to carry out the directions correctly, you will have to concentrate. For some of the directions, you will have to do nothing. Here are the directions:

"**1.** If the sun is cold, hop on your right leg three times.
"**2.** If the rain is wet, touch the toes of your left foot with your right hand.
"**3.** If you have a name that begins like Mary, jump up and down five times, and then clap your hands three times.
"**4.** If stars come out in the daytime, clap your hands twice.
"**5.** If milk comes from a goat, touch your waist with your left hand and at the same time jump up and down four times."

"Children, I am very pleased with you. You all are concentrating very hard. Now I am going to give you some graph paper. You are going to have to listen very carefully so that you can follow the directions. If you follow the directions correctly, you will make a figure. Here are the directions:

"Put your graph paper directly in front of you. Start near the top left side of the paper. Draw a line straight down for four boxes. From the point where you stopped, draw a level line straight across (to the right) for four boxes. From the point where you have now stopped, draw a line straight up for four boxes. From the point you are now, draw a level line straight across to the left for four boxes. What kind of figure have you drawn?" (*a square*)

Summary

The teacher helps the children to pull the main points of the lesson together. She helps them to recognize how important it is to be able to concentrate. She tells them that they will be involved in some more concentration activities the next day.

Skimming

Setting purposes for reading is a crucial factor in reading. Students need to learn that they read for different purposes. If they are reading for pleasure, they may either read quickly or slowly, based on the way they feel. If they are studying or reading information that is new to them, they will probably read very slowly. If, however, they are looking up a telephone number, a name, or a date, or looking over a paragraph for its topic, they will read much more rapidly. Reading rapidly to locate information is called *skimming*. All skimming involves fast reading; however, there are different kinds of skimming. Skimming for a number, a date, or a name can usually be done much more quickly than skimming for the topic of a paragraph or to answer specific questions. (Some persons call the most rapid reading *scanning* and the less rapid reading *skimming*.) Teachers should help students recognize that they read rapidly to locate some specific information, but that once they have located what they want, they may read the surrounding information more slowly.

Skimming
Reading rapidly to find or locate information.

Teachers should also make sure that students do not confuse skimming with studying. Although skimming is used as part of the SQ3R technique when students survey a passage, skimming material is not the same as studying. Studying requires much slower and more concentrated reading.

Skimming is an important skill because it is used so often throughout one's life, and it is many times the only way to get a job done in a reasonable amount of time. Some skimming activities for upper intermediate grade level students follow:

1. Skim newspaper headlines for a particular news item.
2. Skim movie ads for a particular movie.
3. Skim tape or record catalogs for a specific title.
4. Skim the yellow pages of the phone book for some help.

Knowing Your Textbook

Helping children to know about the various parts of their textbooks is an important studying skill that can save students valuable time and effort. Here are some things that teachers should have students do after they have acquired their textbooks.

1. *Survey the textbook.* This helps students to see how the author presents the material. Students should notice whether the author presents topic headings in bold print or in the margins. Students should also notice if there are diagrams, charts, cartoons, pictures, and so on.

2. *Read the preface.* The preface or foreword, which is at the beginning of the book, is the author's explanation of the book. It presents the author's purpose and plan in writing the book. Here the author usually describes the organization

of the book and explains how the book either is different from others in the field or is a further contribution to the field of knowledge.

3. *Read the chapter headings.* The table of contents will give students a good idea of what to expect from the book. Then when they begin to study they will know how each section they are reading relates to the rest of the book.

4. *Skim the index.* The index indicates in detail what material students will find in the book. It is an invaluable aid because it helps them find specific information that they need by giving them the page on which it appears.

5. *Check for a glossary.* Not all books have a glossary; however, a glossary is helpful because it gives students the meanings of specialized words or phrases used in the book.

Activities

Have the students skim to answer the following:

1. Using the index of one of the student's textbooks, have them state the pages on which they would find various topics.
2. Using one of their textbooks, have the students give the meaning(s) of some of the terms that are presented in the glossary of one of their textbooks.
3. Using the table of contents of one of their textbooks, have the students state the pages on which some chapters start.

Reading Maps, Charts, and Graphs

Many textbook writers employ charts, graphs, and maps to make their ideas clearer. A number of teachers use these techniques also because they have learned from experience the power of visual representations. Not only are charts, graphs, and maps used in school; they are used outside school as well, and persons who have difficulty understanding these will be at a disadvantage in our society.

Teachers should help students to gain facility in interpreting and using maps, graphs, and charts. If students are given opportunities to work with various types of illustrative materials, they will be in a better position to decipher these when they are reading. Unfortunately, much important information is lost because many students do not pay attention to textbook writers' charts and graphs. Often students skip over the author's illustrative materials completely. The reason for this may be that teachers have not taken the time to stress their value, so students may feel that they are merely space fillers and, therefore, not too important, or it may be that students do not know how to interpret them. Whatever the reasons are, students need to gain skill in interpreting illustrative materials.

Teachers should not assume that their students are able to interpret illustrative materials. They should make the interpretation of illustrative materials part of their instructional program, and time should be set aside for students to gain experience in working with illustrative materials. It is usually best to present the lessons on interpreting charts, graphs, or maps when students are meeting these in their readings. In practically all subject areas, students will have to be able to interpret various types of charts and graphs; maps are a vital part of social studies.

Maps

A map is a means of communicating information. Teachers must help students learn how to read and interpret maps correctly (Figure 9-3). Students need to recognize that a map is a representation of a flat surface of a whole or part of an area and that it is not an exact replica of an area because it is difficult to portray the round earth on a flat surface. Teachers should help their students recognize the limitations of maps and that relationships are only approximations. There are many different types of maps, and each stresses a particular feature of an area. For example, there are street maps, road maps, political maps, physical maps, relief maps, vegetation maps, land-use maps, product maps, pictorial maps, population maps, historical maps, war maps, weather maps, and so on. All maps have a legend or key that needs to be interpreted; different types of maps require different types of coding. For example, political maps use color coding and definite boundary lines to indicate political divisions; consequently, the map's legend would present a key indicating what various colors represent. A rainfall and tem-

FIGURE 9-3   This teacher is helping students gain map reading skills.

perature map uses a combination of color coding and special types of lines. The color coding is used to represent the amount of rainfall, and the special lines are used to indicate the average temperature in an area. Legends may vary from map to map; the clue lies in being able to interpret the particular legend for a particular map.

Road maps are the ones with which students are probably the most familiar and which they will use the most often. Road maps indicate road and distance information and help persons choose travel routes on land. Teachers could use road maps in class to help students gain facility in map reading and to acquaint them with map scales, which show how the map distances compare to the actual distances. (Any map scale is a ratio between whatever the map is measuring and its corresponding measurement on earth.) Teachers can stimulate students' interest in map reading by using activities such as the following:

1. Teachers could have students bring in a road map of the community in which they live and then have them challenge one another to find the fastest distance to get to a certain destination.
2. Another activity would be for teachers to bring in maps of foreign countries and challenge students to find certain locations or the distance between two different locations.
3. Teachers could have students prepare their own maps of regions they are studying. Practice in constructing maps is probably one of the best ways to have students gain an appreciation of their importance, as well as to help students understand maps better.

Charts and Graphs

Beginning at the intermediate grade level, teachers can help students learn that just as there are different types of maps, so are there various types of charts and graphs. Students need to know how to read or interpret these.

Charts and graphs are used to display data. Here is what one teacher does to help her upper intermediate grade level students understand charts and graphs.

SCENARIO ━━━━━━━━━━━━━━━━━━━━━━━━━━━━━━━━━━━━━

Mrs. Moore Helps Her Students Understand Charts and Graphs

In a recent reading group, the students' selection required them to interpret some charts and graphs. Mrs. Moore asked students a number of questions and found that hardly anyone could read the charts and graphs. She told them that she would spend some time with them to help them become able to interpret charts and graphs.

Mrs. Moore did just that. She showed them a chart of a hypothetical student's study pattern and helped them interpret it. Then Mrs. Moore asked each

Continued

SCENARIO   *Continued*

student to keep a log for a week of the amount of time he or she spends studying each subject. After her students did this, she helped them construct their own charts showing the amount of time each studies.

Mrs. Moore then used the students' charts to introduce them to graphs. She told them that the kinds of information that can be charted are too numerous to state; practically anything that can be tallied can be displayed on a chart. She stated further that graphs are more limited in what they can illustrate than charts because they are usually more structured, but they, too, can display many different kinds of information. Mrs. Moore then displayed the hypothetical student's study pattern chart in a bar graph (see Figure 9-4).

She explained that the bar graph is generally used when people want to compare more than six items or categories. She stated also that the circle graph is used to illustrate parts of a whole; it shows how a total amount of something can be divided. The entire graph is equal to 100 percent, and each segment or part is a fraction of the 100 percent.

Mrs. Moore then asked her students to make a bar graph of their study pattern behavior. After they had done this, she discussed with them what they had learned from their graph about their study pattern. At the conclusion of this

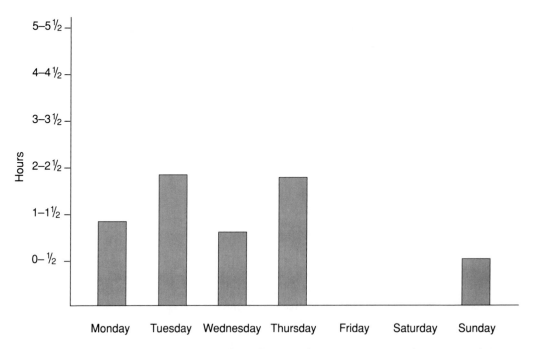

FIGURE 9-4   This bar graph of a sixth-grade student's study pattern compares the amount of time the student spent studying on various days during the week.

activity, she told them that she hoped they realized that charts and graphs are important tools writers use to help illustrate material and that students need to pay careful attention to them.

The School Library and Library Skills

The school library should be an integrated part of the students' ongoing activities. A number of schools have designed their physical plants so that the library is actually in the center of the building, easily accessible to all classrooms. The library, properly utilized, becomes the students' storehouse of information and a reservoir of endless delight for them.

The atmosphere in the library should be such that children feel welcome, invited, and wanted. The librarian is the individual who is responsible for setting this tone. A friendly, warm person who loves children and books will usually have a library which has similar characteristics (see Figure 9-5). Children should

FIGURE 9-5 This librarian is helping a child choose a book.

feel free to visit the library at all times, not just during their regular scheduled periods.

An enthusiastic and inventive librarian will, by various means, act as an invitation to children to come to the library. Some librarians engage in weekly storytelling activities for all grade levels. Librarians should encourage teachers and children to make suggestions for storytelling, as well as to share the kinds of books they enjoy and would like. The librarian should also act as a resource person in helping the classroom teacher to develop library skills in students. Once students gain the library habit, it is hard to break, and it will remain with them throughout life.

Following are some of the library skills that children should achieve in the elementary school.

Primary Grades

In the primary grades children are ready to acquire some library skills that will help them to become independent library users. First, the teacher can help primary children to gain an idea of the kinds of books that are available in the library, for example, fiction and nonfiction books. Definitions of terms should be given, as well as examples of each type of book. For best results, the examples used should be books with which the children are familiar.

Primary grade children who have learned to read and can alphabetize can also learn to use the card catalog. They should learn that there are three kinds of cards for each book: an author card, a title card, and the subject card. The teacher should have samples of these for the children to see and handle. By simulating this activity in the classroom, children will be better prepared for actual library activity. Also, their chances for success in using the catalog properly to find a desired book will be increased. This useful activity can also be programmed to reinforce knowledge of alphabetizing.

Intermediate and Upper Elementary Grades

By the fourth grade children can learn about other categories of books in the library, such as biographies and reference books.

Special Note
Most college and many public libraries are computerized, but not all have terminals for the use of patrons (see Chapter 4). Also, not too many public school libraries are computerized, so learning how to use the card catalogue is still warranted. A computer does not eliminate the need for students to know how to look something up and how to classify or categorize information.

Reference Books

Children in the elementary grades ask many questions about many topics. Teachers should use some of these questions to help children learn about reference sources. Teachers should help children to understand that it is impossible for one person to know everything today because of the vast amount of knowledge that already exists, compounded each year by its exponential growth. However, a person can learn about any particular area or field if he or she knows what source books to go to for help. For example, the *Readers' Guide to Periodical Literature* will help one to find magazine articles written on almost any subject of interest. There are reference books on language and usage, such as Roget's *Thesaurus of English Words and Phrases,* which would help upper grade students in finding synonyms and less trite words to use in writing.

The most often used reference book in elementary school, besides the dictionary, is the encyclopedia. Children should be helped to use the encyclopedia as a tool and an aid, rather than as an end in itself. That is, children should be shown how to extract information from the encyclopedia without copying the article verbatim.

In the upper elementary grades children should learn that there are many reference source books available in the library that can supply information about a famous writer, baseball player, scientist, celebrity, and so forth. The key factor is knowing that these reference sources exist and knowing which reference book to go to for the needed information.

Teachers can help their upper grade children to familiarize themselves with these reference books by giving children assignments in which they have to determine what source books to use in fulfilling the assignment.

The Dictionary: A Special Emphasis

Dictionary
A very important reference tool that supplies word meanings, pronunciations, and a great amount of other useful information.

A dictionary is a very important reference book, not only for elementary school students but for all students. It is helpful in supplying the following information to a student:

1. Spelling
2. Correct usage
3. Derivations and inflected forms
4. Accents and other diacritical markings
5. Antonyms
6. Synonyms
7. Syllabication
8. Definitions
9. Parts of speech
10. Idiomatic phrases

Dictionary Skills: Objectives and Activities
Here are some objectives and activities for primary grade level dictionary skills.

Location of Words

Objectives (Grade 3)   Students should be able to do the following:

1. Open the dictionary halfway and note with which letter words begin in this location.
2. Open the dictionary by quarters and note with which letter words begin in this location.
3. Open the dictionary by thirds and note with which letter words begin in this location.
4. Open the dictionary at certain initial letters such as *g, n,* or *s.*
5. Use key words at head of each page as a guide to finding words.
6. Find brief lists of specific key words.
7. Use key words to find words following the key words.
8. Use key words to find words preceding the key words at end of page.
9. Use key words to find words anywhere on the page.

Activities

1. Children practice opening the dictionary at half, quarters, and thirds.
2. Children open dictionary at half, quarters, and thirds and put down letters with which these sections usually begin.
3. Children practice opening the dictionary according to specific letters.
4. Children are given guide words and asked to find other words on page:

   a. Given guide words *farm—farther,* state which is the first word on the page. State which is the last word on the page.
   b. Given guide words *farm—farther,* would the word *father* be before or after *farm* or before or after *farther?*
   c. Using *can—case* as your guide words, state some words that would be on that dictionary page.

Pronunciation

Objective (Primary Grades)   Students should be able to sound out unfamiliar words, using diacritical markings.

Activities   Children review vowel generalizations and are given new sight words with diacritical markings inserted and asked to pronounce them.

nōté   nēát   nĕt   bōné

Alphabetizing

Objectives (Primary Grades)   Children should be able to

1. Arrange letters in alphabetical order.
2. Arrange words none of which begin with the same letter in alphabetical order.
3. List words several of which begin with the same letters.

Multiple Meanings — Homographs and the Dictionary

Objective (Primary Grades)   Children should be able to use the dictionary to select meanings to fit the context.

Activities

1. Students are asked to list the various meanings of words such as the following:

    train   bark   can

2. Students are asked to write sentences using the words in various ways.
3. Students are given different sentences with the same word and asked to give the meaning of the word in each of the sentences.

Using the Dictionary to Build a Vocabulary of Synonyms and Antonyms

Objectives (Primary Grades)   Children should be able to give

1. the synonyms of stated words.
2. the antonyms of stated words.

Activities

1. Children are given words and asked to state whether they are opposite or similar.

    State whether the following pairs of words are opposite in meaning or alike in meaning:

big – little	old – new	fat – heavy
happy – sad	small – little	sick – ill
good – bad		

2. Children are told a word and asked to give a synonym for the word.

Give words that mean almost exactly the same as the following:

big _____

fat _____

hit _____

small _____

cheerful _____

3. Children are given a common word and asked to consult the dictionary to find a less common word to use in its place.
4. Children are given a word and asked to give an antonym for the word.

Give words that mean the opposite of the following words:

hot _____

stop _____

sad _____

crying _____

5. Children are given a less common word and asked to consult the dictionary to come up with an opposite of the word.[9]

1. Give the opposite of *latter.* _____
2. Give the opposite of *contrary.* _____
3. Give the opposite of *exhausted.* _____
4. Give the opposite of *temporary.* _____

Here are objectives and activities for intermediate grade level dictionary skills. Intermediate grade level students should have acquired the skill to alphabetize words.

Location of Words

Objectives (Grades 4, 5, 6)   Students should be able to

1. Open the dictionary halfway and note with which letter words begin in this location.
2. Open the dictionary by quarters and note with which letter words begin in this location.

---

[9] This section is for highly able third-graders.

3. Open the dictionary by thirds and note with which letter words begin in this location.
4. Open the dictionary at certain initial letters such as *g, n,* or *s.*
5. Use key words at the head of each page as a guide to finding words.
6. Find brief lists of specific key words.
7. Use key words to find words following the key words.
8. Use key words to find words preceding the key words at end of page.
9. Use key words to find words anywhere on the page.

Activities

1. Children practice opening dictionary at halves, quarters, and thirds.
2. Children open dictionary at halves, quarters, and thirds and put down letters with which these sections usually begin.
3. Children practice opening the dictionary according to specific letters.
4. Children are given guide words and asked to find other words on page.

   a. Given guide words *burst—businessman,* state which is the first word on the page. State which is the last word on the page.
   b. Given guide words *burst—businessman,* would the word *burse* be before or after *burst* or before or after *businessman.*
   c. Using *tend—tense* as your guide words, state some words that would be on that dictionary page.

Pronunciation

Objective (Grades 4, 5, 6)   Students should be able to sound out unfamiliar words, using diacritical markings.

Activities   Children review vowel generalizations and are given new sight words with diacritical markings inserted and asked to pronounce them.

   māté   glēám   sōlé   trāīt

Multiple Meanings—Homographs and the Dictionary

Objective (Grades 4, 5, 6)   Students should be able to use the dictionary to select meanings to fit the context.

Activities

1. Students are asked to list the various meanings of words such as the following:

   mean   present   run

2. Students are asked to write sentences using the words in various ways.

3. Students are given different sentences with the same word and asked to give the meaning of the word in each of the sentences.

Using the Dictionary to Build a Vocabulary of Synonyms and Antonyms

Objectives (Grades 4, 5, 6)   Students should be able to give

1. the synonyms of stated words.
2. the antonyms of stated words

Activities

1. Children are given words and asked to state whether they are opposite or similar.

   State whether the following pairs of words are opposites in meaning or alike in meaning.

huge – immense	dark – light
droll – laughable	dusk – dawn
chubby – plump	obese – thin

2. Children are told a word and asked to give a synonym for the word.

   Give words that mean almost exactly the same as the following:

   a. smart _____

   b. fat _____

   c. hit _____

   d. destroy _____

   e. cheerful _____

3. Children are given a common word and asked to consult the dictionary to find a less common word to use in its place.
4. Children are given a word and asked to give an antonym for the word.

   Give words that mean the opposite of the following words:

   a. satisfied _____

   b. dangerous _____

   c. wealthy _____

   d. proud _____

5. Children are given a less common word and asked to consult the dictionary to come up with an opposite of the word.

1. Give the opposite of *obese.* _____

2. Give the opposite of *indolent.* _____

3. Give the opposite of *benign.* _____

4. Give the opposite of *bellicose.* _____

The dictionary riddles that follow can also act as stimuli for initiating other activities. For example, looking up *haiku,* the children will discover that it is a type of poem, and they may decide to try to write some haiku poems. Some children may want to learn more about Mars and other mythological figures, and others may become interested in various mountain ranges.

Dictionary Riddles

Directions   See how well you can answer these ten questions using the dictionary. You should use it to find the meanings of words you do not know and then answer each question.

1. In what countries do centaurs live?
2. Is Mah-Jongg a country?
3. Was Mars the goddess of fire?
4. Is a songstress a man who writes songs?
5. Is Miss. an abbreviation for Missus?
6. Is haiku a Hawaiian mountain?
7. Was Androcles a king?
8. Is a statute a work of art?
9. Is a quadruped an extinct animal?
10. Is a centipede a unit of measurement in the metric system?

Diagnostic Checklist for Reading and Study Skills I

Student's Name: _____

Grade: _____

Teacher: _____

I. Dictionary	Yes	No	Sometimes
A. Grades 1, 2			
The child is able to			
1. supply missing letters of the alphabet.			
2. arrange words none of which begin with the same letter in alphabetical order.			

Continued

Diagnostic Checklist for Reading and Study Skills I *Continued*

I. Dictionary	*Yes*	*No*	*Sometimes*
3. list words several of which begin with the same letter.			
4. list words according to first and second letters.			
5. list words according to third letter.			
6. find the meaning of a word.			
7. find the correct spelling of a word.			

B. Grades 3, 4, 5, 6

The child is able to

	Yes	*No*	*Sometimes*
1. locate words halfway in the dictionary.			
2. open the dictionary by quarters and state the letter with which words begin.			
3. open the dictionary by thirds and state the letters with which words begin.			
4. open the dictionary at certain initial letters.			
5. use key words at the head of each page as a guide to finding words.			
6. use the dictionary to select meanings to fit the context (homographs)			
7. use the dictionary to build up a vocabulary of synonyms.			
8. use the dictionary to build up a vocabulary of antonyms.			
9. answer questions about the derivation of a word.			
10. use the dictionary to learn to pronounce a word.			
11. use the dictionary to correctly syllabicate a word.			
12. use the dictionary to get the correct usage of a word.			
13. use the dictionary to determine the part(s) of speech of the word.			
14. use the dictionary to gain the meanings of idiomatic phrases.			

Library Skills	*Yes*	*No*	*Sometimes*
A. Primary grades			
The child is able to			
1. use the card catalog to find a book.			
2. state the kinds of books that are found in the library.			

Diagnostic Checklist for Reading and Study Skills I   *Continued*

Library Skills	Yes	No	Sometimes

B. Intermediate grades

   The child is able to

     1. state the kinds of reference materials that are found in the library.

     2. use the encyclopedia as an aid to gaining needed information.

     3. find books in the school library.

Building Good Study Habits	Yes	No	Sometimes

Intermediate grades

   The student is able to

     1. plan his or her studying time.

     2. choose a place to study that is free from distractions.

     3. recognize that he or she needs to study.

Study Procedures	Yes	No	Sometimes

Intermediate grades

   The student is able to

     1. use the SQ3R technique when studying.

     2. apply the SQ3R technique when he or she is studying a chapter in a textbook.

Concentration and Following Directions	Yes	No	Sometimes

A. Primary grades

   The child is able to

     1. listen carefully and follow directions.

     2. show that his or her concentration is increasing by being able to pay attention for longer periods of time.

B. Intermediate grades

   The student is able to

     1. read directions and follow them correctly.

     2. fill out some application forms.

Diagnostic Checklist for Reading and Study Skills I   *Continued*

Skimming	Yes	No	Sometimes

A. Primary grades

The child is able to

1. find some information quickly by skimming.
2. skim a paragraph and state its topic.

B. Intermediate grades

The student is able to

1. differentiate between skimming and studying.
2. recognize the role that skimming plays in studying.
3. locate information such as the departure time of trains by skimming train schedules.

Knowing Your Textbook	Yes	No	Sometimes

A. Primary grades

The child is able to

1. use the table of contents to find chapter headings.
2. use the glossary to gain the meaning of a word.
3. list the parts of a textbook.

B. Intermediate grades

The student is able to

1. read the preface to gain information about what the author's purpose was in writing the book.
2. skim the index to gain information about the material that will be found in the book.
3. skim the index to find the page that a specific topic is found on.

Graphic Summary of Chapter

On the following page is a graphic summary of Chapter 9. If you have read the chapter, this graphic illustration should help you remember its main points. Under or beside each heading, you might want to jot down some of the information you recall, as well as some of the key concepts in this chapter. This can act as a good review. You can then check your key concepts against those that follow the graphic summary.

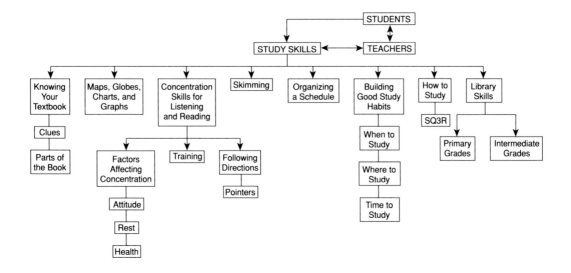

Key Concepts

- The elementary grades are not too soon to help students build good study habits.
- Building good study habits deals with where to study, when to study, and how much time to spend in studying.
- Teachers should integrate study skills in their classes.
- A weekly schedule helps students apportion their time more effectively.
- The SQ3R technique is a viable study method.
- Concentration is sustained attention.
- Individuals cannot concentrate and be relaxed at the same time.
- Following directions is an essential skill.
- Setting purposes for reading is important in reading.
- Knowledge of textbooks is important in studying.
- Graphs, charts, and maps help make ideas clearer.
- Graphs, charts, and maps are means of communication.
- Primary grade children should learn what kinds of books are available in the library.
- Intermediate grade students and above should learn about the many reference books available in the library.
- The dictionary is a very important reference book, which all students should learn to use.

Suggestions for Thought Questions and Activities

1. You have been appointed to a special committee to help to develop a study skills program for your elementary school. What suggestions would you make? What kinds of skills and activities would you recommend for the primary grade children? For the intermediate grade children? For upper intermediate grade children?

2. Develop some concentration activities for primary grade level children.

3. Develop some concentration activities for intermediate grade level students.

4. Prepare a lesson on helping students become acquainted with a specific content-area textbook.

5. Prepare a lesson on map reading for a particular content area.

6. Plan a lesson in which students must use at least three different reference sources.

7. Construct some questions on a specific area that require the students to use the dictionary.

8. Make some suggestions on how you would help students become better direction followers.

9. Choose a story and then develop some skimming lessons based on the story.

10. Some teachers in your school system feel that primary grade level children are too immature to learn study skill techniques. What do you think? How would you convince these teachers that this is not so for many of these children?

Selected Bibliography

Anderson, Thomas H., and Bonnie B. Armbruster. "Studying." In *Handbook of Reading Research,* P. David Pearson, ed. New York: Longman, 1984, pp. 657–679.

Paris, Scott G., Barbara A. Wasik, and Julianne C. Turner. "The Development of Strategic Readers. In *Handbook of Reading Research,* Vol. II, Rebecca Barr, Michael L. Kamil, Peter Mosenthal, and P. David Pearson, eds. New York: Longman, 1991, pp. 609–640.

Rubin, Dorothy. *Reading and Learning Power,* 3rd ed. Needham Heights, Mass.: Ginn Press, 1991.

Rubin, Dorothy. *Teaching Reading and Study Skills in Content Areas.* Boston: Allyn and Bacon, 1992.

Wade, Suzanne, Woodrow Trathen, and Gregory Schraw. "An Analysis of Spontaneous Study Strategies." *Reading Research Quarterly* 25 (Spring 1990): 147–166.

10
Reading and Study Skills II
An Emphasis on Content-Area Reading

SCENARIO: MISS HANSON HELPS HER STUDENTS GAIN STUDY SKILLS

When Miss Hanson was a student at college, she took a reading course that stressed the teaching of study skills to elementary grade level students. Her professor claimed that the intermediate grades were not too soon to help students learn that writing could be used as a mode of learning and that teachers should help students as early as possible to become better test takers and question askers.

Miss Hanson applied all that she learned about study skills to her own studying and found that the strategies helped her tremendously. She felt cheated that she had had to wait until college to attain such essential skills. She vowed to herself that she would not shortchange any students whom she taught, and to this day she has kept that vow.

Throughout the school year, Miss Hanson helps her students acquire various study skills and strategies that she feels will enhance their learning ability. She teaches these study strategies directly using relevant subject-matter material and then gives her students ample opportunities to practice these strategies in school and at home.

This chapter is an outgrowth of the kinds of study skills information that Miss Hanson helps her students acquire.

KEY QUESTIONS

After you finish reading this chapter, you should be able to answer the following questions:

1. Why should children be good question askers?
2. How can teachers help elementary grade level students learn that writing can be a way of learning material?
3. How can notetaking and summarizing be used as modes of learning?
4. What is the role of outlining?
5. How can semantic mapping be used for studying?
6. How can teachers help students be better test takers?

KEY TERMS IN CHAPTER

You should pay special attention to the following key terms:

graphic summary   questions
mnemonic device   subjective tests
notetaking   summary
objective tests   telegraphic writing
outlining   test

Asking Questions

Questions
A good way for students to gain a better insight into a subject; questioning also gives the instructor feedback and slows the instructor down if he or she is going too fast.

A section on question asking is being presented because this is an area in which students need special help. Many students become intimidated early in school about asking questions and as a result hardly ever ask any. Asking questions is an important part of learning! Children must be helped to recognize this, and teachers must provide an environment that is nonthreatening so that students will feel free to ask questions (see Figure 10-1). Knowing how and when to ask questions helps students to gain a better insight into a subject, gives the teacher feedback, and slows the teacher down if he or she is going too fast. Unfortunately, as has already been stated, many students are afraid to ask questions. Sometimes their fear may be due to a teacher's attitude; however, often it's because a student doesn't know how to formulate the question or is "afraid of looking like a fool."

Here are some pointers that teachers should try to get across to their students:

1. Persons who ask the best questions are usually those who know the material best.
2. Asking questions is not a substitute for studying the material.
3. Questions help to clarify the material for students.
4. Teachers usually want and encourage questions.
5. The questions they ask will probably help a number of other students.

Here are suggestions on the kind of questions students should ask about examinations:

FIGURE 10-1 This child is not afraid to ask questions.

1. What kind of test will it be? Will it be an objective or a subjective test?
2. How long will the test be? This will help the students to know whether it's a quiz (a minor exam) or a test (one that usually counts more than a quiz).
3. Will dates, names, formulas, and other such specifics be stressed? (This is important for the student to know because it will influence the type of studying that he or she will do.)
4. Will it be an open-book or closed-book exam? (This is important because it will influence the type of studying a student will do.)
5. What chapters will be covered?

Here are some suggestions on other kinds of questions students should ask:

1. In going over an examination, they should ask general questions or those that relate to everyone's papers. Tell students that if they have specific questions on their papers, they should ask the teacher these questions in private.
2. Tell students that they should not hesitate to ask questions about the marking of their papers if they do not understand it (see Figure 10-2). They should especially ask the teacher about a comment on their paper that they do not

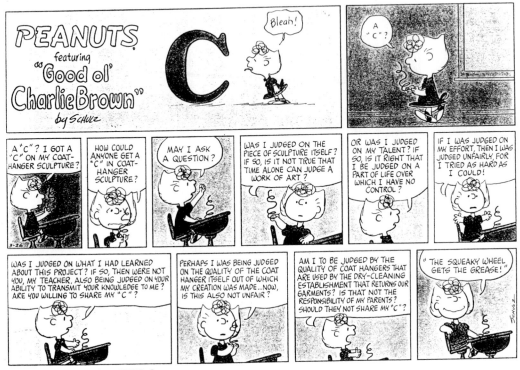

Reprinted by permission of UFS, Inc.

FIGURE 10-2   Sally may not have received a good grade on her sculpture, but she is a good question asker. She deserves an "A" on question asking.

understand. Help them to recognize that they learn from knowledge of results and understanding their mistakes.

Here are some suggestions on how students should ask questions.

1. They should be as specific as possible.
2. They should state the question clearly.
3. They should not say, "I have a question," and then go into a long discourse before asking the question. (The question may be forgotten.)
4. They should make sure that the question is related to the material.

Activities to Enhance Question Asking

1. The teacher constructs some guide questions for students based on a story students have read. The students then construct their own questions based on a story they are currently reading using the teacher's questions as a model.

2. The teacher can have students either individually or in groups formulate questions for an upcoming test.

3. Teachers can have students read a story and then, rather than the teacher

asking questions, the students can be the question askers. Each student writes his or her question on storybook paper and initials the question. Then each student challenges the others to answer the questions. Each question answerer must support his or her answers. At the end of the session, the teacher discusses with the students who has asked the best questions and why.

4. Another question-asking activity is a take-off of Suchman's inquiry method, which has generally been used in science classes. This technique requires students to ask questions in the form of hypotheses. The teacher only answers "Yes" or "No." If students formulate enough correct question hypotheses, they will eventually arrive at the correct conclusion or solution.

Here is how one intermediate grade level teacher uses this technique with his reading groups. He has the students read most of the story but stops them before they get to the end. He then challenges his students to formulate questions that would help give them the author's ending. The teacher answers only "Yes" or "No" to their questions. If the students do not arrive at the author's way of ending the story, they are told to read the ending for themselves. Then they discuss why they had difficulty arriving at the ending. They also discuss whether some of their endings may or may not have been better ones.

Asking Questions of Written Material

SCENARIO

Mrs. Noble Helps Students Become More Alert Readers

Mrs. Noble feels that asking questions of what they are reading will help make students more alert readers. She believes that children not only should be adept at asking questions in class, but they also should ask questions about the material they are reading.

Mrs. Noble introduced her students early in the year to SQ3R (see Chapter 9), a technique in which students use questions to set purposes for their reading. The questioning in SQ3R helps give direction and organization to what students are reading; however, Mrs. Noble feels that students, in order to be actively involved in what they are reading as well as problem solvers, should ask questions about the text material during and after their reading. These questions are generally different from those asked in class and are usually triggered by a number of factors.

She encourages her students to be good critical thinkers and to evaluate what they are reading by presenting them with a short selection and asking them to read it as if they were investigative reporters. While they are reading the selection, they must determine the kinds of questions they would ask and why they would ask these questions. After all the students have finished reading the article, they discuss the kinds of questions that came to their minds while they were reading.

Mrs. Noble recognizes that asking questions of text material is consistent with viewing reading as problem solving, as well as with helping students become better critical thinkers.

Reading and Writing as Modes of Learning

The elementary grades are an excellent place to help students gain a number of reading and writing strategies to help them learn better. These strategies are especially effective when children are reading to gain information in their content areas.

Notetaking for Studying

Notetaking
A useful study and paper-writing tool.

Notetaking is a very important tool; it is useful not only in writing long papers but also in studying. Students are usually not concerned with notetaking until they begin writing long reports or papers. Teachers should help students learn how to take notes. Here is information on notetaking that teachers should convey to their upper intermediate grade level students.

Notes consist of words and phrases that help people remember important material. They do not have to be complete sentences; however, unless an individual's notes are clear and organized, he or she will have difficulty in using them for study purposes. For example, examine this set of notes on an article entitled "Why Home Accidents Occur":

Student's Notes

1. slippery floors
2. bathroom light switch
3. cellar stairs dark
4. ladder broken
5. medicines on shelf
6. light cord bare
7. pots on stove with handles out
8. throw rugs
9. using tools carelessly
10. toys on floor
11. box on stairs
12. putting penny in fuse box
13. thin curtains over stove

Student's List of Main Topics of Article

I. Failure to see danger
II. Failure to use things properly
III. Failure to make repairs

It is difficult to make sense of these notes because the main topics are vaguely stated. The items in the list of notes can fit under more than one main topic. They are not precise enough; that is, they do not contain enough information to identify or distinguish them unmistakably.

In the following lesson plan, a teacher uses these notes to help students become better notetakers.

Lesson Plan: Intermediate Grade Level

Objective

Students will be able to recognize that notes should fit into only one main topic area.

Preliminary Preparation

Overhead projector, transparency of a student's notes, main headings.

Introduction

"We've discussed the importance of having a good outline when we write a long report or composition. What are some of the reasons we gave?" "Yes, good. We also talked about the various kinds of outlines. Who remembers some? Today, I'd like you to look at this transparency. It contains notes from a student report called 'Why Accidents Occur.' You don't know this student because he doesn't go to our school. Look for one moment at the notes that this student took and also his main headings. Today we're going to discuss whether this student took good notes and give our reasons for our opinions. From the discussion we should be able to make some suggestions for good notetaking procedures."

Development

"I'd like everyone to categorize the notes into this student's main headings." (Teacher walks around the room while pupils are working and offers her assistance.) After a while she asks whether anyone is having difficulty classifying the notes. A number of children raise their hands and say that they are. The teacher asks them why. One pupil states that some of the notes fit into more than one main heading, and a number of students agree. Another pupil says that he can't put the notes under the proper heading because he isn't sure about their meaning. The teacher asks some students to read what they have put under main topic I. It turns out that students do not agree. The same is done for main topic II and main topic III. The teacher again asks why this has happened. Students reply that they all interpreted the notes differently, and they could fit under more than one heading.

Summary

The teacher asks students what they have learned that could help them to become better notetakers from this activity concerning notetaking and main topics. Students reply that the main topics must be clearly stated and not overlap. The notes must also be precise and exact, so that there is no question as to where they belong.

    The teacher then states, "Tomorrow we'll look at this student's notes and main topics again. We'll see if we are able to rewrite them so that they can fit properly under the main headings."

Notetaking and SQ3R

1. Notetaking for study purposes can be incorporated in the SQ3R study technique. Here is a suggested procedure combining SQ3R and notetaking:

a. Students should read the whole selection to get an overview of what they have to study. A preliminary reading helps them to see the organization of the material.

b. Students should choose a part of the selection to study, basing their choice on their concentration ability.

c. Students should survey the part chosen and note the topic of the individual paragraph or group of paragraphs. They should write the topic(s) in their notebook instead of the questions they would write in a normal SQ3R procedure.

d. Students should read the part.

e. After they finish reading each paragraph, they should state its main idea. Students should put down *only* important supporting details under the main idea.

(1) Although students do not have to use a formal outline for their notes, they should *indent* their listing so that the relation of supporting material to main ideas is clear.

(2) Students should try not to take any notes until after they have finished reading the whole paragraph. They should remember that *recall* is an essential step in the SQ3R technique. By not taking notes until they have finished reading, they are more actively involved in thinking about the material as they try to construct notes.

2. Good notes are very helpful for review purposes, and they can save students a great deal of time. (See the section on test taking.)

You should help your students to recognize that for study purposes, if the material is new to them, it's usually a good idea to write the topic for each paragraph unless the paragraph is a transitional one. You should also tell your students that textbook writers sometimes list the topics of their paragraphs in the margins and that they should be on the lookout for these helpful clues.

Here is an example of notetaking using the preceding sections, "Notetaking for Studying" and "Notetaking and SQ3R," as the source.

I. Notetaking

   A. A helpful tool

      1. Writing
      2. Studying

   B. Notes must be clear and organized

      1. Whole sentences not needed.
      2. Topics should be clearly distinguished.

   C. Correlated with SQ3R

      1. Follow steps in SQ3R.
      2. Note topics—not questions.

3. After reading, recall main ideas.
4. Insert details under main idea.

D. Useful for review

From this example, you can readily see the four important ideas—namely, *notetaking is a helpful tool, notes should be clear and organized, notetaking is correlated with SQ3R, and notetaking is useful for review.*

A discussion of underlining textbook passages is not presented here because this is a technique that students do not generally engage in until they enter college. Public school children do not own their textbooks, so they cannot write in them.

Semantic Mapping (Graphic Organizer) and Notetaking

A number of students find that a visual representation of the material helps them to remember information they have studied. Here is a scenario of how one upper elementary grade level teacher presents this technique to his students.

SCENARIO ━━━━━━━━━━━━━━━━━━━━━━━━━━━━━━━━━━━

Semantic Mapping (Graphic Organizer), Notetaking, and Studying

Mr. Troy tells his students that rather than taking notes using an informal outline of what they have studied, they could make a graphic illustration of what they are studying and combine this with the SQ3R technique. Mr. Troy tells his students he will model for them what he would do if he were constructing a semantic map to help him in studying. What follows are the steps Mr. Troy models for his students.

Step 1: Mr. Troy tells his students that, as in SQ3R, he chooses the amount of information he will be studying. (This is usually more than a paragraph.) He asks his students to look over their assignment and do the same.

Step 2: He then tells them he sets purposes for reading. He asks them to do the same.

Step 3: Now, he says, we have to read the material. Let's all do that now.

Step 4: After reading the material, Mr. Troy tells his students that they are now ready to construct their semantic map. First, he says, we have to determine the central idea of what we have read and put that in the center of a blank sheet of paper.

Step 5: Next we have to reread each paragraph, state the main topic of each, and append it to the central idea.

Step 6: For the last step, we go over the material once again and append the important supporting details to its main topic.

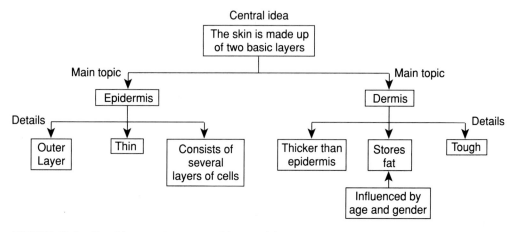

FIGURE 10-3   Graphic organizer as an aid to studying.

Figure 10-3 is an example of the semantic map that Mr. Troy did with his class.

Special Note
Rather than stating the topic of every paragraph, teachers could have the students state the main idea of each one and append supporting details to each main idea. There really is no correct way to construct a graphic illustration. The test is whether it helps students recall a significant amount of information. In this text, at the end of each chapter, graphic summaries are used for this purpose. (See the section on "Graphic Summary: A Special Review Study Aid.")

Notetaking for Writing a Paper

Many children at the intermediate grade level and higher are beginning to write reports and papers. Teachers should help these children to acquire some good notetaking skills at this time because notetaking is helpful in writing reports and long papers. Good notes save time and effort, and they should begin when the paper is begun. Here is some important information that you should convey to your students concerning notetaking:

1. The notecard is an essential aid in recording notes for papers. The card size that the student chooses should be based on his or her style of writing. If the student writes large and intends to use some long quotes, a larger size (five- by seven-inch card) is better than smaller sizes (three-by-five- or four- by six-inch cards). Whichever size card the student chooses, he or she should be consistent; that is, he or she should use cards of only one size. The student should use one card for each note. You should help your students to learn not to record two different ideas on the same card.

Notecards are better than slips of paper because they are easier to handle.

They are superior to regular notepaper because they are not only easier to handle but are also more convenient to organize, store, and edit.

2. To save having problems when students write papers, they should acquire good habits. They should make sure that each notecard contains this information:

a. Each card should contain the topic they are writing on or that topic and the subtopic to which the particular note applies. (If the student doesn't know this information for certain when he or she begins to take notes, he or she should leave room to fill it in later.)

b. Students should be sure to write down the exact source of their information at the bottom or top of each card. Bibliographical forms vary, but by fourth grade, children usually use the following form: The author's last name is written first, a comma separates the last name from the first name, and the title of the book is capitalized and underlined. A comma and page numbers follow the title. For example:

Wiese, Kurt, *You Can Write Chinese,* pages 45–50.

By sixth grade the bibliography also includes the date of publication. The teacher should initiate a discussion on the importance of knowing this factor. The teacher should also tell the students that they only have to record the author's last name and the page from which the information was obtained if they have used the source before. They should, of course, include the first name if there are two authors with the same last name.

c. Students should record the information as clearly as possible. The information may be a summary in their own words, figures or statistics, a definition, a direct quotation, or some other bit of relevant information.

(The notecard in Figure 10-4 contains a summary of the following paragraph by J. A. Hunter.)

In many parts of Africa, the use of traps, poisons, and dogs has virtually exterminated the leopard. In my youth, we thought that the only good leopard was a hide stretched out for drying. But now we are discovering that the leopard played an

---

Topic	The Protection of Leopards
Main idea	Leopards are now widely protected because they play an important part in maintaining nature's balance.
Important details	Leopards used to kill thousands of baboons every year, until the leopard was virtually wiped out. Leopards are now needed to control the baboon population problem.

Hunter, J. A., *African Hunter,* Harper & Brothers, 1952, p. 52.

FIGURE 10-4 Notecard on "The Protection of Leopards."

important part in maintaining nature's balance. Leopards used to kill thousands of baboons every year, and now that the leopards have been largely wiped out baboons are proving to be a major control problem in many parts of the colony. The perfect way to keep them in check is by allowing their natural enemy, the leopard, to destroy them. So leopards are now widely protected and allowed to increase in numbers. Such is the strange way that man works—first he virtually destroys a species and then does everything in his power to restore it.

3. Teachers should impress upon students the importance of writing each note as clearly as possible so that they will not have difficulty understanding it or why they wrote it. Here are some pointers that teachers could give to their students:

a. Tell students if they are quoting an author's exact words, they should make sure they put them in quotation marks.
b. Tell students to try to summarize what they have read, but to be careful that they are stating facts, not opinions. (See section on summaries.)
c. Tell students if they are giving their or someone else's opinion, they should make sure they record this on their card so that they will not confuse the opinion with fact.
d. Tell students not to take notes on matters of common knowledge.
e. Tell students not to take notes on the same information twice. If two or more sources give the same facts or ideas, they should note the idea only once. This rule should *not* be followed, however, if they are collecting evidence to prove or disprove something. The more evidence they can uncover that points to a single conclusion, the better they will be able to defend their position on the question.

Activities

1. Present a number of notecards to your children that do not have topic headings. Have them read each card and determine the author's topic. Have them determine also whether a source has been used before.
2. Present a number of notecards to your students without topic headings, and have them state the idea or ideas recorded. If more than one idea is recorded, have them write or state that this is so.
3. Present a number of notecards to your students that have enough information for one or two paragraphs. Have them use the notecards to write the paragraph(s).

Notetaking for Listening to a Talk

It is not too soon to learn in the intermediate grades how to listen to a talk and how to take notes on talks. Research has shown that children in elementary school spend at least 57.5 percent of class time in listening.[1] This percentage

[1] Miriam E. Wilt, "A Study of Teacher Awareness of Listening as a Factor in Elementary Education," *Journal of Educational Research* 43 (April 1950): 626–636.

rises to about 90 percent in high school. Teachers should make sure that their children have good listening skills as well as notetaking skills because without good listening skills students will not be able to take good notes.

You should help your students to recognize the importance of taking good notes as well as how to take good notes while listening to a talk. If students learn good notetaking habits while they are young, they will carry these with them when they go to high school and college, where students spend most of their class time listening to lectures. Here are some pointers that you should try to get across to your students. (Notice that the pointers given here, as well as in other parts of this chapter, would not change even for college students. As stated earlier, it is important that students acquire good habits as early as possible. It is also important that what students learn at an early age they do not have to unlearn at a later age.)

1. Help your students to understand that many teachers present material in their talks that simplifies, clarifies, and otherwise highlights the key points of the information that they have read in their textbooks.

2. Help them to recognize that it is more difficult to take notes while listening to someone talk than it is to take notes while reading a textbook.

3. Explain to them that there is no single notetaking technique that is best for every student, but there are a number of basic principles that apply to everyone:

a. Students should have a positive frame of mind to what is being presented. This does not mean that they should not be good critical thinkers. It does mean that they should listen to a talk with an open mind and with the desire to learn something.

b. Students need to be well rested and well fed in order to listen to a talk.

c. Students should be sitting where they are able to *see* as well as *hear* the speaker. The speaker's facial gestures and body movements help give meaning to what he or she is saying. Students should also not sit near other students who distract them.

d. Students should have the proper instruments to record a talk; that is, they should have paper and pencils.

4. You should help students to note the following helpful clues that speakers usually give during a talk:

a. Emphasis announced with the words "This is a key point," "This is very important," "This is vital information," and so on. Students should write these points down and underline them.

b. Emphasis implied by time spent on a subject. Obviously, the speaker feels something is important if he or she dwells on it. Students should underline or box their notes on the topic explained at length.

c. Announcements that students neet *not* take notes. Perhaps the topic is a digression, a sideline of discussion; perhaps the speaker knows that the matter is covered thoroughly in the text. (Help students to learn not to tire themselves with needless recording of notes.)

d. Outlines of the topic the speaker is talking about written up on the chalkboard. Students should copy them and leave room to insert additional points that arise in the talk.

e. Guides in the form of main ideas listed on the chalkboard. (Sometimes only the main topic of the lecture is given.)

f. Handouts containing points to be covered in the talk. Be sure to remind students to insert these in their notebooks.

5. Help your students to realize that teachers' quizzes and tests give them vital information about what the teachers feel is important. They should use quizzes and tests as learning experiences. After a quiz or test, they should go over it and then go over their notes to compare them with what was on the quiz or test.

6. Again emphasize to your students the importance of asking questions during class. Tell them that they should never hesitate to ask a question if they don't understand a point. Also, tell them that a question slows down the teacher, it gives the student a chance to catch up, and it gives the teacher some clue as to whether he or she is getting the material across to the students. (See the section in this chapter on "Asking Questions.")

7. Tell students that it is a good idea to go over their notes from the previous day to set up continuity between the old and new material. Tell them that in reviewing their notes, they should look at their "telegraphic writing" (see item 8) and try to *recall* the key ideas presented the day before. Remind them that they learn more from recall than from the immediate rereading of their notes.

8. Emphasize to students that the notes they take while listening to a talk must make sense to them when they read them later, and they should be organized. Tell them that they do not have to use a formal outline, nor do they have to write in sentences. Here are some other suggestions on taking notes during a talk that you should convey to your students:

Telegraphic writing
The use of one or two words to recall a complete message.

a. Tell your students that they should not write every word that a speaker says. Tell them to use telegraphic writing instead. *Telegraphic writing* involves the use of one or two words to recall a complete message. The words that are used are the content words—that is, the words that contain significant information. Stress that economy of writing is important in taking notes while listening to a talk, but the notes should not be so bareboned that the student has difficulty remembering what he or she meant.

b. Help your students to learn how to make generalizations (statements or conclusions based on an accumulation of specific data) because these will help them to retain the information. Also, if students are concentrating on making generalizations, they will be more actively involved.

c. Impress upon your students the importance of spacing out their notes so that they can add material if necessary.

d. Tell your students that it is a good idea to reread their notes right after a speaker has finished to see if the notes make sense. If the notes do not make sense, your student can ask the speaker to clarify a point for him or her. Tell students that they should also get into the habit of dating their notes because the date will be a good reference point if it is needed.

Here is an example of lecture notes:

Jan. 15	Few absolutes in mythology, if any
	What the word "Myth" means:
	(Greeks have other meanings)
Many diff.	Mythology — body of myths or <u>collection</u> of all myths of
meanings of	God; mythology of God; collection; (no complete def.
myth:	because of diverse uses)
	Mythology — "other people's religion"; myths — used to mean
	a lie, untruths, but not simply untruths, fables, stories,
	etc.; myths aren't really true or untrue for people who
	tell them
Myths used to	<u>Myths can be valid or invalid, in sense that interpret experi-</u>
structure	<u>ence</u> — genuine myths are narratives that tend to provide
reality:	structure or order; every person's order is not the same,
	but each has some system of order
	Myths — explain how world came into being, provide struc-
	ture
	If can't provide an explanation, categorize it as "myths";
	examples: 1. botany/zoology structure of classifying
	plants and animals; 2. the idea that you can look at
	world objectively — can't prove or disprove myths

You should caution your students not to expect to find someone else's notes helpful if they did not attend the lecture. The sample lecture notes are composed mostly of generalizations. When students read them, if they attended the lecture, the notes should bring forth a great amount of other information.

Activities

1. Practice notetaking with your students. Present a short talk to your students on a specific topic, or read a short article to them. Have them take notes on the talk or article being read. After they have finished, ask various students to give a summary of the talk or article, using their notes as a guide.
2. Have your students practice notetaking with a partner. Have each take turns

reading a short excerpt and taking notes on it. After they have both had a chance at doing this, they could compare their notes.

3. Read an article to your students, and have them take notes on it. After they have finished, give them a quiz on the article. (The students can use their notes while taking the quiz.)

4. Read an article to your students, and have them take notes on it. Tell them beforehand that they will have a quiz on the article and that they will be able to use their notes to take the quiz. See if they do better on the quiz when they know beforehand that they will have a quiz on the material.

Outlining

Outlining
Helps students organize long papers; serves as a guide for the logical arrangement of material.

Outlining helps students organize long written compositions or papers. An outline should serve as a guide for the logical arrangement of material. Closely related to classification and categorizing, outlining should begin to be developed in the primary grades.

In the middle and upper grades, these skills in outlining should be developed:

Beginning with grade four, pupils often need to use and make outlines for reporting information found in reading a variety of references; listening to tape recordings, radio, and television; experimenting to find answers to questions; observing; and interviewing people who can help with the question at hand. *As the need for making an outline arises,* pupils may consult their English books to find out about the rules involved. Such suggestions as the following can be put in the pupils' own words and kept on a chart for reference:

- Use Roman numerals for the main topics, putting a period after each Roman numeral.
- Use capital letters for subtopics, with a period after each capital letter. Indent the subtopics.
- Use ordinary (Arabic) numerals for details under subtopics and small letters under the details for less important topics. Put a period after each number and letter.
- Begin each topic with a capital letter, whether it is a main topic, a subtopic, or a detail. Do not put a period after a main topic, a subtopic, or a detail. Do not put a period after a topic unless it is a sentence.
- Keep Roman numbers, capital letters, ordinary numbers, and small letters in straight vertical lines.
- Topics are usually phrases, sometimes sentences. Do not mix phrases and sentences in the same outline.

Sets and Outlining

An exercise involving sets can be used with both primary and intermediate grade students to help them recognize that outlining and classification are closely related. Ask students to think of the set of all the books in the library. This is a very general set:

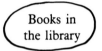

Next ask students to state the kinds of books one would find in the library. By doing this we are becoming less general:

Now ask students to state what kinds of books one would find in the set of fiction books and what kinds of books one would find in the set of nonfiction books:

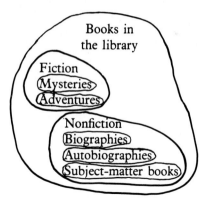

Ask the children to name a particular mystery or adventure book. At this point we are becoming very specific:

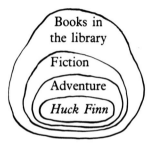

Now ask the students to put this information in outline form.

Outlining Activities

Here are samples of exercises, according to grade levels, that should help children develop the skill of outlining through understanding classification.

Family Names (Primary Grades)

Directions   On the line above each group write the appropriate family name or main topic. Although the different groups in each exercise belong to the same general class, the differences between the groups may be indicated by adding a descriptive word to the family name you choose.

_____

Horse
Cow
Dog

_____

Tiger
Wolf
Bear
Moose
Fox

Organizing (Fourth or Fifth Grade)

Directions   At the head of the exercise is a list of words. Take each word and ask: "Does this word belong in Group I or Group II?" When you are sure of your answer, write the word under its main topic.

Chicago, Arizona, Vermont, California, Los Angeles, Tulsa, Georgia, Baltimore

I. States
   A.
   B.
   C.
   D.

II. Cities
   A.
   B.
   C.
   D.

Time Order – Changes in Transportation

Directions   Study the following list. Select your main topics, and arrange them in time order. Then arrange your subtopics.

horseback, pioneer forms, modern forms, covered wagon, railway express, pony express, motor truck, airplane

I.
   A.
   B.
   C.

II.
   A.
   B.
   C.

Levels of Abstraction (Fifth or Sixth Grade)

Directions   Here are some items in columns. Each column describes one item. Each word tells you more, or less, information about the item than all the others. Put a "1" in front of the word that tells the least, a "2" in front of the word that tells the next least, and so on until the highest number is placed beside the word telling the most. The word that tells the least is the most general word – such as *animal*, whereas the word that tells the most is the most specific – such as *John Doe*.

Example

    __3__   A – John Doe

    __1__   B – Animal

    __2__   C – Human

    _____   A – Animal

    _____   B – Lassie

    _____   C – Collie

    _____   D – Dog

    _____   A – Rock

    _____   B – Nonliving

Continued

Levels of Abstraction (Fifth or Sixth Grade)   *Continued*

_____ C – Rock formations

_____ D – Mt. Everest

_____ A – Tree

_____ B – Living organism

_____ C – Spruce

_____ D – Plant

_____ E – Evergreen

_____ A – Mammal

_____ B – Living organism

_____ C – Arthur Hale

_____ D – Human

_____ E – Animal

_____ A – Machinery

_____ B – Automobile

_____ C – Cadillac

_____ D – Vehicle

_____ A – Wheat

_____ B – Grain

_____ C – Plant

_____ D – Living organism

Summarizing as a Mode of Learning

Summary
A brief statement of the essential information in a longer piece; usually contains the main or central idea.

Many teachers help their intermediate grade level students and above learn how to summarize passages because they recognize this as a viable means of having students gain essential information. Summarizing material is a mode of learning that helps persons to retain the most important concepts and facts in a long passage. It forces students to think about what they have read and to identify and organize the essential information. Also, if the summary is a written summary, it helps to integrate the reading and writing process.

Teachers can help their students learn how to summarize by having students begin with summarizing single paragraphs and then working up to longer passages. Teachers should inform students that a good summary ought to be brief and ought to include only essential information. The main idea of the paragraph (if only a paragraph is being summarized) or the central idea of an article and the important facts should be stated, but not necessarily in the sequence presented in the passage. The sequence in the paragraph or article must be followed in the summary *only if* that sequence is essential. Teachers need to help their students to include only the information stated in the paragraph or article and not their opinions or what they think should have been included.

Before teachers work with summaries, it might be a good idea for them to review with their students how to find the main or central idea of passages. (The passages that are used should be content material that the students are studying.)

Teachers can also convey to their students that in writing a summary, it is sometimes a good idea to begin with the writer's conclusion and work backward to pick out essential points leading to that conclusion.

After teachers have conveyed pertinent information about summaries to their students, they should give students practice in writing summaries, using content material the students are studying. One technique the teacher could use might be to have the students read a paragraph or a section from the textbook that they are presently studying and then have them write a summary of it in class. After they have written their summaries, they could read some of them and discuss which are good summaries and why they are good. Another technique is to have students read a selection from their textbook and then to present them with a few summaries on the selection and have them determine which is the best summary and then explain why. Still another technique the teacher could use would be to have students write a summary of a selection they have read and then to have them compare it with a sample summary that is shown on the overhead projector.

Some teachers may want to have students write a summary together before having them write one individually. Some teachers may merely present students with a sheet that contains tips on how to write a summary, as well as two sample summaries of a section from their textbook. As has been stated many times in this text, the specific tactics teachers employ will depend on the uniqueness of the subject matter, as well as on the individual differences of the students and their past experiences.

Some teachers may give their students a mock test after they have written their summary to illustrate to them how helpful the writing of summaries is in retaining and explaining information.

Graphic summary
A visual representation of the material presented in a selection, section, or a chapter; helps students recall information; an excellent review tool.

Graphic Summary: A Special Review Study Aid

The well-known saying "A picture is worth a thousand words" is true for many people. Because of this, each chapter of this book ends with a graphic summary, which is a visual representation of the material presented in the chapter. The graphic illustration should help you recall the information you have studied because it organizes the major points in a logical way. It is an excellent review tool.

Teachers can help students gain skill in using this technique for study purposes by having their students do the following:

Step 1: Choose a short selection from the students' textbook.

Step 2: Use the SQ3R technique on the short selection, but tell students to omit the last step of SQ3R, which is the review.

Sample Selection: States and Properties of Matter

Our present understanding of the changes we see around us, like the melting of ice and the burning of wood, is intimately tied to our understanding of the nature and composition of matter. Matter is the physical material of the universe; it is anything that occupies space and has mass.

Matter exists in three physical states: gas (also known as vapor), liquid, and solid. A gas has no fixed volume or shape. It takes the volume and shape of its container. A gas can be compressed to fit a small container, and it will expand to occupy a large one. A liquid has a definite volume but no specific shape. It assumes the shape of the portion of the container that it occupies. A solid is rigid. It has both a fixed volume and a fixed shape. Neither liquids nor solids are compressible to any appreciable extent.

Step 3: After they have done all the steps in SQ3R except the last one, have them make a semantic map of what they have read. (See "Semantic Mapping [Graphic Organizer] and Notetaking.") In this book, a semantic map that presents a summary of material is called a *graphic summary.* A sample graphic summary is shown in Figure 10-5.

Step 4: Now have them look at the graphic summary of their selection. They should note that the illustration organizes the material presented in the selection, and the main topic is in the center of the illustration with related material appended to it. Without looking back at their selection, have them use the graphic summary to help them recall the material in the selection.

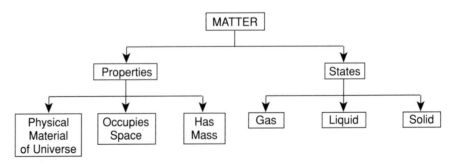

FIGURE 10-5   Sample graphic summary

Test Taking

Test
A standard set of
questions to be
answered.

The word *test* seems to make most students shudder. However, tests are necessary to help students learn about their weaknesses so that they can improve and learn about their strengths; they help give students a steady and encouraging measure of their growth; and tests are helpful for review.

The more students know about tests, the better they can do on them. The information that follows on tests is provided for you the teacher so that you can help your students to be better test takers. The amount of information that you present to your students will depend on the grade level that you are teaching as well as on the students with whom you are working. Many intermediate grade level students are ready to learn about test-taking techniques and how to study for them. As a matter of fact, so are some primary grade level children. Although children today seem to be test-wise, most really are not.

Teachers should help students to be better test takers. The first thing that teachers should try to help students to understand is that the best way to do well on a test is to be *well prepared.* There are no shortcuts to studying. However, research has shown that persons do better on tests if they know certain test-taking techniques and if they are familiar with the various types of tests.

Here are some general test-taking principles:

1. Students should plan to do well. They should have a *positive* attitude.
2. Students should be well rested.
3. Students should be prepared. The better prepared an individual is, the less nervous and anxious he or she will be.
4. Students should look upon tests as a learning experience.
5. Students should look over the whole test before they begin. They should notice the types of questions asked and the points allotted for each question. (Students have to learn not to spend a long time on a one- to five-point question that they know a lot about. They should answer it and go on.)
6. Students should know how much time is allotted for the test. (Students need to learn to allot their time wisely and to check the time.)
7. Students should concentrate!
8. Students should read instructions very carefully. (Students need to be helped in this area because many times they read into the questions things that are not there. Students must learn that if a question asks for a description and *examples,* they must give the examples. Students also need to learn that if they do not understand something or if something does not make sense, they should ask the teacher about it because there may be a mistake on the test.)
9. Students should begin with the questions they are sure of. This will give them a feeling of confidence and success. However, as already advised, they must learn not to dwell on these at length.
10. If students do not know an answer, they should make an intelligent guess. As long as the penalty for a wrong answer is the same as for no answer, it pays to take a calculated guess.

11. After students answer the questions they are sure of, they should work on those that count the most, that is, that are worth the greatest number of points.

12. Students should allow time to go over the test. They should check that they have answered all the questions. They should be leery about changing a response unless they have found a particular reason to while going over the test. For example, they may have misread the question, they may have misinterpreted the question, or they may not have realized that it was a "tricky" question. If the question is a straightforward one, it's probably better for students to leave their first response.

13. After the test has been graded and returned, students should go over it to learn from the results. Unless students find out why an answer is wrong and what the correct answer is, they may continue to make the same mistake on other tests.

14. Students should study the test after they get it back to determine what their teacher emphasizes on tests.

Objective Tests

Objective tests
Those that usually
have only one
correct answer for a
given question.

The information that follows is presented for you, the teacher, so that you will have the background information to help your children to be better objective test takers.

An objective test is any test involving short answers, usually one or two words. Among the variety of objective test questions are true/false, multiple choice, matching items, completion or fill-in, and short answers. As there is usually only one correct answer for a given question, objective tests are, on the whole, easier to take and easier to grade. They can cover a good deal of subject knowledge but not in the depth a subjective test permits. One system of study preparation is appropriate for objective tests and another for subjective tests.

Because an objective test is comprehensive and aimed at discovering powers of *recognition* and *recall,* you should help students prepare for it by concentrating on details. Have them review important definitions, principles, concepts, formulas, names, dates, and terms that relate to the material to be covered on the test. *As students go over the details, they should be sure to review the relation of the details to the whole.* Unless students know their facts and how the facts relate to the general content of the subject, they will find any examination difficult, if not bewildering.

1. Studying for objective tests:

a. True/false, multiple choice, and matching tests call for *recognition.* Fill-in or completion tests call for *recall.* Recall tests are usually more difficult than recognition tests because students have to produce the answers from memory. Recognition tests are usually easier because students have answers from which to choose. However, research has shown that students who do best on recognition tests also do best on recall tests. Presumably, those who know how to distinguish between items in a list also know the material thoroughly enough by memory to recall the right choices.

b. Although objective tests deal with recognition and recall, test questions can be devised to look for such things as students' ability to think critically, to solve new problems, to apply principles, and to select relevant facts. Students need a *fund of knowledge* and *reasoning ability.* If students have the reasoning ability but no fund of knowledge, they either have not studied the material or have not approached their studying from the right angle; they will probably not do well.

c. Research has shown that students *remember* generalizations longer than material memorized by rote with no attempt to make associations.

d. Research has indicated that people forget information mainly because in learning new information they put the old mentally to one side. If students *overlearn* the old material, learn the new material *and its relation to the old,* and continue to use the old as they work with the new, they are less likely to confuse the old with the new or forget the old altogether.

e. Overlearning (continuing of practice after students feel they know the material) the basic information in a field is essential. For example, in some subjects certain definitions, formulas, axioms, or concepts that are often used are worth overlearning.

f. Studying for generalizations does not mean that students should not memorize certain definitions, formulas, principles, and so on. The key thing is for students to understand how to use the material they memorize and to see its relationship to the whole.

g. The following steps are helpful in memorizing material:

(1) Students should read through the whole passage they wish to memorize. It's important to see the relationship of the parts to the whole and to make associations.
(2) If it's a long selection, students should break it up into manageable parts and memorize each part, but they should always remember to relate the part to its whole.
(3) As students learn a new part, they should go back over the old part, and relate it to the new.
(4) Students should go over the whole selection a number of times. Students should remember that to *overlearn* something means that they should practice it beyond the point when they feel they know it. They should remember also to distribute their practice over a period of time.

Mnemonic device
A memory association trick that helps students to recall material.

(5) Students should use mnemonic devices. A mnemonic device is a memory association trick that helps students to recall material. For example, *HOMES* is a mnemonic device to help them to remember the five Great Lakes. Each letter of *HOMES* is the first letter of the

name of one of the Great Lakes—Huron, Ontario, Michigan, Erie, and Superior. Students should be careful not to use a mnemonic device that is more complicated than the fact to be remembered. "Thirty days hath September, April, June, and November" is adequate. Who knows all of this?

Thirty days hath September,
April, June, and November;
All the rest have thirty-one,
Excepting February alone,
and that has twenty-eight days clear
and twenty-nine in each leap year.

And who needs it? (Help your students to remember that the best way to commit information to memory is to learn generalizations and to look for relationships within the material they are studying.)

2. True/false tests:

a. Students should not leave a true/false question unanswered. They have a 50 percent chance of getting the answer correct by guessing (see Figure 10-6). (On some standardized tests, students may be penalized; that is, more points may be deducted for an incorrect answer than for no answer.)

b. Students should *always* read carefully any true/false questions that say *always, never, all, none, impossible, nothing,* and so on. These are usually giveaways that the answer is false. Almost every rule has exceptions. Of course, there are times when inclusive categories such as *all, no, always,* or *never* are accurate. *Examples:*

All humans are mortal. (T)
No human is without vertebra. (T)
Children always learn to speak. (F)
All people who study do well on exams. (F)
All true/false tests are considered objective tests. (T)
All children need ten hours of sleep. (F)

Help your students to notice that when the answer is true for such categories as *all, no, always,* or *never,* the statement is usually a definition or a rule.

c. Help your students to recognize that rather than use giveaways such as *always* or *never,* teachers usually make true/false questions more difficult by stating only part of a definition or by inserting something incorrect in a definition; that is, part of an accurate definition is given but the other part is left out or misstated. Obviously, students should be *well prepared* on details such as definitions for true/false tests. They should be very alert. *Examples:*

(1) Language is defined as a shared, learned system used for all communication. (True or *False*)

Although what is said is correct, the statement is not *complete* enough to be marked true. The complete definition is *Language is a learned, shared, and pat-*

terned, arbitrary system of vocal sound symbols with which people in a given culture can communicate with one another.

(2) An amoeba is a single-celled plant. (True or *False*)

An amoeba is single-celled, but it is an animal, not a plant.

d. Help your students to recognize that statements that use words such as *sometimes, often, usually, many, generally, frequently, as a rule, some,* and so on are usually true. *Examples:*

Usually children learn to speak. (*True* or False)
As a rule, small children need ten hours of sleep. (*True* or False)

Special Note

Make sure that your students make their *T*'s and *F*'s very clear. It may be a good idea to tell them to write out *true* or *false* so that there is no question of misinterpretations. If the *T* or *F* is not clear, the instructor may mark it wrong.

3. Matching items tests:

a. In a matching items test students must usually match the items in one column with the items in another. Help your students to recognize that teachers commonly use this kind of test to match the following elements: words with their meanings; dates with historical events; persons with their achievements; authors with their books; rules with their examples; and so on.

b. Help your students to recognize that if the teacher uses a variety of material on the same matching test, students have a better chance of doing well. For example, if authors are matched with titles of books, wars or major events

© 1968 United Feature Syndicate, Inc.

© 1968 United Feature Syndicate, Inc.

Reprinted by permission of UFS, Inc.

FIGURE 10-6   Poor Linus! He'll learn that even on a true/false test you must be prepared. Guessing does not guarantee a correct answer.

with dates, terms with definitions, and rules with examples on the same matching test, students' choices are more limited.

c. It is often useful to use the process of elimination to help students solve difficult matches. That is, once students have completed all matches they are certain of, they will have a much smaller list from which to choose.

4. Multiple-choice tests:

a. Help your students recognize that multiple-choice tests are not as easy to guess on as true/false tests are. But even on a multiple-choice test, if students have only four answers from which to choose for each question, they have a 25 percent chance of being correct by guessing. Therefore, students should attempt to answer each question (see Figure 10-7).

b. When taking a multiple-choice test, students should read the statement or question, and then before reading the choices think for a moment about what they feel the answer should be. They should read the choices carefully to determine if one matches.

c. Students should read the complete or incomplete question or statement to be answered very carefully. If a negative is contained in the question or statements, they should note it. It may help students to check off mentally each item in the positive. *Example:*

Which of the following is *not* an example of a vowel digraph?

(1) ea   (2) ie   (3) oa   (4) oy

Students could very quickly say the following: *ea* is a digraph; *ie* is a digraph; *oa* is a digraph; therefore, *oy* has to be the answer.

Here are examples of syllabicated nonsense words. Choose the one that is *correctly* syllabicated:

(1) bloa/me/tten   (2) cr/oy   (3) rein/tle   (4) plom/ant

In this example, three are incorrect and only one is correct. Although students may feel that they know their syllabication generalizations and they come to the correctly syllabicated word quickly, they should take a moment to look at the others to make sure that they do indeed have the correct answer.

d. Students should look for teachers' clues in multiple-choice tests. Here are some giveaways: (1) a choice that is much longer and more detailed than the others is usually the correct answer; (2) a word in a choice that also appears in the statement or question usually implies that that choice is the correct answer; (3) ridiculous choices among the items allow students to arrive at the answer by elimination (usually, students can easily eliminate two items, but then they are left with a choice between the two remaining items); (4) a special part of speech required in the answer will identify the correct choice. *Example:*

The definition of *optimist* is: (a) cheerful (b) looking at the bright side (c) one who looks at the bright side of things (d) being cheerful.

The answer must be (c) because *optimist* is a noun.

5. Fill-in or completion tests.

a. The fill-in or completion test is one in which students receive a statement that omits a key word or phrase. Students must produce from memory the missing item. *Example:*

The sixteenth President was _____.

b. The fill-in or completion test is one in which students must *recall* the correct answer. Recall items, like recognition items, can test either for simple facts or for more complex understandings. For such a test, students should concentrate on details, but they should understand how the details are organized—that is, how they are related to what they are studying. Memorizing isolated details will not help students to retain the information or to understand it.

c. You should help your students to recognize that sometimes the teacher intentionally or unintentionally gives them grammatical clues. Students should be on the lookout for these. *Examples:*

A person of high birth is called *an* _____.
A man who has many wives is called a _____.
The authors of the paper describing the first transistor were _____.

In the first two sentences, the indefinite article *an* is a clue that the answer begins with a vowel and the indefinite article *a* is a clue that the answer begins with a consonant. In the third sentence, the plural noun and verb tell students that the answer must be in the plural; that is, there is more than one author involved.

6. Short-answer tests. The short-answer test is very similar to the completion or fill-in test. It is similarly based on recall, and the correct answer is usually

Reprinted by permission of UFS, Inc.

FIGURE 10-7 When you're not prepared, all tests are "mystical."

a word or phrase. However, in the short answer test a question or a simple statement is used rather than a statement with a blank for a missing word or phrase.
Examples:

> Name the sixteenth President of the United States.
> What is the capital of California?

Special Notes

1. Tell your students that if they feel that a recall or recognition test item can
   be answered by more than one answer, they should bring this to the attention of their teacher. It may be that the test question is incorrectly written.
   If the teacher tells them that the question *is* correctly written, they should
   try to choose the best answer. However, they might write a note in the
   margin of their paper (if there is time) explaining why they think it could be
   the other answer, also. Then, when the test is gone over in class, the students can bring this question up or discuss this point after the exam with the
   teacher.
2. Although an objective test question is usually supposed to have only one
   answer, it's possible that there may be more.
3. Completion and short-answer tests lend themselves to more subjectivity
   than the other types of objective tests because students' recall responses
   may be worded in many different ways. The teacher must interpret whether
   the response is the desired one or not. Wherever there is interpretation,
   there is usually some subjectivity.

Subjective Tests (Essay Tests)

Subjective tests
Usually essay tests;
answers are not
merely right or
wrong; tests are a
demonstration of
reasoning, thought,
and perception.

The information that follows is presented for you, the teacher, so that you will
have the background information to help your students to be better subjective test
takers. Although the information is primarily for upper intermediate grade level
students and above, some of the information would also be helpful for earlier
grade level children.

Essay tests are usually given when a teacher wants to see that students
know the material thoroughly enough to organize it and use it to draw conclusions, which goes beyond merely knowing material well enough to recognize it.
Subjective tests are more difficult to take and to grade than are objective tests.
Their answers are not merely right or wrong but are demonstrations of reasoning,
thought, and perception.

1. Comparison of essay tests to objective tests:

   a. On an essay test students spend most of their time thinking and writing,
   whereas on an objective test they spend most of their time reading and thinking.

   b. Students are more free to express their ideas and be creative on an essay
   test than on an objective test.

c. Objective tests allow students to guess at an answer; essay tests may encourage bluffing.

d. Both essay and objective tests can measure simple and complex concepts and knowledge.

2. Studying for an essay test:

Essay tests require students to recall material and to be able to express their ideas logically. Here are some study suggestions for your students:

a. They should look for broad, general concepts (ideas) and for relations between concepts. They should study for main ideas and generalizations. They should note the organization of details that develop the main ideas.

b. They should distribute their studying time. (See the sections on studying.)

c. They should study in particular the material their teacher emphasized or spent much time on in class.

d. They should try to anticipate some of the essay questions. It may be a good idea for them to work up one or two essays answering questions that they think their teacher is likely to ask (see "Special Notes"). Also, their text may contain "questions for discussion" at the end of each chapter. These questions are usually subjective questions. Students should go over them because they may appear on the test as they are or thinly disguised. If they are not given on the test, students' study of them will at least have prepared them for the *kind* of question given.

Special Notes

1. Although it may be a good idea for students to try to anticipate essay questions and prepare one or two in advance, they should be careful! They should not spend too much time doing this. It's better to spend more time on studying generalizations and relations between concepts.

2. If the essay that students prepared in advance is not related to the question that is asked, they should *not* give their prepared essay answer as the answer on the test. They should answer the question. Perhaps they can use a small part of their prepared essay. (After the test, they should study the essay questions asked on the test and compare these with their text and lecture notes to try to determine why their teacher asked these questions. This will help them anticipate questions better next time.)

3. Taking an essay test:

a. Students should read the question. They should make sure they understand it. They should not read into it what is *not* there. They should check to see if examples or illustrations are asked for. They should check to see if their opinion is asked for. If they are asked to list, name, or identify, they should do exactly that. They should not give more information than is asked for. If they are asked to summarize, they should give an overview. If they are asked to analyze, they must break down the question into its parts. The most general type of question is one that asks students to discuss or explain. In a comparison/contrast question, students must give similarities, differences, or both. If students are asked to evaluate, they must make a value judgment. This type of question is the most difficult to answer because it requires that students know a great amount of information on the topic to determine what is best or correct.

b. Students should put down on a scrap sheet of paper any special formulas, principles, concepts, or words that they have memorized and that they think will be relevant to the question. They should do this immediately so that they will not forget to include the important details that they have memorized.

c. They should *think* about the question.

d. They should plan their answer. (Again, they should make sure that they are answering the question.)

e. They should prepare an outline for their answers.

f. They should write out their answer. They should use lists where applicable.

g. They should check the time available to them.

h. They should not spend all their time on a single essay if there is more than one question.

i. They should reread their essay to make sure that their ideas are clearly and logically stated. They should make sure that they have used complete sentences and that each of their paragraphs expresses one main idea.

Special Note

Although it's usually permissible to list items in an essay test, some teachers frown on students writing their complete essay in outline form. Tell students to be sure to check with their teacher whether they can answer by outline *before* they proceed to do so. (See section on questions.) However, tell students if they are pressed for time, and if they have no choice, it's a good idea for them to present their essay in outline form.

4. You should give your students examples of some of the different ways essay questions can be worded. Here are some:

a. Give the reasons for . . .

b. Explain how or why . . .

c. Present arguments for and arguments against . . .

d. Compare the poem _____ to the poem _____ in terms of the author's ability to portray fatalism.

e. Analyze the male character in _____.

f. Give the events that led to the _____ War.

Special Note

You should help your students to recognize that many tests are composed of both objective and subjective test items. On such tests they must plan their time especially wisely. Here are some suggestions for them:

1. They should read the whole test through.
2. They should notice how many points each part of the test is worth.
3. They should put down any special formulas, principles, ideas, or other data they have memorized that they think may be relevant to their essay question.

Diagnostic Checklist for Reading and Study Skills II

Student's Name: _____

Grade: _____

Teacher: _____

Asking Questions	Yes	No	Sometimes

A. Primary grades:

The child is able to
1. formulate questions that will give him or her the information that he or she desires to obtain.
2. ask questions that are pertinent to the topic under discussion.

B. Intermediate grades:

The student will be able to
1. ask questions that will help him or her to study better for a test.
2. ask questions that will help him or her to gain more information about what to study.

Test Taking	Yes	No	Sometimes

A. Primary grades:

The child is able to
1. read questions very carefully so that they are answered correctly.
2. follow directions in taking a test.

B. Intermediate grades:

The student is able to
1. recognize that he or she studies differently for objective tests than for essay tests.

Diagnostic Checklist for Reading and Study Skills II *Continued*

Test Taking	*Yes*	*No*	*Sometimes*
2. take objective tests.			
3. take essay tests.			
4. go over his or her test so that he or she learns why he or she did or did not do well on a test.			
5. to ask questions about a test so that he or she will learn from the mistakes.			

Summaries	*Yes*	*No*	*Sometimes*
Intermediate grades:			
The student is able to			
1. summarize a passage			
2. use a summary for study purposes.			

Notetaking	*Yes*	*No*	*Sometimes*
Intermediate grades:			
The student is able to			
1. explain why notetaking is a useful study tool.			
2. explain why notetaking is helpful in writing long papers.			

Graphic Summary of Chapter

On the following page is a graphic summary of Chapter 10. If you have read the chapter, this graphic illustration should help you remember its main points. Under or beside each heading, you might want to jot down some of the information you recall, as well as some of the key concepts in this chapter. This can act as a good review. You can then check your key concepts against those that follow the graphic summary.

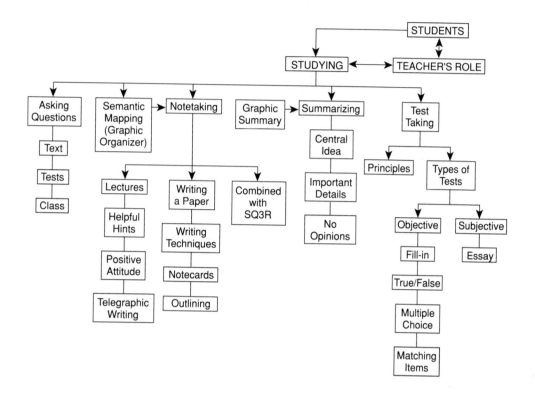

Key Concepts

- Asking questions in class is an important part of learning.
- Asking questions slows teachers down.
- Teachers should help students gain skill in asking questions.
- Asking questions of text material is consistent with viewing reading as problem solving.
- Elementary grade teachers should help children gain reading and writing strategies to help them learn better.
- Notetaking is a good studying tool.
- Intermediate grade level teachers should begin to help students gain notetaking skills.
- Teachers can help upper elementary grade level children combine SQ3R with notetaking for study purposes.
- Visual representations can help children organize and remember information.
- Summarizing is an excellent mode of learning that helps students gain essential information.

- A good summary usually includes the central idea and the important details.
- Notetaking can be used for writing long papers.
- Notecards should be clearly written.
- Outlining helps students retain and organize information.
- Teachers should help students to be better test takers.
- Tests help students learn about their strengths and weaknesses.
- Being well prepared is the best way to do well on a test.

Suggestions for Thought Questions and Activities

1. You have been put on a special committee to try to develop a study skills program in your elementary school that would integrate the reading–writing process. What kind of program would you advocate? What kinds of activities would you recommend for grades 4 through 6?
2. Parents are unhappy with the results of their children's achievement test scores in a number of areas. What kind of program can you recommend to help students achieve better?
3. Discuss how visual representations can help students.
4. Develop a lesson plan using visual representations.
5. Brainstorm some ideas to help your students be better test takers.
6. Brainstorm some techniques to help your students be better question askers.
7. You have students who seem to make careless errors on tests. What would you do to try to help them to be better test takers?
8. What kind of program would you set up to help your students to be better notetakers?

Selected Bibliography

Anderson, Thomas H., and Bonnie B. Armbruster. "Studying." In *Handbook of Reading Research,* P. David Pearson, ed. New York: Longman, 1984, pp. 657–679.

Gillespie, Cindy. "Questions about Student Generated Questions." *Journal of Reading* 34 (December 1990–January 1991): 250–257.

Hill, Margaret. "Writing Summaries Promotes Thinking and Learning Across the Curriculum—But Why Are They So Difficult to Write?" *Journal of Reading* 34 (April 1991): 536–539.

Rubin, Dorothy. *Reading and Learning Power,* 3rd ed. Needham Heights, Mass.: Ginn Press, 1991.

Rubin, Dorothy. *Teaching Reading and Study Skills in Content Areas,* 2nd ed. Boston: Allyn and Bacon, 1992.

___11___

Reading Approaches

SCENARIO: MRS. PERRY REMINISCES ABOUT HER FIRST YEAR AS A TEACHER

Mrs. Perry started teaching in 1959. Even though she did not have a teaching certificate, she was allowed to teach on a provisional one while she went to school to complete the necessary courses to qualify for certification. What is amazing is that she was placed in a first-grade classroom, even though she had no background in reading. When she mentioned this to the principal and others who had hired her, she was told that she did not need to worry because she would teach reading using basal readers and that these were teacher-proof. In other words, if she were to follow the Teacher Edition of the basal readers exactly, she would have no problems. She was told also that she should not allow children to go ahead in the basal readers because that would infringe on the second-grade teacher's domain.

The advice she received was very disconcerting to Mrs. Perry, who had a strong literature and learning theory background. When she looked at the basal readers, she was impressed with the wealth of material they contained; however, she was dismayed at the limited vocabulary and unimaginative stories. (In the 1950s, the vocabulary load was not very high.) She felt the readers would be stultifying for some of the children; however, she did like a number of features, such as the controlled vocabulary, because this would give the children the reinforcement they needed for success. She especially liked the big books that came with the basals. (At that time the preprimers also came as big books, as well as in regular book size.)

Mrs. Perry did use the basal readers, but she did not use them as ends in themselves. She used her judgment as to whether the material was best suited to the needs of her students and then supplemented the basals with other materials and books. She brought in many of her favorite poems and stories to share with her students and invited them to do the same. She read aloud many books to children that had repetitive refrains and had children interact during the reading aloud. She had children writing stories and used their stories for reading. She remembers with great joy the stories they cooperatively wrote and which the children subsequently read. She also remembers how she treasured meeting individually with each of her students and discussing with each what he or she

SCENARIO   *Continued*

was doing and having each one share with her a favorite book or story. She used these informal sessions to assess her students' reading and writing needs.

Looking back, Mrs. Perry realizes that many of the things she did at that time are in vogue today. This is probably because they made sense then, and they still do.

Good teachers are good teachers in any era! Mrs. Perry is a good teacher, and, even as a novice, she was able to use her judgment to develop an excellent eclectic reading program for her students. However, we must remember that she was taking reading courses at one of the state colleges and that she had a strong literature and educational psychology background.

This chapter will present information on reading approaches that teachers use in their classrooms to teach reading. Emphasis will be given to literature-based basal readers; the language experience approach, which utilizes all the language arts areas; and the individualized reading approach, which is probably the most difficult to implement. The next chapter discusses whole language. Most teachers usually use a combination of the three approaches presented in this chapter, as well as elements of whole language.

KEY QUESTIONS

After you finish reading this chapter, you should be able to answer the following questions:

1. What is a literature-based basal reader?
2. What materials are usually used in basal reader programs?
3. How have basal readers changed in the past few decades?
4. What is guided or directed reading?
5. What is a controlled vocabulary?
6. How does the language experience approach incorporate all the language arts areas?
7. What are the steps in developing an experience story?
8. How are word recognition skills taught in the language experience approach?
9. What are some examples of experiences that can be used to develop an experience story?
10. What are the characteristics usually associated with individualized reading?

KEY TERMS IN CHAPTER

You should pay special attention to the following key terms:

basal reader program
controlled vocabulary
experience story
guided reading
individualized reading approach

language experience approach
literature-based basal readers
oral reading
silent reading
vocabulary load

Basal Reader Programs

Basal reader program
A program involving a basal reader series. This program is usually highly structured; it generally has a controlled vocabulary, and skills are sequentially developed.

Basal reader programs involve basal reader series, which usually incorporate a highly structured approach to reading instruction, a controlled vocabulary, and sequentially developed skills. The basal reader program has been the most common approach used by elementary grade teachers to teach reading. It has been estimated that "basal reading programs, with their diverse ancillary materials, such as workbooks and tests, account for at least two-thirds of all expenditures for reading instruction and are used in more than 95 percent of all school districts through grade six. About 66 percent of teachers in grades seven and eight also use basals."[1] A number of teachers claim that they generally use the basal reader program in conjunction with library books and other materials, whereas some school districts report that they adopt multiple basal reader series rather than just one for their reading programs.[2]

The impact of whole language is definitely affecting the use of basals in schools, but it is still too soon to say how much of a decline there will be in the use of basals. Many teachers seem to feel more secure with a reading series than with an approach that is less structured, more open-ended, and not based on a sequential development of skills. However, even though many school districts across the country still do use basal readers, the whole language movement has influenced greatly not only how teachers teach reading today but also the basal reader programs themselves. (See the following section and Chapter 12 on "Whole Language.")

Comparison of Programs for the 1990s with Earlier Programs

The basal reader series published in the late 1970s and early 1980s were more sensitive to the needs and interests of students than earlier series had been. These series provided for the individual differences of students, parental involvement was included, and reading was looked upon as an integral part of the total language arts program rather than a separate component of it. These series also cautioned teachers to accommodate for dialect and language differences. Helping students to become more independent readers was recognized as more important

---

[1] Jeanne S. Chall and James R. Squire, "The Publishing Industry and Textbooks," in *Handbook of Reading Research*, Vol. II, Rebecca Barr, Michael L. Kamil, Peter Mosenthal, and P. David Pearson, eds. (New York: Longman, 1991), p. 123.

[2] Ibid., p. 125.

than before, and an effort was made to guide children beyond the textbook. The stories that were chosen were based on the developmental needs and interests of students, and an attempt was made to avoid sexist, ethnic, and racial biases in stories. There also seemed to be more of an emphasis on the development of higher level comprehension skills than in earlier series, and the vocabulary load was greatly increased.

The series published in the 1980s did make great strides over earlier series. However, it was the whole language movement that actually brought about the greatest changes in basal readers. In the late 1980s and early 1990s a number of literature-based basal reader series have emerged to counteract criticisms of the whole language movement. Rather than using contrived stories, these basal readers use literary works and make literature the focus of their program. For example, in the *World of Reading,* it is stated that "great literature, everyone agrees, is the foundation of a successful reading program."[3] Therefore, in their series, "classic and contemporary literature was carefully selected for both its beauty and its power to inspire children to discover the lifelong rewards of reading."[4]

Literature-based basal readers Use literary works and make literature the focus of their program.

In the *World of Reading,* the student text includes "stories, poems, myths, folktales, songs, plays, biographies, science fiction, essays, speeches, informational articles, parodies, and interviews."[5] In addition, suggestions for optional reading are given, as well as an offer of two classroom collections of popular trade books.

It appears that most of the literature-based series encourage teachers to integrate trade books into their reading lessons and believe in a strong integrated language arts program with special emphasis on the reading–writing connection.

Special Note

Because the cost of producing a basal reader program is exceedingly high, it is not surprising that publishers are so sensitive to what is taking place in the reading field. If a publisher misgauges the marketplace, it could mean the demise of the company.

Materials

Basal reader series include an abundance of materials in addition to the actual readers and the Teacher Editions. If you were to order a complete basal reader program to be delivered to your home, you would probably have to delegate a special room to hold all the materials. "A complete basal reader program today can consist of as many as 150 to 200 separate items. . . ."[6] Obviously, not many schools buy all the materials.

Basal readers in the 1990s usually include an early literacy program (early

---

[3] Theodore Clymer, "10 Ways to Recognize Great Children's Literature," in *World of Reading Teacher Edition* (Needham, Mass.: Silver Burdett & Ginn, 1991), p. M6.

[4] *World of Reading,* p. M5.

[5] Ibid., p. M12.

[6] Chall and Squire, "The Publishing Industry and Textbooks," p. 124.

readers) for kindergarten that stresses shared reading experiences, oral language development, print awareness, letter formation, auditory and visual discrimination, and letter–sound correspondence. The programs usually have three pre-primers (beginning readers), a primer, and Reader 1 for grade 1. From grade 2 to grade 3, there are usually two readers for each grade. From grade 4 on, there are usually one reader for each grade. The readers are all designated by particular levels, beginning with the preprimers (beginning readers) at first grade. Each student text has an accompanying Teacher Edition, replete with all the information a teacher needs to teach each reading lesson.

Here is a listing of some of the materials the *World of Reading* offers besides the student texts and Teacher Editions: workbooks that contain interest inventories, book logs, and checkpoints for informal assessment; a reader's journal for more open-ended personal responses to literature; an interactive teaching kit; a World of Books classroom libraries; a Time Out for Books collection and teacher guide; and a host of other materials.

An especially exciting part of the literature-based basal readers is their trade book guides.

Special Note

Different basal reader series may have different ways of keying their books to reader grade levels. In one series Level 7 is equivalent to the second half of second grade, whereas in another series, Level 6 is equivalent to the second half of second grade.

Vocabulary and Concept Load of Basal Readers

Basal readers are based on graduated levels of difficulty; that is, each subsequent level is supposed to be more difficult than the previous one. Publishers take great pains to try to ensure that the material is suited to the age and developmental level of the children at a particular grade level. They use a number of tools and techniques such as readability formulas and vocabulary guides to try to determine the difficulty of the text material at various grade levels. (See "Readability and Interest Levels" in Chapter 4.)

Vocabulary load
The frequency of difficult words; the degree to which the number of hard words, their rate of introduction, and the ability to understand them affects readability.

Studies on the vocabulary and comprehension difficulty of basal readers used in the 1920s and 1930s found that the readers were actually too difficult for their intended audience. "An analysis of the vocabularies and the readability of texts published after these early studies show that the textbooks did, indeed, become easier"[7] until the mid-1960s, when the emphasis was on sight words. Then, from the late 1960s to the early 1980s, the vocabulary loads seemed to increase when the emphasis on phonics instruction was increased. It has been hypothesized that the vocabulary loads seem to increase with an increase in phonics instruction, and that the load decreases with an emphasis on sight words.[8]

[7] Ibid., p. 127.

[8] Ibid.

One of the biggest criticisms of basal readers has been their use of a controlled vocabulary. At this time, however, this is unwarranted because basal reader programs have greatly lessened this practice since the increased emphasis on story content and especially with the advent of literature-based basal readers.

It will be interesting to see what the studies report on the vocabulary loads of the literature-based basal readers.

Special Note

Controlled vocabulary
The limiting of the number of new words that appear in successive pages in a particular lesson in a basal reader.

A controlled vocabulary is a limit on the number of new words that appear in successive pages or in a lesson and the repetition of these words to ensure that they are learned.

Instructional Technique: Guided Reading

Guided reading
Instructional technique used with basal readers that includes a number of steps under the direction of the teacher; also known as the **directed reading activity (DRA)**.

The teaching techniques used with basal reader programs is a guided one under the direction of the teacher. Although programs may vary in the number of steps they use to present the lesson, in the use of terminology, in the sequencing of presenting steps, and in the length of their lessons, most basal reader programs have some of the following common features:

1. *Preparing for reading or prereading:*

    - Learn a new comprehension or word recognition skill using familiar material or story previously read.
    - Learn new words needed to read the selection.
    - Relate to past experiences or prior knowledge of children.
    - Identify purposes for reading.
    - Use motivating technique to stimulate interest in story.

Silent reading
Reading to oneself; not saying aloud what is read.

2. *Guided silent reading:* Questions and statements are used before, during, and after to direct students to read silently. Questions vary as to purpose. Some questions are concerned with helping students gain insight into the story's events, characters, relationships, problems, solution, and so on, whereas others focus on helping students monitor their reading comprehension and focus on students making predictions, summarizing, and so forth.

Oral reading
Reading aloud.

3. *Guided oral reading* (in some series this is done in the follow-up step or in conjunction with guided silent reading [see Special Notes]): This is similar to guided silent reading except that the questions are used as motivating techniques to stimulate students to read aloud.

4. *Discussion of material read:* Students reflect on what they have read and determine whether they have achieved their objective.

5. *Follow-up activities* (comprehension and/or vocabulary, phonics, structural analysis, or study skill development)

FIGURE 11-1   This teacher uses the basal reader program effectively.

Special Notes

1. Most new series include a section on the modeling of a skill whereby the teacher "thinks aloud" in order to help children gain insight into the skill being taught. Also, the new series are emphasizing strategic thinking and metacognition, where the student monitors his or her thinking processes.
2. Teachers can use the same guided approach in teaching a reading lesson without using a basal reader. In addition, teachers can adapt the guide to use in any way that they feel will best suit their purposes (see Figure 11-1).
3. In some series the second step is called Guided Reading, and both silent and oral reading are included in this step.

Sample Lesson from a Language-Based Basal Reader

Figure 11-2 is a sample lesson from the Teacher Edition of the *World of Reading*.[9] From looking at the Lesson Organizer (p. 364) presented at the beginning of each lesson in the series, you will note that only the first page of Part 3 has been given. The rest of Part 3 has been omitted here because of space limitations. In spite of this, you can see the extraordinary amount of detail that this literature-based series contains. Nothing is taken for granted or left to chance. (See the commentary that follows the example.)

[9] *A New Day,* Level 5 in *World of Reading* (Needham, Mass.: Silver Burdett & Ginn, 1991), pp. 326–342.

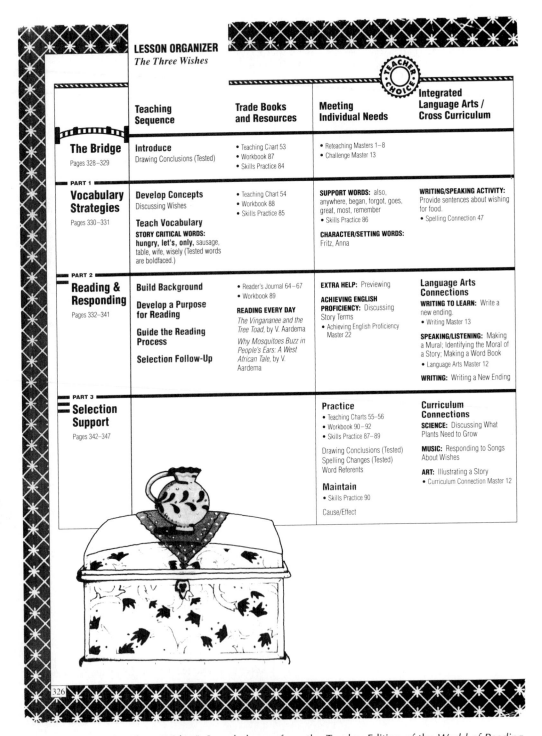

LESSON ORGANIZER
The Three Wishes

	Teaching Sequence	Trade Books and Resources	Meeting Individual Needs	Integrated Language Arts / Cross Curriculum
The Bridge Pages 328–329	Introduce Drawing Conclusions (Tested)	• Teaching Chart 53 • Workbook 87 • Skills Practice 84	• Reteaching Masters 1–8 • Challenge Master 13	
PART 1 **Vocabulary Strategies** Pages 330–331	**Develop Concepts** Discussing Wishes **Teach Vocabulary** STORY CRITICAL WORDS: hungry, let's, only, sausage, table, wife, wisely (Tested words are boldfaced.)	• Teaching Chart 54 • Workbook 88 • Skills Practice 85	SUPPORT WORDS: also, anywhere, began, forgot, goes, great, most, remember • Skills Practice 86 CHARACTER/SETTING WORDS: Fritz, Anna	WRITING/SPEAKING ACTIVITY: Provide sentences about wishing for food. • Spelling Connection 47
PART 2 **Reading & Responding** Pages 332–341	**Build Background** **Develop a Purpose for Reading** **Guide the Reading Process** **Selection Follow-Up**	• Reader's Journal 64–67 • Workbook 89 READING EVERY DAY *The Vingananee and the Tree Toad,* by V. Aardema *Why Mosquitoes Buzz in People's Ears: A West African Tale,* by V. Aardema	EXTRA HELP: Previewing ACHIEVING ENGLISH PROFICIENCY: Discussing Story Terms • Achieving English Proficiency Master 22	**Language Arts Connections** WRITING TO LEARN: Write a new ending. • Writing Master 13 SPEAKING/LISTENING: Making a Mural; Identifying the Moral of a Story; Making a Word Book • Language Arts Master 12 WRITING: Writing a New Ending
PART 3 **Selection Support** Pages 342–347			**Practice** • Teaching Charts 55–56 • Workbook 90–92 • Skills Practice 87–89 Drawing Conclusions (Tested) Spelling Changes (Tested) Word Referents **Maintain** • Skills Practice 90 Cause/Effect	**Curriculum Connections** SCIENCE: Discussing What Plants Need to Grow MUSIC: Responding to Songs About Wishes ART: Illustrating a Story • Curriculum Connection Master 12

326

FIGURE 11-2 "The Three Wishes": Sample lesson from the Teacher Edition of the *World of Reading.*

Student Text pages 160–169

The Three Wishes

by Verna Aardema

SUMMARY   *When a hungry woman asks a poor farmer and his wife for food, the couple generously shares their soup with her. The woman then grants them three wishes, but advises them to choose wisely because their wishes will come true. Fritz and his wife, Anna, decide to each make one wish and then one together. Without really thinking, Fritz and Anna individually wish for sausages and they get more than they can handle. After using the last wish to get rid of the sausages, the couple realizes they can be just as happy with what they have always had.*

327

Continued

FIGURE 11-2 *Continued*

USING THE KNOWN SELECTION   **TO PREPARE FOR THE NEW**

The Bridge

SKILL TRACE: DRAWING CONCLUSIONS				
Introduction	Practice	Test	Reteach	Maintain
TE 328	342	366	385	390	See Level 6

COMPREHENSION

Teaching Drawing Conclusions

OBJECTIVE   Drawing conclusions from text.

1. WARM-UP

Use a passage to draw conclusions orally.

Explain to children that when they read, they think about what happened and why. Tell them this kind of thinking is called drawing conclusions. Read the following paragraph aloud. Have children listen to find story clues about how Alanike, from the familiar story "Alanike and the Storyteller," felt.

> **When Alanike left the storyteller, she smiled and hugged her grandfather. She didn't feel so tired anymore.**

Discuss with children the story clues. *(Alanike seemed happy.)* Have children tell you how they know this. *(Because she smiled and was not so tired anymore. When someone is smiling you know that he or she is happy.)* Explain that you can draw the conclusion that the storyteller must have made Alanike happy.

Discuss story clues and "What I Know" clues.

Explain to children that as they read, they can use story clues and "What I Know" clues to help them draw conclusions. "What I Know" clues are clues that you can use from things you already know or have happened to you before. Story clues are clues written right into the story.

State the objective.

Tell children they will learn to use story clues and "What I Know" clues to draw conclusions about what they are reading.

2. TEACH

Explain why drawing conclusions is important.

Learning how to draw conclusions helps readers better understand what they read.

Present a strategy for drawing conclusions.

Explain to children that there is a strategy they can use to help them draw conclusions about what they read. First, read a passage from a story and look for clues. Then think about what you know about things or events like these. They may be "What I Know" clues. Next, use story clues and "What I Know" clues to draw a conclusion about the passage. Finally, keep reading to find out if your conclusion is correct.

TEACHING CHART 53: DRAWING CONCLUSIONS **53**

1. Billy wrote a story about a boy and his dog. Then Billy got out some paper, crayons, and paints. He wrote his story on each of the pages. He left a lot of room at the top of each page. Then he began using the crayons and paints. What will Billy do?
2. Billy had a new pet kitten. He left his pictures on the table. He went to get a glass of water. When he came back, there were footprints going from one picture to the other. (Conclusion: the kitten walked all over the pictures. Story clues: new kitten, he left the room, footprints. "What I Know" clues: kittens jump up on things.)

328

FIGURE 11-2 *Continued*

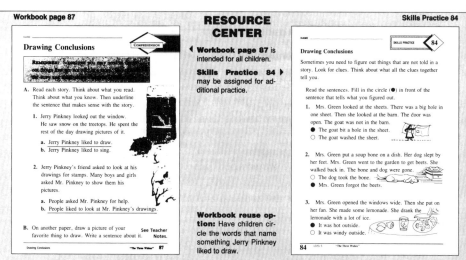

THE THREE WISHES (160–169)

Model the strategy. Display the Teaching Chart. Read passage 1 and point out the story clues. *(story, paper, crayons, paint, wrote story, left room at the top of each page)* Explain the "What I Know" clues. *(Most stories have pictures; you can use crayons and paints to draw pictures.)* Tell children that from both kinds of clues you can draw the conclusion that Billy is going to draw or paint pictures to go along with his story.

3. GUIDED PRACTICE

Check for understanding. Before going on, have children explain how to draw conclusions. *(look for story clues and think about "What I Know" clues)*

Guide children in using the strategy. Have children use the strategy to draw a conclusion for passage 2 on the chart. Discuss story clues and "What I Know" clues that helped them draw a conclusion.

4. WRAP-UP

Summarize instruction. Review that readers draw conclusions to help them better understand what they read. Remind children that sometimes they may need to figure out things that are not told in a story. Ask children to describe the clues they should use to draw conclusions.

5. APPLICATION

Children will draw conclusions as they read "The Three Wishes." The symbol ✔ marks specific questions and activities that apply this skill.

Meeting Individual Needs **RETEACHING** Use the activity on page 390 and Masters 1–8 in the Teacher Resource Kit.

CHALLENGE Use the activity on page 390 and Master 13 in the Teacher Resource Kit.

Workbook page 87

Drawing Conclusions   COMPREHENSION

REMEMBER: *Sometimes you need to figure out things that are not told in a story.*

A. Read each story. Think about what you read. Think about what you know. Then underline the sentence that makes sense with the story.

  1. Jerry Pinkney looked out the window. He saw snow on the treetops. He spent the rest of the day drawing pictures of it.
     a. Jerry Pinkney liked to draw.
     b. Jerry Pinkney liked to sing.

  2. Jerry Pinkney's friend asked to look at his drawings for stamps. Many boys and girls asked Mr. Pinkney to show them his pictures.
     a. People asked Mr. Pinkney for help.
     b. People liked to look at Mr. Pinkney's drawings.

B. On another paper, draw a picture of your favorite thing to draw. Write a sentence about it.   See Teacher Notes.

Drawing Conclusions   "The Three Wishes" **87**

RESOURCE CENTER

◄ **Workbook page 87** is intended for all children.

Skills Practice 84 ► may be assigned for additional practice.

Workbook reuse option: Have children circle the words that name something Jerry Pinkney liked to draw.

Skills Practice 84

SKILLS PRACTICE ◄ 84

Drawing Conclusions

Sometimes you need to figure out things that are not told in a story. Look for clues. Think about what all the clues together tell you.

Read the sentences. Fill in the circle (●) in front of the sentence that tells what you figured out.

  1. Mrs. Green looked at the sheets. There was a big hole in one sheet. Then she looked at the barn. The door was open. The goat was not in the barn.
     ● The goat bit a hole in the sheet.
     ○ The goat washed the sheet.

  2. Mrs. Green put a soup bone on a dish. Her dog slept by her feet. Mrs. Green went to the garden to get beets. She walked back in. The bone and dog were gone.
     ○ The dog took the bone.
     ● Mrs. Green forgot the beets.

  3. Mrs. Green opened the windows wide. Then she put on her fan. She made some lemonade. She drank the lemonade with a lot of ice.
     ● It was hot outside.
     ○ It was windy outside.

84 LEVEL 5   "The Three Wishes"

329

Continued

FIGURE 11-2   *Continued*

Vocabulary Strategies

Developing Concepts

***Build on children's
prior knowledge of wishes.***

Discuss with children a situation where they may have three wishes. Have
them tell what their wishes would be and why they would choose these
particular wishes. Children's wishes may be listed on the chalkboard. Elicit
Story Critical words throughout the discussion. Give children an example of
a situation where they might have to make a choice about something. For
example, tell children they must choose between the toy they have wanted
most of all or a book they have always wanted. Have children tell why they
would make the choice they decided on.

Teaching Vocabulary

***Discuss meanings of Story
Critical words.***

Read each context sentence on the Teaching Chart and have children identify
the new word. Then use the questions below to help children understand
each word. When necessary, provide a definition.

> **TEACHING CHART 54: VOCABULARY**   **54**
>
> 1. **hungry** (wanting food)
>   If you are *hungry*, you want something to eat.
> 2. **only** (without any other)
>   Maybe there are *only* two foods you can have.
> 3. **sausage** (meat stuffed in a casing)
>   Do you want eggs or a *sausage* full of meat?
> 4. **wisely** (with good judgment)
>   You should try to pick *wisely.*
> 5. **wife** (the woman a man is married to)
>   What might a poor man and his *wife* wish for?
> 6. **let's** (let us)
>   *Let's* wish for a good breakfast.
> 7. **table** (a piece of furniture with legs)
>   Oh! Sausage and bread are on the *table.*

hungry   **1. When you are hungry for breakfast what do you eat?** (Possible
answers: cereal, eggs, pancakes) **When you are hungry after school what
do you like to eat?** (Possible answers: fruit, peanut butter)   STRATEGY:
PRIOR KNOWLEDGE

only   2. Point out that the final *y* in *only* has the long *e* sound. **If you could
choose only one thing to do after school, what would it be?** (Possible
answers: to play with a friend, to read)   STRATEGY: PHONICS

sausage   **3. What does a sausage look like?** (It is long and round like a hot dog.) **Do
you eat sausages for breakfast, lunch, or dinner?** (Sausages can be eaten
at any meal.)   STRATEGY: PRIOR KNOWLEDGE

FIGURE 11-2 *Continued*

THE THREE WISHES (160–169)

wisely   **4. What word means the opposite of *foolishly*?** (wisely) Have children
describe something that they have done wisely. (Possible answers: did
homework as soon as they got home from school, rode their bicycle safely)
STRATEGY: ANTONYMS

wife   **5. What word describes a woman who is married?** (wife) Have children
tell what word tells about a man who is married. (husband)   STRATEGY:
PRIOR KNOWLEDGE

let's   **6. What two words mean the same as *let's*?** *(let us)* **What kind of word is
let's?** (contraction) **What letter does the apostrophe replace in *let's*?** (u)
STRATEGY: STRUCTURAL ANALYSIS

table   **7. What does a table look like?** (It has four legs and a top.) **What do you
use tables for?** (Possible answers: to eat at, to do homework on)
STRATEGY: PRIOR KNOWLEDGE

**Discuss Support and Character   Write the words: *began, most, goes, also, anywhere, forgot, remember,
words as needed.**   great, Fritz, Anna*. Read them aloud and define them as necessary. Have
children use each word in an oral sentence.

Provide independent practice.   Options for independent practice are shown in the Resource Center below.

WRITING OR SPEAKING ACTIVITY   *Have children provide orally or in
writing two sentences about a food they might wish for if they were
hungry. Suggest to children that they use the words* began *and* hungry *in
their sentences.*

Workbook page 88

SELECTION VOCABULARY   NAME _____
Using New Words

Circle the word that best completes each sentence.

1. Fritz just had lunch. He wasn't ____ .
   hot   (hungry)   hugged

2. Anna, Fritz's ____ , just had
   lunch, too.
   (wife)   wise   tree

3. There was ____ one bit of meat left.
   two   old   (only)

4. "We will save this for another day,"
   Anna said ____ .
   (wisely)   will   strong

5. Then she put the ____ away.
   (sausage)   strong   snuggles

6. Fritz and Anna cleaned off the
   kitchen ____ .
   (table)   ground   talked

7. "Now, ____ go work in the garden,"
   said Fritz.
   leaves   left   (let's)

88   "The Three Wishes"   Selection Vocabulary

RESOURCE CENTER

◀ **Workbook page 88**
provides practice with
Story Critical words.

Skills Practice 85 ▶
provides additional prac-
tice with Story Critical
words.

Skills Practice 86
provides practice with
Support words.

**Spelling Connection
Master 47** may be
used for spelling instruction with new vocabulary
from this lesson.

**Workbook reuse op-
tion:** Have children un-
derline all the words that
have the long *e* sound,
as in *heat*. Then have
them circle the letter(s) in
each word that made the
sound.

Skills Practice 85

NAME _____   SKILLS PRACTICE 85

Vocabulary: Story Critical Words

A. Read the words.

hungry I was **hungry**, so I ate   table We set the **table** for
        a sandwich.   dinner.
let's   let us   wife   Mr. Fry lives with his
only   Bert used **only** three   **wife**, Mrs. Fry.
        colors in his picture.   wisely She **wisely** did not go
sausage I ate a **sausage** at   out in the rain.
        breakfast.

B. Write the word from the list to finish each sentence.

1. Are you hungry ____ ?

2. Let's ____ eat some food.

3. I can cook only sausage ____ and eggs.

4. Will you set the table ____ ?

C. Draw a line from the sentence to the word that finishes
the sentence.

5. Mrs. Li is the ____ of Mr. Li.   wisely
6. Stuart saves his money ____ .   wife

LEVEL 3   "The Three Wishes"   Content clues   **85**

331

Continued

FIGURE 11-2 *Continued*

PART

Reading & Responding

Building Background

Motivate discussion with quote.

Read aloud the following excerpt from "Alanike and the Storyteller." Have children listen for the advice the storyteller gives Alanike.

> **"Oh, grandfather," said Alanike. "The storyteller told me not to work so hard that I forget to save time for my friends."**

Discuss with children the meaning of the word *advice*. Tell them that it is an opinion about what to do or how to do something. Discuss advice children may have given or received.

Developing a Purpose for Reading

Option 1
Children set purpose.

"WISH" LISTS   Tell children they will read a story about a husband and wife who get to make three wishes. Ask children what three wishes they would make if they had a chance to make three wishes. List their wishes on the chalkboard. Have children read to find out if the characters in the story made any of the same wishes.

Option 2
Teacher sets purpose.

Have children read to find out how the husband and wife used advice. Tell children that in the story, a woman gives Fritz and Anna some advice before they make their three wishes. Have them read to find out whether Fritz and Anna followed the woman's advice.

Meeting
Individual
Needs

EXTRA HELP   Explain that some stories tell about silly or ridiculous things that readers will laugh at and enjoy. Have children preview the illustrations to discover something silly that will happen in the story they are about to read. Direct their attention particularly to the illustration of the sausages raining down on the characters. Then brainstorm with children about how this silly event might have happened. After reading, have children complete Story Map Form 1 and use the map to create an oral summary. Distribute the Story Map Form 1, found in the Teacher Resource Kit.

ACHIEVING ENGLISH PROFICIENCY   Write *sausage* and *porridge* on the board and have children repeat them after you. Use pictures from the story to help you identify these foods. Write *to grant a wish* on the board. Tell children this means "to give someone what they asked for." Say "I wish for a pencil." Have one of the pupils give one. Say, "(Name of pupil) granted my wish." Have children cut out a picture of a food or drink they would like to have. Collect the pictures. Have children request the food saying, "I wish for _____." Return picture to child saying, "I grant your wish." For additional help in story comprehension, use Master 22 in the Teacher Resource Kit.

FIGURE 11-2   *Continued*

Here is a story about two people who had three wishes!

The
Three Wishes

by Verna Aardema

Fritz and Anna lived on a farm. It was a small farm. It was also very dry, and things did not grow well. So Fritz and his <u>wife</u>, Anna, were poor.

One day there was a tap, tap, tap on the door. A woman had come to the farm. She had been walking most of the day, and she was <u>hungry</u>. She asked Fritz and Anna to give her something to eat. Fritz and Anna had a pot of soup. They let the woman come in to eat.

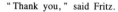

"Thank you," said the woman. "You have been most kind. I will grant you three wishes. Remember to use your wishes <u>wisely</u>. Each wish you make will come true."

"Thank you," said Fritz.

"Thank you very much," said Anna.

The woman left.

AWARD WINNING AUTHOR

| P 160 | THE THREE WISHES | P 161 |

Reader's Journal   **p 64**
Preparing for Reading

**WISH
UPON
A STAR**

Children listen to a poem and write about a wish.

GUIDED READING

Page 160   How do you know that Fritz and Anna were kind people? (They were poor, but shared their food with the hungry woman.)   EVALUATE: CHARACTER

Page 161   How does the woman reward Fritz and Anna for their kindness? (She grants them three wishes.)   RECALL: DETAILS

Page 161   What does the word *grant* mean? How do you know? (The word *grant* means "give." Fritz and Anna will have three wishes that the woman granted them, or gave them.)   ANALYZE: CONTEXT

HIGHLIGHTING LITERATURE

Pages 160–161   Discuss with children the characteristics of a folk tale. (good actions being rewarded, events that happen in groups of three, and happy endings) Have children think about these characteristic as they read the story.

333

Continued

FIGURE 11-2 *Continued*

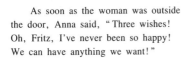

As soon as the woman was outside the door, Anna said, "Three wishes! Oh, Fritz, I've never been so happy! We can have anything we want!"

Fritz said, "Let's have one wish for you, and one wish for me. Then we will have one wish left for the two of us together."

"I like that," said Anna. "It will be fun to have one wish that is all mine."

For most of the day, Fritz and Anna talked about the three wishes they would make. They talked long after it was time to eat again, and they forgot to cook. They began to get hungry.

By the time Anna and Fritz made soup, they were both very, very hungry. As they sat down to eat, Fritz said, "I wish we had a sausage to go with this soup."

And there on the table was a great big brown sausage!

| P 162 | THE THREE WISHES | P 163 |

GUIDED READING

Page 162   How do Fritz and Anna plan to use the three wishes? (They will each make one wish by themselves and then they will make one wish together.)   RECALL: DETAILS

Page 162   Do you think they made a good plan? Why or why not? (Possible answer: yes, because the plan is fair to both of them.)   EVALUATE: CHARACTER

Page 163   What makes a sausage suddenly appear on the table? (Fritz says, "I wish we had a sausage to go with this soup.")   INFER: CAUSE/EFFECT

✔ **Page 163   Do you think that Fritz really meant to make that wish? Why or why not?** (Possible answer: no, because he was so hungry, Fritz said what he said without really thinking.)   SYNTHESIZE: DRAWING CONCLUSIONS

STRATEGIC READING

✔ **Page 163**   Have children close their eyes and try to imagine the expressions on Fritz's and Anna's faces as the sausage suddenly appeared on the table. Have children share their mental pictures. If children have trouble visualizing, remind them to go back to reread the parts of the text that may be confusing to them.
METACOGNITION: VISUALIZING

✔ Skill from The Bridge applied through this question.
✔ Informal Assessment Opportunity: VISUALIZING

FIGURE 11-2   *Continued*

"Oh, Fritz," said Anna, "there goes your wish! And we have <u>only</u> ONE sausage! I wish we had many, many sausages."

There was Anna's only wish!

PUM, PUM, PUM! Great big sausages rained down on them. They both ducked and tried to get the sausages off them.

"Enough! Enough!" cried Anna. "Get the sausages off me!"

"I can't help you," said Fritz. "I can't get the sausages off me!"

PUM, PUM, PUM, came the sausages. Soon the sausages were all around them.

"What can we do?" asked Anna, from under the sausages.

From under the sausages, Fritz said, "Let's eat them."

P 164	THE THREE WISHES	P 165

GUIDED READING

✔ **Page 164   Do you think that Anna really meant to make that wish? Why or why not?** (Possible answer: no, she said it without really thinking, just like Fritz.) SYNTHESIZE: DRAWING CONCLUSIONS

Page 165   What suggestion does Fritz make to help them get rid of the sausages? (He says they should eat them.)   RECALL: DETAILS

✔ **Page 165   Do you think Fritz and Anna have followed the woman's advice to use their wishes wisely?** (Possible answers: no, they have not because they said "I wish" without really thinking.) SYNTHESIZE: DRAWING CONCLUSIONS

Page 165   What do you think will happen next? (Possible answers: they will wish for all the sausages to be gone: they will make another wish that is not wise.) SYNTHESIZE: PREDICTING OUTCOMES

STRATEGIC READING

Pages 160–165   Have children summarize what has happened so far in the story. (Fritz and Anna share their food with a woman and the woman grants them three wishes. They plan how to use their wishes, but without thinking, they both wish for sausages.) Have children tell how Fritz and Anna will get rid of the sausages and how they will use their last wish. (Children may predict that they will use their last wish to get rid of the sausages.) Point out that summarizing and predicting can help readers understand what they read. Suggest that when children have trouble summarizing, they reread those parts of the story that are confusing. Have children go back and verify their predictions after having read the story.   METACOGNITION: SUMMARIZING AND PREDICTING

✔ Skill from The Bridge applied through this question.

335

Continued

FIGURE 11-2   *Continued*

"Don't talk that way," said Anna. "This is not funny! I've had enough sausages. What can we do to get out of this?"

"Well," said Fritz, "your wish is gone, and mine is gone. But together we have one wish left. Let's WISH to get out from under the sausages."

Then they both said, "We wish the sausages would go away."

Just as they had come, the sausages went away. There were no sausages anywhere! The big sausage was also gone from the table.

Fritz and Anna were at the table, with only the soup to eat.

| P 166 | THE THREE WISHES | P 167 |

GUIDED READING

Page 166   How does Anna feel about Fritz's suggestion to eat the sausage? (She does not think it is funny.)   INFER: FEELINGS/ATTITUDES

Page 166   What does Fritz suggest they do next? (He suggests that together they wish to get out from under the sausages.)   RECALL: DETAILS

Page 167   What is Fritz and Anna's third wish? (They wish the sausages would go away.)   RECALL: DETAILS

Page 167   How do you think they feel when the sausages disappear? (They are happy, but upset because they did not use their wishes wisely.)   INFER: FEELINGS/ATTITUDES

HIGHLIGHTING LITERATURE

Pages 160–167   Discuss with children the interesting use of language throughout the story. Have children tell what they think of the use of expressions such as "tap, tap, tap," "pum, pum, pum," and "the sausages rained down on them." Tell children that this kind of language helps readers to visualize what is happening in a story and also makes the story more interesting and fun to read.

FIGURE 11-2   *Continued*

"Oh, Fritz," said Anna, "I am so sad! Here we are without any more wishes."

"Anna," said Fritz, "we were happy before the woman came. We can be happy again. Most of all, I wish we had a sausage to eat with this soup."

"Oh, Fritz," said Anna, "I don't want to SEE a sausage for a long time!"

◆ LIBRARY LINK ◆

If you liked this story by Verna Aardema, look for her book Why Mosquitoes Buzz in People's Ears.

▶ **R**eader's Response

How do you think Fritz and Anna felt when it began raining sausages? How do you think they felt when they used their last wish and the sausages disappeared?

See next page for suggested answers.

SELECTION FOLLOW-UP

The Three Wishes

◆ **T**hinking It Over

1. How did Fritz and Anna use up their three wishes?
2. If Fritz and Anna had three more wishes, what might they wish for? What makes you think this?
3. Why do you think the woman told them to use their wishes wisely?

◆ **W**riting to Learn

THINK AND PLAN   In this story, Fritz and Anna used up their wishes. Think about what could have happened.

1.	They could have wished for bread.
2.	They could have wished for more wishes.
3.	They could have not used the wishes.

WRITE   Use one of the ideas on this page or your own ideas to make up a new ending for the story.

169

P 168 — THE THREE WISHES — P 169

GUIDED READING

✔ **Page 168   What lesson do you think Fritz and Anna have learned?** (They can be happy with what they have always had.)   SYNTHESIZE: DRAWING CONCLUSIONS

RETURNING TO THE READING PURPOSE

OPTION 1   Have children go back to the "wish" lists they made prior to reading. Ask them to tell if any of the things they would have wished for were wished for in the story. Then ask children to tell whether, if Fritz and Anna had used their wishes more wisely, they would have wished for some of the same things.

OPTION 2   If you set the purpose for reading, remind children that the woman told Fritz and Anna to use their three wishes wisely. Discuss the choices they made. Then ask children if they think Fritz and Anna used the woman's advice. Help children conclude that the woman's advice was not really followed.

✔ Skill from The Bridge applied through this question.

Reader's Journal   p 65
Responding to Reading

FRITZ
AND **A**NNA

Children circle words that they think tell about Fritz and Anna. Then they choose one word and write about why they think it tells about the story characters.

337

Continued

FIGURE 11-2 *Continued*

SELECTION FOLLOW-UP

The Three Wishes

THINKING IT OVER

1. **How did Fritz and Anna use up their three wishes?** (They made their first two wishes by accident. Fritz wished for a sausage with his porridge and Anna wished for many sausages. Then they both wished that the sausages would go away.)   RECALL: RETELLING THE STORY

2. **If Fritz and Anna had three more wishes, what might they wish for? What makes you think this?** (Possible answers include any of the following: better soil to grow things in, a larger farm, a new house, more money, a cow. Children may cite additional information from the story to support their answers. For example, Fritz and Anna were poor. Their farm was small and things did not grow well. Accept all reasonable answers.)   SYNTHESIZE: PREDICTING OUTCOMES; METACOGNITION

3. **Why do you think the woman told them to use their wishes wisely?** (She knew that they had only three wishes. After they had used them up, they would not have another chance to wish.)   SYNTHESIZE: DRAWING CONCLUSIONS

WRITING TO LEARN

Use Writing Master 13 to support this activity.

THINK AND PLAN   In this story, Fritz and Anna used up their wishes. **Think about what could have happened.** (To prepare for writing, help children think of additional things Fritz and Anna could have wished for.)

1.	They could have wished for bread.
2.	They could have wished for more wishes.
3.	They could have not used the wishes.

Extend comprehension through writing.

WRITE   Use one of the ideas on this page or your own ideas to make up **a new ending for the story.** (Have children share their new endings with the group.)

FIGURE 11-2   *Continued*

THE THREE WISHES (160–169)

More Ideas for Selection Follow-Up

CRITICAL AND CREATIVE THINKING QUESTIONS

Encourage a variety of responses and points of view.

Use these open-ended questions to encourage critical and creative thinking about the selection.

1. If Fritz and Anna had used their wishes wisely, how do you think the story might have ended?

2. Do you think Fritz and Anna lived happily ever after? Tell why or why not.

REREADING ORALLY

✔ *Have children reread for expression.*

Have children find and reread sections of the story in which Fritz and Anna make their three wishes. Remind children to read with the same expression that Fritz and Anna would have used in their situation. Allow children time to practice their oral rereading with a partner prior to reading the passages aloud to the entire class.

SELECTION COMPREHENSION

Provide comprehension check.

A workbook page to check comprehension is shown in the Resource Center below. It may be used for informal assessment.

✔ **Informal Assessment Opportunity:**   SELF-MONITORING

Workbook page 89

NAME _____   SELECTION
                                         COMPREHENSION

The Three Wishes

Write a word to complete each sentence about "The Three Wishes."

    before   farm   Fritz   wishes   woman

Anna and Fritz lived on a _____ **farm** _____
They were very poor. One day they gave a

hungry _____ **woman** _____ some food. The

woman gave them three _____ **wishes** _____ .

First _____ **Fritz** _____ wished for a
sausage. Then Anna wished for more sausages.
Soon sausages rained down on them. Then they
wished for the sausages to go away. In the end,
Anna and Fritz were left just as they

were _____ **before** _____ the woman came.

Selection Comprehension   "The Three Wishes"   89

RESOURCE CENTER

◄ **Workbook page 89** is intended for all children.

Writing Master 13 supports the Writing to Learn activity.

339

Continued

FIGURE 11-2   *Continued*

PART TWO

LANGUAGE ARTS CONNECTIONS

CREATIVE THINKING: WRITING A NEW STORY ENDING

Discuss possible story endings.

Remind children that Fritz and Anna used their third wish to get rid of all the sausages. Have children brainstorm other ways in which Fritz and Anna could have solved their problem without using their last wish. List suggestions on the chalkboard. Then have children discuss how the story characters might have made good use of their third wish.

Have children write a new story ending.

Work as a group to write a new ending to the story. Have each child contribute at least one sentence to the new ending.   CHALLENGE: WRITING

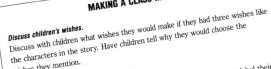

MAKING A CLASS MURAL

Discuss children's wishes.

Discuss with children what wishes they would make if they had three wishes like the characters in the story. Have children tell why they would choose the wishes they mention.

Have children draw a mural of their wishes.

Have each child draw their three wishes on a class mural. Have them label their wishes and tell why they would wish for what is shown in their pictures. Display the mural on a wall in the classroom.   WHOLE CLASS ENRICHMENT

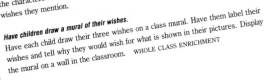

MAKING A BOOK OF WORDS

Discuss the language of poetry.

Read aloud the following sentences from the story:

   One day there was a tap, tap, tap on the door.
   PUM, PUM, PUM came the sausages.

Use the sentences to point out that *tap* and *pum* are words that sound like actions they describe. Introduce a list of other sound words that the children might be familiar with, such as *hiss, whiz, yap, hum, creak, plop,* and *slam.* Have children illustrate these sounds in a class book entitled *Words That Make Sounds.*   LISTENING

FIGURE 11-2   *Continued*

THE THREE WISHES (160–169)

IDENTIFYING THE MORAL OF A STORY

Discuss stories with morals.

Recall with children that "The Three Wishes" is a story that teaches a lesson, or has a moral. The moral of this story is: Be happy with what you have. Explain that a fable or folk tale is a story that teaches a lesson. Tell children they will listen to a story to find out what lesson it teaches.

Have children listen to find a moral.

Read aloud an Aesop fable such as "The Town Mouse and the Country Mouse" or "The Grasshopper and the Ant." Have children tell what the lesson, or moral, of the story is. **Language Arts Master 12** can be used with this activity.   LISTENING/SPEAKING

READING EVERY DAY

Verna Aardema is an author who specializes in folktales. Children will enjoy reading her two colorful folktales from Liberia and West Africa.

The Vingananee and the Tree Toad written by Verna Aardema. Frederick Warne, © 1983. Rat, Buck Deer and Lion are unsuccessful at protecting their stew from the hideous Vingananee. It takes tiny Toad to finally lay low the huge monster in this story of strengths and weaknesses.

Why Mosquitoes Buzz in People's Ears: A West African Tale written by Verna Aardema and illustrated by Leo and Diane Dillon. Dial Press, © 1978. A chain reaction (beginning with Mosquito telling a lie to Iguana and ending with Owl refusing to tell the sun to come up) helps explain why we are annoyed when mosquitos buzz.

Reader's Journal   pp 66, 67
Extending Reading

TAP, TAP, TAP!/ SAUSAGE WISHES

Children decide what Fritz and Anna should wish for when the woman comes back and grants them three more wishes. Then children use their imaginations to change sausages into animals.

Continued

FIGURE 11-2 *Continued*

Selection Support

SKILL TRACE: DRAWING CONCLUSIONS				
Introduction	Practice	Test	Reteach	Maintain
TE 328	342	366	385	390	See Level 6

COMPREHENSION

Drawing Conclusions

OBJECTIVE   Drawing conclusions from text.

Review drawing conclusions.   Remind children that when they read they think about what happened and why in order to understand what the author means. Explain that clues from the story and "What I Know" clues will help them draw conclusions. Read the following paragraph from "The Three Wishes" aloud to children. Have them tell whether or not Fritz and Anna's plan was a fair one.

> **Fritz said, "Let's have one wish for you, and one wish for me. Then we will have one wish left for the two of us."**

Explain to children that the plan was fair. Have children give the story clues and the "What I Know" clues that helped them decide. *(The story clues are: they each had one wish, together they would make a third wish. "What I know" clues are that Fritz and Anna had one wish each and one to share, so they had the wishes divided fairly.)*

Model drawing conclusions.   Read the first passage on the chart aloud to children. Then explain that as you read, you look for story clues and "What I Know" clues. Show your thinking by telling children what the story clues and "What I Know" clues are for the passage. Explain that you were able to draw the conclusion that Fritz had wished for a dog using these clues.

TEACHING CHART 55: DRAWING CONCLUSIONS   55

1. Fritz and Anna talked about wishing for a pet. Fritz liked dogs and Anna liked cats. Anna went out for a walk one day. When she got home, she heard barking in the back of the house. What had Fritz done? (Story clues: talked about wishing for a pet; Fritz liked dogs. "What I know" clues: dogs bark. Conclusion: Fritz wished for a dog and got one.)

2. Fritz was painting the outside of the house blue and yellow. The dog was sleeping near Fritz as he worked. Fritz left the paint cans on the ground and went into the house. When he came out, the paint was spilled and the dog was blue and yellow. What happened? (Story clues: Fritz was painting; he had blue and yellow paint; dog was sleeping near Fritz; Fritz went inside; dog was blue and yellow. "What I know" clues: dogs like to play. Conclusion: the dog spilled the paint.)

Commentary

If teachers were to use all the materials and follow all the steps of the basal reader series, they probably would not have time to do anything else during the school day. However, teachers have the power to use what they feel is best for their students' needs; they are the decision makers. They should feel free to deviate from a lesson, to use a lesson as a springboard for their own creative ideas, and to use other approaches and materials.

Workbooks or skillbooks should not be used as ends in themselves or as busywork. Teachers should use the workbooks or skillbooks as diagnostic instruments to identify those children who are having difficulty with certain skills and those children who are ready to advance to more difficult skills. If teachers have properly instructed the children in the use of the workbook and if they act as guides, the workbook can help the children in developing independence.

Even though the basal reader series are attempting to provide for more individual differences, including cultural and language differences, and they have significantly increased their vocabulary loads, teachers still need to use some individualized approaches to better accommodate the individual differences of their students. It appears that the best reading program is one that incorporates an eclectic-pragmatic approach. In such a program, teachers use skill and ingenuity to mold many approaches into a workable whole. They are not afraid to discard any approach that does not seem to work for the students, and they incorporate reading with the rest of the language arts program.

Basal Reader Checklist

Even though a number of school systems may be moving away from using basal readers, a large percentage of schools still do use them. Therefore, teachers need to be critical textbook consumers. Although in the past two decades basal readers seem to be becoming more similar than different, textbook series are generally unique in what they tend to emphasize, the terminology they use, and usually in the presentation of their material.

Here is a general checklist for choosing basal readers that should help you if your school system uses basal readers.

General Checklist for Choosing Reading Series

	Excellent	Good	Fair	Poor
1. *Physical characteristics*				
a. Print				
(1) Clear				
(2) Readable				

General Checklist for Choosing Reading Series   *Continued*

	Excellent	Good	Fair	Poor
(3) Proper size				
(4) Proper spacing between lines				
b. Paper				
(1) Good weight				
(2) Durable				
(3) Nonglossy				
c. Binding				
(1) Reinforced				
(2) Book held firmly in its cover				

2. *Content (general characteristics)*

	Excellent	Good	Fair	Poor
a. Valid information; that is, information is related to topic being studied.				
b. Covered in proper depth for particular grade level.				
c. Based on objectives that have been chosen for specific reading areas.				
d. Emphasis on interrelating reading with other language arts areas.				
e. Word recognition skills are presented clearly.				
f. Vocabulary expansion skills are developed throughout the various reader levels.				
g. Literal, interpretive, critical, and creative comprehension skills are presented at each reader level.				
h. Study skills appropriate to each reader level are presented.				
i. Activities and other provisions are provided to help students gain an appreciation of reading.				
j. Comprehension selections include material from content areas such as social studies, science, and so on.				

3. *Readability*

	Excellent	Good	Fair	Poor
a. Vocabulary is suitable to particular grade level.				
b. Sentence length is suitable to particular grade level.				

4. *Features*

	Excellent	Good	Fair	Poor
a. Variety of activities.				
b. Creative presentation of material.				
c. Objectives presented at beginning of each lesson.				
d. Index is complete.				
e. Glossary—special terms used in text are defined.				
f. Bibliographies—include up-to-date materials.				

General Checklist for Choosing Reading Series   *Continued*

	Excellent	Good	Fair	Poor
g. Summaries at end of each chapter.				
h. Stories and poems are interesting and have literary value.				

5. *Visual content or illustration*

a. Charts and graphs are included.				
b. Pictures and cartoons are included.				

6. *Treatment of minorities*

a. Every group of people is treated with dignity and respect.				
b. No group is stereotyped.				
c. Each group is accurately portrayed.				

7. *Treatment of gender*

a. Males and females are treated as equals.				
b. Stereotypes are avoided.				

8. *Provisions for individual differences*

a. Special aids for slow learners.				
b. Challenging material for the gifted.				

9. *Teacher's manual*

a. Includes helpful suggestions.				
b. Provides extra activities.				
c. Provides activities for special children.				
d. Provides creative ideas.				
e. Includes suggestions for parents.				
f. Student text is on same page as teacher instructions and answers.				

The Language Experience Approach

Language experience approach
An emerging reading program based on students' experiences, which incorporates all aspects of the language arts into reading.

The language experience approach utilizes the experiences of children and incorporates all aspects of language arts into reading. It is an emerging reading program, based on the inventiveness of both teacher and students. In sharp contrast to approaches predetermined by exact guidelines and materials, the language experience approach to reading brings together all the language arts skills. Persons advocating this approach do not attempt to distinguish between the reading program and other language activities.

In the language experience approach, children's speech determines the language patterns of what they will read, and the children's experiences determine the content. The emphasis is not on decoding from the printed page but, rather, on speaking to express a thought, followed by the encoding of that thought into written form. As the written material is made up of the children's experiences, they will have more of an incentive to learn to read it.

A word of caution is in order. The teacher must be careful to determine whether the children can actually decode the written symbols or whether they have just memorized what they have said. The children may act as though they are reading, but they may not be making any grapheme–phoneme associations.

The teacher using the language experience approach must also help students gain facility in word recognition skills. One difficulty is that word attack skills are often neglected because the needs of the children are not as clearly recognized as when other approaches are used. Nor does the experience approach have a sequential, predetermined guide. As a result, the teacher must know the sequence of skills and teach them as part of the program. The word attack skills needed for independence in the language experience approach are similar to those necessary for any other approach—phonics, structural analysis, context clues, and so on. And all the skills that make an effective reader should be emphasized.

Teachers do not have to use an exclusive language experience approach for their whole reading program. Even for the very experienced teacher, it is not recommended that this be the only approach. A varied reading program is the most likely to be successful for the greatest number of students.

The Experience Story

Experience story
A basic teaching technique in reading founded on experiences of students; story is cooperatively written under the guidance of a teacher; students dictate sentences about a common experience, which the teacher writes on a large chart or the chalkboard.

One tool used as a basic teaching technique is the experience story, which provides for the development and expression of concepts on a very personal and meaningful level. It has the added virtue of permitting growth in most of the language skills.

The experience story is written cooperatively after the class has had a real or vicarious learning experience. The technique is useful with all students at various ability levels. When used with able students, it provides a model against which individuals can evaluate their own writing efforts. The time spent on the experience story may vary from one class period to several days, depending on the complexity of the concept and the ability of the students.

Types of Experiences Used for Experience Stories

The opportunities are unlimited, but the best are those that provide for the development of meaning in a stimulating discussion. Examples include picture description and interpretation; map explanation and interpretation; report on a field trip; summaries of answers to problems; summaries of stories, television shows, and movies; original stories; explanation of the facilities in a new school; descriptions of holidays or special events.

Steps in the Development of an Experience Story

Preparation   The teacher structures the actual experience for the group or individual. Following the first-hand or vicarious experience, the teacher guides a discussion during which together they do the following:

1. Review the experience.
2. Choose the vocabulary to be utilized in writing the story.
3. List the important points to be included in the story.
4. Set up standards for the construction of the story.

Writing the Story   The pupils suggest sentences, which are discussed and probably improved before being written on the board or a chart by the teacher. Then the organization follows. A listing is made of the important points described, based on the natural sequence of the experience. The entire story is read, evaluated, and improved by the students working together.

Example of an Experience Story

The children have visited a local dairy, where they were given samples of some dairy products. The children were taken on a tour of the modern dairy. They saw how clean everything was. They also saw how machines were used to milk the cows.

When the children came back from their field trip to the dairy, the teacher had them go over their experiences. The teacher also had them discuss the differences between how cows were milked a long time ago and how they are milked now. The children also went over the kinds of foods that would be considered dairy foods.

After the children discussed their experiences, the teacher went over some of the special terms that they would need to write their experience story. Here are some of the words that were listed:

cows	milk	local
dairy	bus	taste
enjoy	ice cream	tour
machines		
dairy products		

The words *local* and *tour* were explained.

Here are some of the points that were listed that would help in writing the story:

Going to the dairy.
What we saw at the dairy.
What we tasted at the dairy.
Coming back to school.

The teacher and the children discussed the standards for the story. They decided that each child should have a chance to give a sentence for the story, that the sentence should fit into the story, and that the sentence should make sense.

The children suggested the following sentences for the story:

Today we went to visit a local dairy.
We went on the bus to the dairy.
A man met us at the dairy.
He took us on a tour of the dairy.
We saw lots of cows.
We saw the cows being milked.
Machines were used to milk the cows.
The dairy was very clean.
The man gave us some dairy products to taste.
They tasted good.
We went back on the bus.
We came back to school.
We enjoyed our visit to the dairy.

After each sentence was given, it was read aloud again by the teacher. The teacher then had the child who dictated the sentence read it aloud. After the whole story had been written, the teacher called on the children to read each sentence. She then asked if anyone thought that he or she could read the whole story. The teacher encouraged the children by telling them that she felt that they could read the story and that if they needed any help, she would supply it.

The Individualized Reading Approach

Individualized reading approach Students work at own pace on material, largely trade books, based on the needs, interests, and abilities of each student; emphasizes self-selection of books and individual teacher conferences.

The individualized reading approach has been undertaken in the instruction of reading to better satisfy the individual differences of students. The characteristics usually associated with individualized reading include the individual pupil–teacher conference (Figure 11-3), self-selection of books, self-pacing in reading, record-keeping, and the availability of a wide variety of books and other reading materials. Individualized reading programs may vary from a completely individualized approach to ones using some group instruction as part of the program. When the individualized approach was first initiated, the teacher was supposed to work only in a tutorial manner with the child—that is, in a one-to-one relationship. Children were supposed to choose their own books and work at their own pace, and they were taught the skills of reading in relation to what they were reading rather than in a sequential order. Although some teachers may still follow a completely individualized reading program, many have modified the program

FIGURE 11-3   This teacher meets individually with each of her students.

to include some group instruction to allow for more teacher–pupil contact. Also, many teachers help children choose their books, and skill development is also generally presented in a more sequential manner. Whether individualized reading is practiced alone, in conjunction with another approach, or in some other modified form, the one constant that remains for all is the easy accessibility of a wide range of books based on the interests and reading levels of the students (see Chapter 4).

Of course, books at various interest and reading levels should be made easily accessible regardless of the approach or program in use. (See "Who Are Whole Language Teachers?" in Chapter 12 and "Individualized Instruction" in Chapter 14.)

Graphic Summary of Chapter

On the following page is a graphic summary of Chapter 11. If you have read the chapter, this illustration should help you remember its main points. Under or beside each heading, you might want to jot down some of the information you recall, as well as some of the key concepts in this chapter. This can act as a good review. You can then check your key concepts against those that follow the graphic summary.

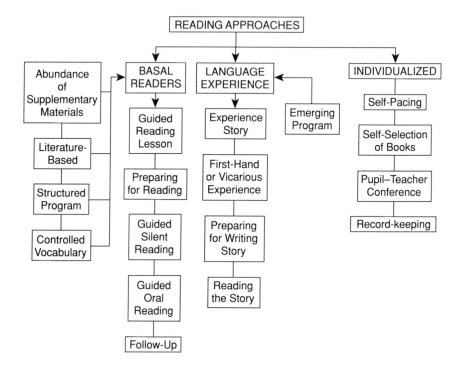

Key Concepts

- Basal reader programs have been the most common approach used by elementary grade teachers to teach reading.
- Usually teachers use basal reader programs in combination with other approaches.
- Whole language has influenced how reading is taught today as well as the basal reader programs.
- The basal readers for the 1990s seem to be literature-based.
- Literature-based basals use whole pieces of good literature rather than contrived text.
- Basal reader programs have an abundance of materials in addition to their readers.
- The guided or directed lesson is the instructional technique used in basal readers.
- The guided or directed approach used in basal readers can be used with trade books or any other materials.
- Basal readers are based on graduated levels of difficulty.
- The language experience approach uses all the language arts.
- The language experience approach is an emerging reading program based on the inventiveness of both teachers and students.

- The language experience approach uses the experience story as its teaching technique.
- The individualized reading approach is used to satisfy the individual differences of students.
- In a completely individualized program, children work on a one-to-one basis with the teacher; they choose their own books and they work at their own pace.
- All individualized programs must have easy accessibility of a wide range of books based on the interests and reading levels of students.

Suggestions for Thought Questions and Activities

1. You have just been appointed to a special primary grade reading committee. Your task is to acquaint the teachers with the language experience approach to reading. How would you do this so that teachers would want to incorporate this type of approach into their reading programs?
2. There is talk in your school of separating reading from the rest of the language arts program and perhaps having a special teacher for reading instruction. How do you feel about this? Present arguments pro or con.
3. Make a comparison/contrast of three different basal reader programs developed for the 1990s. Choose a similar level for all three programs.
4. Choose a basal reader program developed for the 1990s. Compare this basal reader program with the ones prepared ten and twenty years before. Use the *same* basal series and use the *same* level for the comparison.
5. You have just been told that you will be responsible for developing an individualized reading program for your school. How do you feel about this? How would you go about doing this? What kinds of information would you need?
6. The principal in your school has decided on using one approach only in the teaching of reading, and she wants every teacher to adhere to this approach. How do you feel about this? How would you try to persuade her to change her mind? What reasons would you give?

Selected Bibliography

Adams, Marilyn Jager. *Beginning to Read: Thinking and Learning about Print—A Summary,* Steven A. Stahl, Jean Osborn, and Fran Lehr, eds. Urbana, Ill.: Center for the Study of Reading, 1990.

Allen, Elizabeth Godwin, Jane Perryman Wright, and Lester L. Laminack. "Using Language Experience to ALERT Pupil's Critical Thinking Skills." *The Reading Teacher* 41 (May 1988): 904–910.

Anderson, Richard, Ian A. B. Wilkinson, and Jana M. Mason. "A Microanalysis of the Small-Group, Guided Reading Lesson: Effects of an Emphasis on Global Story Meaning." *Reading Research Quarterly* 26 (1991): 417–441.

Barr, Rebecca, and Marilyn W. Sadow. "Influence of Basal Programs on Fourth-Grade Reading Instruction." *Reading Research Quarterly* 24 (Winter 1989): 44–71.

Chall, Jeanne S., and James R. Squire. "The Publishing Industry and Textbooks." In *The Handbook of Reading Research,* Vol. II, Rebecca Barr, Michael L. Kamil, Peter Mosenthal, and P. David Pearson, eds. New York: Longman, 1991, pp. 120–146.

Durkin, Dolores. "Is There a Match between What Elementary Teachers Do and What Basal Manuals Recommend? Technical Report No. 44, Urbana, Ill.: Center for the Study of Reading, 1983.

Stauffer, Russell G. *The Language-Experience Approach to the Teaching of Reading.* New York: Harper & Row, 1970.

12

Whole Language

SCENARIO: MISS GERBER RESEARCHES "WHOLE LANGUAGE"

Miss Gerber has been teaching reading for thirty-five years. She started teaching right out of college and is still teaching in the same elementary school. She prides herself on keeping abreast of her field and especially likes to note new trends and compare them to the approaches she has used over the years. (Miss Gerber has kept a diary of her teaching practices and has also recorded the trends that have been heralded as new.)

She has an open mind and is always willing to try something new if it makes sense to her. However, she has often found that the supposed new practices are merely new terms masquerading as new practices. An unmasking of the terms usually reveals old practices in new masks.

For a number of years the term *whole language* has bombarded the field. The principal of her school asked Miss Gerber and two other teachers if they would research the literature on whole language and report their findings to the rest of the teachers. The principal is thinking of making her school a whole language school. (In Miss Gerber's school district each school has the autonomy to decide on the kind of instructional program it uses.)

Miss Gerber and her colleagues went steadfastly to work. They read almost everything they could get on whole language, and there was a lot. (It seemed as though everyone was writing a book on whole language.) They also attended a number of whole language workshops and observed some teachers supposedly teaching in whole language classrooms. They felt well prepared to make their report to the rest of the teachers.

This chapter is an outgrowth of that report; it will present information on what whole language is and can be. It will also present scenarios of how whole language is practiced in some classrooms.

KEY QUESTIONS

After you finish reading this chapter, you should be able to answer the following questions:

1. What is whole language?
2. What is the whole language movement?
3. What is the whole language debate
4. Are there any definitive whole language programs?
5. How are teachers practicing whole language in their classrooms?
6. What is the place of whole language in the schools?
7. Is whole language just a passing fad?

KEY TERMS IN CHAPTER

You should pay special attention to the following key term:

whole language

What Is Whole Language?

Listen to the following discussion among a group of student teachers:

Student A: I'm in a whole language classroom.

Student B: So am I. We use a whole language basal reader series.

Student C: Oh, in my whole language classroom, we only use trade books — you know, library books.

Student D: I'm in a whole language classroom, too, but my teacher uses a combination of trade books and basal readers.

Student E: You know, everyone uses the term *whole language,* but I really don't know what whole language is.

Student A: Neither do I. It seems as if whole language is whatever you say it is.

Whole language
A movement to influence how reading and writing are taught in school; a set of beliefs in which the emphasis is on the wholeness of things.

Interestingly, Student A may be closer to the truth than she thinks. The term *whole language* is omnipresent, and it seems to connote different meanings to different people.

The whole language movement is an effort on the part of a number of individuals to influence how reading and writing are taught in school. The leaders of this movement have put forth a number of beliefs that focus on the wholeness of things. They advocate a more student-centered view of teaching and more power to teachers and students.

Educators have developed programs based on their interpretation of what whole language is. However, there is no specific program that one can point to and say that it is the quintessential whole language program. This is as it should be, but it has caused a great amount of confusion in the reading field.

Kenneth Goodman, one of the prime movers of the whole language movement, states: "Whole language is clearly a lot of things to a lot of people; it's not a dogma to be narrowly practiced. It's a way of bringing together a view of language, a view of learning, and a view of people, in particular two groups of people: kids and teachers."[1] He says further that any teacher or group of teachers should develop his or her own version of whole language.[2] Also, "whole language cannot be packaged in a kit or bound between the covers of textbooks or workbooks. It certainly can't be scripted."[3] For Goodman, "whole language ideas and concepts become reality only at a point where a teacher is alone with a group of learners. Only there does a whole language program exist."[4] The irony is that many publishing houses, and even some of the major advocates of whole language, are developing prepackaged versions of whole language.

The Whole Language Debate

Whole language has generated a debate in the reading field that has often caused more heat than light:

> To some, the very term 'whole language' is translated to mean an uninformed and irresponsible effort to replace necessary instruction with 'touchy-feely' classroom gratification — and worse. Similarly, the term 'code-emphasis' is translated by others into an unenlightened commitment to unending drill and practice at the expense of the motivation and higher order dimensions of text that make reading worthwhile — and worse. By misinterpreting each other, the two sides prolong a fruitless debate, and they do this at the cost of precious progress and of children's potential reading achievement.[5]

Many of the beliefs put forth by the proponents of whole language are not new. Good teachers have embraced a number of these beliefs for years and have incorporated them in their teaching. Let's look at some of these:

- Give children many opportunities to express themselves.
- Listen to children.
- Involve children in activities that are of interest to them.
- Give children opportunities to ask questions.
- Give children many, many opportunities to read and write.
- Have children write about things they know about.
- Have children read whole pieces of literary works.

[1] Ken Goodman, *What's Whole in Whole Language?* (Portsmouth, N.H.: Heinemann, 1986), p. 5.

[2] Ibid.

[3] Ibid., p. 63.

[4] Ibid.

[5] Marilyn Jager Adams, *Beginning to Read: Thinking and Reading about Print — A Summary*, Steven A. Stahl, Jean Osborn, and Fran Lehr, eds. (Urbana, Ill.: Center for the Study of Reading, 1990), p. 7.

- Help children gain an appreciation of reading.
- Teachers and students should work together.
- The materials used should be based on the needs of students.
- Student–teacher planning should be encouraged.

Some teachers, however, have developed whole language programs that have gone to extremes to embrace every facet of whole language. These purists have eschewed anything that smacks of skill development. For them, basal readers and the teaching of phonics are looked on with disdain. However, even though Goodman claims that "basal readers, workbooks, skills sequences, and practice materials that fragment the process are unacceptable to whole language teachers,"[6] and that "controlled vocabulary, phonic principles, or short, choppy sentences in primers and preprimers produced non-texts,"[7] he also states that "whole language teachers do not ignore phonics. Rather, they keep it in perspective of real reading and real writing."[8]

Goodman states that "teachers guide, support, encourage, and facilitate learning, but they do not control it."[9] He says further that teachers "are aware of the universals of human learning, of language and cognitive processes, but they understand the different paths each learner must take."[10] He claims that teachers "expect and plan for growth and do not impose arbitrary standards of performance."[11]

The whole language view of student-centered education, where the teacher is seen as coequal with learners and where the student's interpretation has as much merit as the teacher's, has caused problems for a number of educators because this "view of the role of the teacher is in many ways the antithesis of the teacher-as-deliverer-of-explicit-instruction view. . . ."[12] In other words, teachers who embrace whole language wholeheartedly would not tell students what to do or when to do it. At this point in time, however, "research supports direct and explicit teacher action. . . . Conversely, there is no research support for inexplicit teacher actions or for instruction in which teachers assume passive or covert roles."[13]

Another area of confusion deals with whole class instruction and ability

6 Goodman, *What's Whole in Whole Language?*, p. 29.

7 Ibid., p. 28.

8 Ibid., p. 38.

9 Ibid., p. 29.

10 Ibid.

11 Ibid.

12 P. David Pearson and Linda Fielding, "Comprehension Instruction," in *Handbook of Reading Research,* Vol. II, Rebecca Barr, Michael L. Kamil, Peter Mosenthal, and P. David Pearson, eds. (New York: Longman, 1991), p. 850.

13 Laura R. Roehler and Gerald D. Duffy, "Teachers' Instructional Actions," in *Handbook of Reading Research,* Vol. II, Rebecca Barr, Michael L. Kamil, Peter Mosenthal, and P. David Pearson, eds. (New York: Longman, 1991), p. 877.

grouping. Some teachers and even entire school systems have interpreted whole language to mean whole class instruction – reading is taught to the whole class regardless of the mix of students in the class. And an important part of the lesson consists of all the children reading aloud, in unison.

According to Goodman, whole language teachers are professionals "who draw constantly on a scientific body of knowledge."[14] In addition, Goodman states that "individual growth, not achievement of absolute levels, is the goal"[15] and "whole language teachers accept individual differences."[16]

Teaching reading to a whole class of heterogeneously mixed students seems to be at odds with Goodman's tenets as put forth in his book about whole language, as well as with what we know about learning principles and individual differences. Most heterogeneous classes have children with ability levels that can range from borderline intelligence to gifted (see Chapter 14, "Organizing for Instruction," and Chapter 15, "Special Children in the Classroom"). What happens to the children at the low end of the ability continuum? Do they become hidden? Do they lose their identities by becoming anonymous?

In addition, when a school system imposes its prescriptive and restrictive version of whole language on all teachers and students, as some have done, and does not allow teachers to use their professional abilities and knowledge, it is violating the spirit of whole language and diminishing teacher empowerment.

Who Are Whole Language Teachers?

The teacher is the key to the success of any program, and this is no different for those who decide to become whole language teachers. When Miss Gerber and her colleagues, the teachers in the scenario at the beginning of the chapter, researched information on whole language, they learned that they were already embracing many of the principles inherent in whole language. However, they also learned that the "true" whole language teachers considered prescriptive teaching material, basal readers and standardized tests, taboo.

Whole language teachers are supposed to wean their students from basal readers to a personalized, individualized reading program that emphasizes writing as well as reading. In whole language programs, the teachers as well as the students are learners.

Teacher empowerment is at the heart of whole language; teachers are seen as major decision makers, and their judgment is highly respected. Prescriptiveness is viewed as antithetical to whole language, whereas flexibility is its strength. With flexibility, however, comes the uncomfortable feeling that anything goes; "it leaves unclear the boundaries between the genuine and the masquerade and between a commitment based on deep understanding of whole

[14] Goodman, *What's Whole in Whole Language?*, p. 28.
[15] Ibid., p. 30.
[16] Ibid.

language principles and a trendy allegiance to slogan and bandwagon."[17] Because of this "fuzziness," a number of people have tried to prescribe what they feel are the "true" whole language programs. This, however, violates the spirit of whole language.

When Miss Gerber and her colleagues met with the school staff to present their report, they told their peers that many may be closer to being whole language teachers than they think. First, they had each teacher answer the following questions:

1. Do you use learning centers?
2. Are your lessons organized around theme units?
3. Do you include pupil–teacher planning?
4. Are your students engaged in all aspects of the language arts?
5. Do you integrate the language arts?
6. Are your students engaged in problem solving?
7. Do you take the individual differences of your students into account when preparing lessons?
8. Do you integrate reading and writing?
9. Do you have many books available on various interest and readability levels?
10. Do you give students many opportunities to read and write?
11. Do you have a Sustained Silent Reading program?
12. Do you read aloud to your students? (See Figure 12-1.)
13. Do you use whole pieces of literature?
14. Do you allow students to choose their own materials?
15. Do you encourage the sharing of books through dramatizations?
16. Do you use children's writing as a springboard for reading?
17. Do you include parents as partners in learning?

Most of the teachers answered "yes" to almost all the questions. Miss Gerber and her cohorts said that they, too, found that they were incorporating many of the beliefs of whole language in their teaching because these tenets are germane to all good reading programs. However, they told their colleagues that after researching whole language, they found a great deal of confusion in the field and found that some practices springing up in the name of whole language are suspect. Miss Gerber and her colleagues said that they felt that the best kind of approach to take would be to continue to have an eclectic program whereby the classroom teacher incorporates the best elements of whole language with a sequential development of skills based on students' needs, while also continuing to use any and all instructional materials that they feel will help their students achieve. They stated further that they felt that what they were doing in their school district was closer to the spirit of whole language than the approaches of

---

[17] Dennis Sumara and Laurie Walker, "The Teacher's Role in Whole Language," *Language Arts* 68 (April 1991): 276.

FIGURE 12-1   Reading aloud to children is an important part of all reading programs.

some other school districts that had embraced whole language, because the teachers in their school district were involved in decisions concerning all aspects of curriculum and instruction, and they had a great deal of autonomy in their classrooms.

Whole Language in the Early 1960s

This section begins with three premises:

1. Anything in the extreme is not good.
2. Whole language and skill development can coexist very well.
3. The whole language movement is not new.

SCENARIO

Mrs. Davis taught in a demonstration school in the early 1960s which embraced all the principles of whole language; at that time, however, it wasn't called whole language.

The principal, teachers, and librarian in this school were firmly committed to a strong language arts program; children were given many opportunities to

Continued

SCENARIO   *Continued*

read and write. Teachers and students planned together the kinds of activities they would have, and children's writings were omnipresent. Everyone appeared happy.

When Mrs. Davis arrived on the scene, she was impressed with the joy children took in reading and writing; however, she was astounded to find that at fifth grade, most lacked basic writing skills and, even though many had a good vocabulary, they did not have the ability to figure out an unfamiliar word independently.

All the students in the demonstration school came from homes where parents were interested in their children's education. Many came to school already reading and writing, and the teachers in this school had kept alive the love of books with which the children came to school. However, these children were shortchanged. Not only did they lack basic skills, but content areas such as science, social studies, and mathematics were neglected.

Mrs. Davis found it exciting to have the power to do all those things she felt would provide an ideal education for her students, but she also felt frustrated that her students had so many lacks that they should not have had.

There is no reason that children cannot enjoy good literature, write their own scripts, engage in dramatizations, and at the same time gain a broad content base and have a strong skills program based on their needs. These things are not mutually exclusive.

Being responsible for children's education is an awesome task; being completely responsible for individualizing instruction for each child in a class without using commercially produced materials makes the task almost impossible.

Whole Language in Action: A Modified Approach

SCENARIO

Mrs. Flynn Is a Whole Language Teacher

Mrs. Flynn, who teaches in a self-contained fifth-grade classroom, has a mix of twenty-five students whose IQs range from borderline intelligence to highly gifted. At the beginning of every year, Mrs. Flynn spends the first few weeks getting to know her students and establishing a nonthreatening environment where creativity can flourish and students are not afraid to be risk takers. She tries to imbue her students with the idea that creativity is a thing of the mind and that each student is unique and can be creative in his or her own way. During the first few weeks, she also helps her students establish certain routines and procedures so that they can live together in harmony during the school year. (Mrs. Flynn likes to explain to her students the reasons for everything she does and encourages them to offer suggestions so that they feel they are part of the deci-

SCENARIO   *Continued*

sion-making process.) Mrs. Flynn knows that establishing a good affective environment takes time, effort, commitment, and sensitivity, so she takes great care in the way she greets her students, what she says, and how she says it.

During the first few weeks Mrs. Flynn engages her students in numerous activities to learn as much as she can about them. For example, she has them brainstorm topics such as the ideal school and the ideal teacher. She has them finish open-ended phrases such as "I wish . . . ," "The best . . . ," and "The book . . ." to learn about their interests. She also has them do lots and lots of writing to gain information about both their reading and writing ability.

Mrs. Flynn uses the data she collects to organize a program for her students that is based on their needs. She recognizes, for example, that Carla, who is a slow learner, will need a program different from the one appropriate for Celeste, who is academically gifted. However, she realizes that even though these two students have different mental ages and cognitive styles, both children need many, many opportunities to read and write, positive feedback, direct instruction based on their needs, encouragement, and on-task activities, as well as opportunities to do things together.

If you were to enter Mrs. Flynn's class about eight weeks into the school year, you would be greatly impressed with the students' activities. Mrs. Flynn's students are working in a number of groups on various projects based on their interests. The students work cooperatively to gain background information on a topic they have chosen to learn more about. Each student, with the help of the teacher, chooses a topic to study, which he or she researches. After extensive reading and notetaking, each student is responsible for sharing his or her information with the rest of the group. The group then writes a joint report, which is presented to the teacher. Then Mrs. Flynn helps each group think of creative ways to present its joint report to the class. Some children use puppet shows; others use role playing; and still others have used various discussion techniques, debates, and some have even simulated a trial with a judge, jury, defense attorney, prosecuting attorney, witnesses, and so on. Mrs. Flynn uses these student projects as springboards to help students gain any needed skills.

During the school day Mrs. Flynn works with the whole class, with individual children, with small groups of children, and with large groups of students.

Let's spend part of the day in Mrs. Flynn's classroom.

Mrs. Flynn's class always begins with a special poem that she or a child reads to the class. Today, because it's a beautiful fall day and varicolored leaves are omnipresent, Mrs. Flynn reads Amy Lowell's poem "Falling Leaves." She tells her students that this is one of her favorite fall poems and she would like to share it with them. After the reading there is a short discussion on the beauty of nature. Mrs. Flynn puts the term *deciduous* on the chalkboard and states that trees that lose their leaves are called deciduous trees. She asks them to be on the lookout for the kinds of trees that are deciduous trees because they will be discussing this in class. She also invites her students to bring in any poems that they would like to share with the class, and she reminds them to ask their parents if

Continued

they have any favorites. If so, the students could bring their poems in to share with the class.

One student raises his hand and says that he lived in another part of the country where the seasons are the same all year. Another student raises her hand and says that she likes a change of season. Before long there is an animated discussion. Mrs. Flynn encourages the children to express their views. She then tells them that they will be studying why different parts of the world and even of our country have different climates during the year. She goes to the globe and points to the lines running north to south and then to those running from east to west and says that the class will be learning about longitude and latitude, which will help them understand why different places have the kinds of seasons they have.

Mrs. Flynn then invites her students to help in the general planning of the day's activities. This is what their schedule looked like:

Newspaper reporting
Reading in groups
MIND BIND (a word riddle game)
Mathematics
Newspaper project
Lunch
Science projects
Independent reading
Social studies projects
Recess
Class magazine (if time is available)
Television reviews (if time is available)

Mrs. Flynn thanks the students for their help. She then calls on her student reporters (each week different students are chosen to report on various parts of the newspaper). Two students are responsible for national news for the week; two others are responsible for local news. There are also sports and weather reporters. (This is part of the ongoing newspaper unit.) After the various reporters have presented the news, Mrs. Flynn asks students if they have any questions about what they are supposed to be doing while she works with each reading group. (Children have special assignments and work based on their individual needs. Some children will be working in groups on special projects, some will work on the computers, others will work in the various learning centers, and still others will be working at their desks completing some unfinished assignments.)

Mrs. Flynn calls a group of children to come to the reading corner, where they will continue to read their soft-cover trade book and discuss the writer's portrayal of his main characters. (Mrs. Flynn uses a combination of trade books, newspapers, and basal readers as reading materials and various approaches to help her students get the most from their reading [see Figure 12-2].)

SCENARIO   *Continued*

Today she begins by having her students go over some more vocabulary words she feels may be a problem for them. She then asks someone to give a brief synopsis of what they have read so far. Next she asks her students a provocative question to stimulate their interest. She asks them how they feel the main characters would fare if they lived in this age rather than in the early 1900s. She then asks them to make predictions about how they feel the main characters will behave when they learn about the secret plan. Next she asks them to read the rest of the chapter to see whether their predictions are correct. Mrs. Flynn observes her students for a few moments while they are reading silently. She then looks around the room to see what the rest of her students are doing. She tries to make eye contact with a number of them. When she does, she smiles and gives them nods of approval.

She looks back at her students and notices if they have finished reading the chapter. It appears they have. She asks them if their predictions were correct. Then she asks them to compare the author's version to theirs. She also asks her students to find clues that help us gain an insight into the characters' behavior. She calls on various students to read aloud their clues and to explain how they help us gain an insight into the characters.

Mrs. Flynn asks the students to think about what they have read so far and to go back to their seats and try to write a very short version of the next chapter. Tomorrow they will read their versions and then they will read the author's version.

The students go back to their seats, and Mrs. Flynn calls another reading group. She works with these students in a similar manner, but they are reading a different trade book. She does the same with the next group, who are reading still another trade book. (Mrs. Flynn chooses the trade books based on the students' reading ability levels.)

After reading, Mrs. Flynn divides the class in half and has them play a word meaning and verbal reasoning game called MIND BIND. Mrs. Flynn presents the students with a word riddle, which they have to solve. The group that gets three correct answers first wins.

FIGURE 12-2   These children are reading their weekly newspaper.

SCENARIO   *Continued*

After the game, Mrs. Flynn tells the students that today she would like to show them how mathematical skills and terms are related to English-language skills and terms. She presents them with the following sentences:

Please train your dog not to bark at the train.
The bark from the tree is peeling.

She asks them to notice the words *bark* and *train* and asks them whether these words have the same meanings in the two sentences. She helps her students recognize that word meanings depend on word order and that the same word in a different position has a different meaning in the sentence.

Mrs. Flynn tells her students that mathematics has a special word order, too; that is, the way the terms are presented in relation to other terms influences the meaning of each term. In mathematics the order (*syntax*) is usually rigid. If you deviate in mathematical syntax, the meaning is usually changed. For example:

$$A > B$$
$$B > A$$

She then presents her students with the following sentences.

The cat scratched the child.
The child scratched the cat.

Mrs. Flynn asks her students to compare the two statements. Are they the same? She helps them recognize that they have the same terms, but the order (syntax) is different. The meanings of the sentences are entirely different.

Mrs. Flynn wants students to see that small deviations can lead to misunderstandings in mathematics, and to recognize that imprecision in language can also lead to lack of communication or misunderstanding.

Mrs. Flynn has the students create a number of sentences that have the same word in different positions. She then has them do the same using letters and symbols to show how mathematical meanings can change based on syntax. Tomorrow, she tells her students, they will analyze mathematical word problems.

Mrs. Flynn tells her students that by now they should see how important it is to be precise in their language so that they say what they wish to say. She says further that their newspaper project should be helping them to recognize this even more. She then engages her students in a discussion of the roles of the various people who work on a newspaper. She asks about the differences between a news story written by a reporter and an editorial written by an editor. A number of hands shoot up to answer. This pleases Mrs. Flynn because she is very proud of this project, which she initiated to teach higher level thinking skills, especially critical thinking.

Today Mrs. Flynn tells her students that she has brought three articles from

SCENARIO   *Continued*

three different newspapers to class. She places the headline from each on the chalkboard and asks the students what they expect to follow from each headline. She asks them also which is a negative, positive, or neutral headline. She then presents the three articles without their headlines on a transparency so that all the children can see them. She asks the students to read each carefully and see if they can match the article with its headline. She again asks the students the role of the reporter, which is to be objective and present facts only. Then she asks them to compare the three articles, which are written about the same event. Mrs. Flynn helps her students recognize that the terms the writer uses can influence the reader and that good readers must be alert to these techniques.

Next she gives them a topic and tells them that they will write three headlines for the same topic. First, they write a neutral headline, next a positive one, and finally a negative one. Mrs. Flynn asks all her students to look at two different newspapers and by the end of the week to bring in two articles on the same topic that have been presented differently.

It's now almost lunchtime, which is the time when Mrs. Flynn reads aloud to her students. She has been reading a Sherlock Holmes mystery, *The Scarlet Band,* to her class. She asks her students if they have figured out the mystery yet. After a short discussion, she begins to read.

Whole Language Reading Instruction: A Modified Approach

Mrs. Smith believes strongly that the concomitant learnings her students gain while learning to read can influence greatly whether they will acquire a lifelong reading habit. Because she recognizes the important role of attitudes, Mrs. Smith is especially cautious about the methods she uses to help students learn to read.

Mrs. Smith has been using basal readers and trade books in her class to teach reading for almost a decade. Whether she is using a basal reader series or a trade book, she usually employs a directed or guided reading activity, which stresses reading as a thinking act. She also uses an eclectic approach in teaching word recognition; that is, she uses a combination of context clues, phonics, and "look and say" in helping students learn new words.

SCENARIO

Mrs. Smith Teaches First-Graders to Read Using Trade Books

Using trade books with her students requires Mrs. Smith to engage in a great amount of preliminary preparation.

Preliminary Teacher Preparation

Step 1   Decision making is an important first step. Mrs. Smith must choose a book or story that is at the interest and attention span level of her students. At the

Continued

SCENARIO   *Continued*

same time, the story must have a controlled vocabulary—that is, one that is repetitive so that students can overlearn the words. The concept load must be at the students' comprehension level, and the story should be characterized by predictability. She also wants a short story that they could read in one or two sessions.

After much investigation and thought, Mrs. Smith chooses "The Little Red Hen."

Step 2   Mrs. Smith reads carefully the story she has chosen. She notices there are a number of words that would not be in her students' reading vocabulary but would be in their listening vocabulary. She also sees some words that would not be in their listening vocabularies; that is, it is unlikely that the children would know the meanings of these words if they were said aloud. Mrs. Smith must decide which words she should retain and for which ones she should substitute other words.

Step 3   Mrs. Smith rewrites the story of "The Little Red Hen" to suit the needs of her students; however, she makes sure the flavor and essence of the story remain the same (see pages 406–408 for Mrs. Smith's rendition of "The Little Red Hen").

Step 4   Mrs. Smith makes a big book out of "The Little Red Hen" by putting the story on large newsprint paper. She makes the letters large enough so that the children sitting around the easel that holds the "home-made" big book can all see the writing easily.

Step 5   Mrs. Smith culls all those words from the story that she will introduce to her students as new words. Now she is ready to present a directed or guided reading lesson to a group of her students. These are the steps she follows whether she uses a basal reader or a trade book.

Preparing for Reading

Mrs. Smith shows the children a little nest with a little red hen sitting in the nest. She asks her students where they would find chickens. A discussion ensues about farms and the kinds of animals you would find on a farm. Mrs. Smith directs the children to the following sentence on the board.

A pig lives on a farm.

She points to the word *pig* and tells them that this is an animal that likes to eat a lot. It also rhymes with *big*. She then asks for someone to read the sentence. A child reads aloud the sentence.

Mrs. Smith then directs the children to another sentence on the board. She points to the word *goose* and tells the children that a goose is a water bird that also lives on a farm. It rhymes with *loose*. The children have no difficulty reading the sentence correctly.

Mrs. Smith asks her children if they know what a lady chicken is called. She puts the word *hen* on the board. She asks the children if they can figure out what the word is. She reminds them that they have worked with the *en* word family. She puts the following words on the board:

    ten   men
    then   pen

A number of children raise their hands. She calls on Jordan, who says, "Hen." "Good," says Mrs. Smith. "Yes, a lady chicken is called a hen. What do you think baby chickens are called?" she asks. She puts the word *chicks* on the board. A number of children raise their hands and call out, "Chicks." "Good," Mrs. Smith says again.

Mrs. Smith then puts the following words on the board.

    flour   wheat
    bread   grain
    mill   plant

She uses the same procedures to help the students acquire each word.

After Mrs. Smith has presented all the new words to her students, she uses a "look and say" approach whereby she frames each word with the index fingers of both hands and says aloud each word. She then has the children say the word aloud. She does the same for each of the new words.

Now she tells the students that they will be reading a story about a little red hen. This little red hen has three friends. Mrs. Smith tells the students that at the end of the story they will find out what kind of friends they are.

Guided Silent Reading

Mrs. Smith tells the students to read the first page silently to find out who the little red hen's friends are and what the little red hen finds.

As the children read silently, Mrs. Smith looks to see if they are subvocalizing or if they are using their fingers to read word by word. (While Mrs. Smith is working with her group of children, at the far end of the room, her teacher's aide is reading a story aloud to the other children.)

When the children finish reading silently, Mrs. Smith asks them to answer the questions. She also asks them to make predictions about what they think will take place.

Mrs. Smith follows the same procedure for the whole story; that is, Mrs. Smith asks the students a question, the children read the page to answer the question, and she then asks them to predict what they think will happen next.

Before the children come to the end of the story, Mrs. Smith asks the children to predict how they think it will end. She then asks them how they would end the story. She writes their endings on the chalkboard. Mrs. Smith has the children read the final page to find out what happens. She then has them compare their endings with the story's ending.

Guided Oral Reading
After the children have silently read the whole story, Mrs. Smith asks them a number of other questions. She has them find the parts in the story that help answer the questions and then calls on a child to read the part aloud. When she asks questions that do not have answers directly stated in the story, she has the children find clues in the story and then has a child read aloud the clues that help answer the question.

Follow-up
Mrs. Smith and the children discuss the various characters in the story and come up with traits for each one. She then has the children think of another character they could put in the story to change the story. She asks them to write about this character and tells them that tomorrow they will read their stories aloud in their reading groups. The children go back to their desks to write their stories.

Special Note
At times, Mrs. Smith combines the guided silent and oral reading. For example, she asks her students to read silently to answer a question. After they have done this, she has them find the answer or clues to the answer in the story and has a child read aloud the part or parts that help answer the question.

The Little Red Hen: Mrs. Smith's Rendition

There was once a little red hen. She was a happy little red hen. She lived with her baby chicks in a small house. She took good care of her house. She took good care of her chicks. She worked hard.

One day she was walking with her friends, the goose, the cat, and the pig. She saw something on the ground. It was a few grains of wheat.
"Who will plant this wheat?" she asked her friends, the goose, the cat, and the pig.
"Not I," said the goose.
"Not I," said the cat.
"Not I," said the pig.
"Then I will plant it myself," said the little red hen. And she did.

The little red hen took good care of her garden. Every day she looked to see if

The Little Red Hen   *Continued*

the seeds were growing. One morning the little red hen saw something green. The seeds had grown. She called her chicks.

"Oh, look, the wheat is growing!" They were very happy.

All summer long the wheat grew. It grew taller and taller. It turned colors. It turned from green to gold. Finally, the wheat was ready to be cut.

"Who will help me cut this wheat?" she asked her friends, the goose, the cat, and the pig.

"Not I," said the goose.

"Not I," said the cat.

"Not I," said the pig.

"Then I will do it myself," said the little red hen. And she did.

Next the little red hen had to beat the wheat. This gets the grain from the wheat.

"Who will help me beat the wheat?" asked the little red hen.

"Not I," said the goose.

"Not I," said the cat.

"Not I," said the pig.

"Then I will do it myself," said the little red hen. And she did.

At last the little red hen had all the grain. She put the golden grain into a large sack. Now she was ready to go to the mill. At the mill the grain would be made into flour. She asked her friends, the goose, the cat, and the pig, "Who will help me take this grain to the mill?"

"Not I," said the goose.

"Not I," said the cat.

"Not I," said the pig.

"Then I will do it myself," said the little red hen. And she did.

The next day the little red hen was ready to bake a loaf of bread with her flour. She asked her friends, the goose, the cat, and the pig, "Who will help me bake this bread?"

"Not I," said the goose.

"Not I," said the cat.

"Not I," said the pig.

"Then I will do it myself," said the little red hen. And she did.

The bread was ready soon. It smelled very good. The little red hen called to her friends, the goose, the cat, and the pig,

"Who will help me eat this bread?"

"I will," said the goose.

"I will," said the cat.

"I will," said the pig.

"Oh, no," said the little red hen.

Continued

The Little Red Hen   Continued

"I found the wheat. I planted it. I watched the wheat grow. I cut it down. I beat it. I put the grain in a sack. I took it to the mill. There it was made into flour. I used the flour to bake this bread.

"Now my chicks and I will eat the bread."
And they did!

Graphic Summary of Chapter

Here is a graphic summary of Chapter 12. If you have read the chapter, this graphic illustration should help you remember its main points. Under or beside each heading, you might want to jot down some of the information you recall, as well as some of the key concepts in this chapter. This can act as a good review. You can then check your key concepts against those that follow the graphic summary.

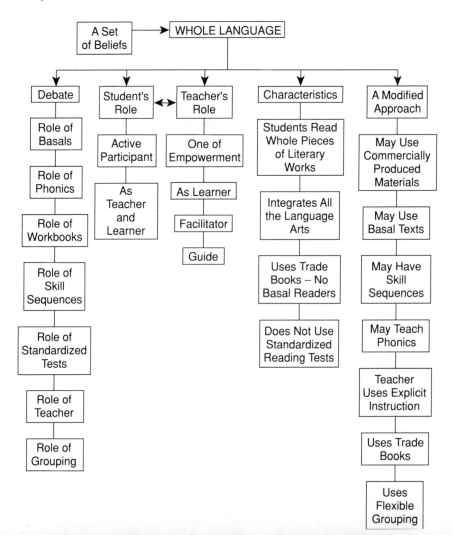

Key Concepts

- Whole language is an effort by a number of individuals to influence how reading and writing are taught.
- Whole language is a set of beliefs.
- Whole language focuses on the wholeness of things.
- Whole language teachers use trade books to teach reading.
- How whole language is presented may vary from teacher to teacher.
- Good teachers have embraced many of the views put forth by whole language proponents.
- Whole language purists eschew anything that smacks of skill development.
- The teacher is the key to the success of any program.
- Whole language teachers are supposed to wean students from basal readers to a personalized, individualized reading program that emphasizes writing as well as reading.
- Teacher empowerment is at the heart of whole language.
- Prescribing what should be "whole language" violates the spirit of whole language.
- A modified whole language program combines elements of whole language with basals, skill development, and other approaches or programs.
- A guided approach to teaching reading can be used with trade books as well as with basal readers.

Suggestions for Thought Questions and Activities

1. Choose three teachers who claim to be "whole language" teachers. Observe each for at least one-half day. Discuss what the teachers did in their classrooms; then discuss the similarities and/or differences among them.

2. Observe a teacher who uses a basal reader program and another who uses trade books only to teach reading. Discuss their method of teaching reading. Use the following questions as a guide to help you evaluate them.

   a. How do they prepare students for reading?
   b. How do they introduce vocabulary?
   c. Do they use interactive instruction?
   d. Do they use a modeling strategy?
   e. Do they use a guided reading approach?
   f. If they teach specific skills, are they taught in relation to what students are reading?

3. You have been appointed to a special committee in your school to help decide whether your school should abandon basal readers and embrace whole language. What will you say?

4. Give a talk on your views concerning a modified whole language reading program.
5. What do you feel whole language proponents have contributed to the field of reading?
6. You have been asked to represent your school in a debate concerning whole language. Which side will you take? What are your views?

Selected Bibliography

Blake, Robert W. *Whole Language: Explorations and Applications.* Urbana, Ill.: National Council of Teachers of English, 1990.

Dudley-Marling, Curt, and Don Dippo. "The Language of Whole Language." *Language Arts* 68 (November 1991): 548–554.

Goodman, Ken. *What's Whole in Whole Language?* Portsmouth, N.H.: Heinemann, 1986.

Seavey, Tom. *Invitations.* Portsmouth, N.H.: Heinemann, 1991.

Weaver, Constance, Diane Stephens, and Janet Vance. *Understanding Whole Language: From Principles to Practice.* Portsmouth, N.H.: Heinemann, 1990.

13

A Diagnostic-Reading and Correction Program

SCENARIO: MR. JARVIS NIPS READING PROBLEMS IN THE BUD

Mr. Jarvis has been a very successful elementary school teacher for over four decades. At his retirement dinner, he was asked to what he attributes his success. This is what he said:

"I chose teaching because I love to work with children, and I enjoy the excitement and drama of teaching. Teaching is hard work, and I have tried to give it everything I have. My reward has been that my students do well. I feel that good teachers make an extremely significant contribution to society and that makes me feel good.

"Most of you have heard me say the following many times: Good teachers do not take anything for granted, and prevention is the key to a good instructional program. Therefore, I have always had a very aggressive diagnostic-reading and correction program in my classes. I know that learning takes place in some kind of relationship, so I have tried to provide a good affective environment—one in which students do not feel threatened. It's an environment conducive to growth, and one in which students are involved in their own learning.

"My maxim has been, 'Success breeds success.' I have achieved this by having continuous diagnosis and by combining diagnosis with instruction. Most of the time I have been successful. Not all the time, but, gratefully, most of the time."

This chapter presents information on a diagnostic-reading and correction program that teachers should have in their classes and discusses the kinds of assessment techniques teachers can use to learn about their students' reading behavior.

KEY QUESTIONS

After you finish reading this chapter, you should be able to answer the following questions:

1. What is a diagnostic-reading and correction program?
2. What is the role of the teacher in diagnosis?
3. What kinds of reading assessment techniques does the teacher usually employ?
4. What is portfolio assessment?
5. What is the role of diagnosis and correction in the content areas?

KEY TERMS IN CHAPTER

You should pay special attention to the following key terms:

appraisal
cloze procedure
cloze test
diagnosis
diagnostic pattern
diagnostic-reading and correction
   program
diagnostic-reading test
disabled reader

identification
observation
portfolio assessment
pull-in program
pull-out program
reading expectancy formula
Reading Recovery program
underachievement

What Is a Diagnostic-Reading and Correction Program?

Diagnostic-reading and correction program
Reading instruction interwoven with diagnosis and correction.

Teachers who have a diagnostic-reading and correction program[1] in their classes continuously diagnose students' reading behavior to nip in the bud any potential problems (see Figure 13-1). *Prevention* is a key term for these teachers; they believe in early intervention and interweave diagnosis with instruction in the regular classroom. The emphasis in such a program is on determining students' strengths and weaknesses, the conditions causing them, and the strategies needed to overcome the difficulties. A diagnostic-reading and correction program requires an environment where students do not feel threatened and are not afraid to ask for help.

The definition that is chosen for reading also influences the diagnostic program. If we are looking upon reading as a total integrative process, then diagnosis should also be looked upon as a total integrative process. If a global definition

[1] See Dorothy Rubin, *Diagnosis and Correction in Reading Instruction,* 2nd ed. (Boston: Allyn and Bacon, 1991).

FIGURE 13-1   This teacher is working with this child to help "nip a problem in the bud."

is chosen, then the diagnostic program will be a broad one (see Chapter 1). Under a global definition, when one does diagnosis, it is recognized that a reading problem is due to many different causes.

The Role of the Teacher in Diagnosis

The role of teachers in a total integrative diagnostic-reading program is broad. The teacher must observe individual children, understand individual differences, build background for reading, and combine diagnosis with teaching.

Teachers must have knowledge of the various word recognition and comprehension skills at their fingertips and be able to teach these effectively. They must know the techniques of observation and be aware of the factors that influence children's reading behavior. Teachers must be able to administer and interpret such diagnostic techniques as the informal reading inventory (see "Special Note") and word analysis tests. If teachers cannot construct their own informal diagnostic tests, they should be aware of those that are commercially available. Obviously, teachers in a total integrative reading program must be well prepared and well informed.

Special Note

In diagnosis the teacher needs to use techniques and instruments that break down complex skills into their component parts so that they can gain information about a student's strengths and weaknesses. An informal reading inventory is an excellent tool that a teacher can use to learn about a student's strengths and weaknesses. However, it is beyond the scope of this book to go into all the information a teacher would need to administer an informal reading inventory. Many excellent diagnosis and correction texts are available that give in-depth information on informal reading inventories (see the "Selected Bibliography").

A Diagnostic Pattern[2]

Step I: Identification

Diagnostic pattern Consists of three steps; identification, appraisal, and diagnosis.

Identification Part of diagnostic pattern; the act of determining the student's present level of performance in word recognition and comprehension for screening purposes.

The teacher must first *identify* the student's present status in a particular problem area. The teacher does this by describing in detail the individual student's performance in the specific problem area. For example, if a student is having difficulty in reading, the teacher would describe in detail what phonic skills the student possesses, what word attack method the student consistently uses, how large the student's sight vocabulary is, how well the student reads orally, what difficulties the student encounters when he or she reads orally and what errors he or she makes, how accurate the student is in comprehending silent reading material, or how accurate the student is in comprehending material when it is read to him or her. Teacher-made tests as well as standardized achievement tests are used to help determine a student's present performance in an area.

Step II: Appraisal

Appraisal Part of diagnostic pattern—a student's present reading performance in relation to his or her potential.

After determining the student's performance level in a particular area, the teacher must *appraise* the student's performance in relation to his or her potential. For example, in the area of reading, the teacher first determines the student's reading performance (see Step I), and then the teacher determines the student's reading expectancy. The teacher then tries to determine if there is a discrepancy between the student's reading performance as determined by achievement tests and the student's reading expectancy. (See the section "Who Is a Disabled Reader?" in this chapter.)

Diagnosis The act of identifying difficulties and strengths from their signs and symptoms, as well as the investigation or analysis of the cause or causes of a condition, situation, or problem.

Step III: Diagnosis

At this step the teacher is interested in discovering the specific conditions and abilities that underlie the student's performance in a particular area. The teacher observes the student while the student is in the activity causing him or her difficulty to try to find the conditions influencing his or her performance. For example, while reading, does the student display any anxieties? Does he or she have

---

[2] Adapted from Ruth Strang, *Diagnostic Teaching of Reading* (New York: McGraw-Hill, 1969).

any habits such as subvocalizing (moving lips while reading), pointing to each word, and so on? Next, the teacher tries to determine whether the abilities involved in the specific skill area are causing the difficulty. For example, lack of phonic skills may be due to deficiencies in auditory or visual discrimination (perceptual problems) or lack of memory (retention problems). Through further diagnostic testing and observation, the teacher tries to determine whether the problem is due to organic or experiential factors. Obviously, if the teacher suspects an organic problem, he or she should refer the student to a skilled professional or medical doctor for further testing. The teacher also tries to determine whether the student's problem is due to the student's attitude or motivation.

Student Involvement in Diagnosis

The main purpose for diagnosis is to determine what is causing a student's problem so that a program can be developed to help a student overcome the difficulty. Student involvement is crucial. Unless the student recognizes that he or she has a problem, unless the student understands what that problem is, and unless the student is interested in overcoming the problem, nothing much will probably be accomplished.

The teacher can help the student to become involved in the following ways:

1. The teacher should help the student recognize his or her strengths as well as weaknesses.
2. The teacher should not overwhelm the student by listing all of his or her difficulties at once.
3. The teacher should try to elicit from the student what the student thinks his or her reading problems are, why the student feels that he or she has these problems, and what the student feels are the causes of his or her reading problems.
4. The teacher and the student together should set attainable goals for a specific problem area.
5. Together, the next learning step should be determined.

Assessment Techniques in a Diagnostic-Reading and Correction Program

Diagnostic reading test
Provides subscores discrete enough so that specific information about a student's reading behavior can be obtained and used for instruction.

A good diagnostic-reading and correction program depends on teachers using a variety of assessment techniques throughout the day to learn about their students' reading behavior. These assessment techniques can range from diagnostic instruments to teacher observations (see "Teacher-Made or Classroom [Informal] Assessments" in Chapter 5).

A diagnostic reading test, which is designed to break down a complex skill into its component parts, helps teachers gain knowledge of students' specific reading behavior. Such tests are very important in determining students' strengths and weaknesses.

Portfolio Assessment

Portfolio assessment
A record-keeping device that gives students, teachers, and parents an ongoing view of a child's reading and writing progress; material that is included varies from teacher to teacher.

Portfolio assessment is a record-keeping device similar to those used in the investment community. The purpose is to give students, teachers, and parents an ongoing view of the child's reading and writing progress.

At the beginning of the year, the teacher prepares a large file folder for each student in the class and explains its purpose. The folders are usually kept in a place that is easily accessible to both teacher and students.

The kinds of materials filed in the folder usually vary from teacher to teacher. Some teachers may include only samples of students' work, whereas others may include everything the students do related to reading. Still others may also include teacher observations, comments, tests, and so forth. The portfolios are most useful if they contain a diverse enough sample of material so that an accurate profile of a student's reading behavior emerges. The more teachers know about their students' reading behavior, the better able they will be to help them.

Special Note

Formal portfolio assessment tools are springing up that have specific instructions for the kinds of materials to be collected and a scale for the evaluation of the material. These tools seem to violate the spirit of portfolio assessment, whereby the kinds of materials that are collected are determined by the students and teacher.

Questioning as a Diagnostic Technique

Asking questions is not only an important part of teaching and learning; it is also very useful in diagnosis. Teachers' questions, which can stimulate students to either low- or high-level thinking, give teachers an insight into students' ability to comprehend information. Teachers can learn from their questions whether students need help, whether they are able to see relationships and make comparisons, and whether what the students are reading or listening to is too difficult or too easy.

Students' questions are important in helping students to learn, and they are essential diagnostic aids in giving teachers feedback on students' ability to understand information. In order to ask good questions, students must know their material. As a result, those students who ask the best questions usually are those who know the material best. Confusing questions are a signal that the teacher needs to slow down or reteach certain material.

Teachers can use questioning as a diagnostic technique to learn about their students' thinking ability. Here are some examples.

The teacher has the children read a short story. The story is about a little boy who wants to go to school, but he can't because he is too young. The teacher tells the children that she is going to make up some questions about the story, and the children have to tell her whether the questions that she makes up are able to be answered or not. If a question is able to be answered, the student should answer it; if a question is not able to be answered, the student must tell why. The teacher makes up the following questions:

1. What are the names of Ben's sister and brother who go to school?
2. Why does Ben want to go to school?
3. Make up an adventure for Ben.
4. Why can't Ben go to school?
5. What are the names of the bus driver's children?
6. What does Ben do in the summer?

This technique can help the teacher learn which children are able to concentrate, as well as which children are able to do different kinds of thinking. Questions 1 and 4 are literal questions; question 2 is an inferential question; question 3 is a creative question; and questions 5 and 6 are not able to be answered because no such information was given in the story either directly or indirectly.

A more difficult questioning technique that the teacher could use with highly able children is to have them make up questions for a selection that they have read. After students have read a selection, the teacher can ask them to make up three different questions. The first question should be one for which the information is directly stated in the passage. The second question should be one for which the answer is not directly stated in the passage. The third question should be one that requires an answer that goes beyond the text.

In early primary grades the teacher can use pictures as the stimuli for questions, or the teacher can relate a short story to the children and have them devise questions for it.

Here are some questions that a group of fourth-grade children made up after reading a story about Melissa and her friend Fred, who were always getting into trouble.

1. Who is Melissa's best friend? (literal)
2. What is the main idea of the story? (inferential)
3. From the story what can we infer about the main character's personality? (inferential)
4. Relate an episode that you think Melissa could get into. (creative)

The children who made up the questions challenged their classmates with their questions and then were responsible for determining whether their classmates had answered them correctly. (See "Asking Questions" in Chapter 10.)

Observation of Students' Learning Behaviors

Observation
A technique that
helps teachers
collect data about
students' behavior.

Direct observation is helpful to the teacher who wants to become aware of the attitudes, interests, and appreciations of students. For example, teachers can observe whether students are volunteering to read aloud or to answer comprehension questions. They can observe whether students are volunteering to participate in discussion and to work in group projects and whether they voluntarily take books from the library and read them. Teachers can also learn about students' interests by observing what they do in their free time.

So that observations are of value, teachers must be as objective as possible and avoid making generalizations about students' behavior too early in the process of getting to know them. For example, after observing that Ronda on one or two occasions is reading mystery stories, the teacher states that Ronda likes mysteries. This may be so, but it may also be that she is just "trying them out." Ronda may actually like only a few of them and she may read only one or two a year.

Teachers who are astute observers will also notice the kinds of errors their students make and try to determine if a pattern exists.

Describing Students' Errors

Teachers should recognize that students' errors give them insight into students' thinking and help teachers learn about students' developmental levels. So that evaluation is diagnostic, the nature of student errors must be pointed out as clearly as possible. The student should understand exactly what the teacher is saying.

"Sara, you are reading very poorly," is a statement that will not help Sara read better. The teacher must be very specific and point out to the child the exact area in which the child needs to improve as well as *how* to improve. For example, if Sara has difficulty reading orally, the teacher should diagnose what Sara's problem or problems are and then suggest to Sara specific things that she could do. Some examples of suggestions could be: "Don't read so fast. Slow down when you come to commas, semicolons, and periods. Read with more expression. Notice the punctuation marks. They are signals that help you. For example, an exclamation mark tells you that the sentence should be read with strong emotion, and a question mark means that you must sound as though you are asking a question."

Cloze Procedure, Comprehension, and Diagnosis

Can you supply the _____ that fits this sentence? When you came to the missing word in this sentence, did you try to gain closure by supplying a term such as *word* to complete the incomplete sentence? If you did, you were involved in the process of *closure*, which has to do with the ability of the reader to use context clues to determine the needed word. To gain *closure*, we must finish whatever is unfinished.

Cloze procedure
A technique that helps teachers gain information about a variety of language facility and comprehension ability skills.

Cloze test
Reader must supply words that have been systematically deleted from a passage.

Cloze procedure is not a comprehension skill; it is a technique that helps teachers gain information about a variety of language facility and comprehension ability skills. A cloze test or exercise is one in which the reader must supply words that have been systematically deleted from a text. At the intermediate grades, the passage is about 250 words, and every fifth word is usually deleted; at the primary grades, the passage is about 100 words, and every eighth or tenth word is usually deleted. Variations of the cloze procedure are usually used. For example, rather than deleting every fifth or tenth word, every noun or verb is deleted, or every function or structure word (definite and indefinite articles, conjunctions, prepositions, and so on) is deleted. This technique is used when the teacher wishes to gain information about a student's sentence sense. *Example:*

> Jane threw _____ ball
> _____ Mary. (the, to)

Another variation of the cloze technique would be to delete key words in the passage. This technique is useful for determining whether students have retained certain information. *Example:*

> A procedure in which the reader must supply words to complete what is unfinished is called the _____ procedure. (cloze)

Cloze technique can also be adapted to use in a number of other ways. Students can be presented with a passage in which parts of words are given and they must complete the incomplete word. *Example:*

> Dick r_____ his bike every day. (rides)

Another adaptation is to present the students with a passage in which every *n*th word is deleted. They must then choose words from a given word list that *best* fits the blanks.

Teachers can use the cloze technique for diagnostic, review, instructive, and testing purposes. In the construction of the exercise, the key thing to remember is the *purpose* of the exercise. If the purpose is to test a student's retention of some concepts in a specific area, then the exact term is usually necessary; however, if the purpose is to gain information of a student's language facility, vocabulary development, or comprehension ability, the exact term is not as important because often many words will make sense in a passage.

Here is an example of an exercise using the cloze technique. Notice how explicitly the instructions are stated for the students, and also notice that the first sentence of the passage is given intact.

Directions   Read the first sentence that has no missing words in it to get a clue to what the story is about. Then read very carefully each sentence that has a missing word or words in it. Using context clues, think of a word that would make sense in the story, and put it in the blank.

In the forest there lives a kind old man and woman.

(1) _____ have been living in

(2) _____ forest for almost ten

(3) _____ . They had decided to

(4) _____ to the forest because they

(5) _____ nature.

        The kind old (6) _____ and woman make their

(7) _____ by baking breads and cakes and

(8) _____ them to the people who

(9) _____ the forest. Everyone who

(10) _____ the forest usually buys

(11) _____ bread or cake from the old

(12) _____ .

Answers   (1) They, (2) the, (3) years, (4) move, (5) love, like, (6) man, (7), living, (8) selling, (9) visit, (10) visits, (11) some, (12) couple

Note that the deletion pattern was not the same throughout the passage.

Special Note

Researchers developed the cloze procedure primarily as a measure of readability—that is, to test the difficulty of instructional materials and to evaluate their suitability for students. As already shown, it has since been used for a number of other purposes, especially as a measure of a student's comprehension.

Scoring the Cloze Test

If you wish to apply the criteria for reading levels that have been used in research with the traditional cloze procedure, you must follow certain rules. First, only words must be deleted, and the replacement for each word must be the *exact* word, not a synonym. Second, the words must be deleted in a systematic manner.

    The traditional cloze procedure consists of deleting every fifth word of a passage that is representative of the material being tested. The passage that is chosen should be able to stand alone; for example, it should not begin with a pronoun that has its antecedent in the former paragraph. The first sentence of the passage should remain intact.

    For maximum reliability, the passage should have at least 50 deletions. Using this figure as our criterion, we can see that the passage needs to be at least 250 words long. Shorter passages would not yield as reliable scores.

    If you have deleted 50 words from a passage, the procedure for scoring the cloze test is very easy. All you have to do is multiply the correct insertions by two and add a percentage symbol. For example, 30 correct insertions would yield a score of 60 percent. If you have not deleted exactly 50 words, you can use the following formula:

$$\frac{\text{Number of Correct Insertions}}{\text{Number of Blanks}} \times 100\%$$

Example:

$$\frac{36 \text{ Correct Insertions}}{60 \text{ Blanks}} \times 100\%$$

$$\frac{36}{60} \times 100\% = (36 \div 60)\ 100\%$$

$$= 60\%$$

Reading Levels Scale for Traditional Cloze Procedure

Independent Level	58% and above
Instructional Level	44% through 57%
Frustration Level	43% and below

Who Is a Disabled Reader?

It is not inconceivable to have a sixth-grade class with a span of reading levels ranging from first grade to eighth grade or above. The teacher in such a class must determine who the disabled readers are. Not all students working below grade level are underachievers. A child reading at a third-grade level in a sixth-grade class may be reading at his or her ability level, whereas another child may not be. Similarly, children reading at their grade levels may be reading far below their ability levels. A teacher may be pleased that a pupil is working on grade level, but gifted children working on grade level are *not* working up to their ability levels. A gifted child working on grade level is "underachieving." However, a child with a 70 IQ in the third grade working at the second-grade level would be achieving at his or her expectancy level. The reading expectancy scores presented in Table 13-1 are idealized ones; that is, there are many other variables that affect ability to read in addition to the mental age of an individual (see Chapter 2). Usually a child with a 70 IQ on an individual IQ test would be working more than one year below grade level. As a child with a 70 IQ would usually not be able to work in the abstract, that child would have difficulty with reading skills involving inference, analogies, and so on.

Underachievement Achievement below one's ability level.

From this discussion, it can be seen that a disabled reader may be any student who is reading below his or her ability level; a disabled reader is one who is underachieving.

Disabled reader A reader who is reading below his or her ability level.

TABLE 13-1   Bond and Tinker Formula for Estimating Reading Expectancy for IQs 70 and 120 (Grades 1–6)

$\dfrac{IQ}{\text{Years of Reading Instruction} \times 100} + 1.0$	= Reading Expectancy at End of School Year
(1 × .70) + 1	= 1.7 at end of 1st grade
(2 × .70) + 1	= 2.4 at end of 2nd grade
(3 × .70) + 1	= 3.1 at end of 3rd grade
(4 × .70) + 1	= 3.8 at end of 4th grade
(5 × .70) + 1	= 4.5 at end of 5th grade
(6 × .70) + 1	= 5.2 at end of 6th grade
(1 × 1.20) + 1	= 2.2 at end of 1st grade
(2 × 1.20) + 1	= 3.4 at end of 2nd grade
(3 × 1.20) + 1	= 4.6 at end of 3rd grade
(4 × 1.20) + 1	= 5.8 at end of 4th grade
(5 × 1.20) + 1	= 7.0 at end of 5th grade
(6 × 1.20) + 1	= 8.2 at end of 6th grade

Note: The Bond and Tinker formula begins at grade 1; that is, at the end of grade 1 the child is considered to have been in school one year.

Reading Expectancy Formulas

Reading expectancy formula
Helps teachers determine who needs special help; helps determine a student's reading potential.

Reading expectancy formulas help teachers to determine who needs special help. A child's reading expectancy yielded by a reading expectancy formula is compared to his or her reading achievement level yielded by a reading achievement test score. If the child's expectancy level is significantly higher than his or her reading achievement scores, further diagnosis should be undertaken. (See "Diagnosis" in this chapter.)

Teachers must be cautioned about using reading expectancy formulas as absolute determinants of reading potential. They are not; they are merely indicators of possible reading potential. Most reading expectancy formulas are based on intelligence quotients, which may not be accurate for the child, especially if a group IQ test was used and the child has word recognition problems.

Reading Intervention Programs

Throughout this book, we have discussed the importance of children's early years in reading and how many children come to school already at risk of failing. Children who come from educationally disadvantaged homes need early identification and, as early as possible, special programs that emphasize the language arts. Some early intervention programs are surfacing that appear to hold a great deal of promise.

What Is Reading Recovery?

Reading Recovery program
An early individualized, one-on-one intervention program for first-graders who are experiencing difficulty in learning to read.

Reading Recovery is an early intervention program that was designed to help young readers who are experiencing difficulty in their first year of reading instruction.[3] In this program, which is not supposed to be a long-term or permanent one, a child who is one of the lowest achieving readers in a first-grade class receives daily individual thirty-minute lessons by a specially trained teacher, in addition to the regular classroom instruction. The program is tailored to the individual child, and the emphasis is on engaging the child in reading and writing activities that will help the child catch up with peers.

This collaborative one-on-one early intervention program is very promising; however, as the designers of the program aptly note, there are many variables that determine how well someone will do in school, not least of which is socioeconomic circumstances (see Chapter 2). "There is no one answer to problems in education."[4]

What Are Pull-In Reading Programs?

Pull-out program
A remedial program that takes place outside the regular classroom and is handled by a special teacher.

Many schools have attempted to help students who have reading problems with the use of pull-out programs. These are remedial programs that take place outside the regular classroom and are usually handled by a special reading reacher or a basic skills reading teacher.

The pull-out program is supposed to supplement the student's classroom developmental reading program. Unfortunately, in many school systems the pull-out program becomes an end in itself, and there is hardly any articulation between the classroom teacher and the basic skills teacher concerning the work the child is doing. Also, the child often feels misplaced and confused because he or she spends a great deal of time away from the regular classroom. When the child returns to the regular classroom, he or she will have missed a significant amount of work.

Pull-in program
An intervention program whereby the basic skills teachers work with the regular classroom teacher as a team in the children's regular classroom.

A *pull-in program* is one in which the basic skills teachers work as a team with the regular classroom teacher and teach those children designated as at-risk or basic skills children in the students' regular classroom. The basic skills students have reading at the same time that the children in the classroom have reading.

During the day, the teacher plans an extra reading instruction period for the at-risk or basic skills students. While the teacher is working with these children, the teacher aide reads a story aloud to the other children, using a directed reading approach.

---

[3] Gay Su Pinnell, Mary D. Fried, and Rose Mary Estice, "Reading Recovery: Learning How to Make a Difference," *The Reading Teacher* 43 (January 1990): 283.

[4] Ibid., p. 293.

Diagnosis and Correction in the Content Areas

Diagnosis and correction in reading should not be relegated merely to the reading period. Reading is taking place all through the day at school, and teachers would be losing valuable opportunities to learn about students' reading strengths and weaknesses if they did not observe their students' reading behavior in the content areas. It's in the content areas that teachers can observe whether students are applying what they have learned during the reading period.

A problem in mathematics may not arise because the student is unable to do quantitative reasoning or basic mathematical operations; it may be that the student has a reading problem. The teacher should have students find the main idea of various paragraphs in their subject matter books to discern whether students are understanding what they are reading. Teachers should give students opportunities to read aloud from their content books to determine whether the books are at the proper readability level for the students. Also, teachers should be alert to students' attitudes toward a subject. It may be that the student does not like the subject because he or she cannot read the textbook. A student who is not reading at grade level would probably have difficulty reading a social studies, science, or math textbook whose readability level is at the same grade level. If teachers cannot get subject matter books for their students at their reading ability levels, they will have to make special provisions for them. Teachers will have to provide these students with a special guide. This guide would have an outline of the material that they are supposed to read. It would also have a listing of all those vocabulary words that the teacher feels would cause difficulty for the students. Before the students are asked to read the content material, the teacher should go over the vocabulary words with the students. The words should be pronounced, presented in a sentence, and defined. After the students have read the material, the teacher should go over it with them in the same way that she or he would in a reading lesson. The emphasis, of course, would be on attaining the concepts of the content area rather than on developing reading skills, but the technique of gaining the content concepts includes reading comprehension skills. Content-area teachers who use the knowledge of reading and study skills to help their students acquire the content information are more likely to be successful teachers.

Special Note

It would be very difficult to get a subject matter book for a student who is reading below grade level at the student's reading ability level and have the textbook cover the same material. If a student is in fourth grade, the subject matter book for third-grade mathematics covers different material. Also, the student may be good in mathematics but have a reading problem. If a book from a lower grade level is used, the student would be penalized in mathematics.

Graphic Summary of Chapter

Here is a graphic summary of Chapter 13. If you have read the chapter, this graphic illustration should help you remember its main points. Under or beside each heading, you might want to jot down some of the information you recall, as well as some of the key concepts in this chapter. This can act as a good review. You can then check your key concepts against those that follow the graphic summary.

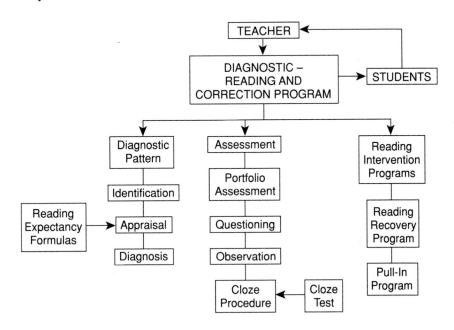

Key Concepts

- A diagnostic-reading and correction program helps nip problems in the bud.
- In a diagnostic-reading and correction program, diagnosis is interwoven with instruction.
- The teacher is a key person in a diagnostic-reading and correction program.
- A diagnostic pattern consists of identification, appraisal, and diagnosis.
- Student involvement is essential in a diagnostic-reading and correction program.
- Teachers can use a number of informal assessment techniques to learn about their students' reading behavior.
- Cloze procedure helps teachers gain information about a variety of language facility and comprehension ability skills.
- A disabled reader is one who is underachieving.

- Reading expectancy formulas help teachers determine who needs help.
- Reading Recovery is an early intervention program designed to help young readers who are having reading problems.

Suggestions for Thought Questions and Activities

1. You have been asked to present a talk to the faculty at your school concerning diagnostic-reading and correction programs. What will you say?
2. Discuss with various teachers how they determine whether a student has a reading problem.
3. Explain why a good diagnostic program is important.
4. Describe the teacher's role in a good diagnostic-reading and correction program.

Selected Bibliography

Harris, Albert J., and Edward R. Sipay, *How to Increase Reading Ability,* 9th ed. New York: Longman, 1990.

Pinnell, Gay Su, Mary D. Fried, and Rose Mary Estice. "Reading Recovery: Learning How to Make a Difference." *The Reading Teacher* 43 (January 1990): 282–295.

Rubin, Dorothy. *Diagnosis and Correction in Reading Instruction,* 2nd ed. Boston: Allyn and Bacon, 1991.

Tierney, Robert J., Mark A. Carter, and Laura E. Desai. *Portfolio Assessment in the Reading-Writing Classroom.* Norwood, Mass.: Christopher-Gordon Publishers, 1991.

Valencia, Shiela. "A Portfolio Approach to Classroom Reading Assessment: The Whys, Whats, and Hows," *The Reading Teacher* 68 (February 1990): 338–340.

14

Organizing for Reading Instruction

SCENARIO: MISS PERKINS PREPARES FOR READING INSTRUCTION

Miss Perkins teaches third grade in a self-contained classroom. During the first few weeks of school she works on establishing good rapport with her students and in organizing for instruction. She collects all kinds of data on her students' achievement through observation and various types of assessment. In addition, Miss Perkins establishes a system of portfolio assessment for her students, in which they keep samples of their reading and writing work.

Miss Perkins evaluates the collected data and uses the information to form tentative groups. When she organizes these groups, she tells her children that they are not permanent; that is, they can and will change from time to time. Miss Perkins also explains the purpose of the groups to her students. (She feels the more her students know and understand about what is taking place, the more she will be able to maintain a nonthreatening environment in her class, which is essential to the success of her reading program.)

Miss Perkins's grouping practices are in accord with the diagnostic-reading and correction program she embraces in her classroom (see Chapter 13). She feels an aggressive diagnostic-reading and correction program requires a flexible grouping philosophy.

Throughout the year, Miss Perkins is flexible in organizing for instruction. She is very sensitive to the needs of her students and adapts instruction on the basis of their ability and interest levels. She recognizes that there is no one best way to organize for reading. There are a number of ways, and some work better for certain groups of students and teachers than others.

This chapter presents information on organizing for reading and discusses how teachers can provide for the individual differences of their students using individualized programs.

KEY QUESTIONS

After you finish reading this chapter, you should be able to answer the following questions:

1. How does organizing for instruction affect the teaching–learning program?
2. What factors are taken into account when organizing for reading?
3. What types of reading groups do teachers generally have?
4. What is the place of student involvement in grouping?
5. For whom does individualized instruction work?
6. What is the role of record keeping in an individualized program?
7. What is the role of learning centers in the classroom?
8. How can teachers use computers as an aid in reading?
9. What is cross-age tutoring?
10. How can teachers use peer tutoring in their classes?

KEY TERMS IN CHAPTER

You should pay special attention to the following key terms:

ability grouping
computer-assisted instruction
cross-age tutoring
group instruction
individualized instruction

learning center
literature study groups
peer tutoring
teacher as classroom manager

How to Organize for Instruction

> *To find one plan of class organization that can be executed effectively by all teachers with all children is as difficult as finding a word to rhyme with orange.*
> —*Emmett A. Betts*

Teachers' decisions concerning how they will organize their classes for instruction are vital because they will affect the entire teaching–learning program. Teachers certainly should take the individual differences of all the students into account and should try to provide for their individual needs. However, it simply is not practical and probably is not possible to provide a completely individualized program for each student in each instructional area. Children need experience in working with small groups, with large groups, and with the whole class. Working with various groups helps children gain learnings that they cannot obtain from working individually.

Teachers in organizing for reading instruction must provide for group instruction as well as individualized instruction. Activities such as choral speaking, creative drama, puppetry, plays, discussion groups, and so on, which are correlated with reading, all require working with others. In a classroom organized for both individual and group instruction, students learn to work both cooperatively and independently. Being courteous and respecting the rights of each individual are the basic tenets of any viable program organized for instruction.

Grouping within Classes

Group instruction
A number of students are taught at the same time; helps make instruction more manageable; students are divided into groups according to some criteria.

Although a combination of individual and group instruction is advocated, we need to look at each separately to get a better understanding of individualized and group instruction.

Types of Groups

Children are organized into groups to make instruction more manageable. During any school day a teacher usually works with the whole class as a unit, with small groups, with large groups, and with individual students. Some groups are ad hoc ones, formed for a specific short-range purpose and dissolved when the purpose has been accomplished, and some groups are ongoing ones.

Factors Teachers Consider in Grouping

There does not appear to be any definitive research on the factors that teachers use to form reading groups. Some researchers have suggested that teachers group according to their conception of the "ideal student"; several claim that teachers use social class as a factor in grouping.[1] Others have found that "teachers consider such information as reading achievement, sex, participation during instruction, and problematic behavior"[2] in forming reading groups. And still others claim that teachers base their grouping decisions on students' achievement rather than social class.[3] One study that investigated teachers' actions rather than what they say they do found that "most teachers assign students to groups on the basis of achievement and work habits and are not influenced by home background."[4]

Teachers usually take a number of factors into account when organizing groups, but the most important factor is generally the student's achievement.

[1] Rebecca Barr and Robert Dreeben, "Grouping Students for Reading Instruction," in *Handbook of Reading Research,* Vol. II, Rebecca Barr, Michael L. Kamil, Peter Mosenthal, and P. David Pearson, eds. (New York: Longman, 1991), p. 897.

[2] Ibid.

[3] Ibid.

[4] Ibid.

Determining Students' Reading Levels for Reading Groups

Ability grouping Dividing students into groups according to similar levels of intelligence and/or achievement; in reading, students are usually grouped according to their reading achievement levels.

Most teachers group their students for reading, and usually they group their students according to their reading achievement levels. Many teachers, however, are confused as to what techniques or instruments to use to determine their students' reading achievement levels. This problem is especially pronounced today because of the controversy surrounding standardized reading achievement tests.

The following scenarios present a number of techniques that teachers often use to group their students. Which method do you feel is a viable one? Why?

Scenario 1

At the beginning of every school year Mr. Kale looks at the standardized reading achievement test scores of each of his students and groups them accordingly.

Scenario 2

Ms. Lane administers a word list composed of words from the glossaries of different reader levels to each of her students. She asks each student to look at each word and then to state the word. She tests her students only on their decoding ability. She then groups them based on their ability to pronounce words.

Scenario 3

Mr. Dole chooses a few passages from the trade books that the children will be reading. He asks his students to read the passages silently and then to answer comprehension questions on the passages. He groups his students based on how well they do on answering the questions.

Scenario 4

Mrs. Crane chooses a short passage from a trade book that the students will be using. She tells her students that she will have them read aloud a very short passage individually and then ask them some questions about the passage. While the student is reading aloud, Mrs. Crane notes any word recognition problem. If there are a significant number, she chooses another passage of comparable difficulty and reads it aloud. She then asks the student to restate what is in the passage and then to state its main idea.

The teacher in Scenario 4 is probably using the best technique for grouping students. However, this method is dependent on teachers being knowledgeable of informal reading inventories and how to adapt these into a shortened version. This technique gives teachers an insight into both the student's decoding and his or her comprehension ability.

The teacher in Scenario 1 is doing what many teachers often do. It is a viable technique, but it doesn't take into account the loss that many children incur in the period from April, when the test is usually given, and the following September, when the children return to school.

The technique in Scenario 3 is also a viable one, but it depends on students' ability to express themselves well in writing. A student who does poorly on such a group written test may have a writing problem rather than a reading one.

The teacher in Scenario 2 is using a completely untenable technique that, unfortunately, a number of teachers use because it's easy and fast. However, this method gives teachers information only on students' ability to decode words. It does not supply any knowledge of students' comprehension ability.

The use of the word list technique to determine groups can result in a mismatch between students and groups. For example, a student who does well on identifying the words on the word list would be put in a top group, whereas a student who does poorly on the word list would be put in a low group. It is possible, however, that the student who did poorly on the word list could have much better comprehension ability than the one who did well on the word list. Because of this problem, teachers should not use word lists alone to determine groups. If word lists are used, they should be used in conjunction with some means of determining students' comprehension ability.

Number of Reading Groups

The number of reading groups depends on the variability within the class. In some classes there may be three groups, in some there may be four, in others there may be two—there isn't really any magic number. In most classes, however, you will usually find three groups. Teachers feel this number is manageable and also gives them the flexibility they need to accommodate the variability in their classes.

Teachers should group their students based on the needs of their particular class rather than looking for a magic number. They should consider all their grouping patterns as tentative and work with a number of different patterns. At times, a teacher may decide to work with the whole class as a unit, at other times on a one-to-one basis with a number of children (see Figure 14-1). When the grouping pattern and groups are viewed as flexible, children can easily flow from one group to another; new groups can be formed and old ones disbanded whenever necessary.

Student Involvement in Grouping

Student involvement is vital for any program to work effectively. To encourage student involvement, the teacher explains to the students the manner in which the groups are being organized and the purposes for the groups. The students are told that they may ask to move to any group at any time if they feel they are ready for something another group is learning. Students may also sit in with any other group to relearn a skill, review a skill, or learn something that they might have missed when it was taught to their group because they were absent. The main factor is that students have the opportunity to move freely from one group to another. Also, by encouraging students to make decisions about their own learning, teachers are helping students to become more self-reliant and independent learners.

FIGURE 14-1   The teacher and child are discussing a funny part in the book.

Grade Level for Student Involvement in Grouping

There is no set level to which one can point and say, *"That* is the correct level at which to include student input in grouping decisions." Some intermediate grade level children who have never had the opportunity to contribute to planning or decision making will not be ready to work in a program with a strong emphasis on student participation, whereas some primary grade level students who have been involved in some planning and decision making will be ready. The teacher will need to involve the inexperienced children gradually in planning and decision making. If teachers encourage some student involvement from the day that children begin school, by the intermediate grades many students should be more independent and involved learners.

Teachers' Responsibility in Student Involvement in Grouping Decisions

Involving students in decision making and planning does not mean that teachers give up their roles as planners and decision makers. Teachers are still the individuals responsible for the major decisions in the classroom. If children wish to plan for activities that are neither feasible nor desirable, teachers must help the students to recognize that they cannot do this. Teachers must help the students to be responsible and discriminating planners and decision makers. This is difficult because responsible decision making and planning require value judgments. A number of primary grade level students, as well as intermediate grade level students, may not be able to make such value decisions. Teachers will obviously have to use their judgment to determine the ability of their students to make certain decisions.

The Stigma Attached to Grouping

The stigma generally attached to grouping is usually discarded when students know that they can move freely from one group to another. If the purposes for the groups are explained and the students are involved in the planning, the students probably will not feel humiliated because they are not at another level. Students do not want to work at their frustration levels; therefore, they usually will not resent working at a lower level, which is at their instructional level. They will also probably not ask to move to a group working at a higher level if they feel that they cannot do the work at that level.

Names usually are chosen for the various ongoing groups rather than numerals, such as one, two, and three. The students usually choose the names for their groups, and this helps give the group a sense of identity. When students understand the purposes of grouping and have information about what the various groups are doing, names such as "Bluebirds," "Robins," and "Jays" are not used as cover-ups for fast, medium, and slow. The names never can act as cover-ups— everyone always knows who the fast, medium, and slow "birds" really are.

Alternatives to Ability Grouping

A number of alternatives to ability grouping are surfacing in the literature. Some of these techniques are viable ones that teachers can use in addition to reading groups rather than as a replacement for ability grouping.

Literature study groups
These are formed on the basis of interest rather than ability.

Literature study groups, which are formed on the basis of interest rather than ability, can be part of the ongoing reading program. Students choose books they would like to read and then discuss these with one another and with their teacher. These discussion groups can meet as often as three times a week or as seldom as once a week. The number of times depends on several factors—the length of the book, the ages of the students involved, the availability of time, and so on.

Groups based on interest are a good idea, but they may cause difficulty for those who are not as good readers as others. Teachers must be careful that the less able readers are not embarrassed and that no undue pressure is exerted on them.

Teacher Management of Groups

A teacher makes the following remarks to the rest of the class: "Don't bother me now. I'm working with this group. It's their turn now. You've had yours."

Is the teacher who made these remarks a good classroom manager? The answer is probably "No." A good classroom manager is able to deal with more than one situation at a time. A teacher working with a group should be aware of what is going on not only in the group with whom he or she is working at the moment, but also with the other children in the class. A teacher cannot "dismiss" the rest of the class because he or she is working with a particular group. Even though the children have been provided with challenging work based on their individual needs, the teacher must be alert to what is going on. A teacher who ignores the rest of the class while working with one group will probably have a number of discipline problems. The following scenario presents an example of a good classroom manager. Notice especially how Mr. Howe is able to manage a number of ongoing activities at the same time. Notice how he is always aware of what is going on in his class, and how he prevents problems from arising.

Teacher as class-room manager
Able to deal with more than one situation at a time; aware of what is going on with all students at all times.

SCENARIO

Mr. Howe Is a Good Classroom Manager

Mr. Howe, a fifth-grade teacher in a self-contained classroom, has just finished working with a reading group. Before he calls another reading group to work with him, he walks around the room and talks to various children to ask if they have any questions or problems. He also stops for a few minutes to listen to some students who are working on a writing project; they are composing a script for a puppet show that they will share with all the fifth grades. He tells them that he is very pleased with their progress. He likes the changes they have incorporated based on their previous conference, and he feels confident that they have a hit on their hands. The latter comment makes the children beam with delight. One child mentions that they are having a problem figuring out the kinds of puppets to use. Mr. Howe says that they will discuss this together, but in the meantime they might want to look at a few books on puppetry, which he suggests to them.

Mr. Howe stops also to listen to some other students who are working on a science project. He asks them some probing questions and to explain why they chose the method they did to carry out their experiment. He asks them if they can think of an alternative way to proceed.

Mr. Howe then stops to talk to a child who is working individually at her desk. He also chats for a moment with the child working at the computer. He walks quietly past a number of children who are deeply engrossed in reading library books. He takes one more look around the room and then calls the next reading group to come to the reading table.

While working with the reading group, Mr. Howe tries to keep close tabs also on what the rest of his class is doing. From time to time, he looks around the room to observe his other students. When he makes eye contact with a student, he smiles and nods approval. When he sees someone looking confused, Mr.

SCENARIO   *Continued*

Howe quietly calls the student to him and asks if he or she needs help. Mr. Howe tells the student that as soon as he is finished with the reading group, he will meet with him or her. Now, however, he would like the student to work on a special project or read a library book.

When Mr. Howe notices that some children are becoming a little too exuberant, he catches their attention and calmly but firmly motions with his hand for them to "keep it down."

Mr. Howe never neglects his reading group. While they read silently to answer questions or to confirm their predictions, Mr. Howe observes their reading behavior to determine whether they mouth words or use their fingers. He listens carefully when they read aloud to notice if they have any oral reading problems. He asks questions that require higher order thinking and constantly challenges them to find evidence for their answers. To make sure students understand how to go about finding answers, he models for them how he does this.

Mr. Howe's students are smart enough to know they are lucky to have him for their teacher. Their parents know it, too.

Individualized Instruction

Individualized instruction
Student works at own pace on material based on the needs, interests, and ability of the student.

The many different types of individualized programs range from informal ones, developed by teachers or teachers and students together for a particular class, to commercially produced or published ones. It is beyond the scope of this book to describe the organizational patterns or the individualized programs that exist; books have been written on these kinds of programs. However, a brief description of some of the characteristics of both informal and commercially produced individualized programs would be helpful.

Teacher-Made (Informal) Programs

Informal programs can vary from teacher to teacher. However, most of the programs use objectives taken from curriculum guides, study guides and instructors' manuals. To accomplish these objectives, the teachers usually select activities and materials from a number of sources, the teacher and student confer periodically, and the teacher keeps a check on the student's progress by keeping adequate records.

Commercially Produced or Published Programs

A variety of commercial programs exist, and they have a number of things in common. Most of the programs use objectives for each curriculum area. Usually each curriculum area is divided into small, discrete learning steps based on graduated levels of difficulty. A variety of activities and materials are generally combined in a multimedia approach, and usually built into the commercial programs is a system of record keeping, progress tests, and checklists.

Some Common Characteristics of Commercially Produced and Teacher-Made Individualized Programs

In almost all individualized programs, students work at their own pace. Learning outcomes in individualized programs are based on the needs, interests, and ability levels of the students. Activities are interesting and challenging, and they usually employ a multimedia approach. The activities are based on desired outcomes, students work independently, and there is some system of record keeping.

For Whom Does Individualized Instruction Work?

Students who have short attention spans, who have difficulty following directions, and who have reading problems will obviously have difficulty working independently. Teachers will have to help these students set limited, short-range objectives. For students with reading problems, the teacher will have to rely heavily on audio tapes to convey directions. Special programs will have to be devised for students who are slow learners (see Chapter 15). Students who have no discernible achievement problems but who have never worked in an individualized program before will also have difficulty unless they are properly oriented to the program. (*Note:* Do not confuse the need to work independently in an individualized program with the need to provide for the individual differences of each student in the class. For example, a child who is a slow learner will usually have difficulty working independently, but the teacher still needs to provide an individual program for this child based on his or her special needs.)

Some Common Sense about Individual Programs

Preparing individual outcomes and a specially tailored program for each student in each specific instructional area can be a monumental task. Therefore, the usual practice is to use outcomes and programs already prepared, either teacher-made or commercially produced, and then match these to the needs of individual students. For such an individualized program to work effectively, teachers must have a variety of individualized programs available for their students, and teachers must know the individual needs of each student. (See the section on "Learning Centers in the Classroom.")

Record Keeping in an Individualized Program

Teachers have many students in their classes who are working in different areas and at different levels. They cannot rely on their memory to recall exactly what each student is doing and at what level each student is working. Therefore, most teachers establish a record-keeping system. They usually have folders on each student in their class in which they keep a record of each student's progress in each area.

The folder usually contains a number of items: standardized achievement test scores, intelligence test scores, samples of students' work in various areas, a checklist of activities, and so forth. (See "Portfolio Assessment" in Chapter 13.)

Learning Centers in the Classroom

Learning center
An integral part of the instructional program and vital to a good individualized program. An area is usually set aside in the classroom for instruction in a specific curriculum area.

The concept of learning centers is not new. Good teachers have always recognized the importance of providing "interest centers" for their students based on their needs and ability levels. However, in the past most of the science, art, library, listening, and fun centers were just "interest attractions"; they usually were marginal to the ongoing teaching–learning program rather than an integral part of it.

As used today, learning centers are an important and integral part of the instructional program. They are more formalized and recognized as vital to a good individualized program. A set area is usually set aside in the classroom for instruction in a specific curriculum area. Aims for learning centers may be developed beforehand by teachers or cooperatively by teachers and students. Some of the requirements for a good learning center are as follows:

1. It is in an easily accessible area.
2. It is attractive.
3. It provides for students on different maturational levels.
4. It has clearly stated objectives so that students know what they are supposed to accomplish (outcomes).
5. It provides for group and team activities as well as individual activities.
6. It allows for student input.
7. It asks probing questions.
8. It has some humorous materials.
9. It provides activities that call for divergent thinking.
10. It uses a multimedia approach.
11. It has carefully worked out learning sequences to accomplish objectives.
12. It has provisions for evaluation and record keeping.

Computer-Assisted Instruction and Reading

Computer-assisted instruction
Instruction using computers.

Ms. Hart, a fourth-grade teacher, recently went to a professional conference and was exposed to some of the latest technological advances in education. At the conference she was especially impressed with the use of computer-assisted instruction in reading. Computer-assisted instruction did not frighten her or make her feel unneeded because Ms. Hart realizes that computer-assisted instruction is mainly a management tool; that is, with the proper program in the computer, a teacher can manage a larger class more effectively. For example, during a reading lesson, students would read a passage and then the computer would question each student simultaneously via terminals. The pupils can answer by menu selection, whereby only one single letter or number needs to be keyed in to indicate the answer. The result to the teacher would be immediate feedback of the responses of *all* the students. This type of questioning and feedback can be repeated for however much depth or breadth of coverage is required by the teacher. The teacher not only can receive immediate feedback, but he or she also can get a pattern of the answers. This would help the teacher to discern immediately those questions that caused the most or the least difficulty for the students. The computer could also display for the teacher a pattern of an individual's responses or compare what an individual student has done over an extended period of time. The possibilities are innumerable. The teacher could use the feedback for evaluation and grouping purposes.

Another possibility of computer-assisted instruction is to use it in a tutorial manner—that is, in a one-to-one situation with the student (see Figure 14-2). In this manner, the student receives immediate knowledge of results in a friendly, nonthreatening way. The student's problem is also diagnosed without the teacher's knowing about it. (Certain programs can be developed so that only the student is apprised of his or her reading difficulties.) Studies have been done that indicate that some students respond more favorably to computer diagnostics than to

FIGURE 14-2   These children are working together on a special computer program.

teacher diagnostics. These students feel that the computer is fairer and more private, and as a result they relate better to an impersonal diagnostic tool.

Ms. Hart was told that the computers of the future may be able to understand and respond to voice input. That would permit students who can't read or write to use the computer as a learning tool. The possibilities are limitless and exciting provided that the software can be developed in a reasonable time frame at an affordable cost.

Special Note

There are computing devices available that respond to voice input, but these devices can accept a limited vocabulary only, and the speaker must be specially trained.

Peer Tutoring

Peer tutoring
A student helps
another student
gain needed skills.

Peer tutoring, which is not new, helps the tutor, the tutee, and the teacher. Peer tutoring usually helps the student who has been encountering difficulty in an area gain skill in the area and gain confidence in working with the skill. It also helps the tutee feel more at ease about participating in a large group. The tutor also gains because it helps him or her overlearn the skill that is being taught, and it helps to enhance his or her self-concept. The tutor is looked upon with prestige and respect by the teacher and his or her peers. Peer tutoring also helps the teacher because it frees the teacher to work individually with more students.

Teachers who use peer tutoring in their classes must be very careful about the pairing of the tutor and tutee. They must be aware of the personalities in their classes and know who the stars and isolates are, as well as which children are in certain cliques. Teachers must also be very sensitive to the fact that some peer tutors, because of their popularity, can be overburdened. They should not allow this to happen.

Cross-Age Tutoring and Buddy Systems

Cross-age tutoring
Students from
upper grades work
with children from
lower grades.

Cross-age tutoring, like peer tutoring, is not a new phenomenon. In the days of the one-room schoolhouse, this practice was used widely. In cross-age tutoring, students from upper grades work with children from lower grades. This type of tutoring is also very effective and frees the teacher to work with greater numbers of students individually. However, cross-age tutoring is somewhat more difficult to implement than peer tutoring because it involves more than one class and teacher. However, the payback is very rewarding, so it is worth the time and effort to develop such a program.

Young children especially enjoy having a "buddy" to whom they can read aloud and with whom they can share books. Teachers who have utilized a cross-age buddy system claim that the young primary grade children enjoy the one-to-one attention they receive from their buddies. And the buddies seem to grow in maturity and become "less self-centered and more considerate of their younger buddies."[5]

Graphic Summary of Chapter

Here is a graphic summary of Chapter 14. If you have read the chapter, this graphic illustration should help you remember its main points. Under or beside each heading, you might want to jot down some of the information you recall, as well as some of the key concepts in this chapter. This can act as a good review. You can then check your key concepts against those that follow the graphic summary.

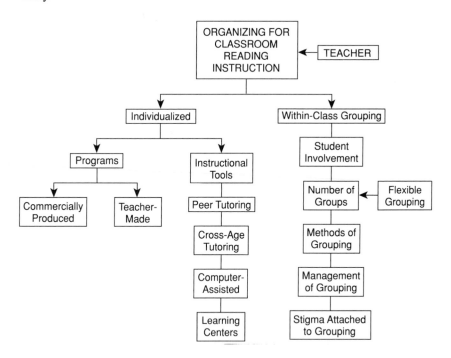

Key Concepts

- Organizing for instruction affects the entire teaching–learning program.
- Teachers organize children into reading groups to make instruction more manageable.
- A number of factors are usually taken into account for grouping, but the most important factor is generally the student's achievement.

5 Connie Morrice and Maureen Simmons, "Beyond Reading Buddies: A Whole Language Cross-Age Program," *The Reading Teacher* 44 (April 1991): 576.

- Student involvement in grouping is important for grouping to be successful.
- Teachers must be good classroom managers.
- Teachers can use other ways to group students for reading in addition to ability grouping.
- Individualized programs are programs in which students work at their own pace individually rather than in a group.
- Learning centers should be an integral part of the instructional program.
- Computer-assisted instruction is a management tool that teachers can utilize to individualize instruction.
- Peer tutoring helps the tutor, the tutee, and the teacher.
- Cross-age tutoring consists of older students working with younger ones.

Suggestions for Thought Questions and Activities

1. Observe various classrooms to determine how teachers group for reading. Prepare a report on your findings.
2. Choose a teacher who has reading groups in his or her class. Then observe closely how he or she manages the class while working with a reading group.
3. You have been asked to present a talk on individualized instruction at a local reading association meeting. What will you say?
4. You have been put on a committee to discuss the pros and cons of technology in the reading program. What are your views on this?
5. Develop a reading learning center.
6. You have been asked to present your views concerning reading groups at a PTA meeting. What will you say?
7. What are your views concerning peer tutoring?

Selected Bibliography

Barr, Rebecca, and Robert Dreeben, "Grouping Students for Reading Instruction." In *Handbook of Reading Research,* Vol. II, Rebecca Barr, Michael L. Kamil, Peter Mosenthal, and P. David Pearson, eds. New York: Longman, 1991, pp. 885–910.

Hiebert, Elfrieda H. "Research Directions: Literacy Contexts and Literacy Processes." *Language Arts* 68 (February 1991): 134–139.

Staab, Claire. "Classroom Organization: Thematic Centers Revisited." *Language Arts* 68 (February 1991): 108–113.

15

Special Children in the Regular Classroom

All the children of all the people have a right to an education.

—Public Law 94-142

SCENARIO: MANY TEACHERS CAN EXPECT A DIVERSE POPULATION OF STUDENTS IN THEIR CLASSES

From as far back as Mrs. Hall could remember, she had wanted to be a teacher. There was no question when she went to college what her vocation would be. Her dream was realized when she accepted a position with a large school system near where she lived. She has been a teacher for twenty years and has never regretted her career choice. Recently her friend's daughter Amy became a teacher. It appears that Amy, too, had always wanted to be a teacher, but now Amy isn't sure.

Amy says that this year, in particular, is a difficult one for her. She just does not feel prepared to deal with all the special children she has in her class. She told her mother's friend Mrs. Hall that she had a child mainstreamed into her class three weeks ago, and she still has not been given the special aid she was promised. She also has a number of at-risk or high-risk students, who require a great deal of help and attention. In addition, she has two highly gifted students. And, as if this were not enough, she has three non-native English speaking children in her class. She also has one child who is considered a slow learner and another who was tested during the term and found to be learning disabled. This child is being kept in her class rather than being put into a special class.

Amy told Mrs. Hall that she remembered her professors talking about teachers having such a diverse population in their classes, but she somehow felt she was immune—that this would never happen to her.

Mrs. Hall tried to help Amy. Besides giving her advice on the kinds of things that worked for her, she suggested that Amy speak to her former professors to see if they could give her some guidance. In addition, she urged Amy to speak again to her principal and to seek help from such people as the reading teacher, the English as a Second Language (ESL)/bilingual people, the language arts supervisors, and also the parents. Mrs. Hall said that often parents can be excellent resources, and they are usually very happy to help their children do better.

This chapter should be of great help to Amy and any other preservice or inservice teachers who need to learn more about how to adapt instruction for students with special needs. In this chapter, reading and other language arts methods are provided that are most applicable to those children whom teachers currently have in their regular classrooms, such as borderline children and gifted children; however, they may also be adapted for children who may be mainstreamed. Public Law 94-142 requires that exceptional children have individualized programs specially prepared for them. These individualized programs are too varied to be presented in a text with as broad a scope as this one. Teachers who have mainstreamed children in their classrooms are, therefore, encouraged to go to special education texts for more in-depth coverage. (See the bibliography for a listing of books that deal specifically with the subject.)

KEY QUESTIONS

After reading this chapter, you should be able to answer the following questions:

1. What is Public Law 94-142?
2. What should teachers know about the mental age span of children in their classes?
3. Who are the "average" children?
4. Who are the exceptional children?
5. What are some of the characteristics of borderline children?
6. What are some of the characteristics of gifted children?
7. What is mainstreaming?
8. What kinds of provisions should teachers make for mainstreamed children?
9. How are learning disabilities defined?
10. What is attention deficit disorder?
11. What are the identification biases of children labeled "educable mentally retarded"?
12. Who are the at-risk children?
13. Why should teachers be cautious about labeling children?

KEY TERMS IN CHAPTER

You should pay special attention to the following new terms:

attention deficit disorder (ADD)
average children
borderline children (slow learners)
educable mentally retarded children
exceptional children
gifted children

learning disability
mainstreaming
mental age
Public Law 94-142
social promotion

What Is Public Law 94-142?

Public Law 94-142
Advocates a free appropriate education for all children in the least restrictive environment.

Public Law 94-142 advocates a free appropriate education for all children in the least restrictive environment. This has brought to the fore the importance of the uniqueness of each child. In the regular classroom there is usually a wide range of ability levels, which generally includes the borderline child (slow learner) and the gifted child.[1] As a result of Public Law 94-142, exceptional children may be mainstreamed into the regular classroom. In order to be able to work with such children, all teachers, not just special education teachers, must become more knowledgeable of exceptional children. The more teachers know about the children with whom they work, the better able they will be to provide for their individual differences and needs.

Mental Age Span in the Regular Classroom

Mental age
A child's present level of development; in intelligence testing, a score based on average abilities for that age group:

$$MA = \frac{IQ \times CA}{100}$$

While the teacher in a regular classroom usually has students with a mental age span of five years, the span can be greater. Mental age (MA) refers to a child's present level of development; it helps to indicate the child's present readiness. As children progress through the grades the span between the borderline, average, and gifted children gets wider.

While children enter school based on chronological age (CA) rather than mental age, instruction needs to be geared to their mental ages rather than their chronological ages. IQ is calculated as MA/CA $\times$ 100, and a child of six, for example, with an IQ of 75[2] has a mental age of 4.5, whereas a child of six with an IQ of 130 has a mental age of 7.8 (see Table 15-1). Obviously, these children need extremely different programs even though both are chronologically the same age.

[1] Although gifted children are classified as exceptional children, they are generally found in the regular classroom. Borderline children (slow learners) are not classified as exceptional children in the revised AAMD definition.

[2] Teachers may have children with IQs as low as 70 in their regular classrooms because borderline children's IQs range approximately from 70 to 85.

TABLE 15-1   Comparison of Mental Ages

Grade	CA	75 IQ MA	85 IQ MA	100 IQ MA	115 IQ MA	130 IQ MA
K	5.6	4.2	4.8	5.6	6.4	7.3
1	6.0	4.5	5.1	6.0	6.9	7.8
	6.6	5.0	5.6	6.6	7.6	8.6
2	7.0	5.3	6.0	7.0	8.1	9.1
	7.6	5.7	6.5	7.6	8.7	9.9
3	8.0	6.0	6.8	8.0	9.2	10.4
	8.6	6.5	7.3	8.6	9.9	11.2
4	9.0	6.8	7.7	9.0	10.4	11.7
	9.6	7.2	8.2	9.6	11.0	12.5
5	10.0	7.5	8.5	10.0	11.5	13.0
	10.6	8.0	9.0	10.6	12.2	13.8
6	11.0	8.3	9.4	11.0	12.7	14.3
	11.6	8.7	9.9	11.6	13.3	15.1
7	12.0	9.0	10.2	12.0	13.8	15.6
	12.6	9.5	10.7	12.6	14.5	16.4
8	13.0	9.8	11.1	13.0	15.0	16.9
	13.6	10.2	11.6	13.6	15.6	17.7

Example: An eight-year-old child with an IQ of 115 has a mental age of 9.2.

$$IQ = \frac{MA}{CA} \times 100$$

$$115 = \frac{x}{8} \times 100$$

$$x = 1.15 \times 8$$

$$x = 9.2$$

Even teachers who believe in individual differences and who attempt to develop an individualized instructional program for each child in their class will not be able to build a meaningful program for their students unless they are knowledgeable of the cognitive styles that children at different intellectual levels possess.

Who Is the Average Child?

Average children
Often referred to children who score in the IQ range approximately from 90 to 110.

The first question that comes to mind whenever anyone labels someone an average child is: Is there really an "average" child? Actually there probably is not. Every child is an individual and as such is unique and special. However, for research purposes we tend to look upon the average child as that individual who scores in the IQ range approximately from 90 to 110. Studies are based on averages. Averages are necessary as criteria or points of reference. Only after we have determined the criteria for "average" can we talk about "above" or "below average."

Who Are the Exceptional Children?

Exceptional children
Those children who deviate so much from the "average" that they require special attention.

The phrase *exceptional children* is usually applied to those children who deviate so much from "average" children that they require special attention: "These children require special education because they are markedly different from most children in one or more of the following ways: they may have mental retardation, learning disabilities, emotional disturbance, physical disabilities, disordered speech or language, impaired hearing, impaired sight, or special gifts or talents."[3]

Even though the emphasis on exceptional children has been on differences, there is a concerted effort today to try also to focus on their similarities. "Exceptional children are not different from 'average' children in every way."[4] It is important that teachers be aware of these differences and similarities so that they can provide for these students' needs if they are mainstreamed into a regular classroom. A discussion of some of the things teachers can do to provide for mainstreamed students is given in this book; however, for an in-depth discussion of exceptional children, students should refer to special education textbooks (see "Selected Bibliography").

The Borderline Child or "Slow Learner"

Borderline children (slow learners)
Children whose IQs usually range approximately from 70 to 85.

The borderline child is usually described as a dull, average child who is borderline in his or her intellectual functioning. As already stated, these children's IQ scores range from approximately 70 to 85. As a result, they generally have difficulty doing schoolwork. Borderline children are not, however, equally slow in all their activities or abnormal in all their characteristics. It is difficult at times to differentiate borderline children and children with specific learning disabilities from underachievers produced by disadvantaged environments.[5]

Providing Instruction for the Borderline Child

Social promotion
Promotion of students based on chronological age rather than achievement.

Teachers in regular classrooms are frequently frustrated because they have children who do not seem to be able to learn material that is considered "average" for the specific grade level. Not only is the teacher frustrated, but so is the child. A child with IQ test scores in the 70 to 85 range would have difficulty working at grade level. Because of social promotion (promotion of children according to chronological age rather than achievement), children are moved along each year into a higher grade. As slow learners go through the grades, their problems gen-

---

[3] Daniel P. Hallahan and James M. Kauffman, *Exceptional Children: Introduction to Special Education,* 4th ed. (Englewood Cliffs, N.J.: Prentice-Hall, 1988), p. 6.

[4] Ibid., p. 2.

[5] Samuel A. Kirk, Sister Joanne Marie Kliebhan, and Janet W. Lerner, *Teaching Reading to Slow and Disabled Learners* (Boston: Houghton Mifflin, 1978), p. 3.

erally become more pronounced and compounded unless they receive special attention.

The term *slow learner* is probably a misnomer because it implies that a child needs more time to get a concept, but eventually will acquire it. Actually, there are some concepts that slow learners cannot acquire no matter how long they work on them because slow learners usually cannot work in the abstract. Obviously, the teacher should not use inductive or deductive teaching techniques in working with slow learners. Slow learners generally can learn material if it is presented at a concrete level. Slow learners usually must be given many opportunities to go over the same concept; they must continue practice in an area beyond the point where they think that they know it, in order to *overlearn* it. The practice should be varied and interesting to stimulate them.

To motivate the slow learners, many games and gamelike activities should be used. Slow learners have a short attention span, so learning tasks should be broken down into small, discrete steps. Generally requiring close supervision, they may have difficulty working independently. Distractions must be kept at a minimum, and each task should be exactly defined and explained. It is necessary to define short-range goals, which slow learners can accomplish, to give them a sense of achievement. Slow learners are usually set in their ways, and once they learn something in one way, they will be very rigid about changing.

The teacher should recognize that individual differences exist within groups as well as between groups. Obviously, there will be individual differences among slow learners.

Reading for the Borderline Child

In Chapter 2 you learned that children who are advanced in language development have a better chance for success in school than those who are not. Slow development of language is a noticeable characteristic of slow learners. The teacher recognizes that these children need many opportunities to express themselves orally and that they learn best at a concrete level. The teacher should, therefore, plan his or her program for slow learners to include many *first-hand experiences* where the children can deal with real things. The teacher can take the children on trips to visit farm animals, zoo animals, the firehouse, the police station, factories, railroad stations, farms, and so on. In planning for the trip, the teacher should use the same good practices that are used for all children. The teacher should discuss the trip with the children beforehand and give them the opportunity to help plan for the trip. After the trip the teacher should encourage the children to discuss what they saw. The teacher and children could then cooperatively write an experience story about the visit (see Chapter 11).

In helping borderline children acquire new words, the teacher should recognize that these children will learn and retain words that they will use in their everyday conversation more readily than abstract words. It therefore helps for the teacher to associate the new words with their pictorial representations, real objects, or actions. Slow learners must repeatedly hear and see these words in association with objects, pictures, or actions in order to learn them. As mentioned in the previous section, the children must *overlearn* the word. (Overlearning takes place when you continue practice even after reaching the point where you feel you know something quite well.) Borderline children not only have problems in working with abstract words, they also have difficulty dealing with words in isolation. Cohen's study has shown that the slower students are in academic progress, the more difficult it is for them to deal with words in isolation, unrelated to a totally meaningful experience. Her study has also found that the reading aloud of stories that are at the interest, ability, and attention span level of the children is an excellent means of helping the children to develop vocabulary and sentence sense.[6] After listening to a story, the children should be encouraged to engage in some oral expression activities. All children need many opportunities to express themselves, and slow learners are no exception. A child who feels accepted and is in a nonthreatening environment will feel more free to contribute than one who feels threatened or embarrassed.

In providing reading and other language arts instruction, the teacher should provide opportunities for the slow learner to work with other children. Oral expression (speech stimulation) activities such as choral speaking, finger play, and creative drama are good for these purposes. The child should be given opportunities to share with the other children; all children seek approval of peers as well as of adults.

Gifted Children

Gifted children
The academically gifted are usually those with an IQ at or above 132 on the Stanford Binet Intelligence Scale; however, *gifted* also usually refers to those whose performance in any line of socially useful endeavor is consistently superior.

Gifted children fall into the category of exceptional children because this group of children deviates greatly from "average" children.

The term *gifted children* evokes a mental image of small children wearing horn-rimmed glasses and carrying encyclopedias. This is a myth. There are many definitions of the gifted. In recent years the definition of *gifted* has been broadened to include not only the verbally gifted with an IQ at or above 132 on the Stanford-Binet intelligence scale (an individual IQ test), but also those individuals whose performance in any line of socially useful endeavor is consistently superior.

Marland's national definition in a congressional report alerts educators to the multifaceted aspects of giftedness:

> *Gifted and talented children are those identified by professionally qualified persons who by virtue of outstanding abilities are capable of high performance. These are children who require differentiated educational programs and services beyond those normally provided by the regular school program in order to realize their contribution to self and society.*
>
>   *Children capable of high performance include those with demonstrated achievement and/or potential ability in any of the following areas:*

[6] Dorothy H. Cohen, "The Effect of Literature on Vocabulary and Reading Achievement," *Elementary English* 45 (February 1968): 209–213, 217.

1. *General intellectual ability.*
2. *Specific academic aptitude.*
3. *Creative or productive thinking.*
4. *Leadership ability.*
5. *Visual and performing arts.*
6. *Psychomotor ability.*[7]

Characteristics of Gifted Children

Gifted children, on the average, are socially, emotionally, physically, and intellectually superior to "average" children in the population. Gifted children have, on the average, superior general intelligence, a desire to know, originality, common sense, will power and perseverance, a desire to excel, self-confidence, prudence and forethought, and a good sense of humor, among a host of other admirable traits.

Instructional Provisions for Gifted Children

Gifted children need special attention because of their precocious learning abilities. However, when gifted children are not given special attention, they still usually manage to work on grade level. As a result, gifted children are often ignored. Regrettably, gifted children are actually the most neglected of all exceptional children. Attention is given to those who have "more need." Margaret Mead, the renowned anthropologist, has written about this attitude toward the gifted, which is still applicable today:

> *Whenever the rise to success cannot be equated with preliminary effort, abstinence and suffering, it tends to be attributed to "luck," which relieves the spectator from according the specially successful person any merit. . . . In American education, we have tended to reduce the gift to a higher I.Q. —thus making it a matter of merely a little more on the continuity scale, to insist on putting more money and effort in bringing the handicapped child "up to par" as an expression of fair play and "giving everyone a break"—and to disallow special gifts. By this refusal to recognize special gifts, we have wasted and dissipated, driven into apathy or schizophrenia, uncounted numbers of gifted children. If they learn easily, they are penalized for having nothing to do; if they excel in some outstanding way, they are penalized as being conspicuously better than the peer group, and teachers warn the gifted child, "Yes, you can do that, it's much more interesting than what the others are doing. But, remember, the rest of the class will dislike you for it."*[8]

Gifted children, like all other children, need guidance and instruction based on their interests, needs, and ability levels. Although gifted children are

[7] S. P. Marland, *Education of the Gifted and the Talented* (Washington, D.C.: U.S. Office of Education, 1972), p. 10.

[8] Margaret Mead, "The Gifted Child in the American Culture of Today," *Journal of Teacher Education* 5 (September 1954): 211–212.

intellectually capable of working at high levels of abstraction, unless they receive appropriate instruction to gain needed skills, they may not be able to realize their potential. Gifted children should not be subjected to unnecessary drill and repetition. Gifted children gain abstract concepts quickly. They usually enjoy challenge and have long attention spans. Teachers who have gifted children in their self-contained classrooms can provide for those children to work at their own pace in many areas through individualized programs (see Chapter 14).

The manner in which material is presented to gifted children should be guided by a knowledge of their characteristics. The atmosphere in the classroom should be one in which gifted students are respected as persons capable of independent work and leadership, and the subject matter that is presented should allow for student involvement, choice, and interaction. Also, the instruction for gifted students should focus on those activities that involve the higher levels of the cognitive domain; that is, gifted children should spend the most time in activities that require analysis, synthesis, and evaluation. They should also be encouraged by their teachers to be intelligent risk takers, to defend their ideas, delve deeply into problems, seek alternative solutions to problems, follow through on hunches, and dream the impossible dream. In short, gifted students will know that their teachers value their talents if they are provided with challenge commensurate with their abilities.

Reading for the Gifted Child

Gifted children's language development is usually very advanced. They generally have a large stock of vocabulary and delight in learning new words. According to Terman, a noted psychologist, who did monumental research on the gifted, nearly half of the gifted children he studied learned to read before starting school: at least 20 percent, before the age of five years; 6 percent, before age four, and 1.6 percent, before age three. Most of these children learned to read with little or no formal instruction.[9] Other studies seem to corroborate these findings. However, these findings should not be taken to mean that gifted children can fend for themselves and that teachers should spend more time with others. It does mean that the teacher must provide alternative programs for gifted children. To fail to recognize that these children are reading when they first enter school and to make them go through a program geared to "average" children can be devastating for the gifted children.

Also frustrating for a gifted child is to be told, "Put your hand down. You're not supposed to know that yet." Such teacher statements can discourage gifted students from participating in discussions, as well as make them feel ostracized. If the teacher feels that gifted students are dominating the discussion or are answering questions too soon, the teacher should take stock of his or her program. Perhaps the teacher could have the gifted students be the discussion lead-

---

[9] Lewis Terman and Melita Oden, *The Gifted Child Grows Up,* Genetic Studies of Genius, vol. 4 (Stanford, Calif.: Stanford University Press, 1947).

ers for certain topics or ask the gifted students to provide special information about the topic that they could share with the rest of the class or group.

Gifted students usually have wide-ranging interests that they like to pursue in depth, and they are generally impatient with detail. Teachers should give their gifted students the time and opportunity to pursue their interests in depth. Also, the teacher should provide a rich and varied program for his or her gifted students because they are usually able to work in a number of activities simultaneously.

While the gifted need opportunities to work with other gifted children, they also need to work with children on all ability levels. Children who work together in activities that tap the special abilities of all the children will usually learn to understand each other better. Speech-stimulating activities such as choral speaking, creative drama, and puppetry give gifted children an opportunity to work with children on all ability levels.

Mainstreaming

Mainstreaming
The placement of handicapped children in the least restrictive educational environment that will meet their needs.

As discussed earlier, the impetus of mainstreaming was triggered by Public Law 94-142, a federal law that is designed to give handicapped children a "free appropriate public education." It requires state and local governments to provide identification programs, a special education, and related services such as transportation, testing, diagnosis, and treatment for children with speech handicaps, hearing impairments, visual handicaps, physical disabilities, emotional disturbances, learning disabilities, and mental retardation handicaps. Public Law 94-142 also requires that whenever possible, handicapped students must be placed in regular classrooms. *Mainstreaming* is the placement of handicapped children in the least restrictive educational environment that will meet their needs.

Handicapped children who are moved to a regular classroom are supposed to be very carefully screened. Only those who seem able to benefit from being in a least restrictive environment are supposed to be put into one. The amount of time that a handicapped child spends in a regular classroom and the area in which the child participates in the regular classroom depend on the individual child. Some children who are moderately mentally retarded may spend time each week in a regular classroom during a special activity such as a story hour.

For mainstreaming to be successful, classroom teachers must be properly prepared for this role, and teachers must enlist the aid and cooperation of every student in their class. Classroom teachers must prepare their students for the mainstreamed child by giving them some background and knowledge about the child. The amount and type of information given will, of course, vary with the grade level. Regular classroom teachers should also have the students involved in some of the planning and implementation of the program for the mainstreamed child.

For example, if teachers are expecting physically handicapped children to be admitted to their class, they can help to prepare their students by reading some books to them that portray a physically handicapped child in a sensitive and perceptive manner. Teachers might read some excerpts from Helen Keller's *The Story of My Life* or Marie Killilea's book *Karen*. After reading the excerpts teachers can engage the students in a discussion of the handicapped child's struggles, fears, hopes, concerns, goals, and dreams. Teachers can then attempt to help the children in their classes recognize that they have feelings, hopes, and fears similar to those of many handicapped children's. Teachers should also help their students to understand that a child with a physical handicap does not necessarily have a mental handicap. As a matter of fact, many handicapped persons are very intelligent and able to make many contributions to society. The teacher can then discuss with the children how they think they can make the new child who is coming to their class feel at home. The teacher might use special films and television programs to initiate interest in the handicapped and to help gain better insights about them.

Instructional Provisions for the Mainstreamed Child

Besides preparing the children in the regular classroom for the mainstreamed child, an individualized program must be developed for each mainstreamed child in cooperation with the child's parents, the special education teacher, or consultants. The program should be one that provides a favorable learning experience for both the handicapped child and the regular classroom students. That is, the integration of a handicapped child should not take away from the program of the regular classroom children.

Children who have orthopedic and other health impairments do not need any special provisions as far as basic reading skills, textbook assignments, or additional instructional materials are concerned. Some students will need special furniture, and their achievement may have to be monitored by using tape recorders; that is, the tests would have to be given orally, and the student would record answers on a tape. Students with speech impairments and those who have emotional disturbances also need no special adjustments except that children with emotional disturbances need an environment that is calm, low in tension, and high in motivation, whereas students with speech impairments need help in making oral reports, so committee assignments should be used for this.

Students who have visual impairment and hearing impairment or deafness will need a number of special adjustments. Students with visual problems should be given front-row seating, and a buddy system should be established for them. The "buddy" would be responsible for making carbon copies of notes and of chalkboard assignments. Students with visual impairments do not need any special help in basic skills for mastering content concepts, but they do need help in visually reading the textbook and other instructional materials. Either the textbook must be read orally to the students, or the students themselves can read it with a magnifier. Some instructional material can be reproduced in large print or put on tape (with the permission of the publisher). Students with visual impairments should have their examinations orally given, recorded on tape, enlarged on a closed-circuit TV, or translated into Braille. Students with hearing impairment, like those with visual impairment, need a number of special provisions. These students need front-row seating so that they can lip-read, and those who are deaf may need a special sign language translator. Students with hearing impairment usually need very well outlined lesson presentations and the rephrasing of complex sentences, as well as special guides to help them interpret what they are reading. Captioned films for the deaf should be used whenever possible, and students with hearing impairment should be assigned to a committee for any type of oral reporting.

Another group of exceptional students who are being mainstreamed into regular classrooms and who need a number of special provisions are students with learning disabilities. Such students require a structured daily schedule and, like students with hearing disabilities, they need well-outlined lessons, rephrasing of complex sentences, and special guides to help them interpret what they are reading. These students also need their written test questions to be rephrased and to be assigned to a committee for oral reports.

Learning Disability

Many teachers have students in their classes who are of average or above-average ability as measured on an IQ test, but who are not working anywhere near their measured ability level. Often, teachers may call these underachieving children lazy or undisciplined. The teachers may be correct, or it may be that these children have learning disabilities that have gone undiagnosed.

Learning disability Difficult to define; the definition best known and acted on is: a disorder in one or more of the basic psychological processes involved in understanding or in using language spoken or written, which may manifest itself in an imperfect ability to listen, think, speak, read, write, spell, or do mathematical calculations; another definition often given is that a learning disability is intrinsic to the individual and presumed to be due to some central nervous system dysfunction.

The concept of learning disability is a confusing one for both professional and lay people. Because of this confusion, it has been difficult to generate a definition that all could embrace. Researchers have found that the characteristics of children labeled "learning disabled" vary so much that it is extremely difficult to list common characteristics. The way the term is used seems to vary not only from state to state but even from school district to school district within a state.

Although to this day there is a great deal of confusion and controversy concerning the term *learning disability* and there are numerous definitions of the term, the one definition that seems to be the best known and acted on is the one that emanated from Public Law 94-142:

"Special learning disability" means a disorder in one or more of the basic psychological processes involved in understanding or in using language spoken or written, which may manifest itself in an imperfect ability to listen, think, speak, read, write, spell, or do mathematical calculations. The term includes such conditions as perceptual handicaps, brain injury, minimal brain dysfunction, dyslexia, and developmental aphasia. The term does not include children who have learning problems which are primarily the result of visual, hearing, or motor handicaps, or mental retardation, emotional disturbance, or environmental, cultural or economic disadvantage.[10]

[10] Federal Register, "Procedures for Evaluating Specific Learning Disabilities" (Washington, D.C.: U.S. Department of Health, Education, and Welfare, December 29, 1977), p. 65083.

A number of professional organizations, dissatisfied with the imprecise nature of the definition endorsed by the federal government, joined together in the early 1980s to form a National Joint Committee on Learning Disabilities to put forth their own definition, which refers to learning disabilities as intrinsic to the individual and presumed to be due to some central nervous system dysfunction. This definition recognizes that although a "learning disability may occur concomitantly with other handicapping conditions . . . , it is not the direct result of these conditions or influences."[11]

Numerous other definitions have been put forth, as well as causes for the various learning disabilities. However, many educators feel that "the field of learning disabilities is in a state of considerable turmoil. Until the field puts its house in order, the term 'learning disability' can have little real meaning."[12]

A Word of Caution

Teachers should be especially vigilant in their classes for those students who are of average or above-average ability who are having some kind of learning problems because these students may have a special learning disability. Teachers should refer these students for special testing. Teachers must, however, be leery of labeling youngsters as learning disabled without adequate and substantive documentation. For example, the Black English trial in Ann Arbor showed that the school district had labeled the Green Road children as "learning disabled" and "emotionally impaired" without due consideration to their racial and linguistic backgrounds. Unfortunately, "the staff was handicapped by their inadequate knowledge of the children's characteristics and the biased nature of the tests they were using."[13] An example is given whereby the "speech therapists weren't aware that the Wepman test included a number of oppositions that are mergers in the Black English vernacular; pin vs. pen, sheaf vs. sheath, clothe vs. clove, and so forth."[14] (See "Dialect and Language Differences" in Chapter 2.)

Attention Deficit Disorder

Concentration, which is sustained attention, is essential for learning. Good learners must be able to attend while listening and reading; they must know what information to ignore and what to process. Unless children can attend, they will be at a great disadvantage in learning to read or for that matter any other learning.

Attention deficit disorder (ADD) Difficulty sustaining concentration at a task.

Children who have an attention deficit disorder (ADD) have difficulty concentrating at a task. They are very easily distracted by the stimuli around them;

---

[11] See Albert J. Harris and Edward R. Sipay, *How to Increase Reading Ability* (New York: Longman, 1991), p. 158.

[12] Ibid., p. 161.

[13] William Labov, "Objectivity and Commitment in Linguistic Science: The Case of the Black English Trial in Ann Arbor," *Language in Society* 11 (August 1982): 168.

[14] Ibid., pp. 168–169.

they do not have selective attention whereby they can ignore the competing stimuli in their environment and home in on the specific task at hand. These children's easy distractibility makes it difficult for them to learn.

The problem of hyperactivity has in the past often been treated with drugs; however, this controversial treatment has been considered by many as a "wolf in sheep's clothing for the child and the family,"[15] and because of a public media outcry this practice has subsided somewhat.[16] (The reason for the outcry is that the drugs the children receive are similar to those commonly referred to as "uppers" or "pep" pills. For some reason these drugs, rather than stimulating the children, have an opposite effect on them. However, many people feel that these children might become addicted to the drugs and that the drugs might have some harmful side effects.) After 1980, ADD was classified into two types, ADD and ADD with hyperactivity. Most of the children diagnosed by clinicians are put in the category of ADD with hyperactivity.[17] A child diagnosed as having an attention deficit disorder is classified as learning disabled and is entitled to special education services.

Clinicians, not teachers, do the diagnosing; however, it is the teacher who often refers the child for diagnosis because of the kinds of behavior the child is exhibiting in class. These kinds of behavior, which have been classified into three categories—coming to attention, decision making, and maintaining attention[18]—can often be disruptive. For example, a child who is constantly inattentive, has poor task-approach skills, has difficulty in getting started on an assignment, has difficulty picking out important information, and is an impulsive decision maker will obviously be more disruptive in class than one who is attentive and works on task. Children who are inattentive would get up more, talk more, fidget more, have difficulty waiting for their turn, call out more, and so on.

The problem is that many times children are diagnosed as having ADD when they are merely frustrated because they cannot read. Children who have reading problems would be prone to have many of the same characteristics as those of children diagnosed as having ADD and then classified as learning disabled.

Misclassification means that children are not given proper instructional help. Unfortunately, the children who seem to be classified as learning disabled are often those who come from educationally disadvantaged homes and who lack the kinds of experiences that are necessary to succeed in school.[19]

---

[15] Walter E. Sawyer, "Attention Deficit Disorder: A Wolf in Sheep's Clothing . . . Again," *The Reading Teacher* 42 (January 1989): 310.

[16] Ibid.

[17] Daniel P. Hallahan and James M. Kauffman, *Exceptional Children: Introduction to Special Education,* 4th ed. (Englewood Cliffs, N.J.: Prentice-Hall, 1988), p. 117.

[18] Barbara K. Keogh and Judith Margolis, "Learn to Labor and Wait: Attentional Problems of Children with Learning Disorders," *Journal of Learning Disabilities* 9 (May 1976): 276–286.

[19] Sawyer, "Attention Deficit Disorder," pp. 311–312.

Identification Biases of Children Labeled
Educable Mentally Retarded

Educable mentally retarded children Children whose IQs usually range approximately from 55 to 70; considered mildly retarded.

It appears that the incidence of educable mental retardation is not equally distributed across all segments of the population. There is a tendency to label more boys as educable mentally retarded than girls. This may be because boys are usually more likely to be mischievous than girls and as a result are more likely to be candidates for referral. There also seems to be a highly disproportionate number of children from a lower socioeconomic status. Studies show, too, that minority children are overrepresented in this group.

For example, in 1980, a class-action suit was "brought by Parents in Action on Special Education on behalf of 'all black children who have been or will be placed in special classes for the educable mentally handicapped in the Chicago school system.' Plaintiffs observed that while 62 percent of the enrollment of the Chicago schools was black, blacks comprised 82 percent of the enrollment of classes for the educable mentally retarded."[20]

The teacher is usually the person who first identifies the child as having a problem. Many times, as already stated, the child is referred for special testing because of nonadapative social behavior. After the referral the child is given a number of standardized tests, of which the IQ test is the most influential in determining whether the child is retarded or not. Since studies have shown that children from minority groups and from lower socioeconomic classes usually do not do as well on IQ tests as children from the rest of the population, it is not surprising to find children from these groups disproportionately represented in the group of children labeled educable mentally retarded.

Children who are second-language learners have special problems because even the most sympathetic teachers often misinterpret children's language and learning abilities. "Perceptions regarding lack of language ability lead to mistaken assumptions about cognitive ability."[21]

There are a number of language assessment instruments available, such as the *Language Assessment Scales—Oral* (LASO), 1990, published by CTB/McGraw-Hill, that can help teachers gain a better insight into their non-English-speaking children's language and concept ability.

It cannot be emphasized enough how careful teachers must be in using such terms as *mentally retarded, emotionally disturbed,* and *learning disabled* to label a child. Once labeled, the child is hardly ever able to shed that label, even if he or she has been incorrectly labeled. Often children so labeled continue to function at a particular level because they themselves have incorporated the image that others have of them.

---

[20] John Salvia and James E. Ysseldyke, *Assessment in Special and Remedial Education,* 4th ed. (Boston: Houghton Mifflin, 1988), p. 45.

[21] Catherine Wallace and Yetta Goodman, "Research Currents: Language and Literacy Development of Multilingual Learners," *Language Arts* 66 (September 1989): 545.

Special Note

Educable usually refers to mildly retarded children; however, the determination for this classification varies from state to state and even from school system to school system.

At-Risk Students: A Final Note

The term *at risk* or *high risk* is heard quite often today; however, the surfacing of another label will not make these students' problems go away. Labels cannot do that! Efforts in the right direction can. Children who come from educationally disadvantaged homes need early identification and special programs that emphasize the language arts beginning in preschool or kindergarten. They need intervention as early as possible. And this intervention must continue throughout the grades.

Teachers at all grade levels must recognize those students who lack learning-to-read as well as reading-to-learn skills. "Students are at risk in reading when they have developed limited cognitive skill in handling the demands inherent in the task of learning from texts. However, another factor, metacognitive in nature, is just as likely to create an at-risk situation for students—a lack of knowledge of their own reading processes."[22] In other words, not only must students who have reading problems want to get help, they must also recognize "when and why they are not comprehending."[23] This is not easy because years of failure have severely damaged these young people's self-images. They do everything and anything to avoid print material, which further compounds their problem.

Teachers can try to enhance these students' self-concept by providing them with a tailored program that will ensure success.

It's good that the term *at risk* is focusing attention on the problems of these students; however, the term *at risk* entails risks of its own. Teachers "must take special care that the term 'at risk' is not used as a prediction of failure, that it does not become a negative label that perpetuates a self-fulfilling prophecy."[24]

Graphic Summary of Chapter

On the following page is a graphic summary of Chapter 15. If you have read the chapter, this graphic illustration should help you remember its main points. Under or beside each heading, you might want to jot down some of the information you recall, as well as some of the key concepts in this chapter. This can act as a good review. You can then check your key concepts against those that follow the graphic summary.

[22] Richard T. Vacca and Nancy D. Padak, "Who's at Risk in Reading?" *Journal of Reading* 33 (April 1990): 487.

[23] Ibid., p. 488.

[24] Linda Gambrell, guest ed., "Journal of Reading: A Themed Issue on Reading Instruction for At-Risk Students," *Journal of Reading* 33 (April 1990): 485.

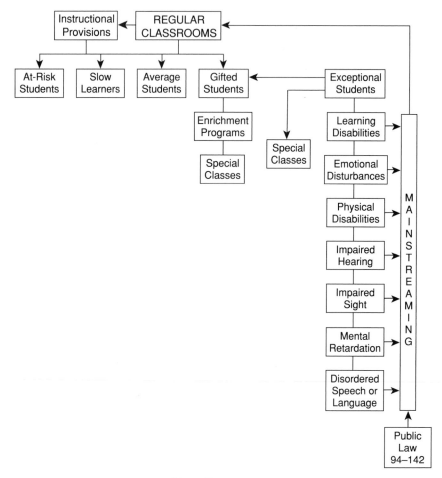

Key Concepts

- Public Law 94-142 advocates a free appropriate education for all children in the least restrictive environment.
- As students progress in school, the mental age among borderline, average, and gifted children increases.
- Average children are those whose IQs range approximately from 90 to 110.
- Exceptional children are those who deviate so much from the average that they require special attention.
- Borderline children are not considered exceptional children.
- Borderline children are those whose IQs range approximately from 70 to 85.
- Gifted children are classified as exceptional children.
- Gifted children are not only the verbally gifted with an IQ at or above 132 on the Stanford-Binet Intelligence Scale (an individual IQ test), but also those whose performance in any line of socially useful endeavor is consistently superior.

- Mainstreaming was triggered by Public Law 94-142.
- For mainstreaming to be successful, teachers and students in regular classrooms must be adequately prepared for the mainstreamed child.
- The definition of learning disability varies.
- Children who have an attention deficit disorder have difficulty concentrating on a task.
- Teachers should be extremely cautious about labeling students.

Suggestions for Thought Questions and Activities

1. You are a teacher who will soon have a child from a special class mainstreamed into your class. How would you go about preparing for this child? To whom would you go for help? How would you involve the children in your class?
2. You have been appointed to a committee that is concerned with the issue of mainstreaming. What are your views about mainstreaming?
3. What recommendations would you make concerning the mainstreaming of children?
4. You have just been appointed to a committee concerned with the development of a program for gifted children. What recommendations would you make?
5. You have two slow learners in your class. How would you help these children gain reading skills?
6. Observe a class in which a child has been mainstreamed. Discuss with the teacher the kinds of help she has gotten and the program she developed for the child. Also discuss the kinds of provisions she made beforehand.
7. You have a child in your class who constantly asks to go to the bathroom. He never finishes his work, and he can't concentrate for more than a few seconds. He always gets up and walks around the room and disturbs other children. What would you do? How would you help this child?

Selected Bibliography

Hallahan, Daniel P., and James M. Kauffman. *Exceptional Children: Introduction to Special Education,* 5th ed. Boston: Allyn and Bacon, 1991.

Kirk, Samuel A., et al. *Teaching Reading to Slow and Disabled Learners.* Boston: Houghton Mifflin, 1978.

Labuda, Michael C., ed. *Creative Reading for Gifted Learners: A Design for Excellence,* 2nd ed. Newark, Del.: International Reading Association, 1985.

Lovitt, Thomas C. *Introduction to Learning Disabilities.* Boston: Allyn and Bacon, 1989.

Parker, Jeanette Plauche. *Instructional Strategies for Teaching the Gifted.* Boston: Allyn and Bacon, 1989.

Schulz, Jane B., C. Dale Carpenter, and Ann P. Turnbull. *Mainstreaming Exceptional Students: A Guide for Classroom Teachers,* 3rd ed. Boston: Allyn and Bacon, 1991.

Terman, Lewis M., and Melita H. Oden. *The Gifted Child Grows Up,* Genetic Studies of Genius, vol. 4. Stanford, Calif.: Stanford University Press, 1947.

16

Parents Are Partners in Learning

SCENARIO: PARENTS ARE THE KEY IN CHILDREN'S EARLY LITERACY DEVELOPMENT

Melissa is a very fortunate child because she has parents who adore her. They realize that with love comes a great amount of responsibility. They have provided a warm, happy, and highly literate environment for their child. And they spend a great deal of time with her.

Melissa's parents are good role models; they love to read and write, and this love carries over to Melissa. Melissa enjoys going to the library with her parents where they all take out books.

Melissa's bedroom is filled with her favorite books, and every night her parents ask Melissa which book she would like to have read to her. Then one of her parents usually reads the book aloud while the other listens. Melissa likes to have both her Mommy and her Daddy present for her bedtime ritual.

For the past week, Melissa has asked for the storybook about a little bear who learns to do things for himself. By the second reading of the book, Melissa can predict the events that follow and repeat the refrain almost verbatim. By the third reading, Melissa can retell the story. By the fourth reading, Melissa takes the book from her parents and "reads" the story aloud, using a falsetto voice to imitate the various book characters. But when Melissa looks at her parents and starts asking them questions about the story or stops at key points for them to repeat the refrain, her parents have difficulty controlling their delight and pride. When Melissa says, "Good," after her parents answer, they can control themselves no longer. They just pick her up and hug and kiss her and tell her how proud they are of her.

Every day is an adventure for Melissa. Her parents are helping her discover the beauty of nature so that she will learn to respect and try to preserve it when she is older. They use her senses of touch, taste, smell, sight, and hearing to gain a simplified understanding of an ecologically healthy environment. For example, they awaken early with her to watch the sun rise. They observe the setting sun, the stars in the sky, and the moon and make up fanciful stories about each. They have gone out after a rainfall and delighted in the scent of the fresh air. They have made snowmen and snowladies together and watched the warm sun melt the snow. They have listened to the song of the trees rustling in the wind, and the music of the crickets. They have held seashells to their ears and heard the roar of the ocean. They have tasted fresh strawberries, melon, and spring water. Melissa's parents even help her discover beauty in such mundane things as rocks and dirt.

Just yesterday while they were out for a walk, Melissa found an acorn. "Mommy," she said, "I want to write a story." They went into the house, and Melissa dictated a story to her mother.

This is her story, verbatim:

Melissa found an acorn.
She's going to be a squirrel and eat the acorn.
Then she's going to climb up the tree.
And her mommy will catch her up the tree.

After her mother wrote Melissa's story, she read it aloud to Melissa. Melissa then "read" it to her mother and drew a picture to go with her story. When her father came home from work, she ran up to him and said, "Look, Daddy, I wrote this story for you."

Yes, Melissa is lucky! Melissa at just three is getting a tremendous start on the road to a good life. Throughout this book, we have cited studies that point to the importance of children's early years and the significant role parents play in their children's literacy development.

This chapter is concerned with the role of parents as partners in their children's learning. We will explore the kind of role parents play and their participation in school reading programs.

KEY QUESTIONS

After you finish reading this chapter, you should be able to answer the following questions:

1. Why is it important for parents to be partners in children's learning?
2. What is the role of parents in their children's emergent literacy?
3. What should parents know about reading stories aloud to children?
4. What does research tell us about parents' role in their children's literacy development?
5. What are the views of teachers toward parental involvement?
6. What are some examples of parental involvement in children's reading programs?

7. What are some examples of parental involvement programs for preschoolers?
8. How do parents feel about television programming?
9. What is the role of the parent–teacher conference?
10. What are some things parents can do to help their children?
11. What is "reality time"?
12. What is the School Entry Questionnaire for parents?
13. What is paired reading?
14. What are Reading Olympics programs?
15. What is the Junior Great Books Program?

KEY TERMS IN CHAPTER

You should pay special attention to the following key terms:

Chapter 1	parent–teacher conference
Junior Great Books Program	Reading Olympics programs
interactive storybook reading	reality time
paired reading	

Parents Are Children's First Teachers

"Mommy, what's this word?" asks Melissa.
"It's *baby*," says her mother.

"Daddy, are the stars far away?" asks Andrew.
"The stars are . . . ," says his father.

"Daddy, is the word on the door *in?*" asks Mathew.
"Yes," and what do you think the word on the other door is?"
"Out," answers Mathew.
"Good," says his father. "How did you know?"

"Mommy, read me a story," says Jennifer.
"Which book do you want me to read to you?" asks her mother.
"I want the one about the moon," says Jennifer.

"Daddy, I want to tell you a story," says Gary.
"Once upon a time, there was a large bear . . ."

"Daddy, Mommy, see what I wrote for you."
"This is very good," says her father. "Can you read it to us?"
"It says, I love you," says Melissa.

And so it goes. . . .

The above dialogues between children and parents should sound familiar because they are taking place all over the world in many homes. Children are curious about the world around them; they have innumerable questions, and the most obvious people to go to for answers are their parents. This is natural. Parents are children's first teachers.

Parents as children's first teachers have a great responsibility. They must recognize that what they do and how they behave toward their children will have a monumental effect on their children for the rest of their lives. Parents who read and write and encourage their children to do the same are being good role models.

Emergent Literacy and Parents

Parents play a very important role in their children's literacy development and especially in that part of the literacy continuum referred to as emergent literacy. (See Chapter 5 on "Emergent Literacy: Children's Early Literacy Development.") Parents who surround their children with books and spend time listening and talking to them are providing the kinds of literacy experiences that are preparing them very well for school. There are many parents, however, who are unsure about the kinds of things they should be doing with their children to help their literacy development. The following four processes should help teachers guide parents in the kinds of activities parents should be involved in with their children to help children attain literacy abilities.

1. *Observation*—Being read to or seeing adults model reading and writing behavior.
2. *Collaboration*—Having an individual interact with the child to provide encouragement, motivation, and help.
3. *Practice*—Trying out what has been learned; for example, the child writes a story or retells it to another child, stuffed animal, or doll without any help or without being supervised by an adult.
4. *Performance*—Sharing what has been learned with an adult who shows interest and support and gives positive reinforcement.[1]

Teachers might also want to share with the parents of their young children the checklist in Table 16-1 that enumerates some of the kinds of things parents should be doing with their young children.

---

[1] Lesley Mandel Morrow and Jeffrey K. Smith, eds., *Assessment for Instruction in Early Literacy* (Englewood Cliffs, N.J.: Prentice-Hall, 1990), p. 3.

TABLE 16-1 The Parent Checklist for Preschoolers and Early Primary Grade Children

	Yes	Needs Improvement
I listen to my child.		
I read aloud to my child every day.		
I discuss things with my child.		
I explain things to my child.		
I spend time with my child.		
I ask my child good questions.		
I ask my child to read picture books to me.		
I ask my child to retell stories to me.		
I write stories with my child.		
I watch special TV shows with my child.		
I talk about TV shows with my child.		
I encourage my child to try things.		
I am patient with my child.		
I take my child to interesting places.		
I take my child to the library.		
I do not pressure my child.		
I read and write in the presence of my child.		
I am a good role model for my child.		

Parents, Literacy, and Research Findings

Studies have consistently shown that "children who grow up in environments that support reading activities develop better reading skills, as do those students who read a lot both in school and at home. Home support appears to be central in fostering higher academic achievement";[2] in fact, one of the clearest predictors of early reading ability is the amount of time spent reading with parents."[3]

Throughout this book we have emphasized the importance of reading stories aloud to children because it is an essential and powerful factor in children's literacy development. Melissa's parents recognize this (see the introductory scenario and Figure 16-1); unfortunately, not all parents do. Investigators claim that there are "homes that do not encourage young children's literacy development."[4] And these homes are best identified "by the values and social styles of the social communities to which they belong."[5] The researchers found that "children from

[2] Ina V. S. Mullis, Eugene H. Owen, and Gary W. Phillips, *America's Challenge: Accelerating Academic Achievement,* National Assessment of Educational Progress (Princeton, N.J.: Educational Testing Service, 1990), p. 55.

[3] Scott G. Paris, Barbara A. Wasik, and Julianne C. Turner, "The Development of Strategic Readers," in *Handbook of Reading Research,* vol. II, Rebecca Barr, Michael L. Kamil, Peter Mosenthal, and P. David Pearson, eds. (New York: Longman, 1991), p. 628.

[4] Marilyn Jager Adams, *Beginning to Read: Thinking and Learning about Print—A Summary,* Steven A. Stahl, Jean Osborn, and Fran Lehr, eds. (Urbana, Ill.: Center for the Study of Reading, 1990), p. 47.

[5] Ibid.

FIGURE 16-1   Melissa's mother and father read to her every day. Their home is filled with books and other print material.

such homes not only miss the literacy coddling of their parents, but they often grow up in a larger environment where reading and writing are peripherally valued activities."[6] What is especially distressing is that parents spend hardly any time during the day in literacy-related activities. For example, storybook time "occupied, on the average, less than two minutes per day, with many of the children not participating in storybook reading at all."[7]

Researches also suggest that parents' expectations play an important role in their children's early literacy development. "Undoubtedly, some of the early encouragement that parents from middle- and high-SES [socioeconomic status] backgrounds provide their children reflects their high expectations for literacy development and their positive value for reading and writing activities."[8]

The lucky children, as stated a number of times in this book, are those who come from homes where parents are providing children with the kinds of literacy-related experiences that prepare them well for school. However, teachers must recognize that not all their students are gaining these kinds of literacy experiences. It is they, the teachers, who must help fill the gap. Unless this is done, these literacy-disadvantaged children will be at risk throughout their years at school.

Storybook Reading and Parents

Storybook reading is important in children's "concurrent writing, intellectual, emotional, and oral language development."[9] Studies have shown "significant positive relations between early childhood experience in being read to at home and such factors as vocabulary development . . . ; level of language development in children viewed as preschoolers . . . ; children's eagerness to read . . . ; becoming literate before formal schooling . . . ; and success in beginning reading at school. . . ."[10]

Interactive story-book reading
Includes a give and take between parent and child while the story is being read aloud whereby the parent tries to help the child gain an understanding of the story.

Parents and Interactive Storybook Reading

When parents read aloud to their children, they are engaged in a socially interactive situation. There is a give and take between the parents and the children whereby the parents try to help the children gain an understanding of the story being read. To do this, parents often change words and add their own renditions. In addition, they encourage their children to supply what they think follows or to

---

6 Ibid.

7 Ibid.

8 Paris, Wasik, and Turner, "Strategic Readers," p. 628.

9 Elizabeth Sulzby and William Teale, "Emergent Literacy," in *Handbook of Reading Research,* vol. II, Rebecca Barr, Michael L. Kamil, Peter Mosenthal, and P. David Pearson, eds. (New York: Longman, 1991), p. 731.

10 Ibid., p. 730.

answer "what" kinds of questions; parents give children knowledge of results by supplying immediate feedback.

Children interact by asking questions and mimicking the language of the text or a parent's rendition of it. Such language play helps children gain facility in language; "children can utilize a strategy of saying what they have heard others say in the same context."[11]

Read the following scenarios:

SCENARIO 1

Mrs. Brown Reads a Story to Her Three-Year-Old

"Listen carefully, Jordan, while I read you this story. Now, remember, don't interrupt Mommy while she reads." Mrs. Brown reads the whole story aloud to her child. She shows her little boy the pictures as she reads, and at the end of the story, she asks her little boy if he liked the story. Jordan asks for another story, but his mother tells him that it is now time for bed.

While reading aloud, Jordan did interrupt his mother and, at one point, tried to turn the page. Mrs. Brown admonished her son to sit still and listen. She also did not allow him to turn the page.

SCENARIO 2

Mrs. Johnson Reads a Story to Her Three-Year-Old

Mrs. Johnson is sitting in a comfortable rocker and her daughter, Patty, is on her lap. Mrs. Johnson asks Patty which book she would like to have read to her before she goes to bed. Patty picks up three books and says, "These." "No," says her mother, "choose one." Patty chooses one. Mrs. Johnson begins to read the story. While she is reading, Patty, who is familiar with the story, completes many of the sentences. When Mrs. Johnson comes to a repetitive refrain that is in the book, Patty says it aloud. After each of Patty's contributions, Mrs. Johnson says, "Good girl." Mrs. Johnson, throughout the story, asks Patty what she thinks will happen next and encourages Patty to answer questions about the story. At the end of the story, Mrs. Johnson asks Patty what she would have done if she were the bunny. She also asks Patty if she would like to be the bunny in the story. She encourages her to tell why. Throughout the story, Mrs. Johnson relates the information from the text to Patty's past experiences. For example, she asks Patty if she remembers where they had just seen lots of rabbits. When the story is finished, Patty says she wants another story; however, her mother tells her that tomorrow she will read the other stories, but now it is time for bed.

11 Ibid., p. 732.

Commentary

Both Mrs. Brown and Mrs. Johnson care for their children and know that reading stories aloud to their children is important. However, Patty is reaping more benefits from her storybook reading time with her mother than Jordan. Patty and her mother are having an interactive storybook experience. Patty's mother involves Patty in the reading aloud of the story; she acts as the bridge between Patty and the storybook.

It appears that differences tend to exist between the way high-SES parents read stories aloud to their children and the way in which low-SES parents read stories aloud. The language and social interaction during the reading aloud of the story and the way the parents mediate the story for their children can greatly influence their children's ultimate literacy achievement.[12]

Studies report that high-SES mothers ask more "what" questions when they read aloud, encourage interaction, and relate the story to the child's past experiences. Low-SES parents, on the other hand, "tended not to extend the information or skills of the book reading beyond its original context."[13]

Outreach programs should work with low-SES parents to help them gain skill in reading aloud to their children.

Parental Involvement in the Schools

Parental involvement in the schools is not a new phenomenon. Parents sit on boards of education; they are involved in parent–teacher associations, parent councils, and parent clubs. Parents help formulate school policy, have say in curriculum matters, and even help to choose textbooks. Parents definitely have a voice in school matters. Until rather recently, however, parents have not been encouraged to take an active role in working with their own children, particularly in the area of reading. Teaching was considered the sole domain of the educator, and parents who wanted to teach their children were usually looked upon as meddlers, troublemakers, and outsiders. At best they were looked upon as well meaning but unknowledgeable, and until the late 1950s parents were admonished not to teach their children to read at home. Today, in many school districts across the country, parents are being looked upon as partners and potential resources rather than as unknowing meddlers. What has caused the pendulum to swing in the other direction?

Some Possible Causes for a Change in Attitude toward Parental Involvement

A number of things have happened not only to change educators' attitudes toward parental involvement in reading instruction, but to change parents' attitudes as

---

12 Ibid., p. 736.

13 Ibid.

well. One strong factor that cannot be overlooked is that parents began to lose confidence in the schools because of the large number of reading failures that were found in the schools. With this loss of confidence in the schools came the desire for more direct involvement in the schools.

Rudolf Flesch's book *Why Johnny Can't Read—And What You Can Do about It,* which was written in 1955, probably helped to raise the consciousness level of parents concerning the role they should be playing in the area of helping their children learn to read. Flesch's book was addressed to parents and was written primarily to help parents help their children learn to read by using a phonic method. Whether or not one agrees with the views expressed in the book is not as important as the impact that the book had, and indeed it did have a great impact. Parents wanted to know more about what their children were doing in reading, and many wanted to be more directly involved.

The increase of reading problems in the schools probably helped to change educators' attitudes as well as parents' attitudes toward parental involvement in the schools. The reading problem may have caused educators to take another look at this great potential resource—parents—because many began to feel that they could use all the help that they could get. However, the greatest impetus for parental involvement probably came about because of the influx of federal monies to fund certain programs related to the improvement of children's reading skills. Practically all of these programs encouraged and urged parental involvement. Head Start, which was initiated in the summer of 1965, is one such program. Its target audience is young children—that is, preschoolers and kindergartners. Follow Through, another such program, was initiated as a pilot project in 1967 and became a nationwide program in 1968. Its audience is the children who participated in the Head Start program. Probably the passage of Title I in 1965 had the greatest effect on parental involvement because the programs under Title I cover a much larger population of children than Head Start, and, as of 1970, parental involvement became a legal mandate for all Title I programs.

Chapter 1
In 1981, Congress replaced Title I with Chapter 1; provides funds for children with major basic skills deficits.

In 1981 Congress replaced Title I with Chapter 1. Interestingly, one of the major differences was the decrease in parental involvement. In the 1987 reauthorization of Chapter 1, the revised legislation states that parents of children in Chapter 1 programs should be involved in decision-making processes.

Research Findings

Research supports parental involvement in their children's school activities because this involvement usually translates into higher achievement for their children. "Research in the 1980s revealed that, typically, when teachers do not specifically seek contact with parents, better educated parents tend to become more involved with the schools, and the result is higher achievement for their children."[14]

[14] Carol Gordon Carlson, ed., *The Parent Principle: Prerequisite for Educational Success,* in *Focus* (Princeton, N.J.: Educational Testing Service, 1991), p. 14.

Investigators in the area of parental involvement feel that schools must play a more significant role in fostering more parental involvement in the schools. They feel strongly that there should be training for teachers and administrators in how to achieve this involvement. In addition, they would like to have research investigate whether "less-educated parents do not want to become involved with their children, or whether teacher practices have inhibited their interactions."[15]

Resistance to Parental Involvement

Even though, as stated earlier, the tide has definitely turned, some teachers still resist parental involvement. Territoriality, the protection of one's domain, may be one motivation behind teachers' resistance to parental involvement. Researchers claim that some teachers feel there should be a separation between the school and the home. They believe it is an intrusion to have parents come into their classroom; if they do invite parents to their classroom, they invite them as observers only, not as participants.[16] Many teachers who feel this way believe they are child advocates. They claim that the separation is for the good of the child because "the separation of home and school will wean the child from the self-oriented atmosphere of the home to the other-oriented outside world."[17]

Investigators suggest that some teachers may resist parental involvement because they "find it an impossible goal."[18] These teachers have had bad experiences with parental involvement, so they are reluctant to encourage it.

Parental Involvement in School Reading Programs

Usually, parents become involved in school programs when their children have a specific reading problem; however, the trend appears to be for increasing parental involvement for children without reading problems.

The participation of parents in many school districts usually depends on how aggressive educators and parents are in demanding such involvement. The involvement of parents in the regular reading program seems to vary from district to district, and even from school to school in some school districts. In one school system you will find an organized program, and in another you will find that the program is up to the individual teacher in each class. The programs that do exist usually are similar in format in that they generally include workshops, instructional materials, and book suggestions. What is presented, however, will vary from district to district. The following is an example of a program that was developed in a local New Jersey school system to incorporate parental involvement in its regular reading program for all children in grades 1 through 5. The program

15 Ibid.
16 Ibid., pp. 9–10.
17 Ibid., p. 10.
18 Ibid.

consists of instructional packets, book suggestions, and three workshops. At the first workshop, a reading specialist explains the reading program that is in use in the school system. The parents are acquainted with the basal reader series, and the terminology that is used is also explained. At the second workshop the parents witness a reading lesson from the basal reader series, which uses a guided reading approach. The third session is entitled "A Book Talk." At this session books at different readability and interest levels are presented, and suggestions are made on how to involve children in reading them.

Another part of the program concerns instructional materials. For children with reading problems, parent packets are produced that consist of activities based on the skills that children are working on in class. Different parent packets are available for different grade levels. For those children who have no reading problems, materials are sent home that help parents to capitalize on their children's reading interests. A special packet that emphasizes more difficult books, especially the Newbery Award winners, is sent home to the parents of children who have been identified as highly able or gifted.

Junior Great Books Program
Program in which parent–teacher teams work together to plan reading discussions for students; sessions take place in regular classrooms during the reading period and are led by both parent and teacher.

A program of special interest was developed in a school system for highly able readers in grades 2 through 6, their teachers, and parents. The program, called the Junior Great Books Program, began in 1979 and included twelve volunteer parents and twelve teachers. A parent and a teacher were paired off and worked together as a team. The parents who volunteered had to take the two-day training session, which was conducted by a special person from the Great Books Foundation in Chicago. The sessions consisted primarily of helping parents learn about the kinds of questions they should ask, as well as how to conduct the discussions. The children who participated in the program were considered "top readers" by their teachers. The criteria that teachers used were teacher-made and standardized test results as well as a child's ability to assume responsibility. The parent–teacher team met every week to plan for the reading discussion, which took place in the regular classroom during the regularly scheduled reading period for forty-five minutes. Both the parent and the teacher helped to lead the discussion with a particular group of children.

Reading Olympics programs
Programs vary; however, most include a contest to challenge students to read the most books they can and the sharing of these books in some way with parents.

An exciting trend in the United States involves the Reading Olympics programs. These programs vary from school system to school system, from school to school, and even from one class to another; however, the important things are that they include reading books and sharing them in some way with parents. Here is how one such program works in the middle part of the year in a first-grade class.

There is a contest in which children are challenged to read as many books as they can. They must read these books aloud to one of their parents, and after they finish reading the book aloud, the parent asks them questions about the story, as well as asking them to retell it. The rewards are obviously manifold. Andrew, the child who won the Read-Aloud Olympics contest in his first-grade class, read 120 books aloud to his parents.

It has been reported that the "home factor that emerged as most strongly relating to reading achievement was 'whether or not the mother regularly heard the child read.' The effect was greater than that of IQ scores, maternal language behavior, or reading to the child."[19] Readers are cautioned, however, that those parents who coached were a special self-selected group, and the success may have been due to parental interest rather than to the practice of reading. Nevertheless, if it works, it's good.

Paired reading
The child reads aloud simultaneously with another person.

Another practice that seems to be gaining favor is that of paired reading (see "Repeated Reading" in Chapter 3). This is a method whereby parents and children read aloud simultaneously. The key to this process is to make sure the child is actually reading rather than mimicking or echoing the parent. This technique is usually used with children who have reading difficulties. At any time during the simultaneous reading, the child may signal that he or she wishes to read alone. The parent should praise the child's desire to do so, and allow the child to read alone. "The child is encouraged to read alone by lack of criticism and by frequent praise for any independent reading."[20]

Many basal reader series, recognizing the importance of learning partnerships, have made a commitment to join in the partnership by providing parents with more than the usual letters that are sent out. Publishers have developed a package that includes the suggestions and activities that are needed to implement a "Parents as Partners" program.

Figure 16-2 is a sample letter that children bring home for their parents. (There are English and Spanish versions of the letters that are sent home.)

Parental Involvement in Preschool Programs

Many parents of preschool children want help for their children. The trend for preschool help gained its greatest impetus from federal funding of programs such as Head Start in the mid-1960s, which mandated parental involvement.

Ira Gordon played a significant role in developing preschool programs in the mid-1960s that included parental involvement. All his programs used paraprofessionals, who visited the home and served as parent educators to demonstrate specially designed home learning activities to the parent.[21]

Gallup's 1979 poll on parents' attitudes toward preschool help asked parents with children who have not yet started school or kindergarten, "Do you think the school could help you in any way in preparing your child for school?"

In the poll, those respondents who have no children in school represent the group most eager to have preschool help for their children (see Table 16-2). When the parents who desired help were asked, "What could the school do?" the suggestion offered most often was to distribute a pamphlet or booklet telling in detail what parents should do to prepare the child for school. One parent is quoted as saying, "I should like to know exactly what they expect of the child, such as the ABCs, numbers, and other areas of learning." Another suggestion that

[19] Kathy Johnston, "Parents and Reading: A U.K. Perspective," *The Reading Teacher* 42 (February 1989): 353.

[20] Ibid., p. 355.

[21] Patricia P. Olmstead et al., *Parent Education: The Contributions of Ira J. Gordon* (Washington, D.C.: Association for Childhood Education International, 1980), p. 8.

Dear Family of _____:

The stories in the second part of the book focus on mountains. To help reinforce this concept, you may wish to share these books with your child:

> ***As Old As the Hills*** by Melvin Berger. Watts, © 1989. This book explains how mountains form and how the earth's plates move in various ways to create and change the earth's topography.
>
> ***Truck and Loader,*** by Helen R. Haddad. Greenwillow, © 1982. The different tasks that can be performed by a dump truck and a steam shovel are explained through detailed illustrations and a clear, informative text.
>
> ***Ming Lo Moves the Mountain,*** by Arnold Lobel. Scholastic, © 1982. Ming Lo consults a wise man to learn how to move a mountain that is troublesome to his wife. Children will laugh at the simple solution.

Through the stories in this unit your child has been learning about certain sounds in words such as short vowel *u* and long vowel *a*. You might enjoy doing the following activities with your child:

1. Short Vowel *u*

> With your child find pictures of the words that have the short vowel *u* sound, such as *tub, cub, rug, bud, jug, bug, cup, bus, sun,* and *duck.*
>
> Combine these words with other words that contain the same vowel sound, such as action words or the names of people, to make up sentence stories about the pictures. For example: Gus and a duck run with a cub in the sun.
>
> Encourage your child to create his or her own stories. You may also wish to cut out, mount, and label some of the pictures you and your child have found.

2. Long Vowel *a*

> Help your child to identify the sound of long vowel *a* by pointing out and pronouncing the names of familiar things or people. For example:

Kate	plane	rake	vase	face
cane	plate	vane	lace	Jane
lake	Blake	race	Nate	cake

> Using the actual objects or pictures, associate them with the sound of long vowel *a* by combining them with action words like *bake, take, rake, make, shake, wade, save,* and so on. Encourage your child to make up sentence stories.
>
> *Example:* Nate and Jane race by the lake.

I hope you and your child have fun sharing these books and activities.

Sincerely,

Source: From Home Connection Letters, Level 2, *Out Came the Sun*, of the *World of Reading* series, © 1991 Silver, Burdett & Ginn, Inc. Used with permission.

FIGURE 16-2 Sample letter to parents.

TABLE 16-2   Parents' Attitudes toward Preschool Help (1979)

	Could School Help with Preschool Child?		
	Yes (%)	No (%)	Don't Know/ No Answer (%)
Parents who presently have no children in school	53	34	13
Parents with one or more children in public school	37	53	10
Parents with one or more children in parochial school	40	40	20

was frequently made was to invite parents and their preschool children to visit the school to see what goes on in a typical day. Some parents thought it would be a good idea to designate a day when a preschool child could actually sit in the kindergarten class with other children to see what it is like. Still other parents suggested that a regular preschool program, such as Head Start, be made part of the education system. Many respondents said that such a preschool program already exists in their community.[22] Many do.

From the 1960s onward, we begin to see a number of programs in which parents are directly involved in teaching their young children some basic beginning reading skills. In some of the programs parents are taught certain skills that they then use to teach their children, and in some they work with preschool teachers and then provide supplementary instruction at home.

Some programs usually have preschool teachers or others model techniques for parents such as how to read aloud to children to encourage interaction and higher level thinking. (See "Reading Aloud to Children" in Chapter 3.)

The trend toward preschool help and parental involvement will certainly continue. President Bush's first national goal in *America 2000* calls for all children to start school ready to learn. This is a direct call for parental involvement and focuses on the importance of children's early years in literacy development.

The 1991 Gallup/Phi Delta Kappa poll, which is the most comprehensive since the series began in 1969, addresses the issue of tax-supported preschools, which is closely related to the first of President Bush's national goals. The poll asks whether the public schools should make tax-supported preschool programs available to three- and four-year-olds whose parents wish such programs. From the results, it appears that the majority in all but a few major demographic groups supports tax-supported preschools.[23]

Special Note

Those conducting the parent involvement programs should help parents recognize that there is a place for "reality time" with children as well as "quality time."

[22] George Gallup, "The Eleventh Annual Gallup Poll of the Public's Attitudes toward the Public Schools," *Phi Delta Kappan* 61 (September 1979): 43–44.

[23] Stanley M. Elam, Lowell C. Rose, and Alec M. Gallup, "The 23rd Annual Gallup Poll of the Public's Attitude toward the Public Schools," *Phi Delta Kappan* 73 (1) (September 1991): 45.

"Quality time" implies a value judgment and is the term most used by those who do not have much time to spend with their children.

Parents' involvement with children is good, and young children especially benefit from being with their parents. However, parents should not get into a frenzy if every moment they spend with their child is not "quality time." Teachers should help all parents recognize that "reality time" is just as important, especially for young children. Reality time is the time that parents spend with their children while making a bed, cooking, baking, going for a walk, swimming, talking, or just quiet time. When children and parents are together, every moment does not have to be filled with "pearls of wisdom."

Reality time
The time parents spend with their children doing different kinds of mundane tasks; the everyday kinds of things parents normally do with their children.

If children perceive that the only times parents and they spend together are those related to trying to teach them something to do better in school, children may begin to react negatively to their parents and to school. They may feel that if they do not do well in school, their parents will not love them.

Parent–Teacher Conferences

Parent–teacher conference
Parent and teacher meet to discuss student's progress in school; may occur at any time during school year, not just at the reporting period.

In some schools the only parent–teacher involvement may be through the parent–teacher conference. This conference is an excellent opportunity for parents and teachers to learn to feel more comfortable with one another, as well as to exchange information. Also, the parent–teacher conference may be the only way for parents to learn about the reading program and the specifics of how individual children are doing.

Some teachers look with dread on parent–teacher conferences; therefore, they structure them so that very little time is allowed for parent input or questioning. Unfortunately, such attitudes are usually conveyed to parents, and a free exchange is generally inhibited. For parent–teacher conferences to work, there must be a feeling of confidence on both sides. The more confidence a teacher has, the more comfortable he or she will feel with parents.

For parent–teacher conferences to be effective, teachers must be friendly, interested, and allow for an exchange of ideas. It is also important for teachers to recognize that although they may have twenty-five or thirty students in the class, this particular child is the one who is important to the parents. Most important, since this conference is primarily an exchange of ideas, teachers should encourage parents to give some insights into the children that would be helpful in teaching them. Remember, it is doubtful that anyone knows these children better than their parents. If the children need any special help, teachers should point this out to parents and explain precisely what they can do.

Parent–teacher conferences need not take place only during the reporting period. Whenever a need for a conference arises is the right time to call for one. However, teachers should remember that successful parent–teacher conferences require careful planning and effort.

Grandparents Should Be Involved, Too

Why not involve the elderly in reading programs in which they could work directly with children as tutors and helpers? Why not have children read aloud to the elderly? Why not bring the grandparents into the mainstream? Why not, indeed?

Interestingly, we are living in an era when a person's life expectancy is the greatest that it has ever been, and as a result there are many more elderly people who are visible. Even though there is an increased interest in gerontology and in more benefits for the elderly, and the elderly have become more vocal, they are usually shunned, especially by young people. Moreover, with the advent of retirement communities and nursing homes, the elderly are probably more segregated from society today than ever before.

The treatment of the elderly in children's literature has probably been the most neglected and the most poorly portrayed of all areas. Children are greatly influenced by the way elderly people are portrayed, especially in fairy tales. When children were asked how elderly people are shown in fairy tales, the children responded, "They are witches."[24] Obviously, these children have been greatly influenced by the portrayal of the old woman as a mean, cross, wicked hag or witch in such famous fairy tales as "Hansel and Gretel," "Sleeping Beauty," and "Snow White and the Seven Dwarfs."

As stated earlier, today the elderly are more visible, but not usually by children, because of the burgeoning of senior communities. It is claimed that the more involved the elderly are, the happier they are and the longer they live. It would seem to be a good idea, both for young people and for the elderly, to have them work together. If young people can see that the elderly are not like the stereotypes portrayed in print, their attitudes toward the elderly could become more positive (see Figure 16-3).

The elderly take part in some community programs developed to foster parental involvement, but their involvement is usually sporadic; that is, it's based more on chance than a concerted effort to get them involved. The programs that incorporate senior citizens as aides or tutors in reading are usually based in a particular school rather than in a districtwide program. For example, in Princeton, New Jersey, some schools have a program in which fifth-graders work in a cooperative effort with the elderly. The fifth-graders eat lunch with the elderly, and at the luncheon they act as the hosts and hostesses. After the luncheon, the senior citizens work with the children as tutors.

Television, Parents, Children, and Reading

Television viewing affects children's reading. We discussed this in Chapter 4, as well as what teachers can do to use television in a positive way. Most television

[24] Myra P. Sadker and David M. Sadker, *Now Upon a Time: A Contemporary View of Children's Literature* (New York: Harper & Row, 1977), p. 77.

FIGURE 16-3 This grandfather enjoys reading to his grandchildren. His grand-children love this time with their grandfather.

viewing, however, is done at home, so we would be remiss if we did not also address this topic in this chapter.

Parents watch television with their children on an average of 7.5 shows a week, and heavier viewing appears to be among parents who have less formal education. In addition, almost 60 percent of the parents who watch television with their children feel uncomfortable at least occasionally about the content of the programs they see (see Table 16-3).[25] It is not surprising, then, that the public ranks the educational value of television lower than family, school, or peers, and that television is perceived as being least positive in influence.[26]

Interestingly, a 1990 Roper survey reports that children aged seven to seventeen are more involved in decision making than ever before because families are so busy today. Of the parents polled, 79 percent claimed that their children decide which television shows the family watches. According to the poll, which was done for *USA Today,* the higher the parents' income and the more educated they are, the more say their children have in family decisions.[27]

[25] George Gallup, Jr., "Parents Disturbed by TV Content; Most See Growth in Problem," *Gallup Poll,* April 9, 1989.

[26] Stanley M. Elam and Alec M. Gallup, "The 21st Annual Gallup Poll of the Public's Attitudes Toward the Public Schools," *Phi Delta Kappan* 71 (September 1989): 47.

[27] Dan Sperling, "Parents Are Listening More to Kids," *USA Today,* January 24, 1990.

TABLE 16-3   Children and Television (1989)

"On the average, about how many television programs do you watch with your children each week?"

TV Viewing with Children

	Average Programs per Week
Nationwide	7.5
Gender:	
Men	6.9
Women	7.9
Age:	
18–29 years	7.6
30 and older	7.3
Education:	
Attended college	5.5
No college	9.1
Income:	
$25,000 and over	6.8
Under $25,000	9.5
Children's age:	
Under 6	7.1
6–12	7.9
13–17	8.0

Parents who watch with their children (83% of parents with children under 18 living at home) were asked:

"About how often would you say you feel uncomfortable about something in a television program that you are watching with your children? Would you say you frequently, occasionally, seldom, or never feel uncomfortable?"

Frequency of Discomfort Caused by TV

Frequently	25%
Occasionally	33
Seldom	25
Never	17
	100%

Helping Parents Gain Literacy

The first goal of *America 2000* states that "all children in America will start school ready to learn."[28] This implies that all children will be in home environ-

[28] George Bush, *America 2000: An Education Strategy* (Washington, D.C.: U.S. Department of Education, 1991), p. 9.

ments that support and encourage those kinds of prerequisite activities necessary to do well in school. This will not happen for those children who come from homes where parents themselves lack basic literacy skills unless intervention takes place.

Fortunately, a number of outreach and intervention programs are springing up that are attempting to help parents gain the literacy skills they need so that they can subsequently help their children. Educational Testing Service (ETS) reports that the Parent and Child Literacy Intervention program, funded by the Department of Education, is one such program. The emphasis in this program is on the parent, and the program takes place in a community center rather than in the school. However, the goal is the same as in other intervention programs— helping the parents so that they can eventually help their children.

A language experience approach is used to help parents gain literacy skills. "Parents talk about family themes with a teacher, and then they dictate or write stories that are ultimately put together in a book or portfolio form and shared with children. Then the parents are shown how to read the stories with their children."[29]

Parental Involvement: A Final Word

The interest of parents in their children's schooling cannot be overstated, especially since a number of studies have suggested that "the potential for parents to help their children in learning to read is tremendous."[30]

However, the success of any program that demands voluntary participation must be based on turnout—not initial turnout, but continuous turnout. It appears that the best turnout is coming from parents from higher SES homes rather than from the lower SES homes. And, not surprisingly, the children from the homes where parents are more involved generally do the best in school. It is unfortunate that parents of at-risk or high-risk children are often not involved in their children's schooling.

There are a number of outreach programs across the country that try to encourage parents who are in low socioeconomic groups to participate. Often these programs try to work with young women before they have given birth and guide them through their pregnancy. Let us hope that these programs have a significant impact on the lives of the children and their parents.

Let us hope also that teachers and administrators will work hard toward making the school climate one in which parents and teachers can work together for the good of the children.

For parents to be partners in learning with educators, "educators" will have to recognize that it's not "them" against "us"; there is no dichotomy. For a partner-

---

[29] Carlson, *The Parent Principle*, p. 18.

[30] Timothy Rasinski and Anthony Fredericks, "Working with Parents: Can Parents Make a Difference?" *The Reading Teacher* 43 (October 1989): 84.

ship to work, there has to be equal give and take. If parents are looked upon as parent-educators, this viewpoint "acknowledges the home–school relationship as a rich potential shared among equals, equals who bring important and divergent experiences to bear upon individual and often limited perspectives."[31]

Graphic Summary of Chapter

Here is a graphic summary of Chapter 16. If you have read the chapter, this graphic illustration should help you remember its main points. Under or beside each heading, you might want to jot down some of the information you recall, as well as some of the key concepts in this chapter. This can act as a good review. You can then check your key concepts against those that follow the graphic summary.

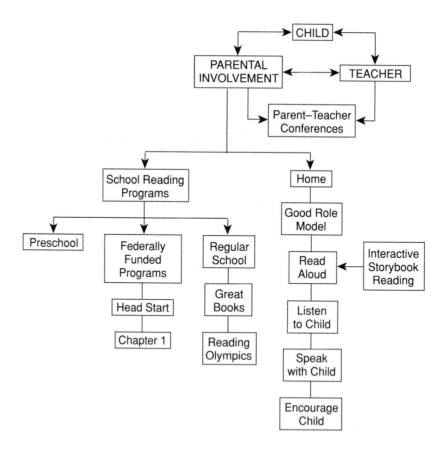

---

[31] Gayle Goodman, "Worlds within Worlds: Reflections on an Encounter with Parents," *Language Arts* 66 (January 1989): 20.

Key Concepts

- Parents are children's first teachers.
- Parents play a very important role in their children's literacy.
- Parents who surround their children with books are preparing them very well for school.
- Reading stories aloud to children is a powerful factor in their literacy development.
- Reading stories aloud is a socially interactive activity.
- Parental expectations influence children's literacy development.
- The young child's language play during the reading aloud of stories helps children gain facility in language.
- Parents are partners in their children's learning.
- Parental involvement in the schools is not new.
- In the past, parents were often not encouraged to teach their children at home.
- A number of factors have changed educators' views toward parental involvement in their children's education.
- The increase in reading problems probably caused educators to look at parents as a potential resource.
- Federally funded programs encouraged and urged parental involvement.
- Research supports parental involvement.
- Some teachers may resist parental involvement because they consider it an impossible goal.
- The participation in school reading programs depends on how aggressive educators and parents are in the district.
- Many parents of preschoolers want to know how to prepare their children for school.
- A major goal for the twenty-first century is for all children to start school ready to learn.
- Reality time with parents is just as important as quality time.
- Parent–teacher conferences should take place anytime during the school year, not just during the reporting period.
- Successful parent–teacher conferences take careful planning and effort.
- Grandparents are an excellent resource to help children in school.
- Television viewing affects children's reading.
- Heavier television viewing appears to be characteristic of parents with less formal education.
- All parents need to be literate.

Suggestions for Thought Questions and Activities

1. Interview the heads of the PTA in two schools in different school districts. Find out their attitudes toward parental involvement in schools. Find out how the parents in their schools are involved in their children's reading programs.
2. What suggestions can you make to get more parents involved in their children's education?
3. Choose two different school districts. Try to set an appointment with an administrator in each school district. Try to determine how each school district involves parents.
4. Conduct an opinion poll in your school district to determine if parents want to be more involved in their children's school programs.
5. Conduct an opinion poll in your school district to determine the kinds of programs parents of preschoolers would like.
6. Conduct an opinion poll in your district to determine what kinds of programs parents who have children in school would like to help them help their children.
7. Brainstorm some questions parents should ask teachers during a parent–teacher conference.
8. Brainstorm some questions teachers should ask parents during a parent–teacher conference.
9. Make a list of the kinds of things teachers should discuss with parents.
10. Try to determine what would make a parent–teacher conference successful.
11. A suggestion was made at a meeting that the elderly should become more involved in working directly with children in your school. How do you feel about this? In what way do you feel the elderly can be used to help children in the reading program?

Selected Bibliography

Carlson, Carol Gordon. *The Parent Principle: Prerequisite for Parental Success.* In *Focus.* Princeton, N.J.: Educational Testing Service, 1991.
Epstein, Joyce L. "School Programs and Teacher Practices of Parent Involvement in Inner-City Elementary and Middle Schools." Baltimore: The Johns Hopkins University Center for Research on Elementary and Middle Schools, 1990.
Griffiths, Alex, and Dorothy Hamilton. *Learning at Home: The Parent, Teacher, Child Alliance.* Portsmouth, N.H.: Heinemann, 1990.
Rasinski, Timothy V., and Anthony D. Fredericks. "Working with Parents: Beyond Parents and into the Community." *The Reading Teacher* 44 (May 1991): 698–699.
Wahl, Amy. "Ready . . . Set . . . Role: Parent's Role in Early Reading." *The Reading Teacher* 42 (December 1988): 228–231.

APPENDIX A

Bookbinding for Books Written by Children

The following section maps out the easy steps to follow in making a handmade book.[1]

Preparation: Decide on the cover size you want and cut two pieces of cardboard to fit. Then select a vinyl-coated fabric wallpaper[2] large enough to cover both pieces of cardboard.

Step 1: Center cardboard covers on wallpaper so that they are about ¼ inch apart and there is a border of about one inch of extra wallpaper around them; then trace with pencil. Paste cardboard covers to wallpaper (see Illustration 1 in Figure A-1).

Step 2: Draw triangle shape at each corner of the wallpaper. Cut off corners of wallpaper (see Illustration 2).

Step 3: Fold and paste wallpaper over cardboard. Press firmly until paste sticks. Be neat. Use a sponge (see Illustration 3).

Step 4: Finish edges of book cover; all wallpaper edges folded and pasted over cardboard (see Illustration 4).

Step 5: Sew or staple 10 pages together (see Illustrations 5 and 6).

Step 6: FINISHED BOOK. Paste the bottom two pages to inside covers of book. Write your full name and room number on inside front page (see Illustration 7).

---

[1] Developed by Ted Lynch, Art Teacher at Community Park School, Princeton, New Jersey.

[2] Cloth may be substituted for wallpaper.

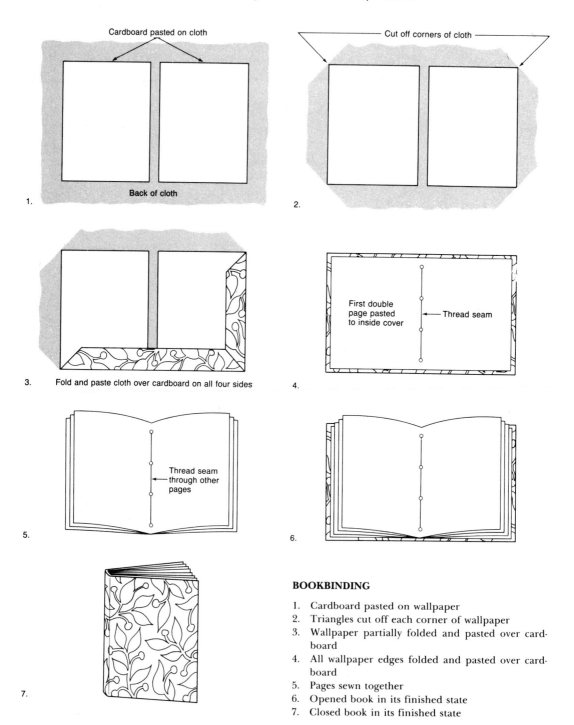

BOOKBINDING

1. Cardboard pasted on wallpaper
2. Triangles cut off each corner of wallpaper
3. Wallpaper partially folded and pasted over cardboard
4. All wallpaper edges folded and pasted over cardboard
5. Pages sewn together
6. Opened book in its finished state
7. Closed book in its finished state

FIGURE A-1   Steps for binding books written by children.

APPENDIX B
Fry Readability Formula

Expanded Directions for Working Readability Graph

1. Randomly select three (3) sample passages and count out exactly 100 words each, beginning with the beginning of a sentence. Do count proper nouns, initializations, and numerals.
2. Count the number of sentences in the hundred words, estimating length of the fraction of the last sentence to the nearest one-tenth.
3. Count the total number of syllables in the 100-word passage. If you don't have a hand counter available, an easy way is simply to put a mark above every syllable over one in each word. Then, when you get to the end of the passage, count the number of marks and add 100. Small calculators can also be used as counters by pushing numeral 1, then push the + sign for each word or syllable when counting.
4. Enter graph with *average* sentence length and *average* number of syllables; plot dot where the two lines intersect. Area where dot is plotted will give you the approximate grade level.
5. If a great deal of variability is found in syllable count or sentence count, putting more samples into the average is desirable.
6. A word is defined as a group of symbols with a space on either side; thus, *Joe, IRA, 1945,* and *&* are each one word.
7. A syllable is defined as a phonetic syllable. Generally, there are as many syllables as vowel sounds. For example, *stopped* is one syllable and *wanted* is two syllables. When counting syllables for numerals and initializations, count one syllable for each symbol. For example, *1945* is four syllables, *IRA* is three syllables, and *&* is one syllable.

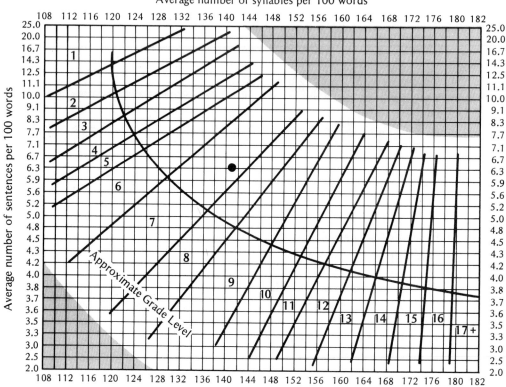

Average number of syllables per 100 words

Note: This "extended graph" does not outmode or render the earlier (1968) version inoperative or inaccurate; it is an extension. (Reproduction permitted—no copyright.)

FIGURE B-1   Graph for estimating readability—Extended by Edward Fry, Rutgers University Reading Center, New Brunswick, N.J. 08904.

TABLE B-1   Example of Fry Readability Formula

	Syllables	Sentences
1st hundred words	124	6.6
2nd hundred words	141	6.6
3rd hundred words	158	6.8
	141	6.3

Average Readability 7th Grade (see dot plotted on graph)

GLOSSARY

Ability grouping. Dividing students into groups according to similar levels of intelligence and/or achievement; in reading, students are usually grouped according to their reading achievement levels.

Accommodation. The individual's developing of new categories rather than integrating them into existing ones—Piaget's cognitive development.

Affective domain. Includes the feelings and emotional learnings that individuals acquire.

Affixes. *Prefixes** that are added before the root word and *suffixes* that are added to the end of a root word.

Analogies. Relationships between words or ideas.

Analysis. Breaking down something into its component parts.

Analytic phonics. Same as *implicit phonics instruction.*

Anecdotal record. A record of observed behavior over a period of time.

Antonyms. Words opposite in meaning to each other.

Appendix. A section of a book containing extra information that does not quite fit into the book but that the author feels is important enough to be presented separately.

Appraisal. Part of diagnostic pattern—a student's present reading performance in relation to his or her potential.

Appreciative reading. Reading for pleasure and enjoyment that fits some mood, feeling, or interest.

Assimilation. A continuous process that helps the individual to integrate new incoming stimuli to existing concepts—Piaget's cognitive development.

At-risk students. Those students who because of their backgrounds or other factors are in danger of failing in school.

Attention deficit disorder (ADD). Difficulty sustaining concentration at a task.

Attitude. Exerts a directive and dynamic influence on an individual's behavior.

Auding. Highest level of listening, which involves listening with comprehension.

Auditory discrimination. Ability to distinguish differences and similarities between sound symbols.

Auditory memory span. Amount of information able to be stored in short-term memory for immediate use or reproduction.

Average children. Often used to refer to children who score in the IQ range approximately from 90–110.

Basal reader program. A program involving a basal reader series. This program is usually highly structured; it generally has a controlled vocabulary, and skills are sequentially developed.

Bias. A mental leaning; a partiality, a prejudice, or a slanting of something.

Bibliotherapy. The use of books to help individuals to cope better with their emotional and adjustment problems.

Big books. Enlarged versions of regular children's books; known for their repetitive patterns which lend to their predictability; they are usually children's favorites.

Bilingual. Using or capable of using two languages.

Black English. A variation of standard English; in the class of *nonstandard English.*

Borderline children (slow learners). Children whose IQs usually range approximately from 70 to 85.

Bottom-up reading models. Models that consider the reading process as one of grapheme–phoneme correspondences; code emphasis or subskill models.

Breve. The short vowel mark (˘).

Caldecott Award books. Books that have received the Caldecott Medal, which is given annually to the book in the United States that has been chosen as the best picture book of the year.

Categorizing. A thinking skill involving the ability to classify items into general and specific categories.

Central idea. The central thought of a group of paragraphs, an article, or a story. All the paragraphs develop the central idea of a group of paragraphs, an article, or a story. See *Main idea.*

Chapter 1. In 1981, Congress replaced Title I with Chapter 1; provides funds for children with major basic skills deficits.

Checklist. A means for systematically and quickly recording a student's behavior; it usually consists of a list of behaviors that the observer records as present or absent.

Classroom assessment. Teacher-made tools or instruments to assess students' strengths and weaknesses; also called informal assessment.

Cloze procedure. A technique that helps teachers gain information about a variety of language facility and comprehension ability skills.

Cloze test. Reader must supply words that have been systematically deleted from a passage.

Clusters. Clusters represent a blend of sounds.

Cognitive development. Refers to development of *thinking.*

---

* Italicized words in definitions are defined elsewhere in the Glossary.

Cognitive domain. Hierarchy of objectives ranging from simplistic thinking skills to the more complex ones.

Combining forms. Usually defined as *roots* borrowed from another language that join together or that join with a *prefix*, a *suffix*, or both to form a word—for example, *aqua/naut.*

Communication. Exchange of ideas.

Comparison. A demonstration of the similarities between persons, ideas, things, and so on.

Compound word. Separate words that combine to form a new word, for example, *grandfather, stepdaughter, sunlight.*

Comprehension. Understanding; the ability to get the meaning of something.

Computer-assisted instruction. Instruction using computers.

Concentration. Sustained attention. It is essential for both studying and listening to lectures.

Concept. A group of stimuli with common characteristics.

Connotative meaning. Includes all emotional associations of the word. It's based on an individual's background of experiences.

Consonant. One of a class of speech sounds; a letter representing a consonant; any letter of the English alphabet except *a, e, i, o,* and *u.*

Consonant blends (clusters). Same as *consonant clusters.* A combination of consonant sounds blended together so that the identity of each sound is retained.

Consonant clusters (blends). A combination of consonant sounds blended together so that the identity of each sound is retained.

Consonant digraph. Two consonants that represent one speech sound.

Construct. Something that cannot be directly observed or directly measured—such as intelligence, attitudes, and motivation.

Content domain. Term that refers to subject matter covered.

Context. The words surrounding a particular word that can shed light on its meaning.

Context clue. An item of information from the surrounding words of a particular word in the form of a *synonym, antonym, example,* definition, description, explanation, and so on, that helps shed light on the particular word.

Contrast. A demonstration of the differences between persons, ideas, things, and so on.

Controlled vocabulary. The limiting of the number of new words that appear in successive pages in a particular lesson in a basal reader.

Corrective reading program. Takes place within the regular classroom.

Creative problem solving. Students using clues are encouraged to generate their own solutions.

Creative reading. Uses divergent thinking skills to go beyond the *literal comprehension, interpretation,* and *critical reading* levels.

Creativity. Difficult to define; one definition that has been given: a combination of imagination plus knowledge plus evaluation.

Criterion-referenced tests. Based on an extensive inventory of objectives in a specific curriculum area; they are used to assess an individual student's performance in respect to his or her mastery of specified objectives in a given curriculum area.

Critical reading. A high-level reading skill that involves evaluation; making a personal judgment on the accuracy, value, and truthfulness of what is read.

Cross-age tutoring. Students from upper grades work with children from lower grades.

Crossed dominance. The dominant hand on one side and the dominant eye on the other.

Decoding. Listening and reading are decoding processes involving the intake of language.

Deductive teaching. Students are given a generalization and must determine which examples fit the rule, going from general to specific.

Denotative meaning. The direct, specific meaning of the word.

Derivatives. Combinations of root words with either *prefixes* or *suffixes* or both, for example, prefix *(re)* plus root word *(play)* = *replay.*

Developmental reading. All those reading skills that are systematically and sequentially developed to help students become effective readers throughout their schooling.

Diacritical marks. Marks that show how to pronounce words.

Diagnosis. The act of identifying difficulties and strengths from their signs and symptoms, as well as the investigation or analysis of the cause or causes of a condition, situation, or problem.

Diagnostic pattern. Consists of three steps: *identification, appraisal,* and *diagnosis.*

Diagnostic-reading and correction program. Reading instruction interwoven with diagnosis and correction.

Diagnostic reading test. Provides subscores discrete enough so that specific information about a student's reading behavior can be obtained and used for instruction.

Diagnostic teaching. The practice of continuously trying a variety of instructional strategies and materials based on the needs of students.

Dialect. A variation of language sufficiently different to be considered separate, but not different enough to be classified as a separate language.

Dictionary. A very important reference tool that supplies word meanings, pronunciations, and a great amount of other useful information.

Digit span. Refers to amount of numbers an individual can retain in his or her short-term memory.

Digraph. Usually consisting of either two consonants or two vowels which represent one speech sound, for example, *ch, ai.*

Diphthongs. Blends of vowel sounds beginning with the first and gliding to the second. The vowel blends are represented by two adjacent vowels, for example, *oi.* For syllabication purposes, diphthongs are considered to be one vowel sound.

Directed listening/thinking approach. Requires teachers

to ask questions before, during, and after a talk; consists of a number of steps; requires students to be active participants.

Directed Reading-Thinking Activity (DRTA). Requires teachers to nurture the inquiry process and students to be active participants and questioners; includes prediction and verification.

Direct instruction. Instruction guided by a teacher, who uses various strategies to help students understand what they are reading; may also be called *explicit teaching.*

Disabled reader. A reader who is reading below his or her ability level.

Divergent thinking. The many different ways to solve problems or to look at things.

Drop Everything and Read (DEAR). Similar to *Sustained Silent Reading (SSR);* practice in independent silent reading.

Dyslexia. Severe reading disability.

Educable mentally retarded children. Children whose IQs usually range approximately from 55 to 70; considered mildly retarded.

Egocentric speech. Child speaks in a collective monologue or primarily in parallel—that is, speech is not directed to another's point of view; concerned with own thoughts.

Emergent literacy. That stage in literacy development concerned with the young child's involvement in language and his or her attempts at reading and writing before coming to school or before conventional or formal reading and writing begin.

Emergent writing. Part of a child's *emergent literacy;* it's preconventional writing.

Environmental psychology. Focuses on behavior in relation to physical settings.

Equilibrium. According to Piaget, a balance between *assimilation* and *accommodation* in *cognitive development.*

English as a Second Language (ESL). Teaching that concentrates on helping children who speak a language other than English or who speak nonstandard English to learn standard English as a language.

Evaluation. A process of appraisal involving specific values and the use of a variety of instruments in order to form a value judgment; goes beyond test and measurement.

Example. Something representative of a whole or a group.

Exceptional children. Those children who deviate so much from the "average" that they require special attention.

Experience story. A basic teaching technique in reading founded on experiences of students; story is cooperatively written under the guidance of a teacher; students dictate sentences about a common experience, which the teacher writes on a large chart or the chalkboard.

Explicit phonics instruction. Each sound associated with a letter in the word is pronounced in isolation, and then the sounds are blended together; also known as *synthetic phonics.*

Explicit teaching. Same as *direct instruction.*

Fact. Something that exists and can be proved true.

Finding inconsistencies. Finding statements that do not make sense.

Gifted children. The academically gifted are usually those with an IQ at or above 132 on the Stanford-Binet Intelligence Scale; however, *gifted* also usually refers to those whose performance in any line of socially useful endeavor is consistently superior.

Good literature. The foundation of any good reading program.

Grapheme–phoneme correspondences. Letter–sound relationships.

Graphemes. The written representation of *phonemes.*

Graphemic base. Same as *phonogram.*

Graphic organizer. Same as *semantic mapping.*

Graphic summary. A visual representation of the material presented in a selection, section, or a chapter; helps students recall information; an excellent review tool.

Group instruction. A number of students are taught at the same time; helps make instruction more manageable; students are divided into groups according to some criteria.

Guided reading. Instructional technique used with basal readers that includes a number of steps under the direction of the teacher; also known as the directed reading activity (DRA).

Home environment. Socioeconomic class, parents' education, and the neighborhood in which children live are some factors that shape children's home environment.

Homographs. Words that are spelled the same but have different meanings.

Homonyms. Words that sound alike, are spelled differently, and have different meanings.

Homophones. Same as *homonyms.*

Identification. Part of *diagnostic pattern;* the act of determining the student's present level of performance in word recognition and comprehension for screening purposes.

Immersion. Complete exposure of a nonnative English speaker to English as soon as he or she enters school.

Implicit phonics instruction. Does not present sounds associated with letters in isolation. Children listen to words that begin with a particular sound; then they state another word that begins with the same sound; also known as *analytic phonics.*

Individualized instruction. Student works at own pace on material based on the needs, interests, and ability of the student.

Individualized reading approach. Students work at own pace on material, largely trade books, based on the needs, interests, and abilities of each student; emphasizes self-selection of books and individual teacher conferences.

Individual tests. Administered to one person at a time.

Inductive teaching. Students discover generalizations by being given numerous examples which portray patterns; going from specific to general.

Inference. Understanding that is not derived from a direct statement but from an indirect suggestion in what is stated; understanding that is implied.

Informal diagnostic reading tests. *Teacher-made tests* to help determine students' specific strengths and weaknesses.

Informal tests. *Teacher-made tests.*

Intake of language. Listening and reading.

Intelligence. Ability to reason abstractly; problem-solving ability based on a hierarchical organization of two things—symbolic representations and strategies for processing information.

Intelligence quotient (IQ). Mental age divided by chronological age multiplied by 100.

Interactive instruction. The teacher intervenes at optimal times to enhance the learning process.

Interactive reading models. The top-down processing of information is dependent on the bottom-up processing, and vice versa.

Interactive storybook reading. Includes a give and take between parent and child while the story is being read aloud whereby the parent tries to help the child gain an understanding of the story.

Interpretation. A reading level that demands a higher level of thinking ability because the material it involves is not directly stated in the text but only suggested or implied.

IPA. International Phonetic Alphabet.

Junior Great Books Program. Program in which parent-teacher teams work together to plan reading discussions for students; sessions take place in regular classrooms during the reading period and are led by both parent and teacher.

Language. A learned, shared, and patterned arbitrary system of vocal sound symbols with which people in a given culture can communicate with one another.

Language arts. The major components are listening, speaking, reading, and writing.

Language experience approach. An emerging reading program based on students' experiences, which incorporates all aspects of the language arts into reading.

Laterality. Sidedness.

Learning center. An integral part of the instructional program and vital to a good individualized program. An area is usually set aside in the classroom for instruction in a specific curriculum area.

Learning disability. Difficult to define; the definition best known and acted on is: a disorder in one or more of the basic psychological processes involved in understanding or in using language spoken or written, which may manifest itself in an imperfect ability to listen, think, speak, read, write, spell, or do mathematical calculations; also defined as intrinsic to the individual and presumed to be due to some central nervous system dysfunction.

Linguistics. The scientific study of language.

Listening comprehension test. Given to assess a child's comprehension through listening; teacher reads aloud to child and then asks questions about the selection.

Listening vocabulary. The number of different words one knows the meaning of when they are said aloud.

Literal comprehension. The ability to obtain a low-level type of understanding by using only information that is explicitly stated.

Literate person. One who can read and write.

Literature-based basal readers. Use literary works and make literature the focus of their program.

Literature-based programs. Reading programs using whole pieces of good literature rather than short excerpts or contrived text.

Literature study groups. These are formed on the basis of interest rather than ability.

Literature webbing. A story map technique to help guide children in using predictable trade books.

Macron. The long vowel mark (ˉ).

Main idea. The central thought of a paragraph. All the sentences in the paragraph develop the main idea. The term *central idea* is usually used when referring to a group of paragraphs, an article, or a story.

Mainstreaming. The placement of handicapped children in the least restrictive educational environment that will meet their needs.

Memory span. The number of discrete elements grasped in a given moment of attention and organized into a unity for purposes of immediate reproduction or immediate use; synonym for *digit span*.

Mental age. A child's present level of development; in intelligence testing, a score based on average abilities for that age group:

$$MA = \frac{IQ \times CA}{100}$$

Metacognition. Thinking critically about thinking; refers to students' knowledge about their thinking processes and ability to control them.

Miscue. Unexpected response to print.

Mixed dominance. No consistent preference for an eye, hand, or foot.

Mnemonic device. A memory association trick that helps students to recall material.

Modeling instruction. Thinking out loud; verbalizing one's thoughts to help students gain understanding.

Morpheme. The smallest individually meaningful element in the utterances of a language.

Morphology. Involves the construction of words and word parts.

Motivation. Internal impetus behind behavior and the direction behavior takes; drive.

Newbery Award books. The books that have received the Newbery Medal, which is given annually to the book in the United States that has been voted "the most distinguished literature" for children.

Nonstandard English. A variation of standard English owing to socioeconomic and cultural differences in the United States.

Notetaking. A useful study and paper-writing tool.

Objective. Desired educational outcome.

Objective tests. Those that usually have only one correct answer for a given question.

Observation. A technique that helps teachers collect data about students' behavior.

Open syllable. A syllable having a single vowel and ending in a vowel. The vowel is usually long, for example, *go.*

Opinions. Based on *attitudes* or feelings; they can vary from person to person, but cannot be conclusively proved right or wrong.

Oral reading. Reading aloud.

Outlining. Helps students organize long papers; serves as a guide for the logical arrangement of material.

Overlearning. Helps persons retain information over a long period of time; occurs when individuals continue to practice even after they think they have learned the material.

Paired reading. The child reads aloud simultaneously with another person.

Parent–teacher conference. Parent and teacher meet to discuss student's progress in school; may occur at any time during school year, not just at the reporting period.

Peer tutoring. A student helps another student gain needed skills.

Perception. A cumulative process based on an individual's background of experiences. It is defined as giving meaning to sensations or the ability to organize stimuli on a field.

Perceptual domain. Part of the reading process that depends on an individual's background of experiences and sensory receptors.

Phoneme. Smallest unit of sound in a specific language system; a class of sounds.

Phonemic awareness. The ability to recognize that a spoken word consists of a sequence of individual sounds.

Phonemics. Deals with the problem of discovering which phonemes are part of the conscious repertoire of sounds made by speakers of a language or dialect.

Phonetics. The study of the nature of speech sounds.

Phonic analysis. The breaking down of a word into its component parts.

Phonics. The study of the relationships between letter symbols of a written language and the sounds they represent.

Phonic synthesis. The building up of the component parts of a word into a whole.

Phonogram (graphemic base). A succession of graphemes that occurs with the same phonetic value in a number of words (*ight, ake, at, et,* and so on); word family.

Phonology. Branch of *linguistics* dealing with the analysis of sound systems of language.

Physical environment. Refers to any observable factors in the physical environment that could affect the behavior of an individual.

Portfolio assessment. A record-keeping device that gives students, teachers, and parents an ongoing view of a child's reading and writing progress; material that is included varies from teacher to teacher.

Prefix. An *affix;* a letter or a sequence of letters added to the beginning of a root word that changes its meaning— for example, *re* plus *play* = *replay.*

Principle. Refers to a rule or a guide.

Propaganda. Any systematic, widespread, deliberate indoctrination or plan for indoctrination.

Proximodistal development. Muscular development from the midpoint of the body to the extremities.

Public Law 94-142. Advocates a free appropriate education for all children in the least restrictive environment.

Pull-in program. An intervention program whereby basic skills teachers work with the regular classroom teacher as a team in the children's regular classroom.

Pull-out program. A remedial program that takes place outside the regular classroom and is handled by a special teacher.

Question Answer Relationships (QARs). Helps students distinguish between "what they have in their heads" and information that is in the text.

Questions. A good way for students to gain a better insight into a subject; questioning also gives the instructor feedback and slows the instructor down if he or she is going too fast.

Readability. Many variables determine how well an individual will comprehend written material.

Readability formulas. Applied directly to the written material to determine the reading difficulty of written material.

Readiness. An ongoing, dynamic process which teachers use to prepare students for various learning activities throughout the school day; *emergent literacy* has replaced concept of readiness in early reading.

Reading. A complex, dynamic process that involves the getting of meaning from and the bringing of meaning to the printed page.

Reading aloud to children. An essential activity for building the knowledge and skills required for reading.

Reading comprehension. A complex intellectual process involving a number of abilities. The two major abilities involve word meanings and reasoning with verbal concepts.

Reading comprehension taxonomy. A hierarchy of reading comprehension skills ranging from the more simplistic to the more complex ones; a classification of these skills.

Reading expectancy formula. Helps teachers determine who needs special help; helps determine a student's reading potential.

Reading Olympics programs. Programs vary; however, most include a contest to challenge students to read the most books they can and the sharing of these books in some way with parents.

Reading process. Concerned with the *affective, perceptual,* and *cognitive domains.*

Reading Recovery program. An early individualized, one-on-one intervention program for first-graders who are experiencing difficulty in learning to read.

Reading strategy. An action or series of actions that helps construct meaning.

Reality time. The time parents spend with their children doing different kinds of mundane tasks; the everyday kinds of things parents normally do with their children.

Recite or recall. The process of finding the answer to a question in one's memory without rereading the text or notes.

Recreational reading. Reading primarily for enjoyment, entertainment, and appreciation.

Reinforcement. Any stimulus, such as praise, which usually causes the individual to repeat a response.

Repeated reading. Similar to *paired reading;* child reads along (assisted reading with model or tape) until he or she gains confidence to read alone.

Reversals. Confusion of letters and words by inverting them; for example, *b* = *d, was* = *saw,* and vice versa.

Role modeling. An observer imitates the behavior of a model.

Role playing. A form of creative drama in which dialogue for a specific role is spontaneously developed.

Root. Smallest unit of a word that can exist and retain its basic meaning, for example, *play.*

Schemata. These structured designs are the cognitive arrangements by which the mind is able to categorize incoming stimuli.

Schema theory. Deals with relations between prior knowledge and comprehension.

Schwa. The sound often found in the unstressed (unaccented) syllables of words with more than one syllable. The schwa sound is represented by an upside-down *e* (ə) in the phonetic (speech) alphabet. A syllable ending in *le* preceded by a consonant is usually the final syllable in a word and contains the schwa sound.

Second-language learners. Children whose parents usually were born in another country and who speak a language other than English; also may refer to a child born in the United States, where English is not the dominant language spoken in the child's home.

Self-fulfilling prophecy. Teacher assumptions about children become true, at least in part, because of the attitude of the teachers, which in turn becomes part of the children's self-concept.

Semantic clue. Meaning clue.

Semantic mapping (graphic organizer). A graphic representation used to illustrate concepts and relationships among concepts such as classes, properties, and examples.

Silent consonants. Two adjacent consonants, one of which is silent—for example, *kn* (know), *pn* (pneumonia).

Silent reading. Reading to oneself; not saying aloud what is read.

Skimming. Reading rapidly to find or locate information.

Slow learners. Same as *borderline children.*

Social promotion. Promotion of students based on chronological age rather than achievement.

Sociogram. A map or chart showing the interrelationships of children in a classroom and identifying those who are "stars" or "isolates."

SQ3R. A widely used study technique that involves five steps: survey, question, read, recite or recall, and review.

Standard English. English in respect to spelling, grammar, vocabulary, and pronunciation that is substantially uniform, though not devoid of regional differences. It is well established by usage in the formal and informal speech and writing of the educated and is widely recognized as acceptable wherever English is spoken and understood.

Standardized reading achievement test. Usually part of a test battery that includes other curriculum areas besides reading; measures general reading achievement.

Standardized tests. Tests that have been published by experts in the field and have precise instructions for administration and scoring.

Starter shelves. The starting of book collections by teachers to which children can contribute.

Story map. A guide that uses questions to help children gain meaning from a story; it logically represents the major ideas of the story; it can also be a guide in writing a story.

Structural analysis. A technique for breaking a word into its pronunciation units; the breaking down of a word into word parts such as *prefixes, suffixes, roots,* and *combining forms.*

Structural synthesis. A technique for building up of word parts into a whole.

Study procedures. (1) Build good habits, (2) devise a system that works for you, (3) keep at it, (4) maintain a certain degree of tension, and (5) concentrate.

Subjective tests. Usually essay tests; answers are not merely right or wrong; tests are a demonstration of reasoning, thought, and perception.

Suffix. An *affix;* a letter or sequence of letters added on the end of a root word, which changes the grammatical form of the word and its meaning; for example, *prince* plus *ly* = *princely.*

Summary. A brief statement of the essential information in a longer piece; usually contains the *main* or *central idea.*

Supporting details. Additional information that supports, explains, or illustrates the *main idea.* Some of the ways that supporting details may be arranged are as cause and effect, examples, sequence of events, descriptions, definitions, comparisons, or contrasts.

Survey. To gain an overview of the text material.

Sustained Silent Reading (SSR). Practice in independent silent reading.

Syllable. A vowel or a group of letters containing one vowel sound, for example, *blo.*

Synonyms. Words similar in meaning.

Syntax. Refers to word order or position of the word in a sentence.

Synthesis. Building up the parts of something, usually into a whole.

Synthetic phonics. Same as *explicit phonics instruction.*

Teacher as classroom manager. Able to deal with more than one situation at a time; aware of what is going on with all students at all times.

Teacher-made tests. Tests prepared by the classroom teacher for a particular class and given by the classroom teacher under conditions of his or her own choosing.

Telegraphic writing. The use of one or two words to recall a message.

Test. A standard set of questions to be answered.

Thinking. Covert manipulation of symbolic representations.

Top-down reading models. These models depend on the reader's background of experiences and language ability in constructing meaning from the text.

Topic sentence. The sentence that states what the paragraph will be about by naming the topic.

Underachievement. Achievement below one's ability level.

Visual discrimination. The ability to distinguish differences and similarities between written symbols.

Vocabulary consciousness. An awareness that words may have different meanings based on their context and a desire to increase one's vocabulary.

Vocabulary load. The frequency of difficult words; the degree to which the number of hard words, their rate of introduction, and the ability to understand them affects readability.

Vowel. One of a class of speech sounds; letter representing a vowel; *a, e, i, o, u,* and sometimes *y* in the English alphabet.

Vowel digraph. Two vowels that represent one speech sound.

Whole language. A movement to influence how reading and writing are taught in schools; a set of beliefs in which the emphasis is on the "wholeness" of things.

Whole word or "look and say." A word recognition technique in which a child's attention is directed to a word and then the word is said.

Word recognition. A twofold process that includes both the identification of printed symbols by some method so that the word can be pronounced and the association of meaning with the word after it has been properly pronounced.

INDEX